THE CRAFT
AND DESIGN OF
MONUMENTAL
BRASSES

THE CRAFT AND DESIGN OF
MONUMENTAL BRASSES

HENRY H. TRIVICK

WITH NEARLY 300 ILLUSTRATIONS,
INCLUDING MANY IN COLOUR

John Baker

5 Royal Opera Arcade, Pall Mall, London

Humanities Press Inc.

303 Park Avenue South, New York

A*

©1969 HENRY H. TRIVICK
FIRST PUBLISHED IN GREAT BRITAIN IN 1969 BY
JOHN BAKER, PUBLISHERS, LIMITED AT
5 ROYAL OPERA ARCADE, PALL MALL
LONDON S.W.1

S.B.N. 212 99820 X

AND IN THE UNITED STATES OF AMERICA BY
THE HUMANITIES PRESS INC.
303 PARK AVENUE SOUTH,
NEW YORK, N.Y. 10010

LIBRARY OF CONGRESS NUMBER 68-47779

THE BLOCKS HAVE BEEN ENGRAVED BY
THE JOHNSTON ENGRAVING COMPANY LIMITED
AND AUGUSTAN ENGRAVERS LIMITED.
THE BOOK HAS BEEN PRINTED BY
THE MILLBROOK PRESS LIMITED
AT SOUTHAMPTON.
THE EDITION HAS BEEN BOUND BY
G. AND J. KITCAT LIMITED

PRINTED AND BOUND IN GREAT BRITAIN

Contents

List of Illustrations

Reproductions are from originals of over 10 feet in depth to as little as 6 inches or less. This accounts for the variation of the thickness of the incised lines in the illustrations

Acknowledgments

To this volume, I have given considerable time and thought during the past few years. I hope therefore that it contains some original comment on the aesthetics of monumental brasses, though it must be regarded as a preliminary introduction.

Since my student days I have read numerous books on the fine arts and more recently books on archaeology. Not only have I been interested in the arts of the Western Hemisphere but of the Eastern Hemisphere as well. This interest was stimulated by some of my art instructors to whom I owe thanks. I am pleased to place on record my gratitude to many friends and to a number of other kind people who have helped me in my labour on this volume.

I do hope, if I have omitted to mention one or two, that I will be forgiven.

I owe a considerable debt to the incumbents of the many parish churches who have so kindly given me permission to make rubbings off the brasses. Over two thirds of the illustrations are taken from my own rubbings.

To the following I wish to tender my thanks for permission to reproduce drawings and photographs.

Asah Shimbun, Tokyo. The Nara Museum. The British Museum. The Victoria & Albert Museum. The Society of Antiquaries. The County Museum, Aylesbury. The Luton Museum. The Reading Museum & Art Gallery. The Berkshire Archaeological Society. The National Monuments Record. *Country Life*. *The Times*. Dr A. Elliott and Mr R. Miles. Institut für Denkmalpflege Arbeitsstelle, Halle. The Dean & Chapter, St Paul's Cathedral.

For very kind assistance in many ways when writing this volume I owe a debt to the following and wish to record my thanks.

Dr H. K. Cameron and Mr F. A. Greenhill, Vice-Presidents, The Monumental Brass Society. Mr K. B. Gardner, Keeper, Dept of Oriental Books and Manuscripts, and Mr J. K. Rowlands, Assistant Keeper, Dept of Prints and Drawings, The British Museum. Mr R. W. Lightbown, Assistant Keeper, Dept of Metalwork, The Victoria & Albert Museum. Mr Vesey Norman, Assistant to The Director, The Wallace Collection. Mr A. B. R. Fairclough, The Council for The Care of Churches. The British Museum Library. The Victoria & Albert Museum Library. Marlow Library. The Ashmolean, Oxford. The Courtauld Institute. The Warburg Institute. Mr John Coales, Hon Secretary, Monumental Brass Society. The Very Rev The Dean, Durham Cathedral. Dr I. Anthony, The Verulamium Museum, St Albans. Mr C. Gowing, County Museum, Aylesbury. Mr T. L. Gwatkin, Reading Museum & Art Gallery. Mr Peter Smith, Luton Museum. Mr F. M. Underhill, Berkshire Archaeological Society. Mr C. Mezulianik. The Rev S. Doran, Vicar, Bray, Berks. Miss Cicely Tower. Miss Meriel Tower. Mrs M. Gaskell for typing my manuscript and Mrs Thomas, writing from France, for giving me information on French brasses and slabs. My thanks to Lady E. M. Richardson for correcting the manuscript and making useful suggestions. Last but not least I wish to thank Mr John Baker my publisher, for showing great patience and understanding of my many requests in the production of this volume; also to Mr Geoffrey Robinson and Mr John Mitchell for assisting in the production.

Bibliography

BOOKS ON INCISED SLABS AND MONUMENTAL BRASSES – a selection of those read by the author, including others for reference.

S. Weever. Ancient Funeral Monuments. 1631.

Gentleman's Magazine. Various issues from 1731.

R. Gough. Sepulchral Monuments of Great Britain, 1786-96.

C. A. Stothard. Monumental Effigies. 1817.

J. S. Cotman. Norfolk and Suffolk Brasses. 1819-28.

T. and G. Hollis. Monumental Effigies of Great Britain. 1840-42.

Cambridge Camden Society. Illustrations of Monumental Brasses. 1846.

C. Boutell. Monumental Brasses and Slabs. 1847.
       The Monumental Brasses of England. 1849.
       Christian Monuments in England and Wales. 1854.

G. E. Kite. Monumental Brasses of Wiltshire. 1860.

H. Haines. A Manual of Monumental Brasses (2 Vols). 1861.

J. G. and L. A. B. Waller. A Series of Monumental Brasses from the 13th century to the 16th century. 1864.

H. Gerlach. Die Mittelalterlichen gravierten messingen Grabplatten in der Domen zu Meissen und Freiberg. 1866.

H. Luchs. Schlesische Furstenbilder des Mittelalters. 1868.

W. F. Creeney. A Book of Facsimiles of Monumental Brasses on the Continent of Europe. 1884.

W. D. Belcher. Kentish Brasses (2 Vols. 1888-1905).

British Museum. Catalogue of Additional Manuscripts (1882-87). 1889.

H. W. Macklin. Monumental Brasses. 1890.

W. F. Creeney. Illustrations of Incised Slabs on the Continent of Europe. 1891.

J. L. Thornley. The Monumental Brasses of Lancashire and Cheshire. 1893.

C. T. Davies. The Monumental Brasses of Gloucestershire. 1899.

E. Farrer. A List of Monumental Brasses Remaining in the County of Suffolk. 1903.

F. Kopera. Monuments de Cracowie. 1904.

E. R. Suffling. English Church Brasses. 1910.

A. S. Cooke. The Date of the Ruthwell and Bewcastle Crosses. 1912.

J. S. M. Ward. Brasses. 1912.

J. Kramer. Metallne Grapplatten in Sachen. 1912.

E. T. Beaumont. Ancient Memorial Brasses. 1913.

A. Oliver. The Incised Slabs of Staffordshire. 1913.

H. W. Macklin. The Brasses of England. 1914.

R. T. Gunther. Brasses and other Funeral Monuments in the Chapel of Magdalen College, Oxford. 1914.

Griffin and Stephenson. Monumental Brasses in Kent. 1923.

W. E. Gawthorne. The Brasses of our Homeland Churches. 1923.

T. W. Morley. Monumental Brasses of Berkshire. 1924.

Mill Stephenson. A List of Monumental Brasses in the British Isles. 1926. (With appendix by M. S. Giuseppi and R. Griffin. 1938.) The two published in one volume. 1964.

Muriel Clayton. Catalogue of Rubbings of Brasses and Incised Slabs. Victoria and Albert Museum. 1929.

E. Eichler. Jarbuc du Pruszishen Kunstsammlungen. Vol. 54. 1933.

W. R. Webster. Notes on the History, Manufacture and Properties of Wrought Brass. An AIME Publication No 1477-E384. Also published in Metals Technology. 1942.

Copper Development Association. Monumental Brasses and Bronzes – a
    Bibliography. 1948.
S. Collon-Gevaert. Histoire des Arts du Métal en Belgique. 1951.
A. C. Bouquet. Church Brasses. 1951.
Sir James Mann. Monumental Brasses. 1957.
F. A. Greenhill. The Incised Slabs of Leicestershire and Rutland. 1958.
J. Franklyn. Brasses. 1964.
M. Norris. Brass Rubbing. 1965.
A. C. Bouquet. In collaboration with Michael Waring. European Brasses. 1967.
Transactions of The Monumental Brass Society. Various dates.
Portfolios of The Monumental Brass Society. Various dates.
Oxford Portfolio of Monumental Brasses. Various dates. (Journal of the
    Oxford University Brass-rubbing Society.)
Journal of The Society of Antiquaries, London. Various dates.
Numerous pamphlets, Church guides and County books have been used for
    reference.
Especially valuable, *Notes on Brass Rubbing* published by The Ashmolean,
    Oxford. It has run into several editions and costs only a few shillings.

A SELECTION OF BOOKS USED OTHER THAN THOSE ON INCISED BRASSES AND
INCISED SLABS.
Charles Winstone. Ancient Painted Glass. 1847.
            The Arts of Glass Painting. 1865.
J. Galliard. Ephemetides Brugeoises. 1847.
            Inscriptions Funeraires de la Flandre. 1861-64.
John Ruskin. Seven Lamps of Architecture. 1849.
            Stones of Venice. 1858. 1867 (Two Vols.) 2nd editions.
            Lectures on Architecture and Painting. 1854-55.
            The Unity of Art. 1859.
            Lectures on Art, 1870.
            The Art of England. 1884.
Facsimile sketch book of Villard de Honnecourt. 1859. Translated by
    R. Willis.
C. Pooley. Notes on Old Crosses of Gloucestershire. 1868.
J. W. Appell. Monuments of Early Christian Art. 1872.
Van Severn Gilliodts. Inventaire des Archives de la ville de Bruges. 1871-78.
A. Rimmer. Ancient Stone Crosses of England. 1875.
R. W. Paul. An Account of Sepulchral Slabs of North West Somersetshire.
    1882.
Fox Bourne. English Merchants. 1886.
G. Baldwin Brown. From Schola to Cathedral. 1886.
J. J. Jusserand. English Wayfaring Life in the Middle Ages. 1891.
J. Cundall. History of Wood Engraving. 1895.
J. Starkie Gardner. Foreign Armour in England. 1898.
C. Headlam. Peter Vischer. 1901.
K. E. Styan. History of Sepulchral Cross Slabs. 1902.
S. Green. Handbook of Church History. 1904.
J. V. Bradley. Illuminated Manuscripts. 1905.
A. L. Jenckers. The Staple of England. 1908.
A. Dryden. Church Embroidery. 1911.
Heeniman. Great Engravers. 1911.
H. W. Davis. Medieval Europe. 1911.
F. J. Snell. The Customs of Old England. 1911.
A. H. Thompson. Historical Growth of the English Parish Church. 1911.
Campbell Dodgson. German Woodcuts in the British Museum. 1914.
P. Nelson. Ancient Painted Glass in England. 1914.
J. Charles Fox. English Church Fittings and Accessories. 1914.
I. Colvin. The Germans in England (In Medieval Times). 1915.

C. Gore. The Church and The Ministry. 1919.

F. H. Crossley. English Church Monuments. 1921.

A. Schulte. Geschichte der Ravensburger Handelgesellschaft. 1923.

L. Norton Brown. Block Printing and Book Illustration in Japan. 1924.

A. Fryer. Wooden Monumental Effigies in England and Wales. 1924.

John Harvey. Gothic England. 1924.

M. Letts. Bruges and Its Past. 1924.

Sir R. Lodge. The Close of the Middle Ages. 1924.

Eileen Power. Medieval People. 1924.

S. Meller. Peter Vischer der altere und seine Werkstatt. 1925-27.

Thomas Carter. The Invention of Printing in China – its spread Westwards.
    1925.

F. Harrison. Painted Glass of York. 1927.

A. Watkins. Old Standing Crosses of Herefordshire. 1930.

A. Peatling. Surrey Archaeological Collection. 1930.

Sir Herbert Read. The Meaning of Art. 1931.

Royal Academy of Arts. French Art. 1932.

J. Aubrey Rees. The English Tradition. 1934.

R. H. Wilenski. The Modern Movement in Art. 1935.

Bernard Rackham. A Guide to the Collection of Stained Glass (V & A). 1936.

A. von Brandt. England and The Hanse. 1937.

F. H. Crossley. English Church Craftsmanship. 1941.

Dr Joan Evans. English Art. 1307-1461. 1947.

Eric Newton. The Meaning of Beauty. 1950.

Arnold Hauser. The Sacred History of Art. 1952.

Bernard Berenson. Seeing and Knowing. 1953.

Royal Academy of Arts. Portuguese Art. 1955.

Lawrence Stone. Sculpture in Britain – The Middle Ages. 1955.

John Betjeman. Guide to English Churches. 1958.

Claude Blair. European Armour. 1958.

Joyce Cary. Art and Reality. 1958.

Professor Francis Wormald and Messrs Sotheby & Co. The Dyson Perrins
    Illuminated Manuscripts. 1958-59-60.

Tempyō No Jihō. Nara Museum. Japan.

Kokuhō (National Treasures of Japan). Mainichi Shimbunsha. 1961.
    Both these volumes are in The British Museum.

A. F. Shore. Portrait Painting from Roman Egypt. 1962.

Sir James Mann. European Arms and Armour. Wallace Collection. 1962.

J. G. Hawthorne (translation by). On Divers Arts. Theophilus
    (11th-12th century). 1963.

F. R. Girling. English Merchants' Marks. 1964.

Sabrina Mitchell. Medieval Manuscript Painting. 1964.

V. Beyer. Stained Glass Windows. 1964.

John Beckworth. Early Medieval Art. 1964.

G. Sourchal, E. Carli and J. Gudiol. Gothic Painting. 1964.

H. Delaborde (Paris). La Gravure. N.D.

CHAPTER ONE

Introduction

THIS BOOK, it is believed, is the first of its kind, in that the majority of the illustrations are reproduced as 'positives' taken 'off the top of the brass originals', using a brass gilt colour base. This method ensures an authentic reproduction of the original design as conceived by the medieval craftsman. The frontispiece shows this correct presentation of the brass on its stone or marble casement. The illustrations are not artists' line drawings but are photographically reduced in size from original rubbings and rendered as positives.

Many books on monumental brasses have been published since Weaver's *Funeral Monuments* (1631) and Gough's *Sepulchral Monuments* (1786) – the first important treatises on the subject. To these pioneers we owe a debt, not only for their works as a whole, but also for recording some brasses and other monuments long since lost. Some writers of the 19th and 20th centuries illustrated their books by the use of steel, copper, wood, or lithographic positive drawings made by artists who employed a yellow base to give the effect of brass. Excellent though these are, they lack the authenticity that can only be obtained by photographic reductions taken from an original 'off the top of the brass' rubbing and presented as a positive. However brilliant and faithful to the original, the artists' drawings are bound to deviate in character and detail, because no artist or craftsman can be entirely accurate in his 'translation' – the human element is bound to intervene, which in this particular instance is a disadvantage. Here only one hundred per cent accuracy of the original can be accepted.

All museums, archaeological societies, and similar institutions holding large numbers of brass rubbings have always had 'negative' rubbings. These bodies used these negative rubbings because they were simple to make and they knew of no other reliable method of recording an incised brass. If a simple, accurate method of obtaining an 'off the top of the brass' positive had been known they would doubtless have preferred it to the negative technique.

The technique devised by the author of this book now makes it possible to obtain in quantity 'off the top of the brass' positive facsimiles of the same sizes as the originals. These facsimiles are not screened and are not photographic copies. They are now widely accepted by museums and similar institutions in this country and abroad.

The introduction of these positives has revealed new features of interest, such as the subtle variations in the original drawings of the faces of the persons depicted, proving that there are more real portraits in brass than had been thought. As every artist knows, a black line on a gilt (or a white) base has a different significance to that of a white line on black, and so the brass effigy when rendered as a positive gives different qualities – but correct ones – to that of the negative heel-ball rubbing.

Monumental brasses have been largely thought of in the past as of interest only to the archaeologist; rarely have they been given serious consideration by the art critic or art historian; yet many of these memorial effigies rank considerably higher as works of art than countless drawings, paintings, manuscripts, and sculptures of parallel date. Today this attitude has changed; the 'brass-rubbing era' is here – with far more adherents than it ever had before. Minds conditioned by 20th-century artistic awareness now fully appreciate the art of the designers who were responsible for the many first-class incised brass effigies that have survived.

More and more books on church brasses are now available, written by

learned amateur and professional archaeologists, which enable their readers
to form a fairly correct assessment of the history of the brasses as well as of the
individuals represented. The present writer makes no attempt to enlarge
upon this latter aspect, but has attempted to show the way to a better understanding of these monuments as recognizable works of art. The illustrations
represent only a small selection of the many available. They have been
chosen for their beauty or for some other special significance in the art
history of brasses. The incised brass memorial is invaluable in that it enables
one to trace the development and decline of a certain art form over several
centuries. Some of our brasses from medieval England are considerable
artistic achievements. Their design and craftsmanship are so excellent and
refined that they surpass the widely acclaimed, large, quadrangular continental brasses; these are indeed remarkable for their detail and craftsmanship but
fall short of the more subtle and simple early English brasses – mostly of the
14th century – which are unrivalled for their aesthetic and poetical qualities.

The study of monumental brasses has often been too restricted in scope
and confined to its own craft. Writers of the last century realized this –
Boutell and Haines included other types of monumental effigy but touched
on them too lightly to give a really comprehensive survey of the artistic and
basic relationships between the various arts and crafts. In such a survey it
would be necessary to include the study of social conditions and trade, both
in this country and on the Continent, the interchange of artistic ideas and
problems, and the more intimate study of the incised stone effigy, the sculptural stone and wooden effigy, brass and copper effigies, embroidery, coloured-
glass windows, mosaics, murals, enamels, illuminated manuscripts, paintings,
and engravings. All these had basic roots which were fed by the social conditions of the time, and by the religious tendencies and architecture of which
these crafts were the handmaidens.

Commercial and trading conditions had considerable influence on artist
and craftsman alike, for varied as their own particular crafts would be, the
circumstances under which they worked would be similar. It would not be
correct, however, to class all the memorial and incised brasses as popular folk
art. The best were inspired by a tradition of intellect and scholarship. The
majority of 16th-century brasses were produced by a band of inferior craftsmen eager to meet a demand from almost all classes except the poorest. This
resulted in the production of a mass of derivative brasses, a popular art or
craft in which the influence of the Christian Church had been lost, but
which was good enough for the large number of people who knew no better.
The 17th century virtually saw the end of the memorial incised brass. The
Renaissance had brought in a new outlook – a classical one, not belonging to
the people or popular art of this country, but an art that had found itself in
Italy and spread northwards through Europe during the 16th century.

The incised effigies and inscriptions on the monumental brass plates in our
parish churches have never been more popular than they are today. No
doubt this is due to the greater interest in archaeology and also to the fact
that people are now more widely aware that they can obtain positive or
negative facsimiles by taking rubbings from these attractive medieval memorials. Once permission has been obtained the technique of making a good
rubbing does not call for a high degree of skill. This volume is largely concerned with the aesthetics of monumental brasses, so it is necessary that the
reproductions should be shown as positives. This is the way in which they
were conceived by the medieval craftsman and therefore the only correct way
in which to read, view or judge them. Aesthetically there is no question of their
superiority as positives; one can say that a negative view is only half seen.

There is no yardstick by which one can measure aesthetics. One can say
'this is beautiful' or 'this is ugly'. The measure of beauty is a personal affair
based on special kinds of emotional experiences, but to write with authority
certain conditions are necessary.

The judgment of the aesthetics of a work of art is heightened and refined in the individual by a sound art training, by the correct environment and the acquisition of further knowledge over a considerable period of time in the arts, and especially by the study of artists and craftsmen and their works.

It is all too true that art criteria varies from decade to decade. It is only the work by the great original artist that reigns supreme from century to century, and even so, these works are subject to rise and fall according to taste and fashion. A great painting by Raphael was considered a great work of art when he created it in the 16th century. Today we still rate it as a great and important work, not only of the 16th century but of all time. R. Gough, a famous antiquary in the 18th century described certain large quadrangular foreign brasses of the 14th century as the product of 'Cellini of the 14th century'. Over a hundred years ago these same brasses were described as the finest examples of the craft and art of the incised memorial brass plate. Today, however, the art or aesthetics of these large designs is not placed so high. Expert opinion now gives pride of place to the designs of the English brasses of the same period, though technically the large quadrangulars are without peers.

On the subject of portraiture in brasses, I am quite convinced that there are considerably more portraits than is usually conceded. I venture to suggest that one who has spent the best part of a lifetime in drawing facial features, as well as in studying portraits by the great masters, is in a strong position when determining what constitutes a portrait on brass or otherwise. In my humble way, I have had that experience, and have projected positive enlargements of many faces from brasses onto a screen and studied them in detail, and by both means have arrived at this conclusion.

H.T.

ERRATA

In the text and lists and in the index an attempt has been made at consistency in name-spelling, often absent in contemporary practice.

p. 28, ON THE CONTINENT, l. 22; *for* Cremon *read* Cremen.

p. 31, plate 21, l. 2; *for* Charlons *read* Châlons.

plate 27, l. 1; *for* KURFÜST *read* KURFÜRST.

p. 35, FRENCH BRASSES, l. 4; *for* Advantage *read* Avantage.

plate 52, l. 1; *for* Aldbury *read* Albury.

p. 46, para. 2, l. 9; *for* Hervey *read* Herwy.

p. 51, plate 70, l. 1; *for* Stanford *read* Stamford.

p. 52, para. 4, l. 1; *for* Curtseys *read* Curteys.

p. 54, *The Tabard*, para. 2, l. 2; *for* (plate 54) *read* (plate 80).

p. 59, para. 3, l. 13; *for* Albury *read* Aldbury.

p. 63, plates 122 and 123; *for* 122 *read* JOHN KENT; *for* 123 *read* JOHN STONOR.

p. 68, l. 21; *for* Advantage *read* Avantage.

p. 82, CHALICE BRASSES, penult. line; *for* Yslyngeton *read* Yslyngton.

p. 87, plate 230; *for* Stanford *read* Stamford.

plate 236, l. 1; *for* Eddlesborough *read* Edlesborough.

p. 90, para. 3, l. 6; *for* Borgoyn *read* Burgoyn.

p. 140, FRANCE, l. 2; *for* Advantage *read* Avantage.

CHAPTER TWO

Early Memorials

IN TRACING the history of the monumental brass it is necessary to consider the subject of memorials as a whole. From the remote past up to the present day almost all civilizations have commemorated their dead, and among the innumerable monuments existing throughout the world, some are very humble and some of great splendour.

In this country there are no *ancient* monuments of real magnificence, but there are numerous cairns, monoliths, cromlechs, circles, barrows, and stone crosses that were erected by our distant ancestors. In Egypt there are the Pyramids containing the tombs of the Pharaohs; and the magnificent treasures of Tutankhamen's tomb discovered by Howard Carter in 1922 are without parallel. The Taj Mahal in India, the ancient mausoleums, the street tombs of Pompeii, the catacombs of Rome – that extensive network of underground galleries where the early Christians buried their dead in sculptural sarcophagi – are all forms of monument peculiar to the circumstances and customs and religion of the people of their time. It is probably in the Christian world that the greatest number and widest variety of monuments have been erected – to all classes of people from the humblest to the most exalted. A visit to any of our churchyards, cemeteries, cathedrals, or parish churches will confirm this statement.

Originally, the church was intended to be the sepulchre of the saint to whom it was dedicated, as well as a place for worship, and it was a principle to allow no other person to be buried in the consecrated ground. It was not long, however, before illustrious persons were permitted to be buried in God's house 'under the protection of the relics of the saints'. The first to be so privileged were highly placed ecclesiastics, kings, princes, and founders of these religious buildings. Once a grave had been allowed in the church it was necessary to indicate its position clearly, usually by a stone slab. Vaults, crypts, chapter-houses, and the cloisters of monasteries were used as places of burial. The dignity of humanity demanded a memorial superior to a plain stone covering, so this slab was later ornamented with an excess of design and craftsmanship. The tombs in early Christian churches consisted of a stone coffin sunk below the floor level and covered with a slab of stone or marble on which was cut a cross, or it was enriched with a foliage design. The memorial effigy came into being as a development of this method of burying the dead under the floor of the building, when the craftsman's art was used to commemorate the deceased by a sculptural, engraved, or painted effigy on the lid of the coffin or on top of the tomb. The Egyptians had done something similar a few thousand of years B.C. The mummies of their dead were placed in a coffin with a painted representation of the deceased on the coffin lid. These were not portraits in any meaning of the word, but some of the later wax paintings (of the early centuries A.D.) found in the tombs are remarkable character paintings – obviously portraiture.*

*See A. F. Shore, Portrait Painting from Roman Egypt (*British Museum*)

INCISED STONE SLABS AND INCISED BRASS PLATES

Three-dimensional sculpture can be traced back to the early days of civilization. A type of early monument was the domed tomb used by the Romans: the tomb of Hadrian is a well-known example. An early Christian example is that of the 3rd century – a small memorial cell in the cemetery of St Callisto. A domed structure of great historical importance is the 'Dome of the Rock'. This was probably erected by Constantine on the supposed site of the Holy Sepulchre, at Jerusalem. Crusader knights, thinking it to be part of the

Temple of Solomon, adapted its form for their own buildings, so where even in the West there appears a church of the Order of the Templars it perpetuates the plan of this Dome of the Rock.

In early Christian times sarcophagi with sculptural figures and gravestones with inscriptions and symbols were used. In Italy in particular we find sculptural sarcophagi dating from the 4th or 5th century. In a few instances the deceased is depicted in effigy form. The custom of the husband holding his wife's hand, or of the couple kneeling, is evidenced on these early sarcophagi as well as on brasses in England dating from the 14th century or later. In these islands only the simplest type of gravestone or slab is found, dating from about the 4th century A.D. These are nothing more than plain covering slabs. The sepulchral cross slab was in use at the beginning of the Christian era: the earliest of these can be seen in the Vatican in Rome. The plain cross appears on some slabs together with a simple inscription. In these islands slabs with crosses and inscriptions can be dated as early as the 7th century.

Two standing crosses, probably the most remarkable in Britain, are the Bewcastle and Ruthwell crosses. The former is in Cumberland and the latter in Dumfriesshire, not more than thirty miles apart. Both these crosses belong to the Northumbrian renaissance of the 7th-8th centuries though there is difference of opinion as to their exact dates and their origin. They are exceptional for their aesthetic qualities and brilliance of execution, and depict scenes from Christian iconography. There is also considerable contention regarding the sculptors who carved them: some experts stating that they are the work of the same person, or at least of the same school, while others claim that they are products of a different school, and are not of the same date – the Bewcastle Cross is estimated to be a hundred years older than the Ruthwell Cross.* The influence of these two standing crosses on the design of later monuments was considerable.

Returning to the coffin stone slab which is related to the standing cross both in material and workmanship, we find that by the 11th century the figure appears on the coffin slab. Crosses cut in relief are found in the centuries prior to this date (from the 7th century). A few iron slabs exist – probably Norman, 10th or 11th century. One of the earliest (if not the earliest) incised stone coffin slabs with a figure (crucifixion) occurs at Llanveynoe in Herefordshire. This was found about forty years ago with another memorial slab which contained an incised cross; they came from a burial ground adjacent to the church. The British Museum dates them 10th century; the lettering is Hiberno-Saxon. The incised stone figure is thought to be a pagan stone later used for Christian burial purposes after re-engraving. On the Continent there are earlier incised tombstones with figures, dating from the 8th and 9th centuries, such as Christ in Majesty, Portugal, 9th century. Another early example of a figure occurs in Perthshire – possibly St Angus, early 11th century.

Searching on the Continent for early dated memorial slabs, we find a few in German churches of the 10th and 11th centuries; some of these were discovered in the crypt of the churches, probably removed there when new churches were erected on old foundations.†

A most advanced form of early memorial is the cast bronze low relief effigy of King Rudolph of Swabia at Merseberg, Germany (1080) (see plate 9). An even earlier memorial in bronze, also in Germany, is the figure of Archbishop Adalbert (981) in the cathedral at Magdeburg. This does not show the skill or craftsmanship of the Merseburg memorial, although Germany was well in advance in metalwork compared with most other European countries.

Coffin slabs were made of various materials as available – alabaster, marble, polished sandstone, gritstone, and other similar stones. Unfortunately a great number of the early stone memorial slabs have perished and most of those remaining are in poor condition.

*Albert S. Cooke, The Date of the Ruthwell and Bewcastle Crosses (Yale University Press).

†There are numerous early memorial slabs prior to the 10th century scattered throughout Europe.

We have seen how the shrine of God was used to contain the shrine of mortals, using various forms and different mediums to perpetuate their memory. The primitive stone slab continued to be used, but simple patterns were added, so that the low-relief cross on the slab, the low-relief effigy, the three-dimensional effigy, the incised stone and the incised brass effigy are all types of memorial placed usually on top of the tomb or coffin. They appeared in this order:

1. Incised stone slab with designs, then the incised stone with effigy
2. The sculptural effigy (various materials)
3. The incised brass effigy (13th century).

The one did not supersede the other: the stone incised effigy, the sculptural effigy and the incised brass effigy were in use together for many centuries. The general characteristics of the incised stone effigy (apart from a few early ones) and the brass effigy are taken from the sculptural effigy and cast tomb effigy.

Just how grand or how humble the monument should be depended on the importance of the individual and the amount of money available. On top of the tomb was placed a slab or a brass with an effigy which often recorded his name, position, and date of death, and begged the passer-by to pray for his soul and that of his wife (and children). The large and imposing brasses on the Continent are restricted to persons of the highest rank or condition: royalty, ecclesiastics, nobility and wealthy merchants. A few of the incised stone slabs, however, appear to commemorate the passing of persons of lower position. It was a very special privilege, even in later times, to be buried within the precincts of the church or cathedral, granted only to persons of great distinction.

By the time the incised brass effigy had arrived in England, sculptors had produced remarkable three-dimensional effigies in wood, stone, and metal. The stone figures of St Mary's Abbey, York (c. 1200), the stone figures of Wells Cathedral (c. 1225), the Purbeck marble effigy of King John, Worcester Cathedral (c. 1225-30), the stone effigy of Longespée, Salisbury Cathedral (1230-40), the recumbent effigy in stone at Pershore (1270), the Purbeck marble effigy of Bishop Kilkenny, Ely Cathedral (1255-60), the many stone relief carvings in Westminster Abbey (1250-60), and in Lincoln and Salisbury Cathedrals, and the wooden effigy of the Duke of Normandy (c. 1285), Gloucester Cathedral, all dating from the second half of the 13th century, and the Crusader Knight at Dorchester, Oxon (c. 1300) are all works of outstanding merit, produced by a variety of craftsmen with considerable French architectural leanings.

The sculptural effigy of John of Eltham in Westminster Abbey (c. 1340) was surely a model for some of the London school of brass effigy engravers in the 14th century. Uncross Eltham's legs and you have the type of effigy in armour that can be seen in many brasses of the second half of the 14th century. The armour changes with the passing of years, but the basic feeling of the Eltham effigy is perpetuated for the rest of the century. Only in the early part of the 15th century does the effigy take on different basic characteristics, enabling one to realize that a new century has brought with it new craftsmen – some of great skill, but less inspired than their predecessors.

*The incised stone memorial slab with effigies can be found on the Continent in increasing numbers from the 12th century onwards, but in decreasing numbers in this country. Here the monumental incised brass slab found favour for various reasons, such as transport, cost and durability, but probably the most important reason was that the English craftsman preferred to engrave on metal rather than on stone – it suited his temperament better.

This country was once very rich in the number of brasses it possessed: some authorities have placed the figure at 150,000 (and 50,000 on the Continent), but only some 10,000 remain today (including inscriptions). There are, however, far greater numbers of incised stone slabs on the Continent,

Those interested in sculptural effigy tombs should read The Street of the Tombs *in* The Stones of Venice *by John Ruskin.*

1. Egyptian funeral portrait (Fayum) 1st century A.D. A portrait full of the intense emotion of a person suffering from illness. The physical attributes of this head are used in such a way by the artist that they give a portrait of the soul or spirit of this lady who died about 1800 years ago. The original is in colour.

2. Crucifixion. Llanveynoe, Herefordshire (c. 10th century).

3

4

5

Three three-dimensional effigies similar to contemporary two-dimensional brass effigies.

3. JOHN OF ELTHAM (alabaster), Westminster Abbey (*c.* 1340).
A model for many incised brass effigies of London workshops.

4. Knight at the Church of Holy Cross, Whorlton, Yorks (*c.* 1305).
Wooden effigy. Note the crossed legs and the bare ankles. The head rests on a cushion. The whole design is similar to contemporary brasses. It is a work of considerable power and carved by an artist of deep emotional feeling.

5. SIR JOHN DAUBYGNE 1346, Brize Norton, Oxon.
A monumental slab – panels sunk at the upper and lower parts. This is similar to a slab with effigy of Sir William de Staunton, Staunton, Notts, 1226, which is an early example of the traditional posture.

6

7

6. THE ROTHWELL CROSS, Dumfriesshire.
Figure of Christ (north face).

7. The Bewcastle Cross, Cumberland. John the Baptist, figure of Christ
and Runes.

8. CHARLEMAGNE (742-814).
An idealistic portrait by Dürer painted in 1512 for the loyal town of Nuremberg. Compare this with the bronze tomb figure of Rudolph, King of Swabia, in Merseberg Cathedral, only 130 miles due north of Nuremberg.

9. THE RUDOLPH EFFIGY c. 1080. Merseberg.

10. ROBERT COURTHOSE, Duke of Normandy, Gloucester Cathedral (c. 1285).
Painted wooden effigy. This altar tomb is slightly earlier than the alabaster crusader Knight in a similar attitude at Dorchester-on-Thames, Oxon. The latter is a more vigorous work.

11. CRUSADER KNIGHT c. 1300. Dorchester, Oxon.

However, if in addition to figure slabs, other types of slabs are included such as cross-slabs, Lombardic and black letter inscriptions, etc., the total would exceed the brass total by four or five times. The total number of recorded brasses of all types on the Continent number about 600.

they are perhaps as numerous as brasses are in this country, although probably 1,000 slabs with effigy exist in these islands today.* For some reason not quite clear, more research has been undertaken in the past on incised brasses than on incised stone slabs. However, considerable work in this connection is now being carried out by knowledgeable individuals and the picture at present is a changing one. Such work is of great value in showing a closer link in the chain, and the picture resolves itself more and more clearly.

It would be appropriate here to clarify the use of terms in connection with the Monumental brass itself. The effigies, inscriptions, shields, canopies, arms etc., are engraved on the flat brass metal plate (or plates). These are set into the stone or marble slab which is called the casement. The countersunk design which has been cut into the casement to receive the engraved brass plate (or plates) is known as the indent. This is sometimes called a matrix. Both terms are correct.

CHAPTER THREE

The Rudolph Effigy

THE FORERUNNER OF THE BRASS EFFIGY?

BY THE MIDDLE of the 11th century German metal workers were the most advanced of their age and had completely mastered the art of metal casting. In fact, Germany has always excelled in the use of metals, and does so to this day.

An outstanding early example of metal casting in Germany is to be seen in Merseburg Cathedral in Saxony. It is a bronze tomb figure in relief of Rudolph, King of Swabia, who died in 1080, the approximate date of this remarkable effigy. It is finely executed, a dignified figure in an excellent state of preservation, and it is *the earliest existing metal tomb figure in Europe*. The inscription runs in border form along the four sides of the rectangle – similar to the method employed on the large monumental brasses 200 years later. This monument is one hundred and fifty years older than the earliest brass effigy, which is Bishop Yso von Welpe* at Verden, Hanover (1231) also in north Germany. In fact, Rudolph's bronze effigy is similar to the single-effigy monumental brasses, and it would appear to be the forerunner of the incised brasses and the incised stone monumental slab with effigy.

*Plate 14

Over a hundred years ago the Reverend Herbert Haines put forward the theory that the incised brass effigy derived from the Limoges enamels.† He cites the early example of the use of Limoges enamels on an effigy of Geoffrey Plantagenet (1150) – or perhaps of some other unknown noble (c. 1196) – in the museum at Le Mans as the probable forerunner of the brass incised effigy. This is on copper, size 24in x 12in and is rectangular in shape. The figure rests on a diapered background, under a canopy with an inscription at the top. The effigy is in low relief in champ-levé enamelled colours. It is dated 1150 and so is eighty-one years earlier than the earliest existing brass, or fifty-eight years earlier than the lost brass at St Paul's, Bedford (see page 24). Haines quotes other examples of enamelled monuments that once existed in French churches but are now lost, though drawings of a number are preserved in Oxford. Haines says that 'towards the 12th century *we find for the first time an attempt made to represent the figure of the person commemorated, by effigy in low relief on the coffin lid,‡* the raised border being still retained, good examples of which are an abbot (Gislebertus Crispinus, Abes, 1114?) at Westminster, and Bishop Roger and Jocelin, 1139-1184, in Salisbury Cathedral.' Later examples are quoted by Haines – an interesting one at the Cistercian Abbey of Villiers in Brabant where both the brass and the copper enamel are used on a stone incised slab. It would appear that Haines was not aware of the existence of the Rudolph memorial. This low relief effigy in Merseburg Cathedral is seventy years earlier than the Limoges figure of Geoffrey Plantagenet, one hundred and fifty-one years earlier than the Verden brass, and thirty-four years earlier than the Crispinus memorial at Westminster. Haines goes on to say that

†A Manual of Monumental Brasses (2 Vols.), 1861, H. Haines. The best publication on the subject in the last century. Haines was a pioneer with original thoughts – his writings demand attention. Knowledge of art, artists, and craftsmen was not so readily available as it is today; it is unfortunate that some subsequent writers have copied Haines without research.

‡My italics.

because the Limoges enamels suggested the adoption of the monumental brasses, it is not to be supposed that these memorials were first made in that city, or even France. It is more likely that the art originated in Germany, in which country the metal was largely manufactured, and in the northern portion of which, especially the kingdom of Hanover and duchies of Mecklenburgh and Brunswick, some of the earliest and finest brasses are to be found. [Haines refers to the large quadrangular brasses.] That the

*My italics.

Flemish were early celebrated for their *skill in engraving** these memorials is evident from the fine specimens remaining at Bruges, Ghent and other parts of Belgium. As their reputation extended also into Germany, it is most probable that many of the finest examples existing in that country, as at Lübeck and Schwerin, are the production of Flemish artists.

CHAPTER FOUR

The Earliest Brasses

As previously mentioned, the earliest *existing* brass with *effigy* is in Germany – the incised brass effigy of Bishop Yso von Welpe at Verden (1231). That there was once a considerable number of brasses with effigies in Western Europe of 13th-century date is almost certain, and all indicates that Germany was the originator and was the first country to produce them in quantity. Sometimes stone and brass were used together on the same memorial.

One of the earliest brasses – if not the earliest existing in England – is an *inscription* at Ashbourne, Derbyshire, dated 1241 (see Inscriptions on Brasses, page 89).* The earliest *existing* brass with an incised effigy in England is that of Sir John d'Aubernoun (1277), which marks the beginning of the 'brass era' in this country, extending to about the mid-18th century when the craft almost died out. A few brasses were put down in the remaining period up to the present day, when an odd one here and there is still laid down.

The Earliest Known Brass?

In St Paul's Church at Bedford there is a casement which once held some metal (brass?). This is thought to be a slab to Simon Beauchamp who died in 1208. This would make it twenty-four years earlier than the earliest existing brass, to Bishop Welpe. The Bedford casement is badly worn. The following description is taken from Macklin's *The Brasses of England* (*an excellent volume*).

In St Paul's Church, Bedford, lies a slab with the worn matrix of a large latin cross, 69in x 30in, with serrated or indented edges; it sprang from a quadrangular plate 17in x 19in and on either side of the head there was a small shield. At the north edge are faint traces of a matrix of a border fillet. This is believed to be the memorial of (Sir) Simon de Beauchamp, 1208, thus mentioned by Leland (*Itinerary*, vol. 1, fol. 116): 'He lieth afore the high altar of St Paul's Church in Bedford, with this epitaphie graven in brass and set on a flat stone "De Bello Campo jacet hic sub Harmore Simon Foundator de Newenham".'

The present writer visited St Paul's, Bedford, and obtained the following information from Mr F. W. Kuhlicke, Director of the Bedford Museum:

The Beauchamp indent is exactly as Macklin describes it. The evidence as to its name is entirely that of Leland, which I have no reason to oppose, seeing that the Beauchamp family was so closely connected with both Bedford Castle and St Paul's Church. The slab is to the south of the high altar and is well protected with felt. It shows very slight markings of the cross and the shields, but I cannot trace any sign of the lettering. As to Simon of the slab, it would be unwise to refer to him as Sir Simon, as although he held a large number of manors and knights fees there is no evidence of his having received the accolade.

How is it that this type of memorial appears in this country at so early a date? It is likely that there were several other such memorials of early 13th-century date that have long since been removed. St Albans or some place not far away with a school of craftsmen could have executed this for Simon Beauchamp. The monks and craftsmen of places of learning like St Albans were widely travelled in the 13th century. They and their fellow artists from Canterbury were in touch with the Rhenish and Mosan schools in the 12th century. The work of the St Albans Psalter proves this. Macklin

The oldest recorded inscription on brass is dated 1189 at Regensburg, Germany. See plate 261.

12. Mosan copper gilt plaque crucifixion. First quar ter 13th century (dated by the Victoria and Albe: Museum). Similar date to Yso von Welpe (see text size 11½" x 8¾".

IHC·NAZA
RENVS·REX
IVDEORV·CO

13

14

13. BISHOP OTTO DE BRUNSWICK 1279. Hildesheim. German work. 77″ x 30″ In his hand he holds a model of the castle of Woloenbergh – he was its builder. He died in his 32nd year. This could well be a portrait of the young bishop. A good objective design. This brass is only slightly more accomplished work than that of Yso von Welpe though nearly 50 years separate them. When viewing these two brasses two points must be taken into consideration. 1. The great ages to which they have attained, during which periods they have become worn, losing some of their definition. 2. Inferior rubbings – it requires more than average skill to 'interpret' these brasses. Breaks, indentations and similar damage should only be restored by a highly skilled artist who understands the meaning of the incised line of the 13th century.

14. BISHOP YSO VON WELPE 1231, Verden, Hanover. German work, a probable portrait. The earliest existing brass effigy – ten years senior to the Ashbourne inscription. The Rev Creeny in 1884 in a description of this brass wrote, 'the drawing might have been better, the lines bolder, firmer, and the whole work more artistic, but not by this artist – not in the year 1231.' The Verden brass is a more accomplished work than Creeny would allow. Victorian standards of judgment were often faulty. The illustration of the Mosan Crucifixion (fig. 12) is dated by the Victoria and Albert Museum (c. 1225). It is an example of metal engraving and design of a very high standard produced in Western Europe – not very far from Verden. 79″ x 29″.

15. THOMAS DE LA MERE, abbot 1349-96, St Alban's Cathedral, Herts.
Size 112″ x 52″. An example of good craftsmanship.

17

17a

100 Miles

BELGIUM to-day

dotted area English

Black.Flanders about 1360

16

18

16. Centre panel of Alton Towers, Triptych, Mosan (*c.* 1150). Champlevé enamel on gilt copper. The diagrammatic, compartmental, encyclopedic, symbolical and literary approach by the designer of this Triptych is similar to the approach of the designers of the quadrangular brasses, 170 years later. Similar characteristics can be found in the Mosan illuminations.

17. SEAL OF ROBERT THE BRUCE OF SCOTLAND 1322
In the Archives, Lübeck.

17a. Arms of the Hanse in London.

18. Flanders in the mid-14th century.

records five other lost brasses in this country of mid-13th century date. It must be remembered that the gaps between the dates of the earliest brasses are considerable. Doubtless quite a large number have been lost to us that would have been invaluable to fit together to form the picture of early 13th-century brasses.

The author has visited hundreds of churches, and it is only too clear that many of the worn casements, some so badly defaced that it is impossible to recognize the design, must have contained brasses of great antiquity. It is known that several brasses existed in Britain which went back at least to the 13th century.

THE HANSEATIC LEAGUE

All the brass that was used in England up to the reign of Queen Elizabeth I was imported from the Continent. The majority of this brass passed through the hands of German merchants who controlled the sea trade between England and Europe. Their rule extended to the far Baltic ports in the east, to France in the west, and to Italy in the south, whence they obtained riches from the Far East. During the 12th and 13th centuries north German towns had formed their own 'Hanse' or guild and only members of it were allowed to trade with England. Lübeck, Hamburg, Bremen, and Cologne were the important ports. The merchandise which passed through the hands of the German traders undoubtedly included quite a considerable quantity of brass for use as memorials in this country. When it is realized that many thousands of brasses were laid down during the 14th, 15th, and the 16th centuries, it is evident that they must have represented a considerable sum of money. Lübeck became the most important port of Germany and controlled all exchange of goods between continental countries, from the Low Countries to Poland and Scandinavia (*The Germans in England*, I. Colvin).

Flanders, especially Bruges, was important to the Hanse. The affairs of the German guild at Bruges became the centre of interest for all German towns from Gotland and Livland to the Rhine.

Bruges, in particular, was the meeting-place of numerous foreign merchants, from England, France, Spain, Portugal, Italy, and elsewhere. A recent book on Bruges* describes the city in the 14th century as 'one of the factories of the Teutonic Hanseatic League. At the time of the formation of the Staple of Calais the city of Bruges had a population of over 35,000. Under the influence of the Hanse, the city chose its coat-of-arms, which it still bears today, the basic red and silver colours of which are borrowed from the Hanseatic cities.' The dominant German traders used and sold raw materials from Flanders. The Germans spoke Flemish, French, or their own language – there was no language problem. The towns of Tournai, Dinant, and Ghent (then the largest town in Flanders, with a population of over 60,000) supplied various types of stone of a dark colour widely used throughout western Europe. It was ideal for monumental work and had been used for a considerable time for this purpose, being employed for fonts, bowls, and sculptural effigies and incised slabs.

The Germans must have supplied the money for the majority of the very large and costly quadrangular brasses discussed in the next chapter. Most of them are situated outside Flanders. Apart from those in England, only four of the 14th century examples are outside Germany or German-controlled states. The Germans must have given their approval for the export of these commodities; indeed, if there are others from this same workshop in other domains it would be due to the encouragement given by the Hanse.

Some of the brasses commemorate individuals who were merchant members of the Hanseatic League and therefore German, as all members had to be of this nationality. In the wills of two 14th-century Lübeck councillors – Warendorp and Gallin – are requests for brass memorials from Flanders. We can assume they were exported from Flanders (via the Hanseatic League).

*Bruges, City of Art (*Gidsen Bond*).

Jacques Couves specifies a design *similar* to the Flemish. It is unfortunate that these brasses did not survive for us to see. Many must have perished over the centuries. Were they really Flemish?

The following brief account of the training of the German apprentice craftsman (*Gesell*) is important because of the close association of the Hanseatic League with the young German student craftsman.

THE GERMAN GESELL

The early German guilds (*Gildwesen*) combined for general advantage, electing a burgomaster as the district head. As these districts developed they formed cities. In the 11th and 12th centuries they were known as Reichstädte or cities of the Empire. Others, though they did not acquire this dignity, maintained privileges and were known as Freistädte, or free cities. From these the Hanse towns developed, to protect their trade, their rights, their arts and crafts, enabling the tradesmen to proceed from city to city without hindrance. Thus it came about that no person would be allowed to follow his handicraft unless he would conform to the regulations of the guild.

The German apprentice (*Gesell*), after training under his master and receiving a certificate from his guild, had to perfect himself by travel and working as he proceeded on his journey (*Wandershaft*). This could last from three to six years and was termed Wanderjahre. On his return he had to submit a 'masterpiece' which, on approval by the masters of the guild, admitted him to become a master himself and entitled him to exercise his profession in the free city. The German apprentice during his wandering years had opportunities to see the extent of other craftsmen's work in his fatherland. He could study the various types of handicraft, visit famous places and buildings, meet a variety of men and manners, acquire a broad understanding of his fellow-creatures and practise his craft as he travelled at public cost. He went from one Herberge to another. The Herberge was a building where the guild had its chest – where the apprentice would lodge and find a local work-master, who, if he required help, would engage and help him and give any information that he might require.

If he were ill he would be cared for at the Herberge. In large towns each trade had its Herberge for the various handicrafts – workers in iron, copper and other metals, cabinet-makers, carvers, locksmiths, stone-workers, goldsmiths, workers in silk, wool, wood and leather, shoemakers, saddlers, glove-makers and other trades. In a small town or village there would be only one Herberge for the use of the Gesell. All the different trades or crafts were under one roof. The travelling apprentice had to carry the tools of his trade with him as well as spare clothes and other necessities.

Providing the apprentice had sufficient money he would be allowed to cross the border into another country. A number of apprentices meeting up together would join forces and cross into the foreign country in strength. The Low Countries were subject to visits by the German Gesell. They would not obtain the same protection and facilities as they had enjoyed in their own fatherland. However they often made contact with some of the towns controlled by their own Hanse. Bruges, Antwerp and other Low Country cities were often their destinations. A few went to France and elsewhere including England. The apprentice, if he decided to cross the border, did this towards the end of his term of apprenticeship, feeling that he had obtained skill in his calling and would be in a position to obtain some work to enable him to make his way. In Bruges for instance he would meet his own countrymen as well as in other towns where the German merchants of the Hanseatic League traded and had their own accommodation and buildings.

At the beginning of the 14th century when the wealthy merchants of the Hanse were living and trading in Flanders, these Gesell soon became familiar with the industries of the Flemish by visiting them at their work. The German merchants explained to their young countrymen, who were fully skilled as craftsmen and designers, the requirements of the prelates and merchant-princes of such items as they could produce in their own country. The method of training the apprentice craftsman by travelling and practising his craft was not confined to the Germans but it was the Germans who organised the system and carried it out with more thoroughness than other nationalities.

In the 14th century it was the Germans who were masters of industry in Northern Europe. They could afford to pay vast sums of money for their large memorials. This they did – others copied and followed.

CHAPTER FIVE

The Large Quadrangular Brasses

THE LARGE 14th-century quadrangular brasses, situated in England and on the Continent and usually called 'Flemish' brasses, form an important section in the history of monumental brasses, so some investigation into their origin is necessary. Fifteenth-century quadrangulars are not included; they are different in character but retain certain traditional trends.

Those listed are as follows:

ON THE CONTINENT

Bishops Godfrey and Frederic de Bulowe, Schwerin, Germany (East)	1314-75	151" x 76"
Bishops Burchard von Serkin and Jon von Mul, Lübeck, Germany (East)	1317-50	142" x 73"
King Eric and Queen Ingeborg, Ringsted, Denmark	1319	112" x 66"
Frau Ramborg de Wik, Vester Åker, Upsala, Sweden	1327	73" x 37"
William Wenemaer and wife, Ghent, Belgium ..	1325-52	84" x 30"
John and Gerard de Heere, Brussels, Belgium ..	1332-98	101" x 62"
Bishops Ludolph and Henry de Bulowe, Schwerin, Germany (East)	1339-47	115" x 71"
Bishop Bernard de Lippe, Paderborn, Germany (West) (*cut to shape*)	1340	97" x 51"
Johann Clinghenberg, Lübeck, Germany (East) (destroyed in 1939-45 war)	1356	
Proconsul Albert Hovener, Stralsund, Germany (East)	1357	100" x 50"
Merchant Johannes von Zoest and wife, Thoun, Poland	1361	124" x 64"
Proconsul Bruno von Warendorp, Lübeck, Germany (East) (*cut to shape*)	1369	103" x 52"
Bishop Bertram Cremon, Lübeck, Germany (East)	1377	115" x 73"
Bishop Rupert, Paderborn, Germany (West) ..	1394	84" x 39"
Bishop Lampertus, Bamberg, Germany (West) ..	1399	63" x 42"
John and Symo Segmund, Nordhausen, Germany (East)	1400	77" x 42"

IN ENGLAND

Adam de Walsohne and wife, King's Lynn, Norfolk	1349	118" x 68"
Thomas Delamere (abbot), St Albans, Herts ..	1360	111" x 52"
Simon de Wensley (priest), Wensley, Yorks ..	c. 1370	64" x 19"
Priest (Kesteven ?), North Mimms, Herts (*small*)..	1360	47" x 19½"
This is listed because it is similar in certain details.		
Robert Braunche and two wives, King's Lynn, Norfolk	1364	106" x 61"
Ralph de Knevyngton, Aveley, Essex (*small*) ..	1370	
Robert Attlath, King's Lynn, Norfolk (*lost brass*)..	1370	
Known by an existing rubbing, Attlath was a merchant.		
Alan Fleming, Newark, Notts	1375	112" x 67"
Thomas de Topcliffe and wife (palimpsest), Topcliffe, Yorks	1362-91	70" x 36"

There are many fragments in existence, some from large quadrangular brasses, as well as other continental brasses of the 15th century 'cut to shape' which are too numerous to list. The two listed above are included because of their dates and locality, which point to other craftsmen producing completely different brasses at the same time that the quadrangulars were executed.

The large brass of Bishop Otto de Brunswick, Hildesheim, Germany (1279) is not included because it is different in conception. It is 77″ x 30″ (see plate 13).

The large quadrangular 'Flemish' brasses of the 14th century cover a period of over eighty years. The small total remaining today suggests that there must have been other similar brasses, long since lost. The majority of those that remain are illustrated in Creeny's excellent volume*. All the illustrations are taken from negative rubbings made almost entirely by Creeny himself. (See List of Continental Brasses.)

These quadrangular brasses are usually made up of several smaller pieces of brass about one-eighth of an inch thick, welded together with expert skill to form one large sheet. The design was drawn or traced out on the polished surface and the engraving incised by the craftsmen. The incised lines were then filled in with a mastic material in red, black, or white. This helped to resist wear by walking feet and also helped to show the design more clearly.

The largest of these brasses is the one to Bishops Godfrey and Frederic de Bulowe (1314-75) at Schwerin, Germany. This brass is 151in by 76in. On an average most of the quadrangular brasses exceed 8ft by 4ft.

The production of somewhat similar brasses continued into the 15th and 16th centuries. With the passing of time, however, the size diminished and the designs changed, becoming more and more akin to the art of the succeeding centuries and of the countries in which they were designed.

On these 14th-century brasses every possible square inch is occupied by some form of engraving, unlike the brasses produced in England in which the figure (or figures) are cut to shape and sunk into the indent in the casement. The extra furnishings are also sunk into the casement, and the intervening spaces are left clear, showing the polished surface of the casement.

These 'Flemish' quadrangular brasses must not be confused with the small English quadrangular brasses of the 16th and 17th centuries.

Artistically these brasses must be considered as a superb craftsman's artistic failure. They are engraved with figures in canopies: more and more canopies and niches with stylized figures 'dead as mutton'. The canopies grow and grow, arch upon arch, gable over gable, crocket upon crocket, finial upon finial, all reaching heavenwards in a confused mass of architecture – a monotonous repetition of brilliant technique by the designers in an effort to hide the obvious fact that invention and originality were not theirs. Shafts with niches containing figures stand one above another and side by side. In the long narrow compartments under the effigies are scenes of the countryside – woodlands, people feasting or hunting, and similar subjects, all within a rectangular plane quite unrelated to the design scheme as a whole and detracting from the main figure to whom the brass is dedicated. Others have spires like mountain peaks reaching higher and higher, and the inevitable canopies supporting superstructure upon superstructure! 'Passion of pinnacle and fret' John Ruskin called it when writing of similar designs of coloured glass windows with canopies. Every possible space is filled in with intricate detail. They were not decorated constructions, which is right, but constructed decorations, which is wrong. These gigantic designs do not hold together as a whole in spite of the attempt to make them do so by keeping the central figure (or figures) simpler in character and in tonal contrast to the rest of the scheme. The concretion of gothic detail – shafts, canopies, niches, figures of saints and angels – is combined with a mass of intricate diaper work

*The Rev W. F. Creeny. A Book of Facsimiles of Monumental Brasses on the Continent of Europe 1884.

19. LAMBIERS D'ABEE et Getrus 1312, Chapel of Abée, Belgium.

124″ x 64″. Incised lime-stone slabs – the faces, the hands and the two hands of God are white marble – inserted and engraved. *The hand of God blessing the persons appears on several slabs, but as far as I know does not appear on brasses.* – H.T.

or reticulated decoration. Remember, these are monuments to the dead placed in a church or cathedral where coloured glass windows would let in little light!

These long narrow compartments with pictorial scenes are mainly copied from pre-Christian times. They are not original interpretations. The peacock feast on the Braunche brass (King's Lynn, 1364) derives from the pagan feast when the peacock of Juno was eaten, which was supposed to exempt one from decay. This is well illustrated on the walls of the tombs of the Roman catacombs dating from the 2nd century, where the artists modified the pagan scene to suit the Christian funeral.

In the compartment under Adam de Walsohne (King's Lynn, 1349) a horseman is carrying grist to the mill; there are similar subjects in the catacomb paintings, mostly taken from pagan scenes but adapted for Christian purposes. Representations of pagan deities are replaced by Christian figures.

The brass of Bishops Godfrey and Frederic de Bulowe (Schwerin) (1314-75) is composed of nine towers with eighty-nine pinnacles at the top, and altogether two hundred and fifty pinnacles and goblets. If these are added to the nine goblets and pinnacles that are above each of the groined roofs of the tabernacles on which stand three dozen saints and prophets in the side and central shafts, this means one hundred and sixty-two more, making in all four hundred and twelve of these architectural enrichments – all pointing heavenwards!

The laying out of this design prior to its execution on the brass surface must have conformed to contrived geometrical laws and dimensions and that is why its perfection is so utterly cold and lifeless. There is far more happiness, warmth and inspiration in many a small English brass than there is in this large, overworked design.

Macklin in *The Brasses of England* comments thus upon the possible origin of these brasses:

It is strange that the origin of such pre-eminent works of art should be so obscure. From whence did they come, and who were their designers, engravers? It is impossible to say with certainty. They have been persistently called 'Flemish' but are *unlike any brasses now existing in the Low Countries*. 'North Germany' is a better term, or perhaps 'Teutonic'. Strong probabilities, however, point to the city of Lübeck. Its citizens elected Eric of Denmark as their lord, and his brass at Ringsted is almost certainly proved to have issued from the same workshop as that of two of its bishops. Stralsund is upon the Baltic coast, within easy reach of Lübeck by sea, and Schwerin, a few miles inland, lies between. The trading towns of the Baltic were nearly all of them connected by the Hanseatic League and looked to Lübeck as their commercial capital. Stralsund was an important member of the confederation. On the business of the League the family of von Zoest is known to have migrated to Poland. This great Teutonic Hanse was founded by Lübeck and Hamburg in 1266, in rivalry with the Hanse of Cologne and was joined by all towns of the Baltic trade. The Flemish towns belonged to a totally distinct league, with Bruges and Ypres as their head, trading chiefly with London. The merchants of Lynn were therefore in special and direct communication with Lübeck, while Newark might be reached by way of Hull and the river Trent. It was Lübeck, we may surely say, which produced the finest brasses in the world and from Lübeck – not Flanders – came those which we are fortunate to possess at Newark, St Albans and King's Lynn.

This was written over fifty years ago and since then a few facts have been revealed but nothing that could establish *beyond doubt* the origin of these brasses. It is interesting to note that Macklin says that they are unlike any brasses existing in the Low Countries. Since then writers have differed about

20. AGNES DE SAINT AMANT 1296, Museum at Rouen, France.
Size 102″ x 49½″. French incised slab. A beautiful example. Compare with one of the large quadrangular brasses which are quickly following in date. The aesthetic quality of these slabs cannot be doubted, far, far ahead of the 'quadrangulars'. Definitely not the same designs or the same craftsmen.

21

21. EUDELINE CHAUBRANT et sa Filles 1338,
Charlons-sur-Marne, France.
Size 126″ x 64″. Another very fine example of an engraved stone slab, contemporaneous to the large
brasses. The superior method of reproducing these
raised slabs as positives must be very apparent when
they are compared to the same examples reproduced
as negative rubbings.

this statement, some claiming that they are alien to German art of the 14th
century and are definitely Flemish in spirit and origin.

Hans Eichler, in *Jahrbüch 1933 der Königlich Preussischen Kunstammlungen*,
makes a strong claim that the majority of these large quadrangular brasses
were the products of a single Flemish workshop, probably in or near Bruges.
Eichler devotes nearly twenty pages (including illustrations) to this theory,
often using archaic German. Other writers since 1933 have copied Eichler.
S. Collon Gevaert, in *Histoire des Arts du Métal en Belgique* (1951), is one of
these. He brings little fresh information to light. Let us consider his views
first.

Gevaert states that monumental brasses originated in Flanders,* but that
this was long in dispute because English craftsmen designed similar works
on 'cullen plates of brass' which they obtained from Flanders (Cullen =
Köln, Germany). There are no records to show when England first imported
brass from Flanders or Germany, but the earliest record available proves that
Germany was exporting to England about 1450. Gevaert says that England
was poor and could not afford large plates of brass, so Dinant sent over
throw-outs which English craftsmen engraved on the reverse side. There is
evidence of late 13th-century brasses in Liége: Bishop Hugh de Pierrepont
and Bishop Jean d'Apo; also a brass (1301) in memory of a canon. These
have long since perished. Gevaert suggests that Bruges was a centre for
engraving brasses after 1300, but it would appear that it had no previous
tradition for the art and craft of engraving precious metals. He thinks that
goldsmiths could have been responsible for the brasses. (Germany had produced brasses in the previous century – England and France also.)

The brass of King Eric and his queen Ingeborg (1319) in Ringsted,
Denmark, is, according to Gevaert, not like the other brasses of the 14th
century. He thinks it derives from stone slabs of the 13th century. The sculptural memorial to Bishop Henri von Bocholt at Lübeck (see plate 33) could
have been made, he claims, in Ghent, Bruges, or England. He mentions
several other of these large brasses but only says 'possibly from Bruges – or
Ghent', but adds that he believes the figures are not by the same craftsmen or
the surrounds and were probably put in at a later date. (Close examination
supports this statement.)

Hans Eichler claims that the Flemish workshop of his theory, or its influence, existed for about a hundred years – from the early 14th to the early
15th centuries. He is not as thorough as one would wish when he tries to
trace the *artistic* background of the brasses. He describes them in detail,
compares them to each other, and gives their location, but fails to take into
consideration the possible influence of German or English brasses of earlier
date: he does not *fully* explain how these brasses may have evolved from earlier
ideas. It is not established beyond doubt that Bruges, or even Flanders, was
the centre of production – more probably Bruges was the selling rather than
the productive centre.

There is little attempt to show how the craft of brass incising developed in
order to produce this type of brass from the 'Flemish' workshop, apart from
the statement that there are similar incised slabs in Flanders. It is suggested
that the inspiration came via French stained-glass windows, possibly from
Rouen and Evreux Cathedrals, and that there could have been an English

*This is very doubtful – there is no proof whatsoever.

Reviewing *The Incised Slabs of Leicestershire and Rutland, 1958*, F. A. Greenhill.
The following is an extract from *Transactions of the Monumental Brass Society*,
Vol IX, Part VII, No. LXXVII, page 390 by H.K.C.:

I too would challenge the author on his bold assertion that Tournai was the origin
of the magnificent slabs and brasses of the fourteenth century. I have long sought
conclusive evidence for their place of origin, without success. Undoubtedly some
of the stone monuments come from Tournai, but the brass case is non-proven.

influence. It is clear that Eichler was undecided as to the originators of these brasses but that he favoured the Flemish designers.

That craftsmen of these quadrangulars did know of the existence of other forms of brasses from other countries seems certain. The great artists of the past, had it not been for the tradition behind them, would have started on a far lower plane. So these large brasses with their superlative craftsmanship must have followed a tradition that was a close forerunner.

Eichler, then, is strongly biased in favour of Flemish workshops as the originators in this case, but has doubts about the artistic similarity of other foreign brasses. He says that a small brass triptych in Susa Cathedral (1368) does not accord with the Italian style of art of the period, and compares the design with the Flemish which he claims is similar. This particular triptych has, in fact, more in common with English illumination and it is possible that the designer used one of the 'sketchbooks' for the design. It could have been created by an Englishman on tour in Italy at that time, as it was a country which English craftsmen often visited.

One would assume that 'Flemish' workshops employed Flemish workers – but not necessarily so; we know that the medieval craftsman moved from place to place. In the 14th century Flanders was under German influence in the commercial field.* These Flemish workshops (if indeed they were as prominent as is suggested) must have had a wide reputation and would have been visited by many craftsmen of other countries. Some of these men would stay to work there for a time and then pass on, as was the custom, leaving behind a little of their influence. Inevitably, therefore, their exclusive qualities could not last. There would indeed appear to be some German and French influence in the designs of the brasses. Flemish artists no doubt preferred to visit France rather than Germany because France had a greater number of finished cathedrals – completed with a host of church 'furniture' inside, which would undoubtedly be a great attraction. The French craftsman or artist probably visited Flanders at the same time. One must, however, keep in mind that her cities were over-run by Germans conducting business and spreading their culture.

ARE THESE 'QUADRANGULARS' BY FLEMISH CRAFTSMEN?

The late 14th-century Flemish were better craftsmen than artists; they were derivative. They borrowed from other countries. In 1375 Hennequin of Bruges was ordered by Louis of Anjou to design a series of tapestries for the cathedral of Angers. It is known that Hennequin applied to the King of France for an illustrated manuscript of the Apocalypse to consult as reference. He used either the manuscript (Bibl. Nat. MS. franc 403) or a very similar one in the Cambrai library. These two manuscripts are Anglo-Norman and probably originated from an English studio in York. Hennequin was not an original artist – he put nothing new into these tapestries, so we see that one of the most important of medieval works (Apocalypse) was obtained from an English source, but executed by a Flemish craftsman.†

THE FLEMISH CRAFTSMEN OF THE INCISED STONE SLABS

The Flemish town of Tournai was undoubtedly a centre of incised memorial stone slabs. The technique of incising a stone slab is not the same as incising

*See The Hanseatic League (previous chapter), also *The Germans in England*. I. Colvin, 1915.

†'Flemish painters were not original. Speaking generally, the painters belonging to the Flemish school had not a great deal of imagination' (Sir Paul Lambotte, K.B.E., late Director of the Beaux Arts for the Belgian Government).

22

23

22. MARTEN FERRADES 1373, Madrid. The small figures and canopies are part of the same brass, but by an inferior craftsman. Note the perspective errors in the roundels and constructions above. At this date perspective was not fully understood as a science (see also plate 23A).

23. A stereotyped head. An example of simplified features executed with a high degree of mechanical precision giving a cold unemotional result. Very typical of numerous continental brasses of this period.

23A

23A. Perspective study of a chalice by Paolo Uccelo (1397-1475) in the Uffizi Gallery, Florence. He was a major artist, mad about perspective. True perspective began to show itself on brass design in the 16th century.

24. BISHOPS GODFREY AND FREDERIC DE BULOWE 1314-1375, Schwerin.
Size of brass 151″ x 76″. The largest existing brass. Note the stylized faces and symbols used in the features. A superb example of late 14th century craftsmanship, 'full of craft but empty of art'.

24

D

25. JOHANNES VON ZOEST AND WIFE 1361 (detail). Thorn (Torun), Poland.
Size of whole brass 124″ x 64″. A further example of the formal stylistic method used by this school of brass engravers. Note the symbols used to illustrate the mouths – they hardly ever change – here the backs of the hands are shown.

26. Part of brass of BURCHARD VON SERKEN (1317) AND JOHN VON MUL (1350), Lübeck dom Kirche.

Size of whole brass 142″ x 73″. Burchard became Bishop in 1276, when he was 80 years of age and died in 1317 at the age of 121 – John von Mul became bishop in 1341. These are very stylized faces – they could be twin brothers! Apart from the stubble beards these two bishops are almost identical with bishops Ludolph and Henry de Bulowe, 1339-1347, on the large brass (115″ x 71″) in the Dom Kirche, Schwerin (East Germany). The gloved hands are confused with the design. Note the symbols used to illustrate the mouths (see page 32). Lübeck and Schwerin are less than 50 miles apart.

27

27. KURFÜST ERNST VON SACHSEN
1486, Meissen, Germany.
Engraved by Peter Vischer (1455?–
1529). Size 97″ x 55″.

28. HERZÖGIN SIDONIEN 1510,
Meissen, Germany.
Engraved by Vischer. Size 95″ x 48″.

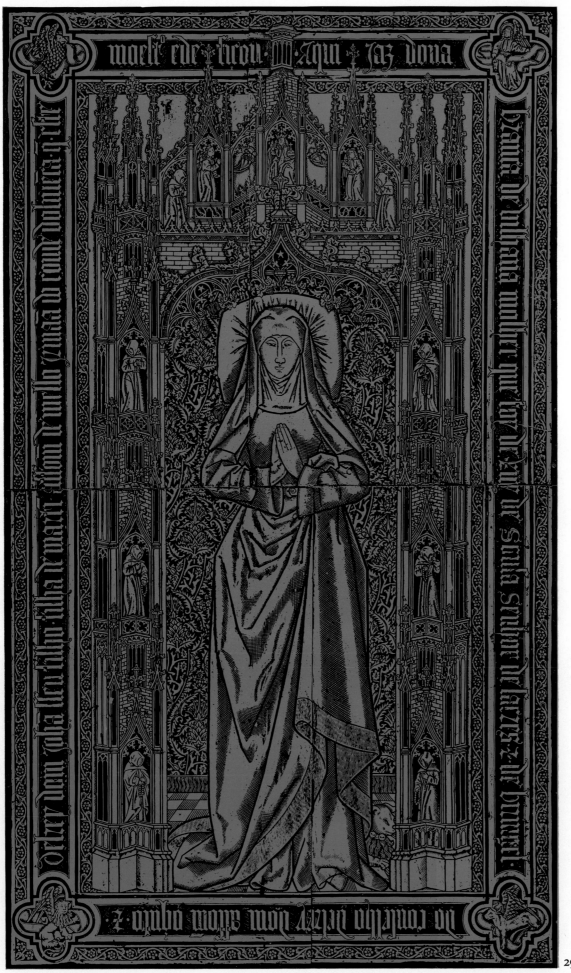

29. DONNA BRANCA DE VILHANA
c. 1500, Evora, Portugal.
75″ x 44″. Certainly not a Flemish
product – very distant in spirit,
though vaguely similar in design –
derivative. Correct in late 15th
century Portuguese metal work.

29

30. Part of a monumental brass. The soul of an abbot or bishop in Abraham's bosom. The engraving filled in with enamel. French; early 15th century (V. & A. Museum).

31. 'JESUS OF LÜBECK'.
An English warship trading between England and Germany (15th century), named after the chief town of the Hanseatic League.

32. HERMAN DE WERTHERE 1395, Nordhausen.
Probably this young man was a Jager in the Schwarzwald (a gamekeeper or hunter). This brass is reminiscent of German folk art of the 18th-19th centuries. The cuckoo clocks, the pipes, ornamented with extravagant designs of hunting scenes and similar souvenirs found in Bavaria belonged to the same category as the late 14th century Wertitere brass. Of similar school are Henrich de Urbech, 1394; Jacob Capillanus, 1395; Katerina Verter, 1397; and Henrich de Urbech, 1397; all at Nordhausen (central Germany) and size 75″ x 19″.

31

30

32

33

33. BISHOP HENRI VON BOCHOLT 1341. Lübeck cathedral.

*Those stone slabs remaining today in Flanders are different in spirit to the quadrangular brasses. The slabs are more aesthetically attractive.

on metal plate – it is very doubtful if the same craftsman would execute both.* The resistance of the metal when cutting necessitates quite a different understanding to that employed when cutting into stone, which chips and powders away. Those who have engraved on these different surfaces, as well as on wood, will understand that perfection in one does not imply perfection in any of the others. Each medium requires a different approach – different in its conception of technique rather than in spirit. It is unlikely that we shall know beyond dispute who were responsible for these 14th-century quadrangular brasses. They are not uniform enough to have come from one workshop. They were not designed by artists who understood the technique of creating a design on such a large scale on a flat metal surface. Great artists understand the limits of their medium; but in this case it is like drawing a 10ft by 6ft mural with a 6H pencil instead of using a broad technique of the brush. The mass of detail, lack of unity and work that is often tentative with little regard for the broad effect suggest craftsmen accustomed to working on a smaller scale – metalsmith or silversmiths, perhaps. Recently the writer viewed a rubbing of the quadrangular Delamere brass (St Albans, 1360) hanging alongside a rubbing of the 'cut to shape' Setvans brass (Chartham, Kent, 1306). The Setvans brass was more beautiful; the form soberly summarized, sensitively expressed by the simple play of the incised lines; the figure noble, full of exquisite grace – a masterpiece. The Delamere brass with all its mass of detail and technical skill became insignificant in comparison. The figure drawing, the face and hands, are not in the same category as the Setvans brass. The Delamere figure is concealed by decorative vestments, there is no 'movement' of the body underneath, such as one finds in Setvans.

It is one of the facts of artistic creation that often artists living far apart in the same decades, and unknown to each other, produce works that are similar but have national characteristics. So with the 'Flemish' brasses – close similarity in design alone does not prove the source: even less so when one country was dominated by another as Flanders was dominated by Germany in the 14th and 15th centuries through the Hanseatic League. Much more study and research are needed regarding these brasses, which are not as identical as some would intimate. They do suggest a common source, but looked at from every angle they reveal differences which point to more than one country as the originator. When all is considered it seems that there were several centres in the 15th century producing a similar type of monumental brass – but with subtle variations. The majority of the continental craftsmen were first-class in their execution, but they made and used designs that were not of high standard, repeating the design again and again with only small basic differences. This derivative method continued for over 150 years. Spain, Portugal, and Italy, where there are only a small number of brasses, suffered in the same way. The German engravers, who as craftsmen were the equal and often superior to the Flemish, made the error of introducing excessive detail. The brasses by the Vischers and the Hilligers are typical of this second-rate style for monumental effigies. At Freiburg the floor of the church is covered with over two dozen brasses by the Hilligers (16th-17th centuries), but none of them is first-class.

The following extracts are taken from writings by leading art historians regarding Medieval Flemish Art and Artists:

But the oldest works that have come down to us are the miniatures or illuminated manuscripts. This art came from abroad. Its history is an indispensable introduction to that of panel painting.† Without this apprenticeship of several centuries the earliest painters, the admirable Flemish primitives, would be inexplicable. *Art in Flanders* – Max Rooses, Director, The Plantin-Moretus Museum, Antwerp. 1931.

Bruges was a probable centre for engraving brasses after 1300, but there is little or no evidence that an earlier tradition existed there for the art of

†The oldest Flemish panel painting existing is the Reliquary of St Odile, 1292. Painted for the Convent of Notre Dame of Koden at Kerniel-Limberg. (This is the far eastern part of Flanders.)

engraving metals. *Histoire des Arts du Métal en Belgique* – Colin Gevaert. 1951. (*Does Gevaert deny tradition? –* H.T.)

In the 14th century, most of the artists of the Low Countries were Germans from the Rhine valley, so it is advisable to preface a study of the 15th century Flemish artists, with at any rate some short general sketch of the earlier school of Köln . . . indeed, ancient records seem to show that most of the artists who worked in the 14th and 15th centuries were Germans. (Sir Martin Conway, *Early Flemish Artists.*)

. . . but they did not come thither to learn their art, the records of the towns in which they took up their abode show that they were already masters who came to practise, not to learn. Bruges and Ghent at that time offered great facilities for the sale of works of art. – *Gerard David* by W. H. J. Weale.*

Weale, a learned Englishman, took up residence in Bruges in the last century and devoted several years to searching the archives and to works of erudition. Known as 'the Father of Flemish Primitives'.

Max Friedländer, an authority on Flemish art, wrote in similar terms.

This, I think, is conclusive. There were no precursors of note. I should require solid evidence before I would assign these 14th century brasses to Flemish craftsmen. We must, I am sure, look south or east, but not far, to find the originators. Enzo Carli in *Gothic Painting* (1965) says that the country of Flanders was subject to French influence in culture – the House of Capet and in ecclesiastical matters was dependent on the bishopric of Rheims.

To the south of the country of Flanders were French centres – Rheims, Verdun and St Omer to name a few, all within easy distance of Bruges – they had long produced ecclesiastical works in various media. To the near east and near south-east were other centres: Aachen in the north to Trier in the south (only a distance of about 120 miles). In this area were Echternach, Huy, Stavelot and Liége, all within 30 miles of each other.

This district north of the Mosel embracing the Ardennes was, I think, responsible for these brasses. Mosan craftsmen, as we know from examples of their works still with us, were craftsmen of the highest skill with a tradition of several centuries behind them. Köln, too, was near, only 50 miles away. It was here that craftsmen made and worked in brass.

Bruges in the 14th century was the most important trading centre in that part of Europe under the heyday of the German Hanse.

I believe that craftsmen from the Mosan area first sent their works to be sold in Bruges. As business increased they eventually settled in or near the city. As time passed they engaged apprentices from France, Flanders, Germany (from Lübeck under the Hanse) and possibly England too. By the third quarter of the 14th century the craftsmen then living had been born near their Bruges workshop. This would explain why traces of French, Teutonic and English workmanship can be detected in these memorial brasses. (See Eichler's and Gevaert's statements.)†

†*Memorial stone slabs are, I feel, by different craftsmen; they are only superficially identical.*

A Rare Memorial at Lübeck

In the cathedral at Lübeck is the tomb of Bishop Henri von Bocholt (1341). This is rare in that it depicts a three-dimensional figure of the bishop in bronze projecting from a base on an incised monumental brass. It is different from the 'Flemish'-made brasses, and one is reminded of the brass of Frau Rambourg de Wik, at Vester Åker, in Sweden (1327). The design of the Bocholt brass, which has a double border of lettering round the edges, is superior in quality. The sculptural figure is a considerable work of art: realistic, bold, broad, simple, with a subtle movement both in the action of the figure and the drapery; the face is full of character, though slightly idealized. The brass slab is made up of thirty-two sections and is different in style from the sculptural figure. This is almost certainly a product of German designers, as is the Wik brass. It has been suggested that it could be English in origin. One is certainly made aware of the importance of other workshops existing at the same time as the 'Flemish' one. France and Germany and England had workshops and craftsmen for making brasses of quantity.

FRENCH BRASSES

The story of the French brasses is a sad one. All those that remain, along with most of the three-dimensional metal tombs, had been melted down by the time of the Revolution. Only two or three escaped. Creeny illustrates only one: Bishop John Advantage, at Amiens (1456) (see Continental list).

André Michel, in *Histoire de l'Art*, says: 'Amiens Cathedral has two metal tombs – Bishop Evrard de Fouilloy (1222), and Geoffrey d'Eu (1236). The former is not flat but is engraved with decorations and Latin inscription around the sides.' He maintains that 14th-century tomb-makers aimed at realism, *portraiture as opposed to purely idealistic and commemorative effigies.* Flemish artists lived near the Porte St Denis in Paris early in the 14th century. In the cathedral of Châlons-sur-Marne is an engraved tomb of a monk – woman and monk with goblet (14th century). Michel says that French churches were tiled with these tombs by the 15th century. Gaignières, in the 17th century, made drawings of hundreds; but these tombs have all been melted down, only stone ones remain. These are simple, sincere and elegant. The face keeps its essential value. The idea of portraiture came slowly. Blanche de Champagne (1283) was represented in an effigy of copper, hammered in thin sheets on to wood. It was made at Limoges early in the 14th century and is now in the Louvre.

Emil Màle in *L'Art religieux de la fin du Moyen Age en France* describes a flat tomb of a knight and his family at l'église collégiale de St Martin, Champeaux (Manche), and describes a tomb (flat?) at Creney, L'Aube, of Jean de Creney, his wife and children – eleven boys and six girls, all lined up under the feet of their parents.

The chief school in France for making funeral monuments in the 14th century was in Paris, near the Porte St Denis, which was known as the Porte aux Peintres. The Abbey of St Denis contains some remarkable tombs of the French Royalty. In a vast country the size of France there must have been several workshops engaged in making funeral brass effigies of all types – alas, all are lost!

CHAPTER SIX

The English Character in the Arts and Crafts

THERE HAVE BEEN barren periods of long duration when only the rarest sons of England produced outstanding works. The English temperament, seasoned by the climatic and political vicissitudes of the land in which we live, has strong natural characteristics: at times dour, mysterious, or noble, it is marked with a warmth that is often slow to show itself. This quality runs like a vein through all English artists, be they painters, poets, sculptors, architects, or craftsmen – sometimes with great vigour, sometimes slow and lethargic. Their minds have often been oppressed by conditions in the land over which they had no control, notwithstanding which they have reached great heights of artistic creativeness.

The fact that they lived and worked on a small island with a limited range of contacts considerably affected their creative vision in past ages when Britain was more insular than she is today. The more spacious an artist's environment, the more he is related to an extensive intellectual community and the greater the breadth of his vision – the more grand and monumental will be his creations. This argument was often used against the English artist whose small country provided fewer opportunities than the vast Continent for seeing and comparing a diversity of artistic creations and developing his intellectual outlook. This is undoubtedly true, but nevertheless the unspoiled vision of the English artist or craftsman was something intimate and comprehensible, original and emotional, expressed in accordance with the English character. He was insular, unspoiled, and expressed himself in a simple, honest way largely untarnished by outside influences.

The 13th century saw the beginning of the finest period of English architecture, when for over 150 years this country produced the most inspired and original edifices in the whole of Europe. The mason, the stone-carver, the sculptor, the wood-carver (none better than the English), the metal-worker – all the craftsmen who played their part in furnishing and decorating the new places of worship with such originality and skill – all shared in the English genius of the period, and their crafts were the handmaidens of architecture.

The English also excelled in embroidery in the 13th century, in illuminated manuscripts in the next century, and our poets from Chaucer to Shakespeare, from Shakespeare to Dylan Thomas, have surely been of the highest international standing. Today, with world-wide communications, no matter where one lives, the swing is towards an art form of quickly changing characteristics and standards that are similar throughout the world – unavoidable consequences of our way of life, our social complexities, and the ever-increasing momentum forced upon us by new discoveries and the progress of mankind.

Although there is much similarity in the designs of our monumental brass effigies, stone slab effigies, and sculptural effigies, there will yet be found a number that are different and original. These departures occur in provincial brasses rather than in the large productions of London workshops and similar centres.

TECHNICAL SKILL AND ARTISTIC ORIGINALITY

Incised brass effigies are invaluable for their technical accomplishment and utilitarian purposes as memorials, but this is not judging them as works of art. The craftsman who has studied and mastered his craft has learned the language by which he can express himself, but something more is needed. He may have astonishing skill, but this by itself is only his language, and not the test of an original artist. It is what he says that is important, how it is represented and stated that stamps it with the hallmark of the original creative artist-craftsman. The man who can be termed such, is a man who has thought about his subject and expressed it with a personal and original approach. For instance, in the brass of Sir Robert Setvans, plate 38 (1306), one of the finest brasses of all time, the technical skill shown in depicting the chain-mail, the man's hair, his face, his hands, his flowing gown decorated with winnowing fans, his beautifully drawn sword, embellished as befits a knight, all these are clean-cut features expressed in a language with a high degree of clarity. But consider his stance, the rhythmic movement of the hair, the placing of his two ailettes and shield, the easy, graceful sway of his surcoat, the positioning of his crossed legs in relationship to the sword and the lion's body, the proportions of the winnowing fans on the gown and shield – all these are individual thoughts expressed by the designer of this excellent brass. They distinguish it from many others of equal merit as far as technical skill and representation are concerned, but also raise it above them, because this designer was an original artist and not an imitator. He understood that the descriptive language and the thoughts of the artist must be amalgamated into a complete whole. Where the one finishes and the other begins cannot be discerned. In great works of art the idea is expressed in as simple terms as possible, not depending on the descriptive language beyond the necessity for understanding.

It is easy for the average spectator to take pleasure in the language or technical skill, but it often requires considerable mental exertion and knowledge to appreciate and distinguish the ideas and thoughts of the artist. An incised brass effigy, for instance, even if executed by an inferior craftsman but with originality, can be more truly a work of art than a brass effigy most skilfully executed but lacking in ideas. The brass of the Earl and Countess of Warwick (St Mary's, Warwick, 1406), for all its technical skill and detail, falls below the small demi-effigy of Walter Frilende (Ockham, Surrey, 1376) as an original work. These two have been chosen because they are vastly different; many might consider the former beautiful because of the technical skill and elaborate detail, and the latter ugly because of the squint eyes and stubble of the beard. Close inspection will reveal that the brass of Frilende has a number of original ideas in the manner of its representation lacking in the brilliant execution of Warwick's brass, which is mechanical and uninspired. (See plates 41 and 42).

The same can be said when comparing the large brass of Burchard von Serken and John von Mul (Lübeck, 1317-50) with the brass of Sir John de Creke and his wife (Westley Waterless, Cambs, 1325). The elongated figures of the latter designed to give an air of elegance and superiority is similar to the method used by El Greco (Doménico Théotocopuli, c. 1542-1614) who elongated his figures to make them appear more saintly. These are qualities of a kind which are not related to the artistic qualifications of the artist's work. (See El Greco, *The Modern Movement in Art*, R. H. Wilenski, 1935.) The English brass is a greater work of art in its refined, dignified simplicity than the gigantic brass at Lübeck with its outstanding technical skill and detail but with little originality.

The original medieval artist, when designing figures of the deity, the Virgin, saints, angels or the devil, was faced with a different problem from that involved in designing a memorial to a contemporary human being. In the former he was relating his figures to the religion of the day; they became idealized types subordinate to the general design on which he was working. Unlike the artist of today who, when depicting a religious subject, feels that he must be in a religious state of mind – in a state of mind, in fact, always suited to his subject – the medieval artist had one state of mind, natural to himself, in which he depicted his subjects according to his vision and know-ledge, and made them look attractive and recognizable to the best of his creative ability. So when the artist was concerned with a known human being he often did produce a portrait using the conventions of his time. 'An attempt at a portrait', an expression often used, is a wrong one – an artist who could design a superb brass would have no trouble in producing a portrait if he so wished (see chapter 13). When an original artist produced a work of art, it was his intense feeling and belief in the purpose of his creation that induced the design.

What had the medieval designer in mind when he set out to produce an *original* memorial effigy? There were certain dogmas that he had to know and had to bring into his design when he was instructed to depict the effigy as a knight clad in the armour of his time: this knight was to be a man in the prime of life, either lying flat on his back, or standing, as some memorials did. At his feet he was to place an animal (often a dog or a lion). He was to include heraldic arms or similar additions.* The designer would be an original artist who understood the craft. He had to devise various patterns which would express his ideas about the memorial effigy – ideas of an emotional type. Next he had to convey to the beholder the various shapes that reminded him of a knight. Then again he would consider all those various shapes that could accommodate themselves happily in the required size of the brass. Lastly, having considered all these problems together, the artist had to think of them as a linear design incised on the brass plates.

In his thoughts about the effigy he would want to express dignity, noble-ness, humility and divinity. These are emotional feelings which are not of material shape, size, or form. How could he hope to solve this? He had to invent shapes and forms of various sizes that would convey these personal emotions. They could only be represented by symbols. A trained artist would be able to draw a knight that would look like a knight, a dog that would look like a dog, a lion that would look like a lion, and so on. This would not be difficult, but to wed them to his own emotions and thoughts about the effigy was a problem of a different nature. What did he do? He introduced certain differences in the usual aspect of the knight effigy. These differences were such that they satisfied his emotions about it without sacrificing his visual aspect of the effigy to too great an extent. In other words, the knight was easily recognizable as a knight but incorporated certain departures that re-flected the personality of the artist. Many 20th-century artists completely abandon the conventional visual aspect in order to give greater emphasis to their emotional feelings about their subject, until this becomes quite un-recognizable because their language is not understood by the average person.

Sometimes the medieval artist introduced a much closer portrait than the idealized type of head; he became fascinated with various other features – the apparel, the heraldic arms, the folds in the drapery, or the hair-style – and when this happened he again compromised. His greatness as an artist was determined by the power of his emotions, his observation and interpretation, his ability to wed these to the visual aspect of his 'model' together with his ability to knit them all together in a unified design. The great classical or romantic artist has an extreme sense of originality, vision and design together with the capacity for very good craftsmanship. As far as the pure craftsman is concerned, he may not be a first-class designer but he would be able to interpret the artist's design in a particular medium to perfection. The genuine artist-craftsman is always a product of his time, and his work reflects the environment and prevailing influences peculiar to the country in which he lives and was trained during his formative years.

The medieval artist-craftsman, however deeply inspired, did not work for

---

*Colour, which was very much a part of medieval art, had to be considered by the artist-designer.

34

34. ROBERT ALBYN 1390, Hemel Hempstead, Herts, with MARGARET ALBYN (right)
Two late 14th century brasses retaining some of the simplicity of the brasses of the earlier part of the century. Effigy 36".

35

35. MARGARET ALBYN 1390, Hemel Hempstead, Herts. Effigy 36".

art's sake. It was his livelihood that mattered. *Away from monastic life*, he derived his inspiration from the world about him. He saw new architectural forms being erected; he observed his fellow-creatures, what they were, what they did, what they used, and how they lived; he was part of it himself. He introduced his observations of forms into shapes and designs that took on a new look. They were quiet, dignified, and lyrical.

THE ENGLISH METHOD

The method employed by early English designers in cutting their brass effigies to shape and mounting down on the indent in the stone casement, together with the other component parts (where required), produced a more satisfactory design than the usual continental method of engraving the whole rectangular shape of brass. The English method was adopted through the entire 'brass era' in this country, with only a few exceptions. There are also a few early instances of a cut to shape effigy appearing on the Continent – such as Margaret Sbrunnen (1352) and William Wenemaer (1325). Both are in the museum at Ghent.*

The excellence of the design and drawing of the first fifty years (1277-1327) of English brasses is something very special and was produced by persons of the highest rank in artistic creation and execution. They were thoroughly conversant with the requirements of the stone and brass medium. These brasses were designed with the idea of incising on a bright brass plate to be laid on the floor of the church. The incised lines, filled in with a black medium and in some instances with enamels, would display the design to advantage. This was related to the medieval artistic concept in which light was a basic part: the 'divine sun', it was termed. These designers were no copiers of the tomb-maker – who would not think easily on the flat plane, nor would be such good draughtsmen: sculptors are rarely first-class figure draughtsmen though exceptions are found in 16th-century Italy. The designers knew how to design on the flat, using simple lines to express three-dimensional form by a series of parallel and crossed lines, and achieving a design of great beauty in a unified pattern by the simple use of the incised line.

These brasses are elegant, clear in arrangement, sure and positive in technical achievement. They show care for detail in a decorative manner, and great sensitivity for the design as a whole. The figures are calm, dignified, and large to express superiority. They are drawn in the stylish manner of English Gothic draughtmanship at its best. These particular brasses were first designed by artists working on the flat and then passed over to the craftsman to engrave. They would be inspired by mural painters or stained-glass window designers, who produced international sketchbooks which were available for all to use; hence the similarity of the designs of stained-glass windows, illuminated manuscripts, sculptured effigies and incised stone slabs and brasses. This statement can be borne out by those who are familiar with the superb figure drawings in the coloured glass windows of Canterbury Cathedral and other churches of the 13th and later centuries. The draughtsmanship is similar in style to that of the d'Aubernoun brass (1277), the Sir Roger de Trumpington brass (1289), Sir John de Creke and wife (1325), and Sir John d'Aubernoun (1327). Similar figures can also be found in murals of the 13th-14th century as well as in illuminated manuscripts.†

It is clear from the later 14th-century brasses that after the artist had completed the drawing, the craftsman would use it over and over again. Copies were made, and as time passed these departed further and further from the original design, resulting in bad draughtsmanship on the brass. There are

*Cut to shape effigies were not confined to English brasses; there are quite a few on the Continent. France once had a considerable number, drawings of which still exist.

†These would be excellent references for colouring brasses, many of which were decorated by the use of coloured enamels.

many thousands of such brasses. The well-designed, well-drawn examples, which are comparatively few, stand out like professionals among a mass of amateurs.

Assessing the Art in Brasses

In making an assessment of the art of individual monumental brass effigies, such as the armour of a particular knight, the dress of a lady or child, or the vestments of an ecclesiastic, one must not confuse the fashion of the clothing with one's appraisal of how the artist-brass-designer interpreted these items in his medium. A 15th-century lady's dress might be considered ugly by a fashion-designer but, on the other hand, the art expert could say that the interpretation of it was a work of art. In art, man responds to the arrangement, the shape, the mass and proportion of things which give pleasure to the vision – this is called beauty. But if the arrangement, the shape, the mass and proportion displease, this is called ugliness. We do not all respond in the same degree to these qualities or even in the same manner; this is usually explained as stages in individual development. An effigy on brass is drawn by an incised line. Line in the hands of a master expresses solid forms, it is sensitive to the shape and to the outline of things. It is selective – a pictorial shorthand. It makes statements, breaks off at the right place and continues later to express just the right forms, converging or tilted planes. It is an abstract medium, it has no relation to the clothing's actual appearance – it only suggests that appearance. It can suggest the light on the dress by a variation in thickness or by gradations of it between black and white.

When looking, therefore, at a monumental brass effigy as a work of art, one looks for forms defined by outlines. This outline must have a movement or rhythmic beauty of its own. If it fails to have this quality it can be called uninspired or dead. It is unfortunate that vast numbers of brasses both of the 15th and 16th centuries were completely dead, owing to the great demand which produced a continuous repetition of similar designs without the slightest regard for their quality. This is very marked in the presentation of the drapery of women's costume. The men in armour were slightly better – quite unconsciously so – due to the shapes of the armour they wore, which sometimes broke up the large outlines to advantage. The abuse of the line technique – the use of two or three lines and of a cross-hatching method of light and shade to indicate form – ruined vast numbers of brasses.

36

37

36. Detail of brass of SIR NICHOLAS DAGWORTH 1401, Blickling, Norfolk.

37. Detail of the brass of SIR JOHN FOXLEY (1378), Bray, Berkshire. The base of a bracket brass which springs from the middle of the fox's back.

38. (opposite) SIR ROBERT DE SETVANS 1306, Chartham, Kent. A masterpiece in brass memorial engraving (see text). Effigy 74″.

39. (opposite) SIR JOHN D'AUBERNOUN the Younger (1327), Stoke D'Abernon, Surrey.
He lies next to his father, Sir John D'Aubernoun (1277). An excellent brass – note the simplicity and graceful movement – so rare in later brasses. What remains of the canopy is of the same high standard as the effigy. Effigy 64″.

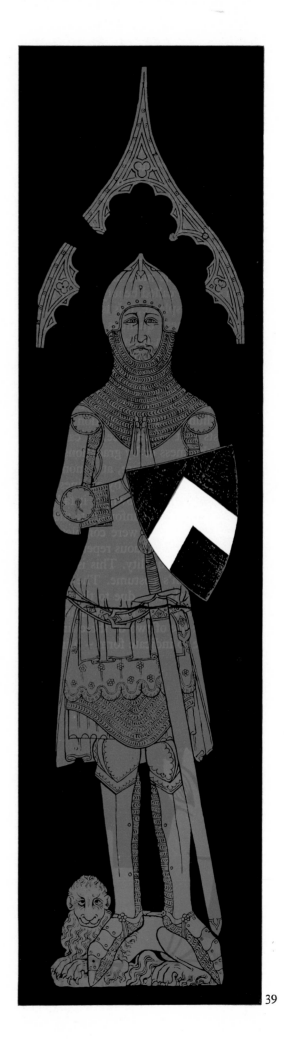

F

38

39

40

40. SIR JOHN DE CREKE AND WIFE ALYNE 1325, Westley Waterless, Cambridgeshire.
A superb brass (see page 37). Male effigy 66″.

41. WALTER FRILENDE, Rector, 1376, Ockham, Surrey.
A first-class brass – don't be misled by the rector's face – it is full of character. Note the lively design of the rest of the brass – a minor masterpiece (see page 37). Effigy 18½″.

41

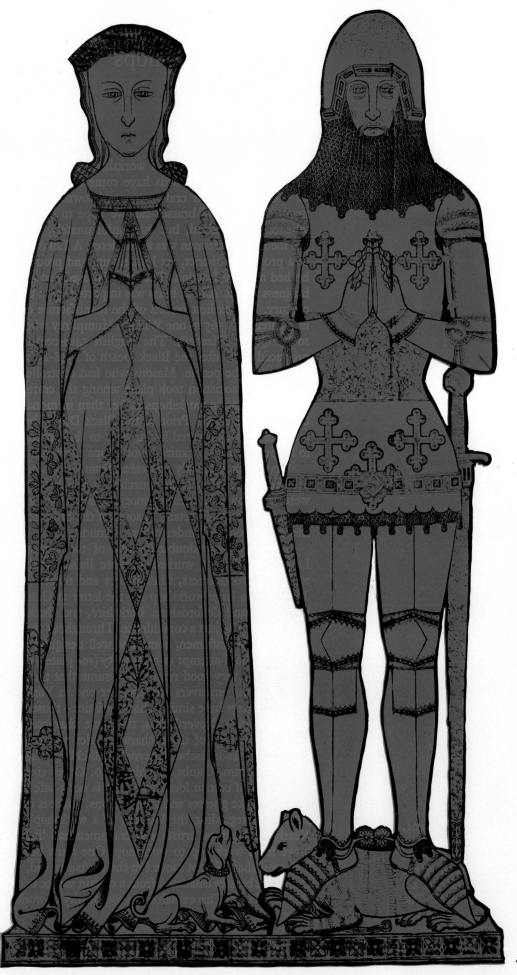

CHAPTER SEVEN

English Workshops

FACTS ABOUT the English workshops of monumental brass designers are obscure. Few records have come down to us and so not many names of designers or craftsmen are known. Only by a close study of the many thousands of brasses can we hope to form a picture of the localities whence they derived, but this, unfortunately, cannot be very reliable since the medieval craftsman was a wanderer. A London-trained man would move to a provincial district, set himself up, and produce designs similar to those he had made in London. The material used had an important bearing on the business aspect. All our brass was imported up to the third quarter of the 16th century. The earliest record of the manufacture of brass in England occurs in a patent of 1565 to one William Humphrey who is given permission to do so by Queen Elizabeth. The English 14th-century brasses were not mass produced until after the Black Death of 1348-49 which killed about seventy per cent of the people. Masons who had controlled the arts and crafts were scarce. A dissociation took place among the crafts – they separated and the work was done in workshops rather than in monasteries. The craft excelled but the art declined. Prior to the Black Death, brass effigies were made by individuals who devoted loving care to their products, but when they came to be produced in organized workshops their individuality had largely gone.

The country quickly recovered from the plague. The wealthy merchants became richer; they built churches in which they were buried and brasses were laid down in their memory. Then more and more 'similar' brasses appeared, many still retaining some of the brilliance of the earlier ones which had been produced under different conditions.

London was undoubtedly one of the centres. The craftsmen at the London workshops worked in close liaison with those of other trades – sculptors, woodcarvers, illuminators and makers of stained-glass windows. There was a large workshop for the latter at Oxford. It is a fact that a few brasses around Oxfordshire, Berkshire, and Buckinghamshire are similar – too similar to be just a coincidence. Throughout the country are found brasses by individual craftsmen, some not well designed or executed, but certainly evincing a bold attempt at originality (see plate 55).

There is very good reason to assume that there was a workshop of East Anglian brass engravers and another one in Yorkshire. Many of the 15th-century brasses have similar characteristics – those in Norfolk and Suffolk are in nearby areas. Nevertheless, the same characteristics are found far from East Anglia! One of these characteristics was the attitude of the women's hands, such as in Isabel Cheyne of Blickling (1485), also Margaret Peyton (1484), Isleham, Cambs, see plate 130. Other similarities can be found on the brasses of certain localities but it is not a safe guide to a local workshop. One can make guesses and suppositions, but it is dangerous to make positive statements regarding the location of a workshop without conclusive proof. Nearly all medieval artists and craftsmen had 'itching feet' – they loved to move from workshop to workshop. One must beware of the 'local' school. The workshop did not move but the craftsman did, so it is not always wise to claim that brasses emanated from a certain source because of the area in which they are found. This explains the conformity of works far removed from each other.

THOMAS DE BEAUCHAMP, Earl of Warwick 1401, AND WIFE MARGARET 1406, St Mary's, Warwick. ...nce on altar tomb. Perhaps a much over-rated brass. ...has considerable refinement in the design of the ...raldic dress of the lady. These two effigies are ...echanical and mathematically considered. The ...ntours of the lady lack imagination making her ...ttle-shaped. Compare her silhouette with that of ...ady Creke (plate 40), which is beautifully conceived. ...he design of the Knight is broken up into bits and ...eces (see text, page 45). Effigy 62".

THE TECHNIQUE

First the artist would sketch his design: his figures in their armour, vestments, or costume, with the architectural canopies (if necessary), heraldic arms, and other accessories. He would space out the inscriptions accurately. All this he would draw on the sheets of brass and paint in a coloured medium, or he would supply the engraver with a complete design which he (the engraver) would copy or trace on to the brass for cutting (late drawings still exist).

We know of this obvious method by a fortunate discovery made at Luton many years ago. On the back of a brass some unfinished lettering was discovered, and it was noticed that the uncut lettering had been drawn in with a painted line ready for the engraving tool to follow the contours. On yet another brass at the same church it was noticed that the engraver, when cutting down the two sides of some letters, had left the middle strip of metal – to be removed later by a different tool. We can see by the two cuts made that the engraver had a similar tool for engraving to that in use today – the *burin graver* or *scorper*. The *scorper*, as well as a flat chisel, was employed to cut away the unwanted metal. The same method would be used for large 'low' areas on the effigy.

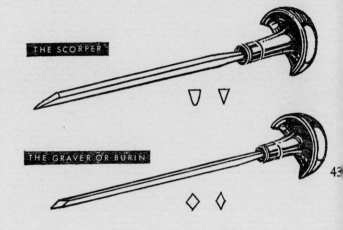

The continental method called for a slightly different technique. Whereas the English cutters preferred the wide curved graver, the continental craftsmen often used the flat graver. A tool similar to the spitzsticker was used for curved lines. This gave the English brasses a deeper channel and greater freedom of movement. Some effigies and inscriptions were cut in relief, that is to say the background was cut out leaving the pattern standing in relief. Such examples exist at Fairford in Gloucestershire on the Thame brass (1534), on the Scrop brass at Hambledon, Bucks (1500), and in the inscription of Geoffrey Kidwelly at Little Wittenham, Berks (1483). Half-sinking was a technique used in depicting materials and in heraldry (Verney, Aldbury, Herts, 1546). It also occupied small spaces such as between legs, or sword and leg, or arms and body, where it usually took the form of cross-cutting. Special care must be taken when rubbing these brasses to get the correct effect.

Small errors of 'confused' engraving occur on a few brasses of armour. These are not usually due to the slipping of the burin (though this does happen) but to the fact that the engraver, possibly tired, incised the line that should have been left in relief. When engraving, the drawing was painted on in colour (as explained above), but in a mass of detail it would be quite easy for the craftsman when tired to forget he was cutting in reverse. Only by close observation of detail in brasses can these errors be noticed. The incised line was filled in with a dark composition showing up clearly on the bright brass plate. In drypoint engraving the copper plate is usually 'blacked' by burning tapers under the plate, the lamp-black deposited making the clean plate quite black and enabling the engraved line to appear bright as the copper was exposed to sight.

ANOTHER TECHNIQUE

The print of St George and the Dragon (B. N., Paris), and that of St Mark (British Museum), both German, are included to show their similarity to designs of brasses: probably the brass engraver was responsible for these unique prints. On the brass of Sir Simon of Wensley (*c.* 1375) a similar technique was used but about one hundred years earlier (see details of this brass on page 44). *I have seen this technique used on one or two other brasses.*

Both these illustrations are in the *manière criblée* or dotted prints. This technique is a combination of an incised line, and a series of engraved dots, stars, or rings made by various punches and stamps. They are white line engravings for relief printing. The areas that would print solid black are relieved by the use of dots or small patterns. When a light tone was required the engraver used the burin to make a series of small lines over the areas that

44. The glass painter, from the east window of College Chapel, Winchester (late 15th century). (See also plate 126 for similar treatment on brass.)

rivets of brass

a method of fixing

wood plug

lead plug 45

had previously been punched on the plate to such an extent that the punched patterns were completely obliterated.

In the print of St George the background has been cut away so that the arabesque shape stands out in bold relief from the white paper. The print of St Mark is of slightly later date than the St George (*c.* 1450-70). These prints are entirely German in origin and Köln was the centre of their production. They are rare, though many designs were made – sometimes from other engravings – and they were often hand-coloured in simple range. They were used, too, as book illustrations though it is seldom that two or three prints exist of the same design. The majority are unique. These *manière criblée* prints ridicule the suggestion that the engravers of the incised monumental brass effigy never thought of taking prints off these memorial plates.

FIXING BRASSES

We know that many brasses when they were originally laid down on their casement indents were decorated with coloured pigments or vitreous enamels. Sir John d'Aubernoun (1277) has a shield in blue enamel. Another example is on the brass of M. Gaynesford (Carshalton, 1503) where parts of the original colouring still remain, *and parts of the red enamel still remain in the belt of Laurence Fyton, Sonning, Berks, 1434.* Enamels were first fixed down on the casement and very carefully and accurately the incised, routed brass was laid on top. This would fit down into the indent and the enamel would be held in position by a lip. A 'tooth' had to be obtained prior to the introduction of a lead base. A tooth is a surface with sufficient key or grain to hold the deposit. On this ground the various designs were cut and filled in according to requirements.

Some of the earliest brasses were not riveted down on to the casement but held in position by their own weight and fixed with pitch. The brass was laid down on the stone or marble casement with its cut indent and marked where the rivet-holes had been drilled in the brass. Then these marked points were drilled into the casement to a depth of about one inch. These drilled holes were undercut to receive the fixing-pins or rivets.

The brass was then placed back on the casement in the original position and the rivets, with an enlarged end, were inserted through the holes of the brass into the holes of the casement. Then molten lead was poured down into the holes to fill the gaps. This was achieved by using a shallow channel cut into the slab from the edge of the indent to the hole, enabling the molten lead to run in and secure the rivet.

Another method was to drive the rivets down with a hammer so as to splay out the bottom end, and lead was poured down to fill the gaps. Hot pitch was then poured over the indents and the brass was replaced with the rivet heads protruding through the holes. These rivets were cut level and punched over to form a rivet fixture. Wooden plugs were sometimes used in place of the lead to hold the rivets. Rivets were generally made of brass, though iron is known to have been used.

46

46. KATHERINE SCROP 1500, Hambledon, Bucks. She is depicted as a widow. The garments in reverse treatment to the rest of the brass. The lines of the drapery are left standing in relief – the base background having been routed away. The rest of the brass is the usual incised technique. The correct way to illustrate this brass is as shown. Note the two rivets. Effigy 9″.

47

48

49

47. Detail from a negative rubbing of SIR SIMON DE WENSLEY *c.* 1375, Wensley, N.R. Yorkshire. The whole dots are incised on the brass plate.

48. Detail from a print from a wood block of Saint Mark *c.* 1460 (British Museum). German. *Manière criblée*. Here again the block has been engraved to produce the whole dots.

49. SAINT GEORGE AND THE DRAGON *c.* 1460-1470 (German, Cologne). B. N. Paris.
Stipple on dotted print shows the similarity between German and technique used on Sir Simon. In 1222, St George's Day – 23rd April – was declared a holiday.

50

50. ST MARK *c.* 1460 (British Museum).
An example of manière criblée. It is coloured. Schr. 2689 B.M.
Schr. = W. L. Schreiber's *Manual de l'Amateur de la Gravure sur Bois
et sur Metal an XV° Siecle* Tome i-iii Berlin 1891-1893.
51. SIR HUGH HASTYNGS 1347, Elsing, Norfolk.
Length 102″. From a facsimile taken in 1782 by Craven Ord (in the
British Museum). A wet sheet of paper was pressed on to the plate after
the incised lines had been filled with printer's ink and wiped clean on
the surface – similar to the technique of taking a proof of an etched
plate. This facsimile has been reversed left to right – the print obtained
by the above method gives a right to left print. This brass is described
in an ancient document of 1408 which is invaluable in that it gives the
nomenclature used in the early 15th century – in Norman French.

51

52. HENRY BARLEY AND WIFE 1475, Aldbury, Herts.
An attractive small two-figure brass. There are not many of this type
of small figure brasses in existence. There is a lively action to Henry's
figure. He wears typical late 15th century armour. On his head he wears
a sallet. The brass is mutilated. There are four daughters but sons and
inscriptions are lost. The achievement above the figures – also damaged
– depicts a rebus on his name – the head of a horse eating barley. Size
of effigies 16″.

53. ISOBEL CHEYNE 1485, Blickling, Norfolk.
A very attractive design – note the action of the hands (see Margaret
Peyton, chapter 12), size 32″ x 18″.

54. HENRY LORD MARNEY 1523, Layer Marney, Essex.
A renaissance altar tomb – a fine example of controlled formal design,
the form of the head is well expressed by the rhythmic lines of the hair
– a convention often used on monumental brasses.

CHAPTER EIGHT

The Art of the Later Brasses

*I think this total rather high. This would mean an average of 500 brasses a year, very few in the 13th century and a tailing off in the 17th century. – H.T.

I F WE ARE to believe some experts who state that at one time some 150,000 brasses were in existence (including inscriptions), it must have meant a full-time job for the busy craftsmen over the centuries.*

In the mid-15th-century a decline in both the technical and artistic quality of brasses is evident. This decline was general except for the three-dimensional sculptural effigies.

The early 15th-century had been a period of increased elaboration on brasses, and their value as memorials of distinction was recognized by the nobility. Several prominent persons who might have been expected to order sculptural effigies favoured decorated brass instead. The brasses became less simple as the artists tried to attract custom by over-elaboration, using various tricks and techniques to make the designs more complicated so that they could demand higher prices for their work. More detail was introduced into the canopies, greater display of heraldic arms, two lines in place of one, a different symbolized technique to express forms and folds in the drapery, and the use of a series of short lines, often crossing each other to express form and shadow – all this to the detriment of aesthetic standards. The work became geometrical and mechanical, lacking inspiration: quite unlike the subtle geometrical rhythm of the figure compositions in the 13th-century windows of Canterbury Cathedral.

The brass of Sir Symon Felbrygge and wife (Felbrigg, 1416), is an example of the early decline. Clean and well-cut, it lacks any original beauty; the figures are stiff but the composition is relieved by the introduction of the flagstaff and standard on the right of the knight. The figure of Thomas de St Quintin (Harpham, Yorks, 1445) is awkward – it lacks any movement, the feet are over-large and in an almost impossible position either for standing or for resting against the hillock of flowers.† The excess of dimension in the incised lines throughout the effigy breaks it up into unhappy shapes and patterns. The slightly later figure at Adderbury, Oxfordshire (1460) is better in that the designer had a good sense of large shapes and poise in the figure.‡ The wife, alas, is a very mechanical product and the introduction of cross-hatching in the drapery does little to enhance the effect. In the figure of the wife of Ralph St Leger (Ulcombe, Kent, 1470) the rot has set in. The figure, especially the face and hands, is crudely drawn, as is the drapery where coarse lines are used to denote the form. A more attractive combination is that at Lower Heyford, Northamptonshire (1487) of the couple holding hands. Considerable thought has been given to the design of the two figures to knit them into one simple shape, and this has been achieved with considerable success. Equally successful is the couple arm in arm at Brown Candover, Hants, c. 1490 (see illustration).

It must be admitted that some of the 15th-century designers possessed a gift for interesting presentation of the figure. This gift would sometimes appear to be an unconscious one, for alongside a simple, well-presented example one would find another which was crude and lacking in artistic values, while yet another would bear witness to a genuine instinct for the beautiful and expressive shapes within the contours. The charming brass to

55. A local brass c. 1630, Launceston, Cornwall. A lady aged 65.

†The figure rose up from his recumbent position. Gone was peace in death. He stood like an actor on a stage surrounded by circumstances of pomp, adulation and flattery. The brass of Sir Roger le Strange, 1506, Hunstanton, Norfolk, and the brass of Sir Thomas Bullen, KG, 1538, Hever, Kent, are two examples.

‡Undoubtedly some craftsmen designed brasses only of ladies, others of men only.

G

Margaret Cheyne at Hever, Kent (1419) is quite exceptional: there is a delightful swing in the movement of the drapery, two open-winged angels hold a decorated cushion behind her head and the whole shape is graceful. Compare this with the stereotyped figure of Lady Howard, St Mary's, Lambeth (1535), or with the lady at St Helen's, Bishopsgate (c. 1535), which are ugly bottle-shaped figures with heraldic display of considerable beauty. Several such effigies occur in the 16th century. Some of the artists delighted in stressing the long perpendicular folds of the costumes of the late 14th and the first half of the 15th-centuries. This extended to dress of all kinds: wherever possible the designer made good use of the folds to create a pattern. It became a trick, so much so that eventually quite impossible folds were evolved reminiscent of 'damp fold drapery' of German origin.

At the base of the figure of the Duchess of Gloucester in Westminster Abbey (1390), the folded drapery as it rests on the ground is elegantly designed into a symbolized pattern of correct shape and function. The same can be said of the figure of Thomas Nelond at Cowfold, Sussex (1453), though it is not so skilfully executed, but as we enter the next century we find confusion taking place owing to semi-mechanical copying of earlier figures without the correct appreciation of the forms. That this happened is quite clear if one studies the base of the folds of the vestment worn by Dame Elizabeth Hervey, Abbess of Elstow (1520).

For the complete understanding of the use of a decorative line to express forms and folds in material study the lovely figure of Lady Creke at Westley Waterless, Cambridgeshire, dating from nearly 200 years earlier (1325). 'The line with the hook at the end' technique of expressing folds in drapery was common in brasses and in other forms of 14th-15th-century art. See the brass of John Seys (c. 1370), West Hanney, Berkshire. This technique can be seen in woodcuts of both German and Flemish artists of about 1460-80 (Virgin and Child Schr. 1029, British Museum.)

The early part of the 16th century produced a mixture of bad and good, or at least bold efforts on the part of some craftsmen to produce better designs and workmanship. Too often we have ill-proportioned figures lacking any good drawing or design, such as the two kneeling figures at Theydon Gernon, Essex (c. 1520), the work of a local engraver but with nothing naïve to redeem it. The brass with five effigies at Ingrave, Essex (1528) is equally bad. Sir Richard Fitzlewes and his four wives form the brass. Sir Richard in the middle is an odd figure complete with heraldic jupon and helm, and his four poor wives are out of proportion. As tall as the knight himself, they are as thin as the proverbial lamp-post – all dressed up in their finery and heraldic mantles (plate 68).

A unique brass of this period (unique for features other than its design and execution, which are poor) is that of Sir Peter Legh and wife at Winwick, Lancashire (1527). Sir Peter, on the death of his wife, became a priest at Winwick church. He is shown wearing the chasuble over his armour and his coat of arms on his breast.

It was often the fashion during the 16th century to represent knights without necks! Many of the effigies wore heavy armour so perhaps this weighed down their heads and necks in agony – the expression on some of their ill-drawn faces suggests such an explanation. A full suit of armour would weigh about 60-90 lb but if made to fit the individual it should not cause any excessive encumbrance. Towards the end of the century we find that the technique of indicating form on brasses had lost its way. Too much line work for this purpose makes the figures 'bitty'. When representing figures in armour the craftsman tried to make the flat plate of brass appear as three-dimensional as the actual armour itself! Unfortunately this technique spread to women's costume and ecclesiastical vestments and gave them a metallic quality. The two figures of a civilian and his wife, William and Audrey Wightman at Harrow, Middlesex (1579) illustrate this point well.

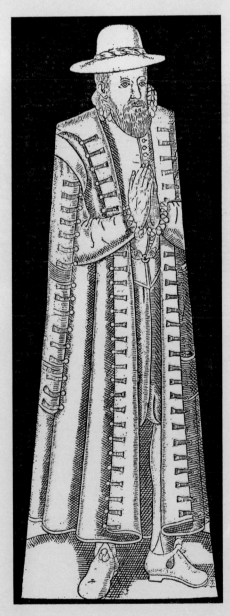

56

56. RICHARD GADBURYE 1624, Eyeworth, Beds.

57. JOHN SAUNDERS 1645, Hambledon, Bucks.
With two wives on tapering rectangular plate not
shown. A sketchbook brass of no great merit but is an
attractive period example similar to various graphic
book illustrations of the first half of the 17th century.
The technique is similar to that of wood engraving.
Effigy 16″.

It is unfortunate that brasses never show the backs of figures, either in
armour, costume, or in vestments. If it were not for contemporary illustrations
and for armour and garments remaining from the past, we should not know
exactly how people were clothed or fastened up behind!

Were the *later* craftsmen who made the sculptured effigies – the alabaster
tomb-makers – the same as those who incised the brass effigies? Visual evidence of 14th-century effigies suggests that they were different craftsmen, but
in the 15th-16th centuries, when the making of memorials had become a well-
organized commercial project, the brass incised effigy, the incised stone effigy,
the sculptural alabaster effigy and probably, to a less extent, the sculptured
wood effigy, were *sometimes* products of the same workshops. Documentary
proof of this fact occurs in 1510, when Henry Harpur and William Moore-
cock, alabastermen, agreed to make an alabaster tomb topped by a brass for
Henry Foljambe of Chesterfield. One assumes that the brass was incised by
these craftsmen and that it was not sub-contracted to a craftsman in brass?

Apart from a few similar examples it is doubtful whether, as is often suggested, this combination of crafts did really exist. Factual evidence would
prove otherwise. Of the large number of brasses produced in the 16th century
none really seems to run side by side with the sculptural effigy of the same
period. The brasses were poorly executed, poorly designed and followed the
same pattern for decade after decade. The sculptural effigies – the tomb sculptures – were more vigorous and adventurous as the century progressed,
though this tendency was halted about 1540 by the dissolution of the monasteries.

The Dissolution and the Reformation had a considerable effect on the
production of brasses. Ecclesiastical brasses, as was to be expected, had almost ceased to be made by the late 1550s. Rectors and vicars and two or three
bishops are commemorated in brass after this date, but their total falls short
of fifty. Brasses to civilians and their wives continued through the 16th century
in very slowly decreasing numbers up to the reign of Mary, but revived during
Elizabeth's reign, when brass was manufactured in England. The quality of
the work was unstable, it showed greater variation but was never outstanding.
Much bad work and a little that was good! An example of some skill in the
17th century is of the Archbishop of York, Samuel Harsnett, at Chigwell
(1631). It is clean and simple without any overstatements.

'Picture' brasses of the late 16th century and of the 17th were for the most
part without any beauty. These often depicted the husband and wife kneeling
on either side of a desk (or pulpit) placed on a floor divided up into rectangular
tiles in perspective. Behind the parents were the sons (on the father's side)
and daughters (on the mother's side). Richard Middleton (Whitchurch, Den-
bighshire, 1565) is an example. Another is John Bowyer (Camberwell, 1570-
1605). Another shows three gentlemen in early 17th-century costume
with three-quarter-length cloaks standing about with their hands in prayer,
rather low, suggesting that they were waiting to attend a banquet and were
saying grace. The men are Dickson, Miller and Cooper (Watford, 1613). In
the three-piece brass of George Coles (St Sepulchre, Northampton, 1640)
the husband is between his two wives and is taking them for a promenade.
Below, the twelve children are all facing right ready to follow their parents!
Has not the reverence and dignity of the memorial brass been lost? The
drawing, however, of this three-piece brass is good and lively.

A few 17th-century brasses drawn in an easy, naturalistic manner are
quite pleasing – as though the artist made an 'honest' drawing from life in
a sketchbook and engraved it straight on to the brass.

HERE LYETH BVRYED THE BODIES OF HENRY DICKSON
GEORGE MILLER AND ANTHONY COOPER WHO WERE LATE
SERVANTS TO Sr CHARLES MORRISON KNIGHT DECEASED &
AFTER CONTYNEWED IN SERVICE Wth DOROTHIE LA: MORRISON
HIS WIFE & Sr CHARLES MORRISON KNIGHT AND BARRONETT
THEIR SONNE, BY THE SPACE OF 40 YEARS IN MEMORY
OF THEM THE SAYD DOROTHIE LA: MORRISON HATH
VOVCHSAFED THIS STONE AND INSCRIPTION

58

58. H. DICKSON, G. MILLER AND A. COOPER, Watford, Herts.
All in civil dress. Servants to Sir Charles Morrison and widow (see page 47).

59. An elephant as a foot base on the brass of SIR WILLIAM VERNON AND WIFE AND CHILDREN 1467, Tong, Salop.
This animal acts as a foot base to Lady Vernon – there are other elephants to be found as foot supports on brasses. Bears, dragons, stags, bulls, horses, hedgehogs, unicorns and other animals also appear as supports on brasses.

59

60. THOMAS DE HORTON *c.* 1360, North Mimms, Herts. Size 47″ deep. The face is similar to that of Johannes von Zoest at Thorn. Note the manière criblée to the left of the chalice. A brass which displays the effigy well but lacks the technical skill of the Thorn brass.

61. SIR THOMAS BULLEN 1538, Hever, Kent.
A brass of skill but of little art – over-realistic in parts. Effigy 60″.

62

62. Unknown Knight *c.* 1460, Adderbury, Oxon.
A good descriptive brass of the armour of the mid-16th century. The armour has become more elaborate and continues in this direction for some decades.

63. FITZROY AND CURSON families. Part of kneeling figure in window at Waterperry, Oxon. Similar position often found on later brasses.

64. NICHOLAS BLACKBURN AND WIFE, 15th century. All Saints', York.
Coloured glass window. The characteristic kneeling position so often found on brasses is here well illustrated.

63

64

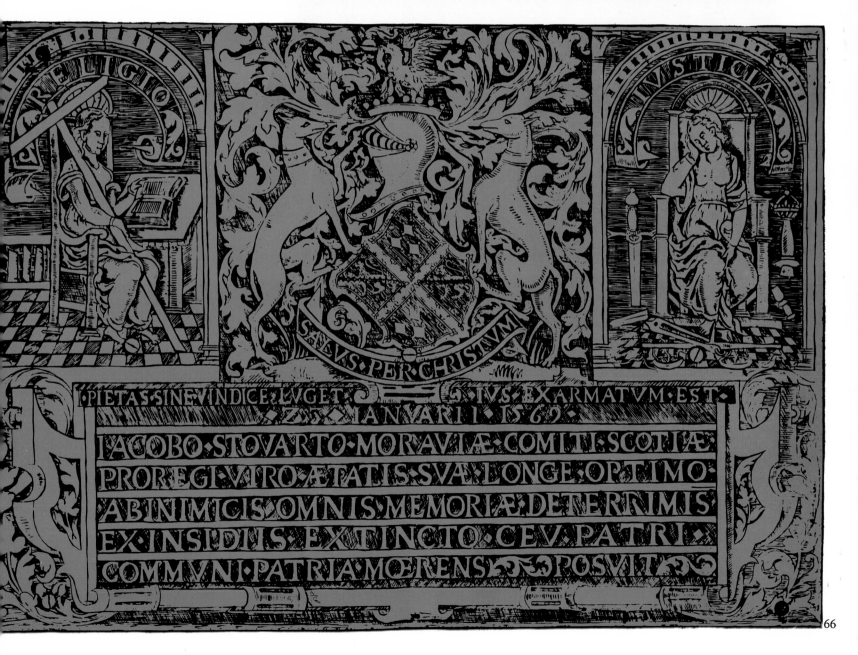

. JOHN BOWYER, WIFE AND CHILDREN 1570-
05, Camberwell, London.
om a group of picture brasses. A brass of limited
ill, size 22″ x 18″.

. JAMES STEWART, Earl of Murry, Regent of Scot-
d, assassinated 1569, Saint Giles, Edinburgh.
e of the few brasses in Scotland. It is a palimpsest.
e figure on the left is Religion and on the right
stice. The brass is engraved by James Gray,
oldsmith.

HERE LYETH BVRIED THE BODIES OF IHON BOWYAR ESQ: & ELIZABETH HIS
WIFE ONE OF THE DAVGHTERS OF ROBERT DRAPER ESQ: THEY HAD ISSVE 3
SONNES AND 3. DAVGHTERS. AND IOHN DIED THE X.TH OF OCTOBER 1570
ELIZABETH AFTER MARIED WILLM FOSTER ESQ: AND HAD ISSVE BY HIM
ONE SONNE AND ONE DAVGHTER. AND DIED THE XXVII OF APRILL 1605

65

RELIGIO

IVSTICIA

SALVS · PER · CHRISTVM

PIETAS · SINE · VINDICE · LVGET ·   · IVS · EX · ARMATVM · EST ·
· Z · · · IANVARII · 1569 ·

IACOBO · STOVARTO · MORAVIÆ · COMITI · SCOTIÆ
PROREGI · VIRO · ÆTATIS · SVÆ · LONGE · OPTIMO
AB · INIMICIS · OMNIS · MEMORIÆ · DETERNIMIS
EX · INSIDIIS · EXTINCTO · CEV · PATRI ·
COMMVNI · PATRIA · MŒRENS · POSVIT

66

67. Unknown civilian and lady arm-in-ar
c. 1500. Brown Candover, Hants. An unusu
brass. Interesting use of form, texture
material, belt and other features combin
to make a homogeneous whole, this is
67 chief and important merit. Effigy 19".

68

68. SIR R. FITZLEWES AND FOUR WIVES 1528, Ingrave, Essex.

CHAPTER NINE

Canopies

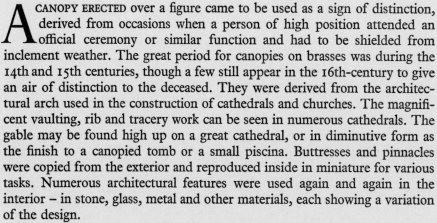

A CANOPY ERECTED over a figure came to be used as a sign of distinction, derived from occasions when a person of high position attended an official ceremony or similar function and had to be shielded from inclement weather. The great period for canopies on brasses was during the 14th and 15th centuries, though a few still appear in the 16th-century to give an air of distinction to the deceased. They were derived from the architectural arch used in the construction of cathedrals and churches. The magnificent vaulting, rib and tracery work can be seen in numerous cathedrals. The gable may be found high up on a great cathedral, or in diminutive form as the finish to a canopied tomb or a small piscina. Buttresses and pinnacles were copied from the exterior and reproduced inside in miniature for various tasks. Numerous architectural features were used again and again in the interior – in stone, glass, metal and other materials, each showing a variation of the design.

Sculptural canopy design is best seen in Westminster Abbey in the famous tombs of Edmund Crouchback (1296) and of William de Valence. They are patterns for the designers of brasses. The tomb of Bishop Bridport at Salisbury (c. 1264) has shafts rising from a base and meeting in an arch with elaborate finials; this is a replica of the conventional church window of the 13th century. The canopy of the tomb of Edward II in Gloucester Cathedral (c. 1334) is an elaborate construction in Caen stone consisting of three gables and a mass of smaller ones, together with pinnacles and niches forming a pattern of perpendicular movement. All these canopies have their counterpart on brasses. The earliest are simple in the extreme, beautifully shaped with straight side shafts (Sir John d'Aubernoun, 1327; Sir John de Cobham, 1354). When, however, we arrive at the 16th-century canopies – that, for instance, of Sir R. l'Estrange at Hunstanton (1506), 'full of craft but empty of art' – progress appears to have lost its way. The canopy designs of the 14th-century, and some of the 15th, were among the finest productions – along with the early effigies and some crosses – of English craftsmen in the monumental brass industry. Taking a broad view, they often surpassed the design of the figures which were placed under the canopies. This simple linear feeling for design is very much an English quality, since the English have always been better artists in line than in tone or colour. In craft work it has always been the same, from Saxon times to the present day.

The church at Cobham, Kent, contains the fine collection of brasses of the Cobham family. There are nineteen brasses in this church – the majority are to this family. Six brasses are ogee-headed; the side shafts are pinnacled. Between these pinnacles and the centre finials is placed, on either side, a shield of arms. The finials are delicately foliated. In the brass of Sir John and of Dame Margaret, the finials terminate in small figures of the Virgin and Child. The narrow marginal fillets contain inscriptions in French. Jone de Kobeham (died 1298, brass laid 1320) was the daughter of Sir Robert Setvans, whose brass at Chartham (1307) has been described elsewhere as one of the finest of all brasses. Lady Joan de Cobham (1433) has no canopy but she had five husbands! Her third husband was Sir Nicholas Hawberk (1407) who is under a fine triple canopy. On top appear (a) left, the Virgin and Child, (b) centre, the Holy Trinity, (c) right, St George and the Dragon.

The brass of Sir Hugh Hastyngs (Elsing, 1343) shows the remains of what was once a beautiful canopy. As the 14th century progressed the canopies became more elaborate. The sides were no longer straight but had ogee arches

69. JANE WILBERTSON 1810, Llangynfelyn, Cardiganshire.
Size 36″ x 29¾″. A very fine example of an exceptionally late brass. Haines records this brass in his list of modern brasses but wrongly states that it is at Machynlleth. The enamel still remains in the incised lines making it almost impossible to rub. Note the engraver's monogram at the bottom of the right of the desk.

70. Gothic coloured glass window (c. 1340), Stanford, Northants. Showing use of canopy. Note the elaborate finial and crockets.

71. Gothic gable, Cologne Cathedral, illustrating the finial at the top and the crockets down both sides of the arch.

of well-balanced curves culminating in tall, slender pinnacles. The foliation became elaborate and lofty pinnacles were the fashion. Super-canopies then made their appearance. These were constructions above the canopy or canopies consisting of yet further small canopied compartments or niches. A typical example is that of the Lincolnshire merchant, Walter Pescod, at Boston (1398). This brass is somewhat mutilated, but originally it had no fewer than fifteen saints in niches – four in niches in each side shaft and seven in the super-canopy – only two of which remain today. This brass is not attractive; with its over-crowding it is brass designing gone mad. A more pleasing canopy brass of later date is that of Prior Thomas Nelond of Crowfold (1453). A quadruple canopy is here illustrated. Robert Ingylton, 1472, Thornton, Bucks.

A quite absurd 'canopy' is that of Bishop Wyvil, Salisbury Cathedral (1375). The bishop is placed inside a castle with battlements. At the castle gate stands a guard on duty. The design is ugly, the drawing bad and the whole conception fragmentary. It hardly reflects the age in which it was executed, for almost any mediocre designer of any period from the 14th to the 20th century could have been responsible for this dreadful brass. The story of this brass is related in Bouquet's *Church Brasses* (pages 94-8).

The brass of Sir Robert de Grey at Rotherfield Greys, Oxfordshire (1387) is surrounded by a border with inscriptions. Sir Robert stands under a canopy of simple design. This brass is typical of many of its period – not inspired, but honest good craftsmanship.

The canopy brass of J. Curtseys and widow at Wymington, Bedfordshire (1391) is a distinguished brass when seen in its full size. It avoids being 'fussy'. The two figures stand out clearly from the shafts of the canopy: the spaces between the figures and the shafts and between the two figures are well-proportioned and asymmetrical which is an advantage. The simple lines used to express the faces are reduced to a minimum; they are excellently drawn and indicate the individual features perfectly. The cushions behind the heads are decorative; they are not quite identical, and have just enough subtle variation to make them different, yet at the same time they form a fitting part of the whole design of the figures and canopy. The animals at the base, too, become an intrinsic component of the design – they do not assert themselves beyond the part they are intended to play. The perpendicular lines of the drapery break up the large shapes in a rhythmic pattern conforming to the perpendicular shafts of the canopy. The space between the two heads and the arches of the double canopy is again well considered and in every way aids the presentation of the two figures. The double canopy is 'clean', crisp, and 'open' in design. It is light and elegant and avoids the confusion so often found in the later canopies. The finials are simple, suitably decorative, and do not assert themselves beyond the exact degree in which they were intended to contribute to the completeness of the whole. This is a quality found only in the best brasses; too often in second-class examples a particular facet is over stressed, bringing ruin to the design (see plate 74).

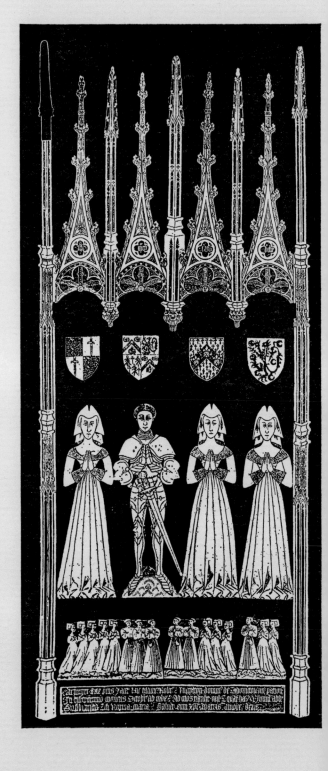

72. ROBERT INGYLTON 1472, Thornton, Bucks. With three wives and sixteen children, six sons and ten daughters. An interesting brass with four canopies. Certainly no portraiture, the wives with horned headdresses are almost identical and appear to be about the same age.

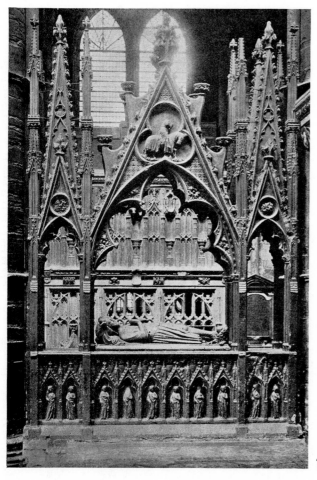

73

73. Tomb of Edmond Crouchback, d. 1296, Westminster Abbey. Edmond was the second son of Henry III and became Earl of Lancaster. A pattern of canopy tomb which illustrates the extravagant use of the canopy in the three-dimensional tomb, and was widely used in brass memorials.

74. J. CURTEYS AND WIDOW 1391, Wymington, Beds. J. Curteys, Lord of the Manor, Mayor of the Staple of Calais, rebuilder of the church.

74

H

CHAPTER TEN

Heraldry on Brasses

To cover this subject fully would require a volume in itself. Heraldry first came into fashion in the early part of the 12th century when knights carried bright colours on their shields in tournaments or in battle. Heraldic arms were intended to distinguish persons and property, to record descent and alliance, and one of the earliest records we have of the use of such devices occurs on the shield of Geoffrey Plantagenet, Count of Anjou (c. 1150). This is an enamelled portrait-figure of Geoffrey and is in Le Mans museum (see page 22).

In the early part of the 13th century it became the fashion to decorate the gown which knights wore over their chain-mail: hence the generic term *coat of arms*. The crest evolved from the idea of painting heraldic devices on the front of the helmet, repeating all or part of the shield device. In the 13th century it was fashionable to paint a fan-shaped metal crest and fix it to the top of the helm. Later this developed into a three-dimensional figure in wood or other material, such as a bird, beast, or some imaginative device. The combination of shield, helm, and crest became a complete entity and has remained so ever since – term 'coat of arms'. Its use became widespread among knights, both on the battle-field and for civic purposes. The arms appeared on tombs and on numerous brasses; the recumbent knight often holds a shield on which his arms are delineated, his head resting on a helm and crest.

The meaning and derivations of the old devices are many and varied and some we do not know. Often they were based on punning – a rebus. Trumpington, trumpets; Fauconer, falcons; Foxley, foxes; Barley, barley; Setvans, seven winnowing fans; Wingfield, wings; Pecok, peacock, are a few examples of many depicted on monumental brasses.

Sir John d'Aubernoun the Elder, of Stoke D'Abernon, Surrey (1277), displays his simple heraldic device on his pennon. The brass of Sir Symon de Felbrygge, at Felbrigg, Norfolk (1443), shows him with the banner of Richard II.

The earlier designers of heraldic devices were the best. They designed in a simple, large, and effective manner, suitable to their purpose, with bold shapes and simple colour schemes. This can be seen in the brasses of D'Aubernoun, Trumpington, Bures, Setvans, Fitzralph and Creke, where the shields display their owners' devices. Unfortunately the enamel has long since gone except for the shield of d'Aubernoun.

Coats of arms on monumental brasses can be classified according to their methods of display – whether on the military figure, on the figure for ceremonial occasions, or as decorations designed as accessories on various parts of the brass, not on the figure. With few exceptions all heraldic brasses were decorated in enamelled colours right down to the 17th century. St George's Chapel, Windsor, contains a remarkable display of coats of arms of Knights of the Garter. These stall plates, which number about 600, date from the reign of Richard III, the earliest plates are enamel on gilt or silvered copper. Brass was used on some later ones. After the 17th century the colours were *painted* on copper but early in our own century the artists reverted to the enamelling technique.

JOHN AND LETTYS TERRY 1524, St John Mad-Market, Norwich, Norfolk.

ry was a wealthy merchant and left monies to ens of the town. Top shield is arms of Norwich the lower a combination of Merchant Adventrs, Mercers, etc. Merchant mark at bottom. early as the 13th century ladies were wearing rnosters or ave-beads as jewellery. A member he Venetian embassy to London in 1500 comted on English ladies' taste for wearing long ries at the waist. Lettys Terry's five decades of beads divided by larger paternoster-beads, hed to an elaborate buckle apparently used only ngland for this purpose, corresponds in general ern to the chief form of the rosary since its ial establishment in 1475. The three formal s of the buckle may symbolise the three sets of Mysteries in the Rosary devotion.

CRESTS ON BRASSES

Crests appear in considerable numbers on brasses. Sir Thomas Brounflet at Wymington, Bedfordshire (1430) carries a crest with tilted helm. Sir Thomas was cup-bearer to Henry V. Sir John de Brewys at Wiston, Sussex (1426) and Sir John de Harpeden in Westminster Abbey (1438), display large striking crests with animals. Sir N. Dagworth at Blickling (1401) has a crest with a long-necked creature, half bird, half animal (see plate 36). It has a beak, beard, long ears, and presumably a feathered neck of great length. Both the figures of Sir W. Moyne at Sawtry, Huntingdonshire (1404) and the mutilated brass of Sir John Segrave at Dorchester, Oxon (1425) have human figures in their crests. Lord Ferrers at Merevale, Warwickshire (1407) displays peacock feathers. The badly-proportioned figure of Sir A. Grey in St Albans Abbey (1480) displays a huge crest; his head is as large as his torso while from his waist downwards he is a dwarf. The brass of Sir R. l'Estrange at Hunstanton (1506) has a most elaborate canopy; the knight stands on a bracket and his crest is of most lively design and gigantic proportions, including the mantling. Another complicated over-elaborate brass with a rather pretentious crest is that to the father of Anne Boleyn, Sir Thomas Bullen, at Hever, Kent (1538). (See page 45, footnote, and plate 61).

The Jupon

The arms of Sir William Bagot at Baginton, Warwickshire (1401) are displayed on his jupon. This was a leather jacket on which the arms were painted. In a similar manner the brass to the Earl of Warwick displays his arms: gules, a fess between six crosses crosslet or. The kirtle of his countess shows the arms of Ferrers: gules, seven mascles or. She was the daughter of Lord Ferrers. Her mantle is ornamented with the arms of her lord (whose feet rest on a bear in chains). Other examples of jupons displaying arms are W. de Aldborough, Aldborough (1360), Sir Dallingridge, Fletching (1380), Sir George Felbrigge, Playford (1400), Sir John Wingfield, Letheringham (1400).

The Tabard

Following the jupon came the tabard. This was a loose garment with short sleeves which came into use in the early part of the 15th century and often bore its owner's heraldic devices. An early example is the brass of John Wantele at Amberley (1424), which has three lions' heads on the garment. The arms are: vert, three lions' masks argent, langued gules. This brass is of interest for the manner in which the background of the tabard was engraved; a deep tooth or key was cut in the brass metal, which was then filled in with lead and silver (plate 78).

A fine example of tabard and mantle is found on the brass of Sir Ralph Verney and his wife at Aldbury, Hertfordshire (1547) (plate 80). The arms are:

Dexter
Quarterly 1 and 4 azure, on a cross argent five mullets pierced gules (Verney)
2 azure, 2 chevron argent, on a canton of the last a Paschal lamb gules (Aignell)
3 argent, a fess vert, over all a lion rampant gules (Whittingham)
Sinister
Quarterly 1 and 4 argent, a chevron between three eagles legs erased sable (Bray)
2 and 3 Vair, three bendlets gules (Bray)
The whole charged with an escutcheon of pretence
Quarterly 1, or, on a bend gules three goats trippaut argent (Halliwell)
2 sable, a chevron between three bulls' heads cabossed argent (Norbury)
3 gules, a fess chequy argent and sable between six cross crosslets of the second (Haversham)
4 or, two bends gules (Sudeley)

76

76. Shield from brass of SIR WILLIAM VERNON 1467, Tong, Salop.
Use of a wood wind instrument on heraldic shield.

76A

76B

76A. RICHARD COLWELL 1533, Faversham, Kent — a rebus.

76B. HENRY(?) CASTELYN 1407, Bexley, Kent. Hunting horn with bawdrick and shield.

77

77. Shield to ROBERT WASHINGTON, gent, 1622, Great Brington, Northants.
The Washington Arms, the origin of the American stars and stripes. Arms: sable, two bars or, three spur rowels in chief. The Washington family lived at Sulgrave Manor in the same county.

Sir Ralph Verney wears a tabard bearing his coat of arms quarterly and impaling the quartered coat of his wife. On Lady Verney's mantle is seen her husband's coat of arms and her own paternal coat with the escutcheon of pretence which denotes that her mother was an heiress.

Collars are various. The SS collar is of doubtful origin (see the Bagot brass, Baginton, Warwickshire, 1401). Many suggestions have been made as to the meaning of SS but none of them can be proved. There are also collars of roses, suns, and a few other devices. Again theories have been advanced about their origin, but as none can be proved decisively one has to come to the conclusion that all three were decorative motifs without any particular meaning. Knights of the Garter appear on brasses. The figure of Sir Thomas Bullen (1538) mentioned above, wears the Garter.

Illustrated in heraldic mantles: Lady Katherine Howard in St Mary's, Lambeth (1535) and an unknown lady in St Helen's, Bishopsgate, of about the same date (plates 81 and 145).

ARMS OF THE STAPLE OF CALAIS

The merchants of the Staple of Calais had their own coat of arms: Barry nebulee of six argent and azure on a chief gules, lion passant guardant or. John Feld of Standon in Hertfordshire (1474, illustrated, plate 228) was one of the merchants entitled to use it. The arms of several of the great London companies appear on many brasses. The Clothworkers, the Drapers, the Fishmongers, the Grocers, the Haberdashers, the Ironmongers, Merchant Tailors, the Mercers, the Skinners, the Salters are some of the most important. (See list at end of book.)

The shield as an accessory to the effigy often appears on brasses and is usually placed in the corners of the casement. A coat of arms in excellent state of preservation, together with inscription, is that at Over Winchendon, Bucks, to John Goodwyn (1558).

Hic iacet Johes Wantle qui obiit xxiiij die Januar Anno dni millo CCCCxxiiij cui aie ipiacetur deus

78

79

78. JOHN WANTLE 1424, Amberley, Sussex.
An unusual heraldic tabard. Effigy and ins. 34".

79. DAME ELIZABETH GORINGE 1558, Burton, Sussex.
A rare instance of a lady wearing a heraldic tabard. The kneeling figure is a common position – found not only on brasses but on coloured glass windows, manuscripts, incised slabs and altar frontals, see plates 126, 127.

80

80. SIR RALPH AND LADY VERNEY 1546, Aldbury, Herts.
Sir Ralph wears a tabard and Lady Elizabeth a heraldic mantle. Both
garments display armorial bearings. The faces are doubtful portraits,
and, as is often the case, the figures are ill-drawn at the expense of the
heraldic display. Effigy 25".

81

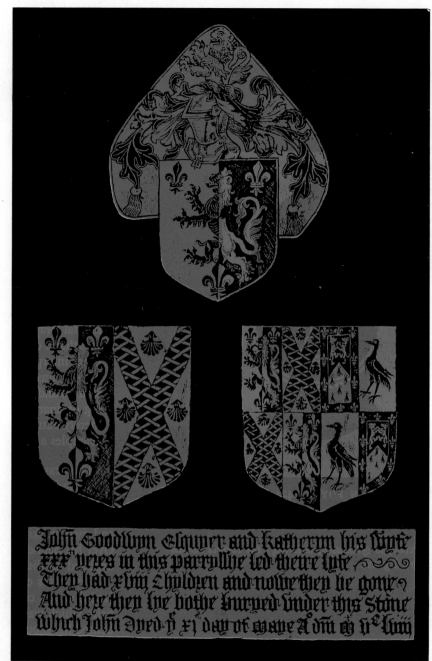

81. LADY KATHERINE HOWARD 1535, St Mary, Lambeth.
A bottle shaped brass designed mainly to show her heraldic mantle.
Similar to several brasses of approximate date (see unknown lady 1535,
St Helen's, Bishopsgate, E.C., plate 145). Effigy 38″.

82. Arms of JOHN GOODWYN 1558, Over Winchendon, Bucks.
This original brass is in a rare state of preservation (countersunk
mural). Very fine. Designed with exceptional clarity and incised with
equal skill. Size 27″ x 17″.

CHAPTER ELEVEN

Knights in Armour and Kings

83

83. Head of JOHN POYLE 1424, Hampton Poyle, Oxon.

Surcoat, so often used, is wrong; the correct nomenclature is gown.

ROM EARLIEST TIMES man has devised methods of attack and defence. Armour was one of the means of self-protection in battle, but when armour plate could be pierced by shot or cannon ball, armour went out of use except for military exercises and ceremonial display.

Before we consider the armour depicted on brasses we should remember that all drawings endeavour to depict three dimensions in the flat (as are all brass effigies and accessories). The late Sir James Mann points out that in the portrayal of chain-mail a warning note is necessary:

> To draw every link on a small scale was impossible and lines of dots or circles were used and sometimes a very close depiction is found on monumental brasses or paintings where there was room for it. But a popular shorthand depiction of mail in the 13th and 14th centuries has in the past been interpreted as mail of another construction called 'banded mail'. This is unsupported by any other evidence, either from finds or written sources and must now be accepted as no more than a facile way of representing ordinary interlinked mail. Mail constructed of links whose ends were merely butted together instead of riveted did not find favour in Europe and examples are almost always of Eastern origin.

The brass of Sir John d'Aubernoun at Stoke D'Abernon, Surrey (1277) is unique in that it depicts the knight with his lance in addition to his sword. This suit of mail is of the type that had been current for over 200 years. The knight wears a hauberk (shirt) of mail with sleeves extending over his hands and mail stockings down to his toes. Strapped to his feet are pointed spurs. Over his hauberk he wears a gown of linen.* This armour is similar to that depicted on the Bayeux Tapestry (see plate 110).

The brass of Sir Roger Trumpington at Trumpington, Cambridgeshire (1289) shows certain differences. He is resting as on a pillow, on a conical helm which was worn over the mail coif (hood). The two rectangular shapes behind his shoulders are known as ailettes, engraved with his arms. They are metal plates and were laced to the side of his shoulders. Note that his shield is convex. Sir Roger was a crusader – not because he is cross-legged but because it is recorded that he went with Prince Edward to the Holy Land.

Numerous suggestions have been put forward to explain the reason for the cross-legged position, including the crusader theory, but we know that some cross-legged knights were not crusaders. One more suggestion may not be out of place. In a 13th-century sketchbook of Villiard de Honecourt is a drawing of a crowned king in a sitting position with his legs crossed. He leans over with a twist to his body to enable him to replace his sword in the scabbard. Before him stand two women. The king is thought to be Solomon delivering justice. So with a knight wearing heavy chain-mail and with flexed legs crossing each other, his hands together in prayer, after a life spent in defence of justice – his image is perpetuated in this position to remind others of his devotion to the right.

Later, when the less flexible plate armour replaced the flexible chain-mail, a stiffer pose was necessary and so knights were then depicted without crossed legs.

The brass of Sir Robert Bures at Acton, Suffolk (1302) is a 'copy-book' description of the armour. It has been referred to as the finest military brass in existence. It certainly shows the knight in all his fine display of armour complete in every detail, but it has not the grace of the figure of Sir Robert

Setvans at Chartham, Kent (1306), who is bare-headed. This figure, along with that of Sir John de Creke at Westley Waterless (1325), is probably one of the most elegant and graceful military brasses ever designed. Setvans' shield and ailettes are charged with winnowing fans (seven fans) – a rebus on his name (plates 38, 40).

By 1325 armour had changed in style in several respects. Two brasses to show this are Sir (not known) Bacon of Gorleston, Suffolk (1320), and Sir William Fitzralph of Pebmarsh, Essex (c. 1323). In both these brasses we find the upper forearms protected by steel plates, small elbow-pieces are attached and round plates fastened in front of the shoulders and at the bend of the arms (plate 93).

The brasses of Sir John de Creke (1325) and of Sir John d'Aubernoun the Younger (1327) show further changes. D'Aubernoun is bearded, they both wear more elegant basinets, Creke bears lions on his shoulders and elbows, the spurs are of a new rowel type, but d'Aubernoun still wears the prick type. The gowns are short at the front and long at the back. Later the back was shortened and was known as a skirted jupon. This was a loose garment but soon it became a tight-fitting one – more military in appearance – and it remained in fashion from about the middle of the 14th-century to the early part of the 15th. The jupon often had the owner's coat of arms embroidered on it. It was laced up at the sides (plates 39, 40).

Moustaches or beards became more popular. Examples are Sir John Foxley at Bray in Berkshire (1378), and Sir Edward Cerne at Draycot Cerne in Wiltshire (1393). Sir Edward wears a pointed type of basinet. His neck and throat are protected by camail which was hung on staples on the lower edge of the basinet. Late in the century a metal strip was used for this purpose. The belt holding the sword disappeared and was replaced by a magnificent baldric worn over the hips; this was often richly jewelled, as was the scabbard. The sword was fixed on the left-hand side in a vertical position, and at the right-hand side was a dagger (plates 104, 100).

For a short time the thighs were decorated with small circles. This is often called studded armour, but wrongly so, because these circles are the same as the rivet-heads of a brigandine (breastplate) defence, made up of small plates riveted to a leather base and faced on the front with a coloured material. An example of this is on the brass of Sir Thomas Cheyne at Drayton Beauchamp, Buckinghamshire (1368). Sabatons – sharp-pointed shoes – had the instep protected by a gusset of mail. Gauntlets were of leather and steel, with steel plates on the knuckles. The armour of this period is almost all plate, the mail which had lasted so long was not considered sufficiently defensive against the methods of attack. Another feature of defence was the visor fitted to the helmet. Few brasses depict the visor because it would hardly be correct to cover up the features for a funeral plate (plate 98).

Most of the continental brasses show weapons fixed to the breast-plate or brigandine, under the jupon. Early in the 15th-century the basinets became rounder. The elbows were protected by coutiers, which became larger and larger, and the armpits were likewise protected by palettes which took on larger proportions as time passed. Belts holding swords were worn transversely. The belt was fixed by a hook on the right hip to one placed lower on the left side. The sword was usually worn on the left-hand side and the knight would pass his right hand across to draw it. On two unnamed brasses at Writtle, Essex (c. 1500), the swords are shown on the right – probably for left-handed users. On the brass of N. Parker at Honing in Norfolk (1496) the sword hangs down the centre between the legs.

Before the middle of the 15th-century the left arm received additional protection, but the right arm was relieved of some of its weight of armour to give the wearer more freedom for fighting or striking. The besagues were superseded by paldrons, massive steel plates to protect the upper arms and shoulders. The body-armour was likewise strengthened by the introduction of

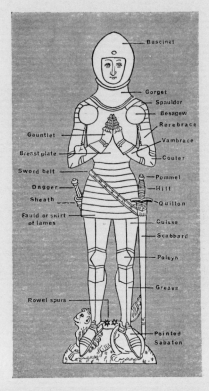

84

84. 15th century armour. This type of armour was in use about the end of the first quarter of the 15th century and with only slight variations lasted well into the third quarter when it became more ornamental and complex.

85

85. SIR RICHARD DE BOSELYNGTHORPE c. 1300, Buslingthorpe, Lincs.
A very attractive early brass – Sir Richard holds a heart and wears chain mail, ailettes and gown.

86. SAINT ETHELRED, King of the West Saxons (Martyr), died 871 (inscription restored in the 17th century gives date 873). Wimborne Minster, Dorset. 1440 approximate date of engraving. Effigy 14¼".

placcates to the upper part of the breast-plate. This became more angular in the centre; it projected forward, the placcate rising to a cusped point. Knee-plates (poleyns) were larger and steel plates at the back added extra protection. By now the armour had become heavier than ever. It was incorrectly stated that if the wearer fell in battle he would be unable to rise unless someone came to his aid: this was most unlikely to happen if he were surrounded by the enemy!* The armour of an unknown knight at Adderbury, Oxon (1460) is typical of that of the mid-15th-century, as is also the Yorkist armour of Sir A. Grey at St Albans, Herts (1480).

Much of the armour of this period came from Milan. The linear representations of this type of armour on brasses are often inaccurate. It is difficult to understand why this should be so, but considering the period in which these brasses were incised one realizes that those responsible for the drawing of the designs were not first-class draughtsmen or artists, but craftsmen more accustomed to working in the round; they knew a certain part of the armour to have certain characteristics, and endeavoured to represent it as they knew it to be and not as they saw it from the front view. This would account for certain exaggerations and inaccuracies.

By the third quarter of the 15th-century armour became somewhat more simple in design. The extravagances were reduced to plainer forms and some left out altogether. The small brass of Thomas Latton at Blewbury (1523) shows a neater arrangement. The shoulder-plate (pauldron) on his left is extended to protect his neck in a forward movement in battle. He wears a mail skirt. The broad-toed shoes took the place of the pointed sabatons. These were extremely ugly and often spoilt the appearance of the incised effigy. The tabard became more popular than hitherto, and was in general use up to the mid-16th-century. The tabard was blazoned with the owner's arms as in the brass of Henry Leyneham at Tidmarsh (1517). He wears the large ugly sabatons and his shoulder-shields as well as his tabard are emblazoned. Another fine example of heraldic display is that of Sir Ralph Verney with his wife, at Albury, Hertfordshire (1546) (see plate 80).

Military brasses of the first half of the 16th-century were generally of poor standard. Many were ugly and badly designed and incised. The development of fire-arms had a pronounced effect on the use of armour in Elizabethan times. The end of armour as a means of defence was in sight, for gunpowder and shot could penetrate the steel; but armour continued to be worn long after it was useless as a means of protection. Even as late as the early 18th-century it was worn, but purely on account of its martial appearance and on ceremonial occasions. Pauldrons were discarded and were replaced by epaulettes. The breast-plate was longer and pointed at the waist in the middle. The skirt of taces disappeared and was replaced by lamboys which were buckled to the cuirass. Ruffs were worn round the neck and often at the wrists too.

The armour of the 17th-century was very like that of the late 16th-century. The head is always depicted bare. Beards and moustaches again came into fashion. The lamboys (steel petticoats) were made of a series of over-lapping plates riveted together. The sword and dagger were still carried. Jack-boots replaced the armour for legs and feet in this century. A good example is the memorial to William Pen, sheriff of Buckinghamshire, at Penn (1638). He is in armour; the brass is well cut, and apart from the feet the drawing is fairly good (see plate 113).

A few brasses of Charles I's reign, with effigies, remind one of the King himself, due no doubt to the fashion of the Van Dyck beard.

Military brasses never depict chargers. This would mean a complete change in the lay-out and evidently no one would undertake this break-away from the conventional design. We hear that some knights had great affection

87. An early brass – 1310. Croft, Lincs. Half effigy of knight in mail and gown. Effigy 18".

*The average weight of a complete suit of armour varied between 60 lb to about 90 lb. Helmets 4 lb upwards.

for their chargers. Various ladies are depicted with their pet dogs, just as knights are shown with different animals, but not horses. A horse appears on an incised slab under the feet of an unknown priest at Chalons-sur-Marne (*c.* 1280).

KINGS ON BRASSES

Kings rarely appear on English brasses except in Hereford Cathedral which has a small seated figure of St Ethelbert, king and martyr,* holding his crowned head in his left hand. This is from the mutilated brass of Thomas de Cantilupe (died 1282, engraved *c.* 1290).

At Wimborne Minster, Dorset, there is another brass of St Ethelred, King of the West Saxons (died 871 – the inscription has 873). It is a half-effigy; the king is in regal robes with crown and sceptre. It was engraved about 1440 and restored in the 17th century, but is only a second-class brass – not worthy of the royal personage it represents. On the brass of Sir Hugh Hastyngs at Elsing, Norfolk (1347) there is a small figure of Edward III in one of the side shafts (see plate 51).

An example on the Continent is King Eric Menved at Ringsted in Denmark (1319).

88. SIR REGINALD DE MALYNS 1385, Chinnor, Oxon (part of brass). 18″ deep. He is between his two wives, see plates 119, 120.

89. From a window at Adderbury, Oxon (15th century).

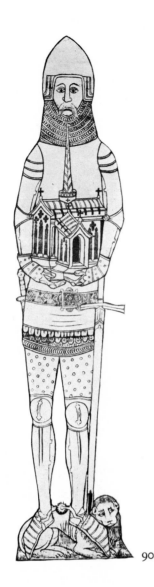

90

90. SIR JOHN DE COBHAM 1365, Cobham, Kent. Holding a church.

91. BRIAN ROUCLIFF AND WIFE JOAN 1494, Cowthorpe, Yorks. They hold the church which Roucliff rebuilt – he was baron of the exchequer.

92. Medieval painting of KING ATHELSTAN holding a model of the church, Milton Abbey, Dorset. (*Courtesy*, *Country Life*)

92

91

93. SIR WILLIAM FITZRALPH 1323, Pebmarsh, Essex.

94. SIR JOHN D'AUBERNOUN 1277, Stoke D'Abernon Church, Surrey. The oldest effigy brass in Great Britain. Effigy 76″.

95. SIR ROBERT DE BURES 1302, Acton, Suffolk. Effigy 79″.

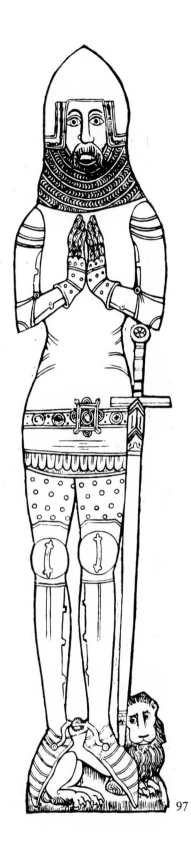

96

97

98

96. SIR ROGER DE TRUMPINGTON 1289, Trumpington Church, Cambridgeshire. Effigy 77″.

97. SIR THOMAS DE COBHAM 1367, Cobham, Kent. Similar to Sir Thomas Cheyne, 1368. Effigy 60″.

98. SIR THOMAS CHEYNE 1368, Drayton Beauchamp, Bucks. The armour is similar to that of Sir John de Cobham, 1365, Cobham, Kent. Note the enriched sword belt (baldric). The circles on the thighs and legs are rivet heads. An attractive brass retaining some of the best qualities of the earlier designs of the 14th century. Effigy 60″.

99

100

99. SIR ROBERT DE GREY 1387, Rotherfield Greys, Oxon.
The shields are missing. A good brass but not first quality. This is typical of the late 14th century and early 15th century brasses when the figures became stiff and mechanical. But they are clear and simple in design and the cutting is good. 58″ deep.

100. SIR EDWARD AND LADY CERNE 1393, Draycot Cerne, Wilts.
A good brass. The lady wears a veil denoting that she is a widow. Sir Edward wears the fashionable moustache. Part of the cushion is missing but has been restored in the illustration. 37½″ deep including inscription.

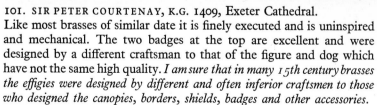

101

102

101. SIR PETER COURTENAY, K.G. 1409, Exeter Cathedral.
Like most brasses of similar date it is finely executed and is uninspired
and mechanical. The two badges at the top are excellent and were
designed by a different craftsman to that of the figure and dog which
have not the same high quality. *I am sure that in many 15th century brasses
the effigies were designed by different and often inferior craftsmen to those
who designed the canopies, borders, shields, badges and other accessories.*

102. JOHN PECOK (?) *c.* 1380, St Michaels, St Albans, Herts.
A symmetrical balance throughout, with a freedom of movement and a
subtle departure from the mechanical. Compare with early 15th century
brasses (see above). A good brass apart from the body of the animal
which is too small for the head. Effigy 34″.

103. SIR NICHOLAS DAGWORTH 1401, Blickling, Norfolk.
A large brass. The borders and inscription are mutilated. A good brass but stiff and cold in conception (for detail of crest see plate 36). 65″ deep.

104. SIR JOHN FOXLEY 1368, Bray, Berks.
Note the fox's head on the helm – a rebus. 29″ deep.

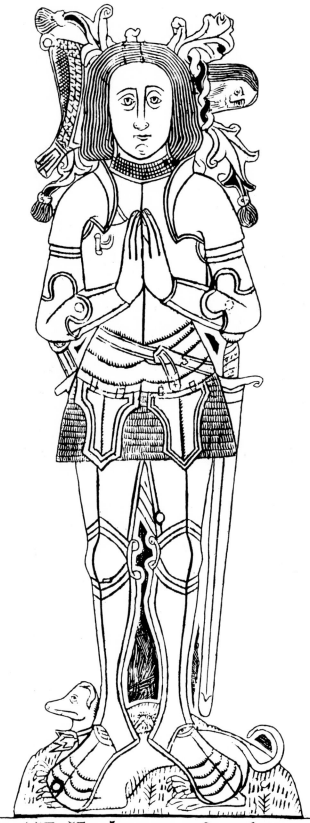

105. LAWRENCE FYTON 1434, Sonning, Berks.
The clean appearance of plate armour of the 1st half of the 15th century is well shown in this brass. Traces of the original red enamel still remain in the belt (1967). Size 39″ x 11″.

106. JOHN LEVENTHORPE 1510, St Helen's, Bishopsgate.
Usher to the chamber of Henry VII. An interesting brass. Note the figure in the helm and the obliteration of the inscription. Size 34½″ effigy.

107

108

109

107. SIR THOMAS DE ST QUINTIN 1418, Lord of the Manor, Harpham, Yorks. Effigy 40″.

108. WALTER GRENE 1456(?), Hayes, Middlesex.

109. THOMAS QUARTREMAYNE c. 1460, Thame, Oxon.
Note the shape of the elbow-plates and pauldrons. Effigy 27½″.

110. Mounted Knights in armour (Bayeux Tapestry), 1066-1082 (*Reading Museum facsimile*).

110

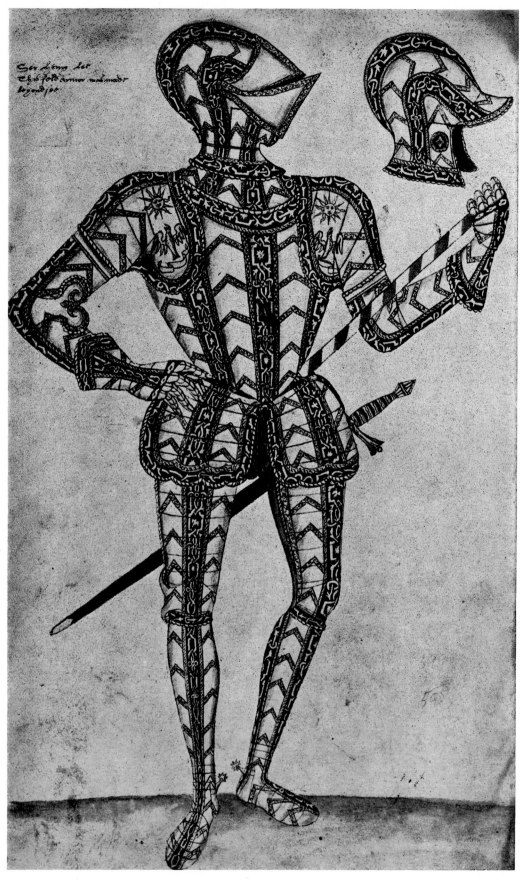

111. Design for suit of armour for SIR HENRY LEE from a 16th century
sketch book in the Victoria and Albert Museum.

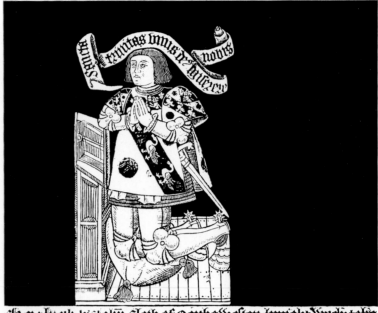

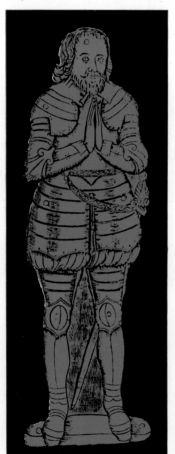

112. SIR JOHN CLERK 1539, Thame, Oxon. An exceptionally well-designed brass. The designer made excellent use of the abstract and decorative values; the scroll is lively and well placed – very much a part of the whole design. The inscription underneath is interesting beyond the usual.

113. WILLIAM PEN, Sheriff of Bucks, Penn, Bucks. A brass typical of its period. 25″ deep.

114. Unknown Knight, Whittle, Essex, c. 1500. Effigy 30″. Of interest because the sword is worn on right hand side – a left-handed individual!

115

115. Fairford, Gloucestershire. Church of St Mary the Virgin, south side. A famous Cotswold church containing the brass of JOHN TAME AND WIFE (1500) and other brasses.

116. THOMAS GIFFORD 1550, Twyford, Bucks.
Part of brass of Knight in Armour. A fine, exciting and well executed
base. The cutting shows a very spontaneous action with the engraving
tool.

117. SIR SYMOND DE FELBRIG 1351, Felbrigg, Norfolk.
In civil dress and with anelace. A fine simple figure and a portrait.

118. DAME ANNE NORBURY (widow) 1464, Stoke D'Abernon, Surrey.
A novel way of illustrating her children.

CHAPTER TWELVE

Women, Children and the Professions

WOMEN'S FASHIONS

IN THE MAIN, the costume of women depicted on brasses is simple; they are shown wearing their everyday clothes. As the brass is a funeral monument, people rightly considered it bad taste to have themselves represented in all their finery, although there are a few exceptions. The garments shown on our brasses are an invaluable guide to the history of the costume of the English-woman over several centuries. Perhaps it is the head-dresses worn by ladies in the 'brass era' that is the most fascinating section of their wardrobe. Continental brasses of women are few and do not tell us much about their clothes. The only brass that I can trace to a queen is one at Gadebusch Mecklenburg, Germany. It is of the Queen of Sweden, 1432. There is, of course, the double brass of King Eric and Queen Ingeburg, 1319, Ringstead, Denmark.

The dresses depicted on brasses of the first half of the 14th-century are simple in the extreme. They were known as kirtles – robes with tight sleeves, pulled in at the waist, the sleeves often being full-length and forming mittens covering the backs of the hands. On our earliest brass of a woman (Lady Camoys, Trotton, Sussex, 1310) she is seen wearing a long flowing mantle hanging loose from the shoulders. This is more attractive on the tall slender figure of Lady Creke (Westley Waterless, Cambridge, 1325). Here the mantle is open, fastened by a cord across the breast, and the subtle swing from the hips gives the figure great charm. She wears a wimple – a kind of kerchief which gives her a queenly appearance. She completely outshines the effigies of Lady Camoys and of Lady Cobham (Cobham, Kent, 1320). Surely there is no other *husband and wife* on brass who express dignity, nobility, refinement, and elegance better than the two figures of Sir John and Lady de Creke (plate 40).

Charming is the figure of Lady Joan de Northwood (Minster, Sheppey, 1330). Not so elegant or dignified as Lady Creke, Lady Joan is, however, very well drawn, the folds of her mantle well selected (taken from a model); her face is pretty (plate 128).

The style of dress worn in the early part of the 14th-century continued to be worn, with only slight variations, up to about the end of the long reign of King Edward III (1327-77). Then the cote-hardie came into fashion. This was a garment that was made to fit the figure both at back and front, but opened at the sides to disclose the under-dress and its girdle. The cote-hardie was a long garment that reached to the ground in straight folds. It continued in use for over a hundred years. Both the wives of Sir John Foxley at Bray, Berkshire (1378) wear this garment. On Lady Maud's, heraldic embroidery is displayed to perfection. Both ladies' dresses carry the long lappets (liripipes) which hang from the sleeves (plate 129).

Widows

Elyne, the widow of Sir Edward Cerne, at Draycot Cerne, Wiltshire (1393 and 1419) is shown (plate 100). Her dress consists of the kirtle, mantle, and veiled head-dress, with a plaited barbe (throat and neck covering) made of pleated linen. Other examples of widows occur on the brass of Alianore de Bohun in Westminster Abbey (1399) and Colubery Mayne (1628), Dinton, Bucks. This habit continues into the 17th-century; the widow could be distinguished by the wearing of a long veil and this has never entirely gone out of fashion. Today a widow often wears a black veil at her husband's funeral.

Head-dresses

The nebule head-dress framing the face and reaching the shoulders was subject to many variations. The plaited hair was enclosed in a net, sometimes made to project on both sides and rest on the shoulders. The two wives of Sir Reginald de Malynes, Chinnor, Oxon (1385) show two variations of this fashion, the nebule and the zig-zag. On the brass of Lady Burton at Little Casterton (c. 1400) the braided hair has a network of decorative design. On top is a tiara of jewels. The head-dress of Eleanor Corp at Stoke Fleming, Devon (1391) shows an unusual style. The hair is enclosed in a netted caul, jewelled at front. Over the head at the top is a kerchief which waves outwards from both sides of the head.

The first half of the 15th-century brought no great change in women's fashions. Joan Peryent, at Digswell, Herts (1415), wears a most unusual head-dress (see plate 132). On her left collar a swan is embroidered and at her feet is a hedgehog. Her long loose robe is gathered in high up by a girdle.

The horned type of head-dress is well illustrated on the brass of Katherine Quatremayne at Thame, Oxon (c. 1420). She died in 1342! There are several variations in this type of head-dress, which continued well after the middle of the 15th-century. Another unusual example is that of Jane Keriell at Ash, Kent (1460) which is more acutely pointed – of horseshoe shape.

About this date a new style of gown came into fashion, which remained in use for a considerable time. This consisted of a long robe worn over the kirtle. The low-cut neck was bordered with fur; it had long full sleeves also edged with fur at the cuffs. It was fitted with a girdle at the waist. This is seen in the brass of Cecilia Kidwelly at Little Wittenham, Berkshire (1472), and Dame Cristine Philip at Herne, Kent (1470).

The butterfly head-dress made its debut at this period. It was a most attractive style, but must have been very difficult to control in windy weather; perhaps it was only worn indoors, though this seems doubtful. (For illustrations of this head-dress see the wife of Henry Barley at Albury, Herts (1475); Margaret Peyton at Isleham, Cambridgeshire (1484); and Margaret Dayrell at Lillingstone Dayrell, Bucks (1491).*) It consisted of a richly ornamented cap at the back of the head in which the hair was confined; over this was placed a veil of light, thin gauze, sometimes decorated, and held in position by a framework of wires! The dress worn with this headgear was a gown close-fitting at the top, low at the neck, with fur and decorative edging and cuffs. The skirt was long and loose and flowing, sometimes gathered up under the arms. A narrow girdle was worn over the hips. Necklaces of considerable beauty were worn with this fashion. The Italian brocade dress of Margaret Peyton is beautifully designed, very graphic – a brass sought after by most brass rubbers. Isobel Cheyne of Blickling, Norfolk (1485) wears the same fashion. Her dress is much more simple than Margaret's, but her poise, the action of her hands and her happy face (surely a portrait!) make her a most charming and attractive personality (plate 53).

Unmarried Women

These were usually depicted with long, flowing hair, sometimes a wreath of flowers encircled the head (for a young maiden). The brass of Agnes Oxenbridge at Etchingham, Sussex (1480) depicts the spinster with her hair drawn back from the forehead into tresses tied behind (see right).

Changes in fashion

The early 16th-century saw the accession of Henry VIII and changes took place in ladies' costume. The heraldic mantle was more in evidence. Examples

*This brass is by a first-class artist-craftsman. The figure is very elegant; it is simple and the draughtsmanship excellent. What a pity 16th century workshops did not use it as a guide! (see plates 130, 131).

119, 120. The two wives of SIR REGINALD DE MALYNS 1385, Chinnor, Oxon.
Part of brass 18″ deep. Two stereo type faces. Only the head dress is different (see also plate 88).

121. ELIZABETH BROUGHTON 1524, spinster, Chenies, Bucks.
An attractive little brass though the figure from the waist downwards is too short. Note the interesting design of the hair.

122. JOHN STONOR (boy) 1512, Wraysbury, Bucks.

123. JOHN KENT of Reading, 1434, Headbourne Worthy, Hants. A scholar at Winchester.

124. ELIZABETH WALROND (ROCHES) 1480, Childrey, Berks.
Part of brass showing the excellent design made by giving the figure a narrow waist and bringing the arms well away from the body. The triangular space between the arms and the body helps to give the required animation to the design.

125. ANNE GAYNESFORD 1490, Checkendon, Oxon.
Part of the brass. This has some considerable character due more to the designer than to the person it represents.

are Lady Katherine Howard at Lambeth, London (1535); an unknown woman at Bishopsgate, London (1535) (see chapter 10); and Lady Verney in Aldbury, Hertfordshire (1546). The pedimental head-dress which made its appearance towards the end of the 15th-century continued into the reign of Henry VIII and examples are many and varied. This consisted of embroidered material, bands of which framed the face, meeting in a sharp angle in the middle of the forehead and hanging down each side of the head. Examples are Jane Sylan at Luton (1513), Elizabeth Perepoynt at West Malling, Kent (1543), and Margaret Fetteplace at Marcham, Berkshire (1540). These remind one of some of the drawings by Holbein in Windsor Castle, as well as of some 15th-century paintings. The dress worn about the middle of the century was open from the centre downwards, showing the petticoat. The sleeves are puffed at the shoulders as in the brass of Ruth Lytkott at Swallowfield, Berkshire (1554). She wears the Paris head-dress, a small ruff, and a small box engraved with a heart hangs in front.

About 1570 we come upon the typical Elizabethan dress. Mary Yate of Buckland, Berkshire (1578), wears a gown open in front and showing an embroidered under-bodice with small ruff round the neck. A girdle is tied at the waist and the front of the gown is open displaying the elaborately embroidered petticoat. A similar dress is worn by Margery Hyde of Denchworth, Berkshire (1562), except that her under-gown has striped sleeves.

Towards the end of the century hats are worn. These are high-crowned. Sometimes a large calash or hood was worn over the head and fell down behind for a considerable distance. Elizabeth Blight at Finchampstead, Berkshire (1635) wears such a head covering. The effigy of Mary Seventhorpe at Sawbridgeworth (1600) exhibits the costume that is usually associated with portraits of Queen Elizabeth, with large ruffs around the neck.

Few brasses illustrate any later fashions, for brasses were going out. The brass dedicated to Anne Dutch at Little Wittenham, Berkshire (1683) is to an infant nine months old, but she is depicted as a full-grown woman in dress of earlier date (c. 1650). The brass of Philadelphia Greenwood at St Mary Cray, Kent (1773) is the only one that we have to a lady of the 18th-century.

CHILDREN

Medieval families often had many children. It is quite common to find inscriptions such as 'Together they lived thirty-five years and had twelve children – seven sons and five daughters.' At Thame, in Oxfordshire, the inscription on the brass of Geoffrey Dormer, a wool merchant (1502), states that he had two wives and twenty-five children.

On 16th-century brasses more children are depicted than in any other century, although the 17th-century also had many brasses with children. Individual children are sometimes seen without their parents, for instance Thomas Heron, aged seventeen, of Little Ilford (1512); but children usually appear with their families, the sons lined up under their father and the daughters under their mother – the children much smaller than their parents. Another method of depicting children was to drape them against their parents. The five daughters of Margery Bosard, Ditchingham, Norfolk, 1490, are shown festooned around their mother's skirt (see also plate 118).

At Quy, Cambridge, the twelve sons of John Ansty, all wearing heraldic tabards, are shown with their father (1460). A long strip frieze of thirteen children appears at Beddington, Surrey (Carreu, 1414). A rubbing of a lost brass once at Wenden Lofts, Essex (1460), shows Abbot Lucas and his three brothers. Unmarried girls usually wear long hair and are bare-headed.

Representations of children in cradles are found on several brasses, for instance, Dorothy King (1630) and William King (1633), daughter and son of John King, both in the Oliver Chapel, Windsor Castle. At Ypres, Belgium (1487), there were three boys, one whipping a top, two walking on stilts and an infant learning to walk with the help of a ring mounted on three legs. On a London brass, John Bowyer and his wife of Camberwell (1570) are seen with their eight sons and three daughters, all kneeling with their parents. Some brasses give the names of both parents and children on scroll labels issuing from the heads or mouths of the individuals (see plate 65).

Sometimes when a mother and child died during childbirth, the mother was depicted holding her dead infant in her arms (Elizabeth Death, Dartford, 1590). On a few brasses the mother is shown in bed with the dead child lying on the bed-covering or similar drapery. A good example is that at Wormington, Gloucestershire, of Anne Savage (1605), and another is Alice Harison at Hurst, Berkshire (c. 1600). The brass of the Feld family (an altar tomb) at Standon, Hertfordshire (1474-77), represents the children as 'individuals' – the children of both father and son all appear to be of about the same age. The father is shown with two sons and one daughter underneath himself and the son depicted next to his father had two sons and two daughters underneath himself. It is assumed, therefore, that the grandfather had three sons! All the children are well drawn, full of action and are quite distinctive, as are their parents, but clearly not by the same designer. These brasses are by first-class artists and are in excellent condition. The brass (plate 151) of Elizabeth Culpeper at Ardingly, Sussex, is dated 1634. Elizabeth died aged seven years. John Stonor at Wraysbury, Buckinghamshire, died in 1512 when only a schoolboy, as seen on the brass, plate 122.

DUPLICATE BRASSES

More than one brass to the same person is found in different churches, and even in the same church! Henry Bradshaw is shown at Halton, Buckinghamshire (1553) with his wife Joan. His widow moved to Noke, Oxon, where she died. Here she is depicted with Henry Bradshaw and a former husband (1598). There are several such instances. Brasses to the same individual or individuals in the same church are frequent: Anne Herbert, alone and with her husband at Lodden, Norfolk (1530 and 1561). John Cottesmore and his wife at Brightwell Baldwin, Oxon, appear together kneeling and again full length (1439). The former is a small mural brass and the latter is large with double canopy (on the chancel floor). At Depden, Suffolk (1572), Lady Anne, widow of G. Waldegrave, and later wife of Sir Thomas Jermyn, is represented with both her husbands on the same brass. Bernard Brocas in armour and tabard at Sherbourne St John (1488) is shown kneeling, and on the same brass is a skeleton in a shroud – both are of the same individual! At Pimperne in Dorset is a brass to Dorothy Williams (1694). She is shown as an effigy as

126

126. JOHN COTTUSMORE 1439, Chief Justice of Common Pleas. Brightwell Baldwin, Oxon.
Nicely engraved but badly proportioned. Effigy 8½″ deep.

127. JOHN SPYCER 1437, Burford, Oxon.
Compare this with the kneeling figure of Judge Cottusmore 1439, Brightwell Baldwin, above. These two brasses were probably produced in the same Oxfordshire workshop.

128. SIR JOHN DE NORTHWOOD AND LADY JOAN DE NORTHWOOD 1330, Minster, Sheppey, Kent.
Knight and his lady, Minster, Kent (once two separate monuments). Date uncertain (c. 1330-1340?). The Knight's lower part is a restoration and a palimpsest. Twice restored — in the 17th century and 19th century when a piece was added to give correct proportion to the figure. This can be best seen in the shield which had been shortened to match that of the lady. At some time the lady has been shortened slightly in in the lower part. The lady's dress is unusual. She wears kirtel and sleeveless cote-hardie and the material hanging down from her shoulders is fur lined. These effigies are not by the same craftsman but show French influence; the lady is a more skilled and rhythmic robust design. Male effigy 71″.

129

130

129. LADY MAUD FOXLEY 1378, Bray, Berks.
Nebule head-dress. The brass once contained coloured enamels (note the 'tooth'). Size 29″ x 9″.

130. MARGARET PEYTON 1484, Isleham, Cambs.
Size 31″ x 10″. An attractive dress – Venetian brocade. The pattern is constant, the folds are obtained by scoring. Note the action of the hands – an East Anglian characteristic.

131

132

131. MARGARET DAYRELL 1491, Lillingstone Dayrell, Bucks.
A delightful brass. A very elegant lady wearing a butterfly head-dress.
A beautifully drawn figure – simple and expressive of dignity and surely
a portrait. Note the delicate drawing of the mouth. Size 31″ effigy.

132. JOAN PERYENT 1415, Digswell, Herts.
Illustration shows only part of the brass which is full length with her
husband John. She wears an SS collar and swan brooch. A most exciting
head-dress (size of part illustrated 34″ x 19″).

The xxy daye of the moneth augufte the yere after the & Incarnacyon &
Of our lord god to reken Iufte = A thoufland fyue hundreth forty faue one
Dyed thys lady whych vnder thys ftone lyeth hereburyed Elyzabeth by name
The wyfe of Iohn ffyneux late gone The whych in thys world had eu good
fam whole foll & pre Ihu throwgh hys grace In heuen maye haue a reftyng place

133

134

133. ELIZABETH FYNEUX 1539, Herne, Kent.
Daughter of Sir John Paston. Widow of Robert C
and of Sir John Fyneux. A 'sketchbook' type
figure and a good attempt at characterization.
inverted T design of the brass would have been
proved by reducing the width of the inscription
extending its depth.

134. THE FELD CHILDREN 1474-7, Standon, H
Full of life and movement.

135 and 136. SIR WILLIAM HARPER AND DAME
MARGARET his second wife, 1573, St Paul's, Bedford.
Lord Mayor of London. A good portrait brass. Sir
William was the founder of Bedford Modern School
and almshouses. Note his mantle thrown back to
display the suit of armour. Effigies 20″.

137. CECILY, wife of SIR JOHN FORTESCUE, 1570,
Mursley, Bucks.
14½″ deep. This could well be a crude likeness. A
typical Elizabethan dress.

138. ANNE SAVAGE 1605, Wormington, Gloucestershire.
22″ wide x 21″ deep. There is a poorly designed inscription under the 'picture' and a heavy border inscription turns along the four sides. A bedstead brass
belonging to a small group of brasses of women who
died in childbirth. Though not of outstanding merit
this brass is very descriptive. The perspective is good
and the design is more in the manner of a woodcut
than a brass engraving. Probably the work of a 17th
century book illustrator. Queen Elizabeth favoured
plain line without heavy shadows in portraiture (in
the Holbein tradition). By 1605 this influence had
weakened.

135   136

137

138

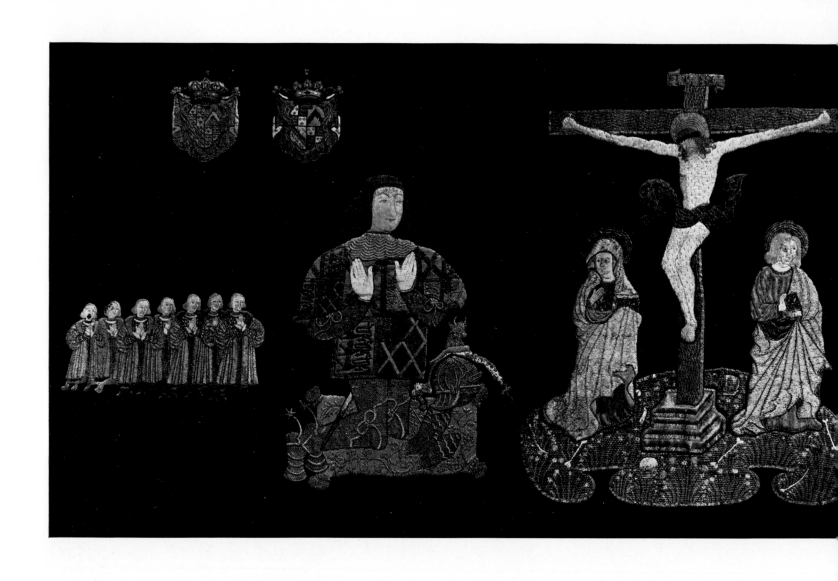

139

139. Altar Frontal *c.* 1550. English silver gilt embroidery. Earl of Westmoreland and wife, seven sons and thirteen daughters. Side of crucifixion (left) the B.V.M. (right) St John. Victoria and Albert Museum. This 16th century altar frontal is reminiscent of family brasses of similar date. The kneeling figures and the boys lined up behind their father and the girls lined up behind their mother is characteristic of 16th century memorials.

140. BUTLER BOWDEN COPE, detail – an Archbishop – (1330-50). Coloured silks and silver gilt thread in split stitch and underside couching on the velvet. A superb example of English work. Copes and works of this nature were unrivalled by any other nation. Effigy, canopy with crockets and finial similar to that found on brass effigies. Victoria and Albert Museum.

140

mgraué Esuuoni dé ṁaṁus ꝼr̃ moune renald dé ṁaṁus·
cĥr̃ ⁊ Ꝯabele̅ ꞇ̃a sẽuie̅ gꞌsouut uⱥ dien dé lo̅s almes̅ eᵵ uⱥ

141

Orate ꝓ aĩabꝰ ꞷr̃i deaud Lloyde ꝯ uⱥ̃o꞊ꞇ uⱥne bacallaꝝ
Eᵵ ꞇ̃ome baker̃ iuꝰ cuuꝭ sꞷlaᵵer qꞷ obueruͭ aṁno
dũ ꞷꞷbuo quagͭe cuuo ⱷ ꞷꝭbꭿ ueꞛo decebꞛꝭ die̅ xxuⱥ

142

143

141. SIR ESMOUN DE MALYNS AND WIFE ISOBEL
1385, Chinnor, Oxon.
Inscription in French. Sir Esmoun was the son of
Sir Reginald de Malyns. Isobel wears the nebule
head-dress. Taller effigy 17″.

142. DAVID LLOYDE, LL.B., AND THOMAS BAKER,
All Souls' College, Oxford.
Both died 24th December 1510. Taller effigy 11¾″.

143. JOHN TEDCASTELL, gent, 1596, Barking, Essex.
A portrait (see inscriptions plate 256).

144. ELIZABETH, JOAN AND JOAN 1506, Leckhampstead, Bucks.
Children of Regenolde Tylney, citizen and alderman
of London. 7¼″ deep. An attractive lively trio with a
good idea of a uniform design though lacking in skill.

144

146

145. Unknown lady, St Helen's, Bishopsgate, *c.* 1535. A bottle-shaped brass. Not a 'pin-up girl' like her neighbour at St Mary's, Lambeth, of similar date. Effigy 34″.

146. The three daughters of WILMOTTA CAREY 1581, Tor Mohun, Torquay. A charming local brass.

145

147

147. KATHERINE QUATREMAYN (engr. *c.* 1420), Thame, Oxon.
She died in 1342, but the brass shows the early type of horned head-dress of the 15th century. The illustration shows only part of the complete figure. Note the high waist-line. Like many brasses of the 15th century, the dress below the waist was shown in over-long perpendicular folds. This gave extra dignity to the figure.

148. ALICE HYDE 1567, St James's, Denchworth, Berks.
Wife of William Hyde with whom she appears on the brass. A fine graceful arabesque of the figure – better than most of this period. There is much character in the face – a portrait. Alice married the son of William and Margery Hyde (see plate 264). Effigy 26".

148

149. DAME CRISTINE PHELIP, 25 May 1470, Hern
Kent.

Her husband Sir Matthew Phelip was a citizen an
goldsmith, Mayor of London 1464. Dame Cristir
wears horned head-dress and mantle. Note the actio
of the hands. Not a very attractive brass but a goo
character study and probably a good likeness (not
'school' brass). Effigy 43″.

150. JOYCE TIPTOFT c. 1470, Enfield, Middlese
In heraldic mantle and coronet. A good brass showir
more figure than usual on these heraldic brasse
Effigy 54″.

151

well as a recumbent skeleton. Here the designer's name appears, 'Edmund Culpeper fecit'.

ACADEMIC DRESS

The distinctive university robes derived from ecclesiastical and monastic dress. Professors of Divinity wore a circular cap, a cassock with fur cuffs, a long gown and over this a hood lined with fur. Examples on brasses are: William Town, DD, King's College, Cambridge (1496); Thomas Hylle, DD, New College, Oxford (1468); and John Sperehawke, DD, Hitchin, Hertfordshire (1474). The latter wears cap and hood and a gown like a chasuble. At Sperehawke's feet is a hawk standing on a spear – a rebus. *This is a lost brass and is known only by a rubbing.*

Professors of Law wore a similar dress to Doctors or Professors of Divinity. A fine bracket brass at Merton College, Oxford, depicts John Bloxham, Bachelor of Divinity (1387); with him is John Whytton, Rector of Wood Eaton (1420).

Masters and Bachelors of Arts wore a less distinctive costume. They wore a cassock, a *short* gown with sleeves, a cape and a hood, such as that of John Motesfont, LLB, at Lydd, Kent (1420). After the middle of the 15th-century the dress of the Master of Arts consisted of a cassock, short gown (sleeveless), a tippet, and a hood – seen on the anonymous brass at Magdalen College, Oxford (1480). The brass of John Spence, BD, Ewelme, Oxon (1517), shows him wearing a combination of the two grades.

LEGAL BRASSES

Legal costume long ago was similar to that of today. A judge wore a cope (at times with a black cap!), a hood, a tippet, and a mantle lined with miniver. Examples are: Sir Hugh de Holes, Justice of the King's Bench, Watford, Hertfordshire (1415), and Sir William Laken, Justice of the King's Bench, Bray, Berkshire (1475). Wigs only came into fashion in the 17th-century. Serjeants-at-law did not wear gowns. They wore the coif, tunic, a long fur-lined robe and hood. Example: John Rede, Checkendon, Oxon (1404). Notaries wore a long robe with open sleeves and a belt at the waist from which was suspended an ink-horn and pencase. Examples: anonymous brass at New College, Oxford (1510) and Robert Wymbyll at St Mary Tower, Ipswich (1506).

The brass of Robert Shiers, Gt Bookham, Surrey (1668), shows him in civil gown, bare headed, with a book in his right hand. He was a member of the Inner Temple and appears to be laying down the law. There are over sixty brasses to the legal profession.

CIVILIANS

Fourteenth-century civilians depicted on brasses wore a simple habit. They wore tight fitting under-dress over which they placed another close-fitting garment. This was the tunic which extended below the knees. The sleeves were also tight, extending to the elbows from which hung down long liripipes.

A long mantle was worn on top. The hose too was tight fitting. The shoes were long pointed.

Forked beards became the fashion. In the next century the tunic extended to the ankles and for a time this went out of fashion and the shortened garment again extended to just below the knees. Later however the fashion reverted to the longer garment. The top of the tunic was buttoned close to the neck and the full sleeves gathered in at the waist.

Examples: Civilian (*c.* 1370), Shottesbrook, Berkshire; Nicholas Canteys (1431), Margate, Kent; Geoffrey Kidwelly (1483), (plate 240), Little Wittenham, Berkshire.

151. ELIZABETH CULPEPER 1634, Ardingley, Sussex.
A charming sketchbook brass of a young girl (died age 7). Similar to plate 196, probably by the same craftsman.

152. COLUBERY (LOVELACE), wife of Simon Mayne, died 1617. Widow died 1628. Dinton, Bucks.
An attractive sketch book brass. Effigy 19½".

152

CHAPTER THIRTEEN

Brasses of Ecclesiastics

P RE-REFORMATION BRASSES of ecclesiastics form quite a considerable proportion of our remaining monumental brasses. Here are archbishops, bishops, mitred abbots, priests in chasuble, priests in cope, priests in almuce, and in alb and stole, priests in cassock and in surplice as well as religious orders, both male and female. Widows who have vowed never to remarry, known as vowesses, are included. The earliest existing brass of an effigy is that of Bishop Yso von Welpe in Verden, Germany (1231) (see illustration). The earliest ecclesiastical brass in England is that to Richard Hakebourne in Merton College (1311). A brass of similar date existed at Oulton, Suffolk. It commemorated a rector . . . de Bacon, in mass vestments. It was stolen in 1857. It is illustrated in Cotman, Boutell and Haines.

VESTMENTS

The Amice, from the Latin *amictus* (an outer garment), is the first robe with which the priest vests himself when preparing for the Eucharist service. It has an oval collar enriched in the centre with an embroidered cross and trimming (apparel) which was sewn to the outer edge. It is said to symbolize the napkin with which Christ was blindfolded at his trial.

Examples on brasses: Richard Hakebourne, Merton College, Oxford (1311); Walter Frilende, Ockham (1376); Walter de Annefordhe, Binfield, Berkshire (1361), and many others.

The Alb. The oldest Christian vestment – usually white. Before it became recognized as the alb it passed through many earlier stages as a covering garment. It took on various embroidered ornaments, but by the 13th-century it had again become a simple white garment without decorations, similar to those we see on brasses. It is rare to find a cleric wearing an alb without the dalmatic or chasuble; however the brass of John West at Sudborough, Northamptonshire (1415) shows him wearing the alb with decorations of apparels on the wrists and at the hem both front and back. It derives its name from *albus* (white) and is symbolical of the garment which Herod placed upon Christ before sending Him to Pilate.

Examples on brasses: Laurence de St Maur, Higham Ferrers, Northamptonshire (1337); Richard Harward, St Cross, Hampshire (1493); John de Limburg, Bamberg, Germany (1475).

The Stole. Dates from the 1st century B.C. *Sudarium, orarium, stola.*

Priests could wear their stole at all times to distinguish them and their vocation.

Examples on brasses: Laurence de St Maur, Higham Ferrers, Northamptonshire (1337); a priest, Shottesbroke, Berkshire (1370).

The Maniple. Became a church vestment in the 6th century. By the 10th century it was embellished with embroidery. It was similar in shape to the stole but smaller, and hung over the left arm. It is a symbol of the towel with which Christ wiped the Apostles' feet.

Examples on brasses: Thomas Cranley, New College, Oxford (1417); Eghard de Hanensee, Hildesheim, Germany (1460); Johannes de la Fontaine (1531), Damme, Belgium.

The Chasuble. The top vestment, oval in shape, pointed behind and before, it has a hole in the top for the head to enter. Its ample folds hang from the arms. It is usually ornamented.

Examples on brasses: William de Herleston, Sparsholt, Berkshire (1353); John de Swynstead, Edlesborough, Buckinghamshire (1395); a priest, Erfurt,

153

153. CANON JAMES COORTHOPP 1557, Christchurch, Oxford.
Canon of Christ Church and Dean of Peterborough, in almuce. Effigy 32″.

66

Germany (1420); Thomas de Horton, North Mimms, Hertfordshire (1360).

The Cassock. This was the everyday dress of the priest. It was a long coat, black, sometimes lined with fur. Usually it was worn open in front, and it had coat sleeves and a girdle round the waist. Later the cassock was made of coloured materials; the Pope wore a white one, cardinals scarlet, archbishops and bishops, purple. For daily use they were black, piped in either scarlet or purple. Cardinal Wolsey wore a longer type of garment which originated in the 15th century.

Examples on brasses: William Geddyng, Wantage, Berkshire (1512); William Lawnder, Northleach, Glos (1530).

The Surplice. This garment was a loose white linen vestment with short, but wide, open sleeves. It was a processional vestment lacking ornament. By the 14th-century it had become what it is today – the white vestment of a lower grade of clerics. In the 15th-century it was shortened, reaching only to the thigh, whereas three centuries earlier it had been a full-length garment.

Examples on brasses: Richard Harward, St Cross, Winchester, Hants (1493); William Dye, Westerham, Kent (1567).

The Cope. A processional vestment, worn over the cassock and surplice. An outer vestment with an ornamental orphrey round the edges. It is fastened at the neck by a morse (or large clasp).

Example: John Martock, Barnwell, Somerset (1503).

The Almuce. Another processional vestment. It had a tippet or hood of white fur. It was only introduced in the 13th-century, and in the 15th-century it took the form of a cape with a pendant and lappets hanging in front. It was, like the surplice, used to protect the wearer from the cold of the church. By the 16th-century the almuce had become a sign of distinction because its colour and material varied – grey for the highest rank and a black silk or cloth for the lower clergy.

Examples on brasses: James Coorthopp, Christchurch Cathedral, Oxford (1557); E. Sheffeld, Luton, Bedfordshire (1515).

MONASTIC COSTUME

The dissolution of the monasteries accounted for the destruction of a vast number of brasses of the monastic clergy. They usually wore tunic, scapular, gown, cowl, and hood. These would differ in colour depending on the order to which they belonged. There are only about thirty brasses of monastic costume left today out of what was once many thousands.

Examples on brasses: Thomas Nelond, Cowfold (Clunic Prior of Lewes, 1433); Robert Beauver, St Alban's Abbey (Benedictine, 1460); Richard Bewfforeste, Dorchester, Oxon (Augustinian, 1510); Joan Clopton, widow, vowess, Quinton, Gloucestershire (1430); Dame Elizabeth Herwy, Elstow (Benedictine abbess, 1501-24, died 1527, engraved *c.* 1520).

ARCHBISHOPS AND BISHOPS

Archbishops, bishops, and abbots wore the same vestments as priests but with the addition of certain distinctive marks or ornaments according to their rank. Over the alb but under the chasuble members of the hierarchy wore a tunic or chimere, a robe similar to the alb but shorter and open at both sides lower down. They wore mitres (some finely jewelled), sandals, gloves, a ring upon the second finger of the right hand, and a crozier. Another vestment they wore was the dalmatic; like the tunic, it was partially open at the sides and in some examples was covered with an elaborate pattern.

The pall was worn by archbishops. It was a narrow band of white wool with a circle to throw over the shoulders from which hung two bands before and behind like the letter Y. These were ornamented with small crosses. (See brass of Bishop Yso von Welpe, 1213, plate 14.) The crozier is the staff with cross or crucifix, carried by archbishops. The gloves were frequently

154. JOHN MARTOCK 1503, Barnwell, Somerset. Fellow of Merton, 1461-1503. Wearing choir dress and cope. Brass restored in the 19th century.

154

embroidered and jewelled. The ring was worn over the gloves, and was set with a precious stone.

Bishops wore scarlet stockings and the sandals were often decorated with jewels and gold. Buskins or garters were made of linen or silk. *The mitre* (already mentioned), the jewelled cap, assumed various shapes. In the 13th-century it was low, small and with straight sides meeting in a point in the middle at the top. A good example can be seen in the brass of Archbishop Grenfelde at York (1315). Later the mitre became higher with curved sides, as in the brass of Bishop Goodrich at Ely (1554). Later again it became still more curved, both down the sides and in the centre; this is shown on the brass of Archbishop Harsnett at Chigwell (1631). There are many good brasses to the hierarchy both in England and on the Continent. The following list includes most of the better known of these:

Thomas Cranley, Archbishop of Dublin, at New College, Oxford (1417).
Bishop H. Spiegel von Dessenberg, Paderborn Cathedral, Germany (1380).
Bishop Otto de Brunswicke, Hildesheim, Germany (1279) – the third oldest brass in existence (with effigy).
Bishop Bernhard de Lippe, Paderborn Cathedral, Germany (1340).
Bishop Bertram Cremen, Lübeck, Germany (1377).
Bishop John Advantage, Amiens, France (1456) – a kneeling figure with Virgin and Child and St John.
Bishop Andreas, Poznan, Poland (1479), (destroyed).
Bishop John Tydeman, Lübeck, Germany (1561).
Bishop R. Wyvil, Salisbury Cathedral (1375).
John de Waltham, Westminster Abbey (1395).
John Bowthe, Bishop of Exeter, East Horsley, Surrey (1478).

No cardinals appear on English brasses. At Cues, in Germany, there is a brass to Cardinal Cusanos (died 1464). He is seen 'standing' behind an eight-line inscription. His hands are crossed, supported by the top of the inscription tablet. He wears a skull-cap and mitre. The pillow behind his head shows two cardinals' hats and two scutcheons with a crayfish (*Flusskrebs*) – a rebus on his name.

At Kracow, Poland, is a large brass (111in x 62in) to Cardinal Cazmiri (1500). This is another large overworked brass full of detail of doubtful artistic merit. Cazmiri was the son of King Casimir IV of Poland. This is a portrait brass, as is the brass of Cardinal Cusanos. Herman Vischer the Younger engraved this brass and used figures from Dürer's woodcuts as models for the figures in the shafts of the canopies (Dürer, 1471-1528). The general presentation of this brass is not conceived as a whole. The introduction of Dürer's figures does not improve the design; whereas in Dürer's woodcut (Nicholas Ulrich and Erasmus) the conception of the whole design is unified and is freely expressed, Vischer's design sadly lacks these qualities.

It is next to impossible for a minor artist to extract a figure from a great artist's composition and incorporate it into a design without ruining that design as a singly conceived unit.

Rings and Gloves

In the 13th century the Pope wore a gold ring with St Peter in the design. He used this as his holy seal. In the 14th-century bishops wore a ring over their gloved finger, following a recent custom of cardinals and abbots, and they sometimes wore several rings. The right hand of Bishop Ludolph de Bulowe (1339) on the Schwerin brass shows him wearing a ring on his middle finger over his glove, as does his brother Bishop Henry de Bulowe (1347). On the brass of Bishop Andreas at Poznan (1479), the right hand, which is raised in blessing, has one ring on the forefinger and two rings on the third finger over the glove. On the brass of Archbishop Jacobus de Senno at Gniezno,

156. SIR RICHARD CATESBY 1553, Ashby St Legers, Northants.
An example of English portraiture executed with considerable skill but less than that of Martin Ferrades (see plate 22). In this portrait the artist shows a warm appreciation of the character of his model.

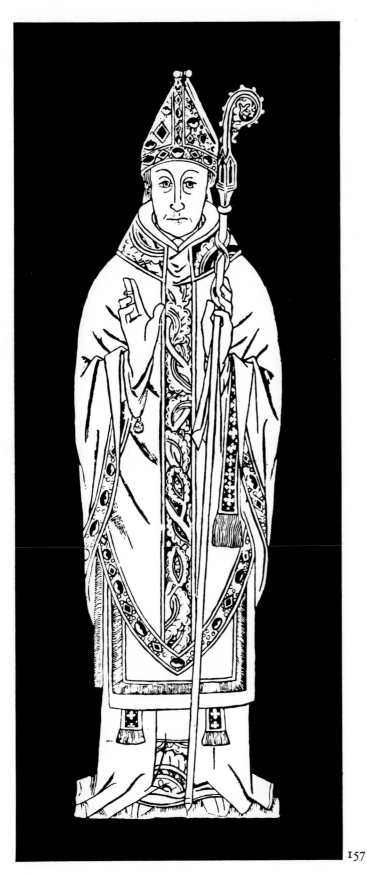

157

157. JOHN ESTNEY, d. 1498, Abbot of Westminster Abbey.

158. LAURENCE DE ST MAUR 1337, Higham Ferrers, Northants.
A much finer brass, one of the best of a priest, similar to the brass of Sir
John D'Abernoun, the younger (1327). Notice the subtle movements
of the body and the movement of the neck in the opposite direction.
The drapery shows the hook technique, at the feet two dogs are fighting
over a bone. Effigy 63″.

158

L*

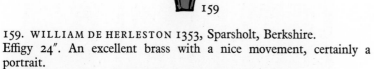

159

160

161

162

159. WILLIAM DE HERLESTON 1353, Sparsholt, Berkshire.
Effigy 24″. An excellent brass with a nice movement, certainly a portrait.
160. Priest, *c.* 1480, Childrey, Berks. In Mass vestments.
161. JOHN SEYS, *c.* 1370, West Hanney, Berks.
In Mass vestments (mutilated). Though nearly 130 years separate these three brasses of Berkshire rectors, there is only a small depreciation in the quality of design and workmanship. The earliest is the best and the latest only slightly inferior. There is little change in the Mass vestments.
162. SAMUEL HARSNETT, vicar 1631, Chigwell, Essex.
In cope with mitre and crozier. Illustration shows figure only but is complete with marginal inscriptions and shields. A very well executed engraving but over realistic to be a first class portrait.

163

163. ANTHONINE WILLEBAERT 1601, St Jacque's Church, Bruges.
An attractive design of a late Flemish brass. Evidence of decline in
standards of engraving; overcrowded with detail which is so often
found on Flemish designs. 29″ deep.

164. Pen drawing – Albrecht Dürer, 1471-1528. Designed for the tomb of Count Eitel and wife Magdalena, Countess of Brandenburg. The pen drawing is in the Uffizi, Florence. The tomb executed by Peter Vischer (1452?-1529) is in the church of Hechingen. Vischer made a second similar tomb for Count Herman VIII and wife. This wife was sister of the Countess of Brandenburg. Doubtless it is due to this relationship that the second tomb was made.

165. Tomb of ALBRECHT DÜRER at Nuremburg, from an old print c. 1835.

166. Tomb of COUNT HERMAN VIII AND WIFE, by Peter Vischer, in the church at Romhild (1500). It is clear that Vischer was not able to translate the qualities of Dürer's design into his own medium (bronze) with much success. Herman Vischer used the figures of the woodcut of Nicholas Ulmich and Erasmus to design the brass for Cardinal Frederick (1510), Cracow, Poland. (Herman was Peter's younger brother.)

167. Six portrait illustrations from various pages of *The Bedford Hours and Psalter*. London School about 1420. The most important surviving English illumination manuscript of 'International Gothic' style (1384-1430). The result of contributions and exchanges between many cities including London, Paris, Cologne, Milan and Prague. The first artist who worked on this book is said to have been William Scheerre. A second artist (Herman?), a greater and more original one than Scheerre, excelled in portraying the human likeness. The book contains 280 portraits taken from life. They depict persons of different classes of early 15th century English society. Here again we have undisputed evidence of 15th century portraiture and also of wide international exchange of artistic ideas in the 14th and 15th centuries. The manuscript was originally owned by John, Duke of Bedford (son of Henry IV), and uncle and guardian of Henry VI and Regent of France. Now in the British Museum.

168. Portrait of GEOFFREY KIDWELLY 1483. Little Wittenham, Berks.

169. Detail from the brass of BISHOP ANDREAS 1479, Poznan, Poland (lost in 1939-45 war).

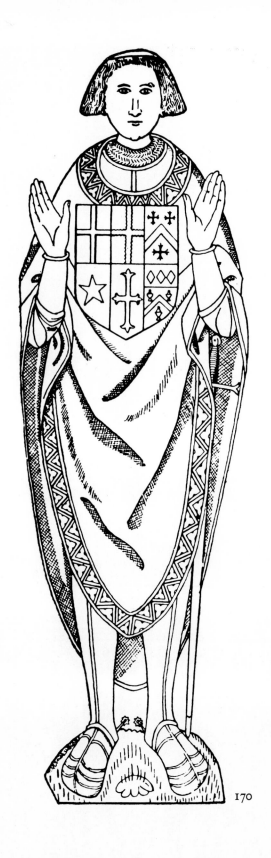

170. SIR PETER LEGH 1527, Winwick, Lancs.
A unique brass in that it depicts a knight in armour over which he wears a chasuble. On his breast he shows a shield of arms. Sir Peter's wife died in 1491. Her brother was Thomas Savage, Archbishop of York. Sir Peter joined the church in 1511. Subsequently he described himself as 'knight and priest'.

171. THOMAS CRANLEY, warden, Archbishop of Dublin 1417. New College, Oxford.
An attractive brass showing figure only – he is under a canopy. Note his ringed glove and chrisma. Effigy 58″.

172

172. SIR RICHARD BEWFFORESTE 1510, Dorchester, Oxon.
The arrangement of the linear pattern to express the vestments
is particularly well designed (50″ x 17″).

173. JOHN DE SWYNSTEDE 1395, Eddlesborough, Bucks.
He was rector and prebendary of Lincoln. This brass was moved to
Pitstone church (Bucks), then to Ashridge House, Bucks, and then
back to its original church. It is a fine brass drawn with great skill. A
good example of the hook technique. The face is a very obvious portrait
(51″ deep).

173

174. SIR JOHN WYNN OF GWEDVR, Knt. Bart. 1626, Llanrwst, Denbigh. A good 17th century portrait.

175. Portrait of LADY SYDNEY, wife of Sir John Wynn, 1632, Llanrwst, Denbigh.

176. Portrait of LADY MARY, elder daughter of Sir John and Lady Wynn, 1658, Llanrwst, and wife of Sir Robert Mostyn of Flint (note 'Silvanus Crue sculp').

177. Portrait of SIR OWEN WYNNE of Gwedvr, Bt. 1660, Llanrwst.

178

179

178. Drawing by Villard d'Honnicourt – an important 13th century French architect who travelled widely making drawings for reference. This figure shows the hook technique widely used in medieval art in depicting drapery. See plates 40, 158, 159, 160, 161, 173.

179. SIR WILLIAM TENDRING 1408, Stoke-by-Nayland, Suffolk.
Effigy 5′ 11″. Acknowledged by all to be a portrait!

Poland (1480), the right hand, holding the crozier, and the left hand, holding the cross staff, both have rings on the thumb and third finger over the glove. In Belgium rings appear on the left hand on the brass of Marie, wife of Francisco de Lapuebla, Bruges (1572); on the left hand of the brass of Jane de la Douve (Bruges, 1515) there are rings on the forefinger and the little finger.

The wearing of gloves is an ancient custom: a glove was found in the tomb of Tutankhamen (14th-century BC). Ecclesiatics wore gloves without any particular significance until about the 12th century, when Pope Innocent III recognized their use and they came to be worn in order that nothing sacred should be touched by the bare hand.

There are several examples on brasses of archbishops and bishops and abbots wearing gloves. Probably the earliest is that of Otto de Brunswick at Hildesheim (1279). Nearly all the large quadrangular brasses of the 14th and 15th centuries of archbishops and bishops show them wearing gloves with a chrisma.*

Abbot Thomas de la Mare, at St Albans, Hertfordshire (c. 1360); Thomas Cranley, Archbishop of Dublin at New College, Oxford (1417); and Robert Pursglove, Suffragan Bishop of Hull at Tideswell, Derby (1579) are examples in England of ecclesiastics wearing gloves with the chrisma. The gloves were also decorated with jewels.

Post-Reformation Period
The Reformation practically saw the end of ecclesiastical brasses in any quantity. After the Reformation the civil dress of the period appears to have been chosen for effigies of ecclesiastics in preference to that of their calling. This was probably done for diplomatic reasons. Some few exceptions do exist. Leonard Hurst of Denham, Buckinghamshire (1560) is in cassock and surplice, and William Dye of Westerham, Kent (1567) in similar attire. Bishop Henry Robinson of Carlisle, at Queen's College, Oxford (1616) is a late example of a bishop wearing rochet and chimere. The rochet was an alb with sleeves of large dimensions.

PORTRAITURE ON BRASSES
It will be appropriate here to state some facts about portraiture on brasses. It has often been said that few portraits exist. The author is of the opinion that there are more than is usually accepted. The heel-ball rubbing is by no means easy to read as far as individual characteristics are concerned. The many illustrations in Victorian books of brasses – engraved by hand as positives – are not reliable. The technique of rendering a brass as a full-sized gilt and black positive taken 'off the top of the brass' has shown this defect. The difference between an individual medieval portrait and a stereotyped portrait is often a subtle one.

We look to brasses to give us an authentic picture of the attire of the period in which the brass was cut, but we fail to appreciate that a considerable number give us a portrait of an individual, though doubtless very many others bear no facial resemblance whatsoever to the person they represent. There are even a few 'twin' brasses in existence to persons who are quite unrelated to each other. Thousands of others were cut without representing any particular individual. Some very obvious portraits do exist however. By a 'portrait' is here meant a face that depicts individual characteristics: portrait, in the accepted conventional sense, means a 'likeness'.

We do not know that a face incised on brass with strong individual features is necessarily a *likeness*. We can only assume this. The brass of Sir W. Tendring at Stoke-by-Nayland (1408) depicts him with a beard and bald

*The chrisma (medieval English) is the symbol on the back of the bishop's glove and symbolizes blessing with the holy oil (chrism) used by bishops in baptism, confirmation, consecration and holy orders.

head. We say it is a likeness. Artists worked from models, and it is not beyond
the realms of possibility that the brass was cut after the death of Sir William
and inspired by another man with a bald head and beard.

DEATH MASKS AS MODELS FOR BRASS PORTRAITURE

In medieval times the deceased person was exposed at the funeral for all to
see; this custom was followed in the 14th century by the practice of bearing
in the funeral procession a quickly-made effigy of the deceased, wearing his
clothes. These effigies were made of wood and the face and hands of wax or
plaster and painted to look likelike. (Later ones, as we know, are preserved
in Westminster Abbey.) These death-masks would have provided excellent
models for those who had to make sculptural or incised effigies. Some 13th
and 14th-century effigies exhibit a marked variety of countenances and portray
individuality and character.* Rarely are elderly people depicted – life was
shorter in the Middle Ages.

DEMI-EFFIGIES OF ECCLESIASTICS AS PORTRAITS

There are numerous examples of medieval portraiture depicted on these
demi-brasses. A few are illustrated in pages 72 and 73. All but the most
prejudiced will be able to distinguish these as portraits. But why these
portraits in an age when portraiture was not supposed to exist on brasses?

There could be good reasons why the brass effigy should depict a portrait
of the priest. The ecclesiastic was an educated man – a scholar, who had a
background of learning, of books (manuscripts), and of the arts. He was an
intelligent man, an honest man – honest in what he believed and preached.
He would not so easily accept the idioms and conventions of his time as the
majority of people. When he saw the brass effigy on the floor of the church of
someone he had known in life, and failed to recognize the features, what was
his reaction? Would he not decide that when his time came he should be
depicted by a portrait of himself as all knew him? He or one of his
colleagues may have had a talent for drawing, or he may have arranged
with the artist-designer from the brass workshop to record his portrait against
the time when it should be required.†

Now consider the well-known portraits (several of them self-portraits) of
the great artists of the past 500 years: Botticelli, Mantegna, Leonardo,
Raphael, Michelangelo, Bosch, Titian, Dürer, Holbein, Rubens, Rembrandt,
Hogarth, Reynolds, Turner, Van Gogh, Cézanne, Picasso, and Braque, to
name a few. These are honest portraits as seen by artists living centuries
apart, with vastly different conceptions and vastly different conclusions.
There is no flattery: one is aware that all show qualities greater than a mere
successful rendering of natural appearances, qualities that we recognize as
the special interpretation of the great individual artist – and by his genius he
shows it to us. Look at the portraits on brasses of these priests – young, old,
bull-necked, obese, resolute, gentle, cruel, self-indulgent! Full of character.
These too are honest portraits, not by the greatest of artists, but with distinctive features that with the passing of centuries remain for us today as
significant as ever.

There are many demi-effigies of priests on brasses that are not portraits
– many are stereotyped – but this does not lessen the likelihood that the dis-
criminating ecclesiastic insisted on his correct portrait for the incised brass
slab. It is wrong to think that portraits on brasses were confined to ecclesiastics, but there would certainly appear to be a larger proportion of these.
The Rev W. F. Creeny, in his book on the brasses of Europe, describes a

*See Albert Fryer, *Wooden Monumental Effigies.*

†Numerous portraits exist in manuscripts. The monks often portrayed themselves
and their fellows to illustrate some of the medieval manuscripts. Portraits also
appear in stained glass windows, in sculpture and carvings of the same period.

180. Figure of SAINT CHRISTOPHER on brass to
William Complyn, 1498, Weeke, Hampshire.
A long inscription appears under this figure.
Effigy 8½″.

few faces as portraits – such as William Wenemaer, Ghent, Belgium (1325).

The full-figure effigies of priests and rectors are uneven in quality in their representation of the individual. The 14th-century effigies are for the most part of a high standard; in the 15th-century, when far more were produced, they are of mixed quality, and the few from the 16th-century indicate a much lower artistic outlook, with the portrait appearing less and less. The Reformation had much to do with this too, in more ways than one. Why, one may ask, did the 16th-century priest not demand a portrait like his predecessor? The answer is that the demi-portraits of the 14th and 15th centuries were the products of certain workshops of brass engravers who specialized in producing portraits of priests. When these workshops ceased to exist the portraits came to an end, as did the production of the demi-ecclesiastical brass.* The portrait oil painting and the portrait drawing became the fashion.

Extract from 'Illustrations of Monumental Brasses' printed for the Cambridge Camden Society. 1840. Page 5. Introductory Remarks by J.M.N.

> But to one question not considered there, a few remarks may, on account of its interest, be here devoted. It is this – Do brass effigies contain likenesses of those whom they commemorate? The writer of this article, after careful investigation of the subject, is compelled (while he stands open to conviction) to return an answer in opposition to that usually given. In his opinion, generally speaking, they do so, more or less. And the three following arguments may be urged in support of that opinion.
>
> 1. The very strongly marked features which occur in many effigies. An instance may be particularized in the present work, that of Archbishop Harsnett.† If such a face were met with in a gallery of portraits, everyone would at once pronounce it a likeness.
>
> 2. Very frequent effigies are found of two or three generations in the same family; and the family likeness is remarkable. Now this, considering that the artists must have been different, is in itself a great presumption that the likenesses are real; but it is rendered still greater by the fact that, if a stranger becomes connected by marriage with the family, and his effigy exists, the character of the face will invariably be found entirely different from the preceding ones.‡
>
> 3. We may ask – Is it likely that the families of the deceased would have allowed so plain a face to be represented as is frequently seen, were it not their desire to preserve the likeness? And why should artists, evidently capable of the highest efforts, deviate in the proportion of their figures so far from the beau idéal of the human form, except for the same reason?
>
> In proportion as this view of the subject is admitted, brasses will assume a still higher interest; and a collection of them will be a kind of portrait gallery of the illustrious of ancient times.

*Since writing the above I have acquired a copy of R. T. Gunther's volume on *Brasses and Other Funeral Monuments in the Chapel of Magdalen College, Oxford.* On page 2 Gunther writes in his description of Ralph Vawdrey, A.M., chaplain, 1476 (Bloxam, ii, 123), 'A fine brass and a convincing portrait'.

†Plate 162.

‡A remarkable example of this occurs in Hatley Cockayne Church, Bedfordshire.

181. SAINT CHRISTOPHER from the Cromwell brass c. 1470, Tattershall, Lincs.
Though barely thirty years separate these two ideas, there is a considerable change in the conception of Saint Christopher. The earlier figure shows a more realistic and vigorous interpretation of both the figure and water.

182

183

184

185

186

187

Of the ten demi-effigies displayed on these two pages, nine are undoubtedly portraits. Hakebourne is the exception and this is a stylized or near portrait. The nine have been chosen at random and dozens of portraits could be found from the large number of medieval brasses of ecclesiastics existing today. To a lesser extent this applies to brasses of knights and civilians and their ladies. The portrait of Annefordhe (1361) is similar – but not exactly similar – to the portrait brass of William de Lound (rector), Althorpe, Lincs. On close inspection there are considerable differences between these two demi-effigies.

182. WALTER DE ANNEFORDHE (rector), 1361, Binfield, Berkshire. Effigy 12".

183. Unknown priest, Wantage, Berks, c. 1360. Effigy 23".

184. ROGER CAMPEDENE (rector), 1398, Stanford in the Vale, Berkshire.

185. THOMAS DE HOPE 1346, Kemsing, Kent. Effigy 21".

186. WILLIAM LYE (rector), 1391, Northfleet, Kent.

187. JOHN EVERDON (rector), 1413, Twyford, Bucks. Effigy 15".

188. RICHARD HAKEBOURNE 1311, Merton College, Oxford. Effigy 21".

189. WILLIAM CARBROK, chaplain, c. 1435, Wilhamstead, Beds.

190. Demi effigy of Brother WILLIAM TERNEMU of Yarmouth c. 1440.
Palimpsest – on reverse is ALICE SWANE 1546, Halvergate, Norfolk.

191. WILLIAM BRANWHAIT 1498 (Master of Hospital), Ewelme, Oxon. Effigy 12½".

188

189

190

191

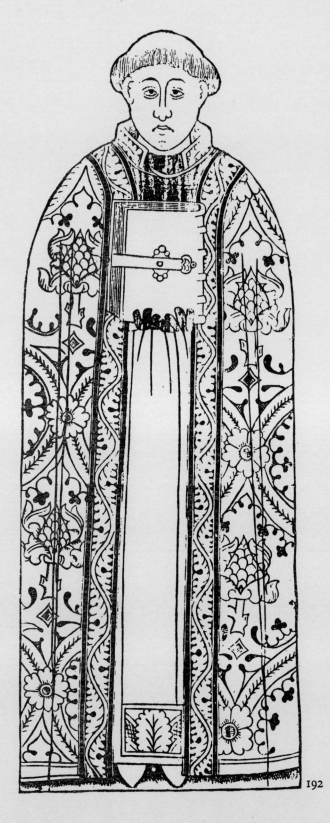

192. THOS. TONGE 1472, Beeford, Yorks.
This brass, though bottle shaped, is better than many – the
diapered cope is well designed as part of the whole composition.

193. SIR SIMON DE WENSLEY (rector 1361-94), Wensley, Yorks.
64″ x 19″. A good chalice brass of continental design, probably
German or Flemish. Note the stipple technique similar to the
manière criblée of the German school of engravers of the 15th
century (see plates 47-50). This was used to indicate the stubble
of the beard on 14th century effigies but was more of a stroke
than a point (see Hakebourne, plate 188).

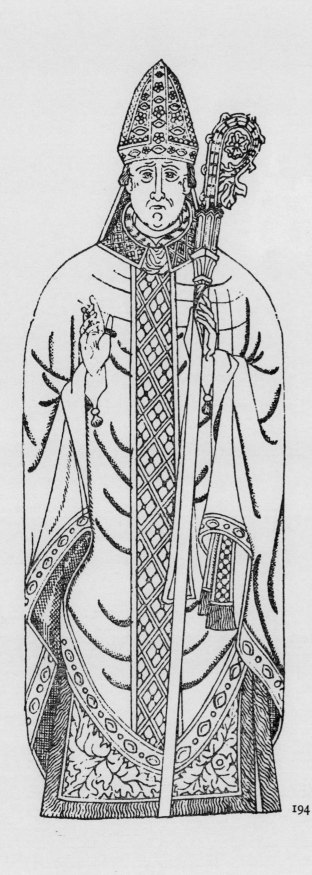

194. JAMES STANLEY, Bishop of Ely 1515.
Manchester Cathedral (lower part lost). A good delicate incised brass
and a portrait.

195. WILLIAM GREY, rector, 1524, Eversholt, Dorset.
In mass vestments with chalice and wafer. Effigy 18″.

M*

196. DOROTHY MANNOCK, widow of Sir Francis Mannock, Bt., 1
aged 42. Stoke-by-Nayland, Suffolk. Another portrait brass. Note
sensitive drawing of the hands. (See plate 151).

197

197. LORD JOHN MARNAY 1524, Little Horkesley, Essex.
An unmistakable portrait. Compare this with the head of Sir Richard
Catesby, 1553, Ashby St Legers, Northants, also a portrait, plate 156.

199

198. GEOFFREY FYCHE, dean, 1537, St Patrick's Cathedral, Dublin.
Brass in the manner of an engraved illustration, its technique more
suitable for a book than a funeral plate. Size 24½″ x 20″. Compare cross-
hatching with stipple on plate 197.

199. Detail of Orphery of Cope from brass. HENRY SEVER 1471,
Merton, Oxford, 'Sacre theologie professor'. Section shown, 12″ deep.

200

200. JOHN HOLTHAM, rector, Provost of Queen's College, Oxford, 1361, Chinnor, Oxon. A good simple brass and an undoubted portrait. Effigy 24″.

201 and 202. Priest with St John the Baptist, *c.* 1415, Apsley Guise, Beds. These figures are successful because their contours are simple and the forms are not broken up beyond requirements for descriptive purposes. Effigies 18″.

201

202

203. THOMAS BURGOYN 1516, Sutton, Beds.
Inscription 22″ wide. A very simple but dramatic
brass. Note the semi italics of the inscription.

204. OLAWS EIKIBY 1316, Eikiby, Gotland, Baltic.
Incised slab (part shown only – the bottom half is mutilated). A beautiful design – the three small crosses at
the top represent the crucifixion. Where the arms of
the cross meet in the centre, the symbol formed is a
swastika!

Crosses and Symbols

CROSSES OF VARIOUS KINDS appear on brasses. The cross was used for crucifixion long before the Christian era and three types came into use for this purpose: the **T** cross (*crux commissa*), the **✝** cross (Latin cross, *crux immissa*), and the **X** cross (*crux decussata*).

The Latin type of cross is more commonly held to depict the crucifixion of Christ. The Agnus Dei – the symbol of Our Lord, or the Lamb of God – shows a lamb statant with one foreleg arched round the base of a long Latin cross. Merton College, Oxford, has a bracket brass to John Bloxham and John Whytton (*c.* 1420), and at the base is the Lamb with cross and banner of St John the Baptist.

Crosses were used on tombs in the early centuries, and it was not until the effigy appeared on the stone slab or brass plate that the cross became less popular. There are many thousands of crosses on tombs, raised or incised, in this country and in Europe. Many of these on stone slabs used as tomb tops are of great beauty (see plate 204).

In this country there are probably fewer than twenty brasses with only crosses, and again fewer than twenty that have crosses with the figure or head of the deceased placed on or within the cross. The earliest, that of Richard de Hakebourne (1311) has been mentioned elsewhere. At Chinnor, in Oxfordshire (1320), the head of the individual is enclosed by the quatrefoil which has floriated terminations. At Buxted, Sussex, the cross to Britell Avenel, priest (1408), retains its stem and has a base of four steps; the three-quarter length of the priest is in the head of the cross! The brass to Thomas Chichele and his wife at Higham Ferrers, Northamptonshire (1400) bears the four Evangelists upon the ends of the arms. The stem is decorated within the cross form and Our Lord is represented in the central crossing.

The fine cross at Granthorpe, Lincolnshire (*c.* 1380) is a magnificent design. The cross rises from a base of rock with fish swimming in the water round it. There is no figure or head, but an elaborately engraved inner cross, and the four floriated ends are large and delightfully conceived. One of the latest cross brasses is to a two-year-old girl, Francisca Shyppe, at North Tuddenham, Norfolk (1625).

An early cross brass at Taplow, Buckinghamshire, to Nicholas Aumberdene (1350) shows a dolphin embowed naiant at the base of the cross. Aumberdene was a London fishmonger.

Kneeling figures on either side of the stem of the cross appear on the brass at Hildersham, Cambridgeshire, to Robert de Paris and his wife (1408). A very simple cross can be seen at Sutton, in Bedfordshire (1516), to Thomas Burgoyn and wife (plate 203).

The effigy of William de Herlestone, priest, at Sparsholt, Berkshire (*c.* 1360) is placed within the octofoil cross. This is one of the most distinguished brass effigies of the 14th-century and was designed by an artist of considerable importance. The movement of this figure is excellent. The weight is taken on the right leg, which dominates the movement. The left leg helps to keep the balance by being placed slightly lower than the right, and so the left shoulder drops lower than the right shoulder. This causes the left arm also to be lower. To complete the balance, the neck and head swing to the right at an angle in opposition to the swing of the shoulders. The drapery conforms to the general movement of the body. Note that the ends of the stole swing in a different direction to that of the alb. The effigy is complete but the cross is mutilated (see plate 159).

81

Nichol de Gore, at Woodchurch, Kent (*c.* 1330), appears within a quatre-foiled circle as a full-length effigy, the arms of the cross terminating in bold fleurs-de-lys. The inscription runs on the circle. The effigy, though earlier than Herlestone, is vastly inferior in design and execution.

Symbols of the Trinity and of Evangelists

Symbols of the Holy Trinity appear on numerous brasses. The Almighty Father is usually in the form of an aged bearded man, seated and holding a crucifix upon which the Dove (the emblem of the Holy Ghost) is alighting. A very fine example exists at Childrey in Berkshire on the brass of Joan Strangbon (1477) (see plate 224). This is very much in the German tradition and research may reveal interesting data. The Trinity brass of M. Fox, Cha-combe (1545), is somewhat similar but has not the merit of the Childrey brass. Another type of symbol for the Holy Trinity appeared in the form of the verbal emblem, on the shield of Thomas Nelond at Cowfield, Sussex (1433). *Evangelistic Symbols* are common on brasses both in England and on the Continent. They are the eagle of St John, the lion of St Mark, the bull of St Luke and the angel of St Matthew, and are generally placed at each of the four corners of the marginal inscription, usually set in circles or quatrefoils and infrequently in shields. Examples are: Richard Charlis, Addington, Kent (1378); Sir W. Calthorpe, Burnham Thorpe, Norfolk (1420); Simon Seman, Barton-on-Humber, Lincolnshire (1433); Thomas Brond, Newport, Essex (1515); John Mershden, Thurcaston, Leicester (1425); Ramburgh de Wik, Vester, Åker, Sweden (1327); John and Symo Segemund, Nordhausen, Germany (1400, 1410); Frederick the Good, Duke of Saxony, Meissen (1464). *Resurrection on Brasses:* there is one at All Hallows, London (1500); also Robert Harding, Cranleigh, Surrey (1503); and Edward Love, Stoke Lyne, Oxon (1535).

The Virgin, Angels and Apostles. The Blessed Virgin appears on numerous brasses. The British Museum has one which shows her kneeling at a desk (*c.* 1500). Richard Bulkley, Beaumaris, Anglesey, has both the Virgin Mary and the Holy Trinity (1530). The brass of Sir Thomas Stathum shows St Anne, Blessed Virgin Mary and St Christopher. The Adoration of the Shepherds appears on a brass at Cobham, Surrey (*c.* 1500) which is often used as a Christmas card (plates 180, 181).

Angels appear on a few brasses. An unusual one is that to Walter Beau-champ, Checkendon, Oxon (1430). The angels are taking Beauchamp's soul (in the form of a female nude) to Heaven! Angels are on the brass of Sir Hugh Hastyngs at Elsing, Norfolk (1343); the Twelve Apostles appear on the Walsoken brass at Lynne, Norfolk (1349); the Virgin and Child are on George Rede's at Fovant, Wiltshire (1492); and individual apostles and saints are depicted on several brasses, such as the fine St George on the Hastings brass at Elsing, Norfolk (1347).

Chalice Brasses

Chalices are quite common on brasses, sometimes alone or with the Eucharistic wafer. The chalice is usually enriched with decorations. The bowl is shallow. Often the wafer is shown with the sacred monogram standing on its edge inside the bowl of the chalice. (The wafer is the thin disc of unleavened bread used in the Eucharist.)

Examples: William Langton, St Michael Spurriergale, York (1466); Thomas Elys, Shorne, Kent (1519); and an anonymous brass at Gazeley, Suffolk (1530) are all chalice brasses without effigy.

The following are with effigies: Sir Simon Wensley, Wensley, Yorkshire (1375); Thomas Wheteaker, Radwell, Hertfordshire (1487); John Wryght, Clothall, Hertfordshire (1519); and John Yslyngeton, Cley-next-the-Sea, Norfolk (1520).

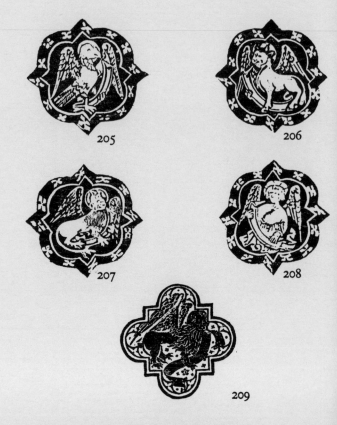

205. SAINT JOHN 206. SAINT LUKE
207. SAINT MARK 208. SAINT MATTHEW
209. SAINT MARK (alternative)

210. SIR THOMAS STATHUM and two wives, 1470, Morley, Derbyshire.
At the top is SAINT CHRISTOPHER, on the left is Saint Anne and the little virgin and on the right the Blessed Virgin and Child. Depth of brass 45″.

211. Brass to JOHN MERSTUN 1446, Lillingstone Lovell, Bucks. Two hands with clouds holding a bleeding heart. 'Ihc' (the first three letters of Jesus in Greek).

211

212, 213. Unknown man and woman in shrouds, c. 1520. Biddenham, Beds. Badly drawn figures – an example of the morbid outlook which is depicted on brasses for about 250 years. Man 17¾", woman 19" deep.

212   213

On the Continent there are also some good effigies with chalice, such as these three in Germany: John de Heringer, Erfurt (1505); E. de Rabenstain, Bamburg (1505); and a priest at Erfurt (1420). A fine chalice on the back of the brass to N. West at Marsworth, Buckinghamshire (1586) is part of a continental brass.

HEART BRASSES

It was often the custom to take the heart out of the corpse and bury the body elsewhere. In the usual type of heart brass three scrolls are seen issuing from the heart bearing in an upward direction, as in those of Thomas Smyth (priest) at Margate, Kent (1433) and Sir R. Kervile, Wiggenhall St Mary, Norfolk (1450). Other heart brasses depict the heart held up by two hands which come through the clouds. Then there are the scrolls on which a text is incised:

Thomas Denton, Caversfield, Oxon (1533); John Merstun, Lillingstone Lovell, Buckinghamshire (1446).

The heart brass of Thomas Knyghtley at Fawsley, Northants (1516) shows the armed and tabarded effigy of Knyghtley together with four shields of arms in the corners. The heart and three scrolls are placed above the head of the figure. At St Albans the brass of Robert Beaumer (1460) shows him holding the heart with drops of blood. This effigy is greatly elongated, a medieval method of expressing divinity. There are numerous variations among heart brasses, too many to describe here.

SHROUD BRASSES AND SKELETONS

These brasses reveal morbid trends from the second quarter of the 15th-century to the early 17th-century – a sentimental type of morbidity which appeared in Victorian times in more subtle guise. This cult of death was not confined to England but was prevalent on the Continent too.* Possibly plague and pestilence had some effect on the outlook of the period, and people attempted to devote their lives to preparation for death. These morbid ideas were reflected in manuscripts, paintings, frescoes and in three-dimensional sculptures. At Ewelme in Oxfordshire is the fine sculptural effigy of the Duchess of Suffolk in the serene sleep of death, but behind the tracery panels is another carving of her dead body in grisly detail! The sculptural effigy of Francois de Sarra is depicted with toads eating his face (c. 1400). Such unhealthy designs on brasses were horrifying in the extreme. A most unpleasant one is at Oddington, Oxfordshire, to one Ralph Hamsterley (1510). It depicts worms attacking his corpse. The artist, to emphasize the horror, draws the worms much larger than life – evidently they have fed well! Let it be said that the majority of the shroud brasses are badly designed, badly drawn, and poorly incised.

Another odd idea was to show the deceased as a skeleton or shrouded figure and the survivors in ordinary costume; an example is John Manfield

*'And therefore we find early tombs at once simple and lovely in adornment, severe and solemn in their expression; confessing the power, and accepting the peace of death, openly and joyfully; and in all their symbols marking that the hope of resurrection lay only in Christ's righteousness; signed always with this simple utterance of the dead, "I will lay me down in peace and take my rest; for it is Thou, Lord, only that makest me dwell in safety". But the tombs of the later ages are a ghastly struggle of mean pride and miserable terror: the one mustering the statues of the Virtues about the tomb, disguising the sarcophagus with delicate sculpture, polishing the false periods of the elaborate epitaph and filling with strained animation the features of the portrait statue; and the other summoning underneath, out of the niche or from behind the curtain, the frowning scull, or scythed skeleton, or some other more terrible image of the enemy in whose defiance the whiteness of the sepulchre has been set to shine above the whiteness of the ashes.' John Ruskin, The Street of the Tombs, *The Stones of Venice*.

at Taplow, Buckinghamshire (1455). On the brass of William Feteplace at Childrey, Berkshire (1516) both husband and wife are shown rising from their tombs. These are very small, the figures are only nine-and-a-half inches high.

The figure of death as a skeleton appears on the brass of Thomas Sparke, D.D., at Bletchley, Buckinghamshire (1616). This is a detailed engraving on a small plate and is nothing more nor less than a large book illustration, so that the objective of a mural memorial incised brass is quite lost. The brass of Bishop Schönberg, Naumburg (1516), depicts a skeleton with entrails exposed. At Hunsdon, Hertfordshire, the brass to James Gray, a park-keeper (1591), is lightly engraved showing death striking a dart into both Gray and the stag (which Gray is shooting).

Shrouded figures are common – mostly perpendicular, though a few are depicted recumbent. The effigy of Alexander Belsyre, Handborough, Oxon (1567) is recumbent, as are Elizabeth Horne, Shipton-under-Wychwood, Oxon (1548) and the unknown effigy at Chicheley, Buckinghamshire (1560). In the small brass of Elizabeth Bligh, with her little daughter at Finchampstead, Berkshire (1635), the mother's hand rests on a skull which is on a pedestal. The two shrouded figures at Biddenham, Bedfordshire (1520), facing each other, are husband and wife.

214, 215 (opposite). Emblem of blessed Trinity from brass of Prior Nelond, 1433, Cowfold, Sussex. Window in Cirencester church using the same design.

216. JOHN CLAIMOND, first president Corpus Christi College, Oxford, 1530. Example of the use of an emaciated effigy in shroud for a distinguished individual.

217. From the brass of THOMAS MAGNUS, M.A. 1550, Sessay N.R., Yorks.

218. 14th century evangelistic symbol – the eagle of St John, in glass window, Shere, Surrey. Similar in design to those used on brasses.

215

218

219. Cross *c.* 1380, Grainthorpe, Lincs. A beautiful large cross. Stem and marginal inscription nearly all lost.

219

N

220

220. GEORGE REDE, rector, *c.* 1500, Fovant, Wilts. A picture brass of the Annunciation. A badly balanced inscription appears underneath. English, derived from incunabula book illustrations and with a decided French influence. 14″ wide. (Rector resigned 1504.)

221. Coloured glass window. Angel from Chartham, Kent (South wall), *c.* 1300. Similar angels appear on brasses such as the Hastyngs brass, Elsing, 1347 (see plate 51), and Margaret Cheyney 1419, Hever, Kent.

221

222. RICHARD DE LA BARRE 1386, Hereford Cathedral.
A popular design of a head of a cross – the figure is too rigid to make a happy combination.

223. Civilian in a cross (*c.* 1395), St Michael's, St Albans, Herts.
Mutilated cross. In this illustration part of the cross has been restored, size 48″ (section shown).

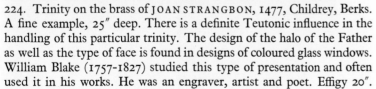

224

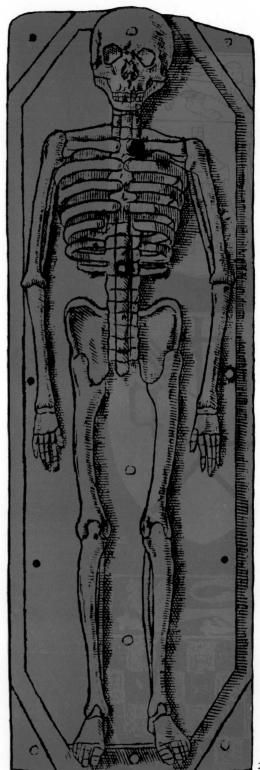

225

224. Trinity on the brass of JOAN STRANGBON, 1477, Childrey, Berks.
A fine example, 25″ deep. There is a definite Teutonic influence in the
handling of this particular trinity. The design of the halo of the Father
as well as the type of face is found in designs of coloured glass windows.
William Blake (1757-1827) studied this type of presentation and often
used it in his works. He was an engraver, artist and poet. Effigy 20″.

225. JOHN MAUNSELL, gent 1605, Haversham, Bucks.
An example of the morbid mentality of the 17th century. Not a good
anatomical study! Inscription:
HERE RESTETH THE BODY OF JOHN MAUNSELL GENT
WHO DEPARTED THIS LIFE THE 25TH OF JANUARYE
1605 WHEN HE HAD LIVED LXVJ YEERES FOWER
MONETHS AND FIVE DAYES WHOSE CHRISTIAN LIFE
AND GODLY END GRAVNT VS TO FOLLOW
Effigy 23″.

CHAPTER FIFTEEN

Parish Churches, Guilds and Wool Brasses

226

227

228

226. Shield of MERCHANT TAILORS 1631, Kirk-leatham, Robert Coulthirst of Upleatham, Yorks, died aged 90.

227. Merchant's mark of LAURENCE PYGOT, Wool-man, 1450, Dunstable Priory Church, Beds. An excellent and simple design.

228. Arms of the staple of Calais on the brass of John Feld, 1474, Standon, Herts.

OUR ANCIENT parish churches contain treasures which are now part of our English heritage. There are over 10,000 ancient churches in the country and in these is found a great variety of memorials which tell us much about the history of our forebears. The majority of our monumental brasses are within these churches. A few are in museums and private collections, a very few on the outside of churches, and one or two in more unusual places.

Outside the church today, if the fields are not built over by a modern housing estate, you may see sheep grazing – a reminder that about 600 years ago a wealthy sheep farmer, whose flocks grazed on these very same fields, hills, or downs, erected the church, and when he died monumental brasses were laid on his tomb to commemorate his passing, and that of his wife and children. Up to the 15th and 16th centuries the wealthy merchants and guilds gave money for the building of churches, chantries, and chapels as well as for their subsequent adornment.

THE GUILDS

The guild was generally a professional organization designed to maintain standards of work and to protect its members against outside competition, having originated for the purpose of keeping together the people of the parish or town or village. It also had a religious purpose.

The earliest record of an English guild is of that formed at Norwich in 1264 for the chaplains of St Mary's church. Other guilds quickly followed; often dedicated to a saint and all of a religious character, they would present a sum of money or effigy or gift of an ecclesiastical nature to the church. Soon these guilds were engaged in the building of churches, bridges, hospitals, schools, and similar projects, and often they had a specific charitable purpose, such as several of the City of London Companies still maintain today.

Guilds extended to trades – tailors, haberdashers, carpenters, mariners, farmers, glovers, bakers, fishermen, and numerous other occupations. Leading men from far afield were later admitted into some of them.

The English Craft Guild of the medieval craftsman was established in 1301. *This fact is of considerable importance to the student of monumental brasses, because it shows that there must have been some liasion between the designers and engravers of the early brasses and the mason builders of the great cathedrals and churches.*

About the middle of the 14th-century, Edward III ordered all guilds to be remodelled with fresh privileges but more stringent rules 'for the greater good and profit of the people'. This was a move in the right direction, and the charters provided that the guilds should meet at least once a year to 'settle and govern their mysteries', to 'elect honest, lawful and sufficient men to direct the concerns of their trade and to correct and amend the same'. This meeting was in addition to four other annual ones, to conduct business and for friendly intercourse. Members were enjoined to be generous towards each other and to that end to hold regular festivals, processions, and other gatherings, and to wear the liveries appointed for each Company. In the County Lists will be found many of the early members of these Companies. Their memorials exist today in the same churches where they worshipped three, four, or five hundred years ago.

The Wool Merchants and their Brasses

Many merchants and tradesmen, together with their wives and children, are commemorated in brasses. Most of them were prominent men who contributed greatly to the prosperity of these islands in the Middle Ages.

One of the most important industries of the period was that of wool, which brought great wealth to those who took part in it and consequently considerable prosperity to the areas involved. The best wool in Europe then came from the black-faced sheep of England and from Spanish sheep. The Merino sheep of Castile originally came from North Africa. The wool from these sheep held its own with English wool, and was in fact imported into England in the 13th-century (the expression 'carrying wools to England' was used in the sense in which we now say 'carrying coals to Newcastle').

It is a matter of interest that the great wool industry of Australia today is associated with both England and Spain. There was a time when Spanish wool was poor in quality, but it was improved by crossing with our famous Cotswold sheep. King Edward VI sent a present of these sheep to Spain, and later Spanish farmers imported them to raise the standard of their flocks. Eventually John Macarthur, an Australian, obtained a number of sheep from George III. These sheep, which were of Spanish origin, were the start of the Australian wool industry, and the Merino sheep of Australia now produce some of the finest wool in the world.

Cotswold Churches

A considerable number of wool merchants are commemorated in brasses which were placed in the churches they built, or partly built, or restored. Usually their wives appear with them, and their children. Sometimes they are shown in the coloured glass windows of the church. One could name a dozen or more wool merchants depicted on brasses and this would represent only a moderate percentage of the total. The church of St Mary at Fairford, famous throughout the kingdom for its collection of 16th-century coloured glass windows, was rebuilt in the middle of the 15th-century by a wool merchant named John Tame and his son Edmond (died 1534) who carried on with his father's great work.

One of the finest of the Cotswold churches is that of St Peter and St Paul at Northleach, a centre of the wool trade in the Middle Ages. Many different languages could be heard spoken there when at the Spring meetings merchants from far and wide came to examine wool samples and to buy and sell. They must have gone to the church to pray. The greatest benefactor of this church was John Fortey, 1458, who added the nave clerestory, the main structure having been rebuilt on a previous foundation early in the same century.

This church contains many brasses to woolmen and others, including those to an unknown wool merchant, his feet on a wool pack (*c.* 1400); Agnes Fortey and her two husbands; William Scors, tailor (died 1420); Thomas Fortey, woolman (church repairer and road repairer) 1447; John Fortey (above mentioned); unknown woolman (*c.* 1485); John Taylour, woolman (*c.* 1490); William Bicknell and his wife, founders of a chantry (*c.* 1500); Robert Serche, civilian (1501); Thomas Bushe, woolman and merchant of the Staple of Calais (1525) and his wife Joan (1526). There are other brasses, including W. Lawnder, priest, *c.* 1530. J. Fortey's feet are on a woolpack as well as on a sheep; his initials and trademark are shown in medallions round the border. William Scors, the tailor, is shown with a pair of scissors at his feet; the border of this brass contains a snail, a crab, a hedgehog, a pig, a falcon and dogs, as well as plants and flowers. The Bushe brass bears the arms of the Staple of Calais on the canopy spandrels, and under the figure is the merchant's trademark, while a pun on the name is made by illustrating sheep among bushes. On the Taylour brass a sheep is shown standing on a woolpack.

229. JOHN FORTEY, Woolman, 1458, Northleach, Gloucestershire. See detail, plate 233A.

In the church at Chipping Campden in Gloucestershire there is a large brass to a famous wool merchant, William Grevel, citizen of London, and his wife, under a double canopy. The town has one of the finest wool houses left in England today – Greville House (1380). In the main street the Wool Hall still stands. At Chipping Norton, Oxon, there is a brass to another woolman, John Yonge, standing on a woolpack (1451); also a brass to John Pergetter, an ironmonger (1484). Winchcombe, in Gloucestershire, has yet another 'wool' church, but it has no brasses to wool merchants. The church has forty gargoyles for which it is famous. Did John Fortey of Northleach help to build this church too?

At Witney in Oxfordshire, in another wool church, is a brass to Richard Wenman and his wife (1500). This woman was the daughter of John Bushe of Northleach. Wenman, too, was a member of the Staple of Calais. In Cirencester, Gloucestershire, is a brass to a wool merchant, Robert Pagge (1440). He also repaired churches and roads. Phillip Marner, a clothier (1587), with shears by his head, stands on a dog. Another clothier, Hodgkinson Paine (1642), has his name punned in verse. In one of the stained glass windows of this church the design includes a weaver's shuttle.

Lechlade has a wool church. An unknown wool merchant with wife and children (inscription lost) stands with his feet on a woolpack (1450). He may have been John Townsend. At Thame is a brass to a wool merchant and a member of the Staple of Calais – Geoffrey Dormer with his wife and twenty-five children! (1502). In this church are brasses to the Quatremayn family who by marriage were related to Sir Robert de Grey of Rotherfield Greys (see plate 99).

Other Wool Churches

At St Albans Abbey, Hertfordshire, Thomas Fayreman and his wife are commemorated (1411). He was one of several wool merchants in that district; as are John Feld, with his son and grand-children on an altar tomb at Standon, in the same county (1474-77); John Hicchecok at Ampthill, Bedfordshire (1450); Lawrence Pygott and wife at Dunstable, Bedfordshire (1450); a merchant of the Staple at Hitchin, Hertfordshire (1452); and another at St Albans Abbey – Paul Rowlatt (1519). At Chicheley, Buckinghamshire there are Anthony Cave and his wife (1558); and at Easton Neston, Northants, Richard Fermer and wife (1552). There are others in and around London: at All Hallows, Barking, Thomas Gilbert and wife (1483); at Ealing, Middlesex, Richard Amondesham and wife (1490).

Another centre for the wool merchants was East Anglia. Here we find at Linwode, Lincolnshire, John Lyndewode and wife (1419) and John Lyndewode the younger (1421), both standing on woolpacks. At All Saints' church, Stamford, Lincolnshire, John Browne and his wife (1442) are both on wool packs and in the same church their son William Browne and his wife (c. 1460) are again on woolpacks and with the device of a stork as decoration. At Algarkirk, Lincolnshire, there are Nicholas Robertson and two wives (1498); at Winthorpe, Lincolnshire, Richard Barowe and wife (1505); at Mattishall, Norfolk, Robert Foster and wife (1507); and at Sawley in Derbyshire, Richard Shylton and wife (1510).

Among wool merchants' brasses that of John Curteys and his wife at Wymington, Bedfordshire (1391-6) is the oldest, and is a specially fine brass of character on an altar tomb in good preservation (see plate 74). Curteys was President of the Wool Staple of Calais. There are a few brass inscriptions to woolmen: the one at Newark in Nottinghamshire, to Robert Whitecoumbe (1447), shows his merchant's mark. The lives of these merchants make interesting reading. Eileen Power in *Medieval People* describes how some of them lived, worked, loved, quarrelled, prospered, and died; for instance, Thomas Betson, a merchant of the Staple, and Thomas Paycocke of

230

230. WILLIAM BROWNE c. 1460, All Saints', Stanford, Lincs. Part of brass. Note woolpacks.

Coggeshall, a master weaver, are two persons who are made thoroughly familiar to us in this lively book.

One of the most important families of merchant traders in the 14th-century was that of the de la Poles of Hull. They first came to England with William I, and various branches of the family fought in subsequent wars and then turned to trading as a means of making money.

They settled in Yorkshire – Ravensrod – and became extremely wealthy, owing to their trade with the Continent. William de la Pole was chosen to be Mayor of the Staple of Antwerp in 1338. He was a friend of King Edward III and was made Baron of the Exchequer and given property in Lombard Street. William died in 1366 aged about eighty. He is depicted in a monument at Hull. Another William de la Pole became Duke of Suffolk and married Alice, daughter of Thomas Chaucer (son of William Chaucer). Thomas Chaucer and his wife are depicted on a brass at Ewelme, Oxon (1436) where they founded a hospital. Sir John de la Pole is depicted on a brass with his wife, holding hands, at Chrishall, Essex (1380). Their daughter Joan became heiress to Sir John de Cobham. She can be seen holding a model of the church in her hands on a brass at Cobham, Kent (1365). Joan had five husbands. Other de la Poles married into some of the richest families in the country.

At St Paul's church, Bedford, is a brass to Sir William Harper (1573), Lord Mayor of London and founder of Bedford Modern School. Harper, as a young man, was apprenticed to a Merchant Taylor and admitted to the freedom of the company in 1533. He lived in Lombard Street. In 1553 he was appointed Master of the Merchant Taylors, and eight years later was elected Lord Mayor of London. Queen Elizabeth knighted him.

In the list of brasses of the various counties given in this book it is worth noting the large number of people of the past who were members of the different companies or guilds, and carried the arms of these on their memorial brasses. However, although trades are often recorded on the brasses of individuals, it is only by tracing records that one can discover how many of the people whose names appear on brasses were actually tradesmen.

MERCHANTS' MARKS ON BRASSES

When a merchant was a member of the Merchant Adventurers his mark indicated the fact.

Merchants' marks were used throughout the wool and cloth trade. In the church of St Peter at Tiverton in Devonshire, where many such merchants lived, there are a number of their marks. This is also true of East Anglia and was noted by Cotman in his *Brasses of Norfolk and Suffolk*. East Anglia was of course one of the important sheep-farming districts.

At Northleach church on the brass of John Fortey his mark is repeated no less than six times, forming part of the decoration of the marginal inscription (see plate 229).

Some merchants' marks were used in the Middle Ages as a rune – a symbol supposed to have the power of dispersing evil or guarding against it, or even of casting a spell on an opponent. It had evidently to be spoken to give full effect – it was a phonetic symbol. The German Hanseatic League was the originator of merchants' marks. A number of these marks contained the Christian cross as part of their design, some were shaped like the figure 4 on its side – the shape of the sign of the cross made by the hand when crossing oneself (top, bottom, left, right). Various other symbols entered the designs.

231. ARMS OF MERCHANTS ADVENTURERS from brass of Andrew Evyngar, 1533, All Hallows, Barking.

232. THOMAS POWNDER 1525, St Mary Quay, Ipswich.

233. JOHN TAYLOR 1490, detail, Northleach, Gloucestershire.

233A. A graphic detail from the brass of John Fortey, Woolman, 1458, Northleach, Gloucestershire. (See plate 229)

234

235

234. JOHN FELD snr. 1474, Standon, Herts.
Size 36″ effigy. A good portrait. Father of John Feld in tabard. He is
standing with his son on the same base. He is shown with two sons and
one daughter (see chapter 12).

235. JOHN FELD jnr. 1477, Standon, Herts.
Size 36″ effigy. A good portrait and tabard brass (altar tomb). He is
shown with two sons and two daughters.

236. Rose brass: JOHN KILLINGWORTH 1412, Eddlesborough,
Bucks. (21″ deep).

236

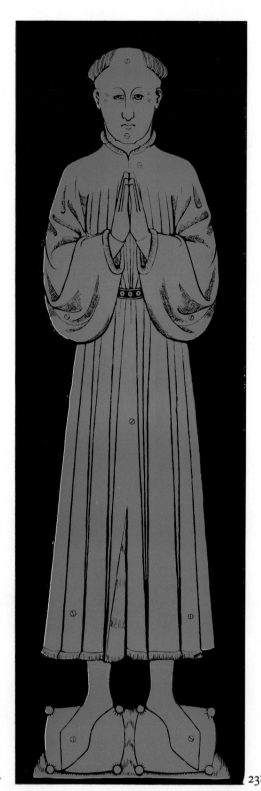

237. NICHOLAS CANTYS 1431, Margate, Kent.
In civil costume – ornamental shoes. Can one doubt that this is a portrait?

238. JOHN YONGE 1451, Chipping Norton, Oxon.
A very well drawn face, a portrait. His feet stand on woolpacks. A good simple brass. His wife is with him on the complete brass. He wears hose and shoes of one piece.

239. Unknown civilian c. 1370, Shottesbrooke, Berks. Wearing tunic and mantle fastened by three shoulder buttons. Another portrait. These three brasses show considerable restraint in the use of linear design. Note the complete lack of hatchwork in the Shottesbrooke brass.

240

240. GEOFFREY KIDWELLY 1483, Little Wittenham, Berks.
A good simple brass to a civilian wearing mantle. Over his left shoulder
a hood. Note his purse – attached to a girdle at the waist. A neat first
class portrait brass. See detail plate 168. In the 15th and early 16th
centuries prayer-beads, displayed as a badge of piety, were often worn
at the belt. The short, open paternoster-string, tasselled at both ends
or with a tassel at one end and a cross at the other, was used almost
exclusively by men. The number of beads varies: ten, eleven, twelve
and thirty are common. The Arnofini Bethrothal (1434) (in the National
Gallery) Jan Van Eyck, shows a rosary hanging on the wall. The
painting by Rogier van de Weyden of Mary Magdalen reading shows a
male figure with a string of two octaves of ave-beads divided by three
larger paternoster beads. Effigy 28″.

241. Merchants' marks for members of the Hanse, 1402. Cotton
manuscripts, British Museum.

241

242. Northleach, Glos. A scene that has changed little during the past five hundred years. A famous wool church, contains the brasses of many famous woolmen including John Fortey (d. 1458) who erected the roof of this church.

243. Algarkirk, Lincs. Church of Saint Peter and Paul. Contains brass of N. Robertson, merchant, of Staple of Calais, 1498.

244. Chipping Campden, Glos. The wool market hall. One of the meeting places of wool merchants in the Middle Ages. William Grevel, 'the flower of the wool merchants of all England', is buried at Chipping Campden.

245. Cobham, Kent. Church of St Mary Magdalene. The famous church of brasses (on floor in photo).

CHAPTER SIXTEEN

Inscriptions and Palimpsests

246. From the brass of JOHN ESTBURY 1485, Lambourn, Berks.

Grotesque animals, birds, floral designs and the like are placed between each word of the chamfer inscriptions.

INCISED inscriptions occurred on stone slabs, crosses, and similar memorials and monuments much earlier than on monumental brasses. Some Irish high crosses from before AD 1000 carry inscriptions, such as that at Bealin, 'Pray for Tvathgall who caused this cross to be erected'. In China and Japan copper tomb-plates with inscriptions date from the centuries BC.

Early incised inscriptions were written in Roman characters, but by the 13th-century Lombardic characters were used. The lettering on Trajan's column in Rome (AD 141) was the basis of Roman lettering in use today.

Incised inscriptions on British monumental brasses are in different languages – Norman-French, Latin and English. Norman-French was used in the 13th and 14th centuries and continued to a very limited extent into the 15th. English inscriptions were introduced at the end of the 14th-century, were used on a limited scale during the next century, but came into general use after about 1500. Some continental brass inscriptions are in Latin, but there was a more practical trend by designers and engravers who used the language of their own country. France used French; Flanders used Flemish and German; Germany used Latin and German; Spain used Spanish, and so on. Basically three types of letter forms were adopted for inscriptions – Lombardic, Old English and Roman.

Many monumental brass inscriptions occupy marginal strips; others – the majority – are on rectangular plates, alone or at the bottom of the effigies; and a few appear on scrolls and similar accessories. The marginal inscription on the brass of Sir John d'Aubernoun (1327) is in Lombardic capitals – these are separate letters beautifully formed. Most of the early inscriptions to accompany the effigies were worked in separately, each having its own indent on the casement. By the middle of the 14th-century the letters were engraved on and not between the fillets of brass. These were mostly capital letters. In the Topcliffe brass (1391) and the Newark brass (1361) the inscriptions are incised in small letters, not capitals. (The terms 'upper case' and 'lower case' in use today to signify capitals and small letters are quite incongruous when used in connection with 14th-century incised lettering. They refer to hand type-setting, being the position in the typesetter's cabinet.)

Two early inscriptions are those commemorating the dedication of the church at Ashbourne, Derbyshire (1241) and the foundation of Bisham Abbey at Denchworth, Berkshire (1333) which is a palimpsest. In Westminster Abbey are two other palimpsests: to Margaret, daughter of William de Valence (1276) and one to her brother John (1277). By the close of the 14th-century the Lombardic style had been superseded by Old English or Black Letter, sometimes called German text.

Not all inscriptions were incised letters. Sometimes the letters were left standing, the surround having been cut away as on Bishop Young at New College, Oxford (1526); at Morley, Derbyshire to G. de Statham (1403); or at Little Wittenham to Geoffrey Kidwelly (1472). A vast number of inscriptions appealed to the reader 'Of your charite pray for the soul of —, who died on —, on whose soul J'hu have merci'. See Sir John Radclif, Crosthwaite, (1527) (plate 253). The form of words used is often archaic, contractions are very common, especially in Latin or in the Old English inscriptions. The contraction is usually marked by the addition of a line above the nearest vowel. Spacing was not always of the best. As the engraver came near to the end of the line some letters were cramped, or excessive contractions were used, making it difficult to read. When there was too much space or a line fell short, some decorative motif often appears. Scrolls or labels with incised lettering grew from the hands or mouth of some of the persons commemorated – see L. Fyton, Sonning (1434); Sir Richard Bewfforeste, Dorchester, Oxon (1510); William Feteplace and wife, Childrey (1516). A simple rectangular inscription in black letter type, cleanly cut, is that to John Fage, Roxton, Bedfordshire (1400). An amusing inscription is on the brass of John Smith, Brightwell Baldwin, Oxon (1370), in early English (see illustration). The sense of it is as follows:*

*With acknowledgments to Dr A. C. Bouquet.

> Man, come and see how all (the) dead shall be
> When to you comes evil and bareness (so as) to
> Have naught when we journey away.
> All that we care for is other men's.
> Except that which we do for God's love
> We have nothing there (i.e. in the grave).
> Under this grave lies John the Smith.
> God give his soul Heaven's peace.

The St Christopher brass to W. Complyn at Weeke, Hampshire (1498) contains a well-cut and well-displayed inscription (see illustration); on the finely-cut arms of John Goodwyn and his wife at Over Winchendon (1558) it is recorded that they had eighteen children.

English inscriptions continue up to the present day. Some of the 'copper plate' inscriptions of the 17th century are beautifully designed and have sensitively spaced lettering, for example, that to Richard Blackford at Dunster, Somerset (1689).

The lettering used in 16th century brasses varied considerably: brasses were popular and the standard poor. It is evident that many engravers were at work, not of the highest skill. 'Semi-italic scripts' occur, which are the result of hurried work, with italics (Italian) letters slanting to the right. 'Lettering artists', if in a hurry, will tend to make their letters slant slightly, almost reverting to handwriting; for example, T. Borgoyn, Sutton, Bedford-shire (1516). Bilingual inscriptions are known – at Wouldham, Kent, is an inscription to Morley (1602), with mottoes in Latin, Italian, Spanish, and French. At Northleach, Gloucestershire, a brass to William Lawnder (1530), has an inscription in Latin and English. There are many inscriptions to almost every trade and profession, to infants, to widows, spinsters, bachelors, brothers and sisters, and all the family. Some of the epitaphs are amusing, some sad, some expressing humility, some humorous, some pathetic – many archaic in language, difficult to read. A collection of these would make an interesting comment on our ancestors' attitude to the passing from this world to the next.

An attractive late brass occurs at Sonning, Berkshire, to Lord Stowell who died in 1836 in his ninety-first year. This 19th-century brass with coat-of-arms and inscription is typical of its date – reminiscent of posters, hand-bills, and painted signs, and hatchments in particular.

PALIMPSESTS

Many brasses are known as palimpsests (Greek: *Palin*, again and *Psestos*, scraped). This term was originally used of manuscripts written on parchment when the writers had erased the first version and written over it. In brasses too, when the original design was erased and a new one superimposed, this was also called a palimpsest, or when the brass was turned over and engraved again on the other side. Sometimes brasses are converted or adapted, cut down and re-engraved and in a few rare instances the brass has been appropriated for someone else. All these come under the heading of palimpsests – incorrectly so, but it has now been accepted.

There are numerous instances of palimpsests in this country as well as a few on the Continent, mostly in the Low Countries. Some palimpsests are obvious – when on the obverse the original work has not been entirely removed. Appropriated brasses, too, are sometimes easy to notice. John Wyborne, at Ticehurst, Sussex (1503) is much larger than his two wives. The brass was originally to a knight of about 1380! Those that have been engraved on the back are by far the most numerous and difficult to detect, unless for some reason they have to be lifted up, or have become loose. If a brass design is of the mid-15th-century or later and is on a thick plate, the odds are that it is a palimpsest. Brass of this date was thin in comparison with the very early plates.

The charming little church of Waterperry, in Oxfordshire, has a most valuable palimpsest. This church is well worth a visit, but it is necessary first to make sure that it will be open. There are many fascinating items of archaeological interest, outside as well as inside. In the churchyard is a tall cross with original 14th-century shaft and pedestal. Inside there are the remains of a Saxon arch. On the north wall of the chancel are two fine carved heads of 13th-century date. There is an effigy of a cross-legged knight under a simple ogee canopy of the first half of the 14th-century (Fitzroy family). On the floor are medieval paving tiles. The ancient glass in three 13th-century lancet windows is dated about 1220.

The church contains three brasses. The palimpsest brass represents Walter Curson and his wife (1527). The head and shoulders of the man have been replaced by a new head and shoulders, representing him as bareheaded with long hair and a collar of mail, while a Vandyke beard has been added. Two oblong besagues which covered the armpits have been worked over to represent pauldrons and these are surmounted with reinforcements. The breast-plate has received the addition of three demi-placcates, and gussets of mail have been added to the insteps. The skirt of taces has been adapted to represent chain-mail, and the two tassets that have been added still show the taces. The feet have been altered; originally they were long pointed sabatons, now they appear as round-toed, but the original long pointed toes still remain. The man has two pairs of feet!

The wife has been cut in two below the waist (on the reverse is a fine half-figure of a lady *c.* 1440). The lower half is a 15th-century figure with a little dog with its collar and bells. The upper half displays a pedimental head-dress with ornamental lappets. The gown is cut square at the neck and has loose sleeves with fur cuffs. The undergarment shows ribbed sleeves and embroidered neck and the lady wears an ornamental girdle from which hangs a pomander on a chain. Beneath Curson are his eight sons, and beneath his wife were (now missing) their seven daughters. The whole is surrounded by a marginal inscription, each word of which is separated by a skull and crossbones.

Walter Curson died in 1527 and was buried in the church of Austin Friars which occupied the site of Wadham College, Oxford. At the Dissolution, in 1539, the brass was removed to Waterperry. It is not quite certain to whom the original was dedicated, but from all available data and much research it is thought to be to one Simon Camp who died about the middle of the 15th-century. The reverse of the marginal inscription has a deeply-cut inscription to 'Simon Kamp'.*

*For further information see the handbook on Waterperry church.

Rubbings should always be made of a palimpsest when the opportunity presents itself. Sometimes electro-type casts are made and preserved in the church or local museum. At Marsworth, in Buckinghamshire, there are some interesting palimpsests of the brasses of the West family. These were originally Flemish brasses and have inscriptions in Flemish. Five other pieces of this brass are at Walkern, Hertfordshire. The casts are in Aylesbury museum. The brass of Thomas Cod, Rochester (1465) shows both sides *almost* identical. For some reason the obverse was not considered correct and it was re-engraved on the reverse with only slight modifications. The brass of Margaret Bulstrode at Hedgerley, Buckinghamshire (1540) came loose and it was found that the inscription on the reverse was about two centuries older – to Thomas de Totyngtone (*c.* 1312). He was abbot of St Edmund's Bury, which monastery was dissolved during the Dissolution by Henry VIII (1536-9). Margaret's brass is dated 1540, so no time had been lost in disposing of the brass to a craftsman's workshop for re-use.

By assembling rubbings of palimpsests it is possible to piece together various brasses widely dispersed, and this suggests that originally the particular brass was sold to a central workshop which re-used the pieces for clients far apart.

An interesting Berkshire palimpsest is that at Denchworth, Bucks (1562). On the obverse is an inscription to W. Hyde (1562), and on the reverse an inscription recording the laying of the foundation stone of Bisham Abbey by Edward III in 1333. Brasses taken up from their slabs were not always re-employed as memorials. Some have been used for diverse purposes. The British Museum has two circular brasses, on the reverse of which mathematical instruments are engraved. The obverse has effigies of priests. Brasses have been melted down to make church bells (as at Meopham), to mend a plough, to make a weather-vane and to act as a foot-scraper; another was used as a poker for a church stove. Some were melted down to make a chandelier and another one was commandeered by workmen for a frying-pan!

As time passes doubtless more and more palimpsests will come to light. Whenever anyone sees a brass loose in a church it should be reported to the incumbent or, better still, write to the Monumental Brass Society, who will see that it is carefully replaced. First, however, make sure that it is a palimpsest, or valuable information may be lost by quick replacement of the brass by local workmen who, unaware of the value of the reverse engraving, would thus conceal it for a long time to come. There are over 200 palimpsests in the U.K.; probably many more will come to light in the future.

247

248

247. **THOMAS PAYNE AND WIFE ELIZABETH** 1528, Hutton, Somerset.
Part of brass in which their sons and daughters are all kneeling. Male
effigy 12¾″ high. Note the semi-italic inscription.

248. **JOHN SMITH** 1370, Brightwell Baldwin, Oxon.
A very early inscription, recently restored (21″ wide). (See page 90.)

249. Brass of HUMPHRIE OKER, 1538, WIFE ISABEL and thirteen children, Okeover, Staffs. Adapted from the brass of William Lord Zouch and two wives, Alice and Elizabeth, Okeover, Staffs, 1447. The front of Zouch was altered for Humphrie's tabard, the effigy of Alice was left for Isabel without alteration but the effigy of the second wife Elizabeth was reversed and the children engraved on this side. Shields were altered and additions made and the marginal inscriptions reversed and engraved to suit. Depth of brass 108″.

250. The original brass of WILLIAM LORD ZOUCH and two wives ALICE AND ELIZABETH, Okeover, Staffs, 1447. About the middle of the 19th century the brass was stolen and broken up for melting. These fragments, 55 in all were reassembled and placed on a board in the church at the end of the last century. The dark areas on Elizabeth's dress are repairs as also are the dark shields.

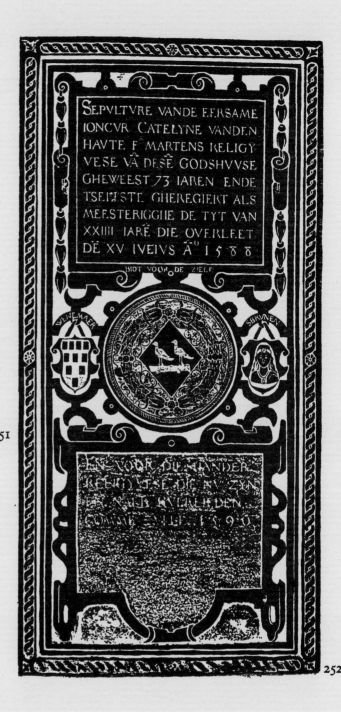

251. ROGER LEGH and six sons 1506, Macclesfield, Cheshire.
Wife Elizabeth and seven daughters (lost). In the rectangular design is
Pope St Gregory in triple Tiara and under is a promise of an indulgence
of "XVI thousand years and XXVI days" for "V pater nost' & V dues
and a cred". Depth of brass 10½".

252. JAMES COTREL 1595, York Minster.
Another portrait brass. A very good, well spaced inscription, excellently
designed. Depth of brass 33".

252A. CATELYNE VAN DEN HAUTE 1588, Ghent.
This inscription illustrates the use of both stone and brass on one
memorial. The whole design is of stone except the round plate in the
middle, which is of brass. This shows a wreath and a lozenge with
Catelyne's armorial bearings. The arms of William Wenemaer and
wife are also displayed – they were the founders of the almshouse in
which the memorial was placed.

253. SIR JOHN RATCLIF AND ALICE HIS WIFE 1527, Crosthwaite, Cumberland.

A typical stereotyped inscription in English of the 16th century. It is strange that the lady's head is well drawn but that of Sir John needs no comment. Effigies 23″.

254. JANE, LADY BRAY 1558, Eaton Bray, Beds.
With one son and ten daughters and lozenge with arms either side.
This is clearly an example of dual craftsmanship. The portrait portion
has excellence but the shields, lower portions of figures and desk are
inferior.

P

255. Chalice on a body. Fragment of a large brass. Continental 15th century. A very bold crisp conception. Palimpsest of brass of Nicholas West, 1586, Marsworth, Bucks. Depth of part shown 13″. See pp. 91-92.

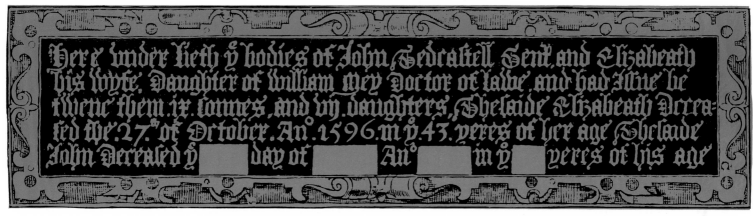

256

256A

256. JOHN TEDCASTELL AND WIFE ELIZABETH 1596, Barking, Essex. 28½″ long. Inscription from a brass depicting John, Elizabeth and children. John's date of death was not recorded on the brass. The blanks enhance the beauty of the design! The letters of the inscription are standing in relief.

256A. Inscription of GEOFFREY KIDWELLY 1483, Little Wittenham, Berks. This inscription is in raised lettering but it is not of any particular skill. It is also upside down to the effigy. Ins. 16″ wide.

257

257. BISHOP JOHN ADVANTAGE. Virgin and Child, the Bishop and Saint John, Amiens, 1456.
One of the few French brasses recorded by Creeny. This type of composition is derived from Flemish and Italian paintings of the 15th century. It is not suitable for a brass memorial. It would have been better if used as a printing plate for a book. The French inscription – clear enough but not well spaced. Notice the close border on the right hand side.

258. Inscription to WILLIAM SHAKESPEARE, died 1616. Stratford on Avon. Engraved 1624.

IVDICIO PYLIVM GENIO SOCRATEM ARTE MARONEM
TERRA TEGIT POPVLVS MÆRET OIYMPVS HABET

STAY PASSENGER WHY GOEST THOV BY SO FAST?
READ IF THOV CANST, WHOM ENVIOVS DEATH HATH PLAST
WITH IN THIS MONVMENT SHAKSPEARE: WITH WHOME
QVICK NATVRE DIDE: WHOSE NAME, DOTH DECK Ꙟ TOMBE
FAR MORE TEN COST: SIEH ALL Ꙟ HE HATH WRITT
LEAVES LIVING ART BVT PAGE, TO SERVE HIS WITT.

OBIT ANO DO 1616
ÆTATIS 53 DIE 23AP

258

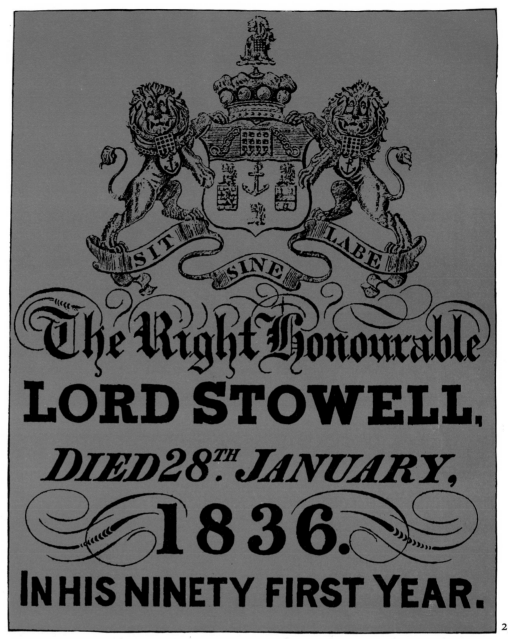

259. LORD STOWELL 1836, Sonning, Berks.
An attractive brass memorial of the first half of the 19th century. The mixing of various types of lettering is similar to that found on billposters and stage coaches of similar date. Lord Stowell (born William Scott), friend of Dr Johnson and a great authority on maritime law. Size of brass 29″ x 24″.

260. JOHN FAGE snr. 1400, Roxton, Beds. 23″ wide.

Orate pro aia Johis ffage senioris de Chalnesterne qui obijt die
Sabbati aut festum Natinitatis sancti Johis Bapte anno dm̄i
mill̄mo CCCC cuius anime propicietur deus — Amen

261

ANNO AB INCARNACIONE DNI M CC XLI
VIII KE MAII DEDICATA EST HEC ECCIA
ET HOC ALTARE CONSECRATVM IN HO
NORE SCI OSWALDI REGIS ET MARTI
RIS A VENERABILI PATRE DOMINO
HVGONE DE PATISHVL COVENTRENSI
EPISCOPO.

262

261. Gilded brass plate. Regensburg 1189. Recording consecration of an altar. The earliest recorded brass in Europe. See p. 89.

262. Ashbourne, Derbyshire. Inscription of dedication and consecration of the church by Hugh de Pateshull, Bishop of Coventry in 1241. Reproduced from the *Gentleman's Magazine*, September 1772. In the October issue of 1772, the translation is given as follows: 'In the year from the Incarnation of Our Lord 1241, May 8, this Church was dedicated and this altar consecrated to the honour of Saint Oswald King and Martyr, by the venerable Father, Sir Hugh de Patishul, Bishop of Coventry'. *The woodcut illustration may not be entirely correct in its rendering.* – H.T.

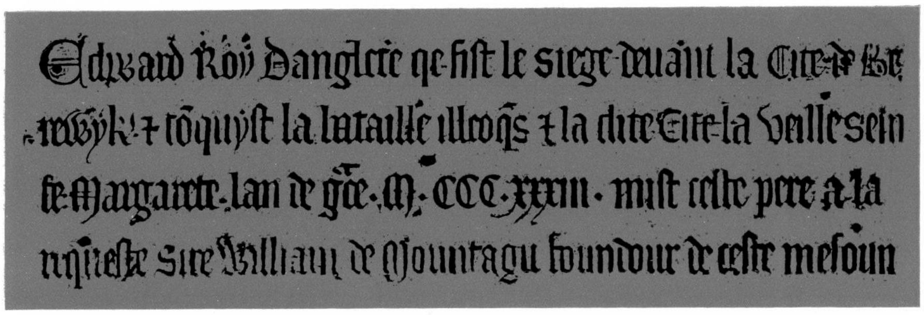

263

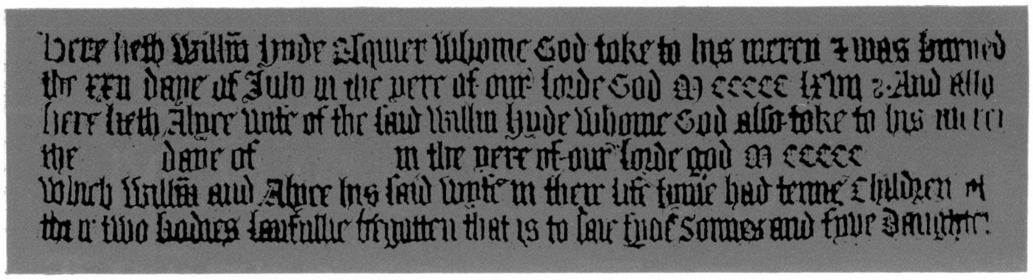

264

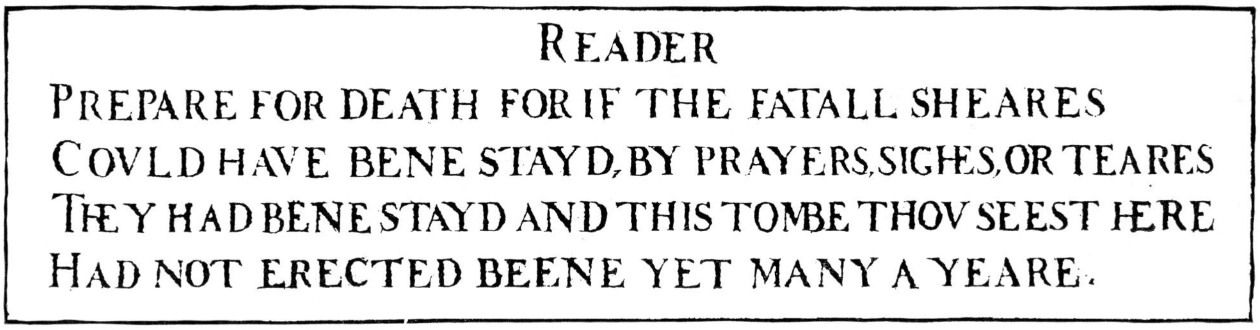

READER

PREPARE FOR DEATH FOR IF THE FATALL SHEARES
COVLD HAVE BENE STAYD, BY PRAYERS, SIGHES, OR TEARES
THEY HAD BENE STAYD AND THIS TOMBE THOV SEEST HERE
HAD NOT ERECTED BEENE YET MANY A YEARE.

264A

263. Records the laying of the foundation stone of Bisham Abbey, Berks, 1333. The Norman French inscription is translated as follows: 'Edward, King of England, laid siege to the City of Berwick and conquered in battle the said city, the eve of Saint Margaret, the year of grace 1333, laid this stone at the request of Sir William de Mountagu, founder of this house.' Reverse side used for plate 264. See p. 89.

264. WILLIAM HYDE 1562, Denchworth, Berks.
This inscription appears on reverse of 263. William Hyde is in armour with wife and 12 sons and 8 daughters. See plate 148.

264A. LADY BROOKE 1600, Kirby Moorside, N.R. Yorks. An interesting stone inscription. Ins. 21″ wide.

CHAPTER SEVENTEEN

Distribution of Brasses

266

266. Devil-bird, from the brass of BOUCHARD and
JOHN VON MUL 1317-50 Lübeck.

266A

266A. From the brass of JOHN LUNEBORCH 1474-5,
Lübeck.

, A LOST BRASS. SIR MILES DE STAPLETON
4 AND WIFE JOAN, once at Ingham, Norfolk and
mpression at the British Museum.
s of exquisite charm. The elongated figures and
naïve quality of the drawing establishes this brass
ne of outstanding quality.

Aᴛ ᴀ rough estimate, based on Mill Stephenson's *List of Monumental
Brasses in the British Isles*, there are approximately 9,500 brasses
in these islands, *including inscriptions*. Mill Stephenson's list is most
reliable, giving names, dates and places. There is not much chance that this
total will change, unless another brass or two should be discovered in an
unexpected place or, on the other hand, some should get lost through becoming
loose or through theft or damage by enemy action.

In England, Kent heads the list with over 700 brasses. Norfolk is second
with about 650 and Essex third with about 450. Oxfordshire, Suffolk, and
Hertfordshire top the 300 mark. There are over 200 in Surrey, Berkshire,
Middlesex, Buckinghamshire, Yorkshire and Northamptonshire. Bedfordshire,
Sussex, Cambridgeshire, Hampshire, Gloucestershire and Lincolnshire
each have 150 to 200. The other counties vary, with Northumberland falling
below ten and Westmorland reaching two dozen. This is also true of Scotland
(six), of Ireland (five), and the Isle of Man (three). The Isle of Wight is included
in Hampshire's list.

Local conditions affected the distribution of brasses. Where there was
more money available, brasses were used in preference to local stone, which
was less durable. East Anglia, the Home Counties and south-eastern counties
have the most brasses. They were the wealthier areas and could afford brass
memorials. As local prosperity attracted more people, they in turn would
demand more and better memorials. Gloucestershire, Yorkshire and Northamptonshire were large and prosperous counties – the first because of its
flourishing wool trade. Northamptonshire was the home of many rich gentry
and it was also a prosperous farming region. Where local stone was available
there is a marked increase in the number of incised slabs used as memorials,
such as in Leicestershire. Scotland suffered the loss of a considerable number
of brasses in the Middle Ages. Some large and elaborate brasses sometimes
occur in counties where the total is not high. This is explained by the fact
that some wealthy individual lived in what was otherwise a poorer area.

The effigies on brasses are usually represented either in a recumbent,
standing or kneeling position. The figures are often full front view or three-
quarter. Only one or two side views are known and back views never. The
hands are usually raised in front of the breast in the act of praying; sometimes
– not often – crossed over the breast. Some of the eastern counties show
brasses of women with their hands apart, palms outward, held breast high.
A few brasses show the husband holding his wife's hand. Priests are easily
recognized by the tonsure – many of these early brasses were demi-effigies.
Inscriptions appear on a vast number of effigies and there are also considerable numbers of inscriptions by themselves.

CONTINENTAL BRASSES

The continental total is less than one-tenth of the total in these islands.
Germany and the Low Countries have several hundreds, France almost
none; Spain, Portugal, and Italy a few. That there were large numbers on
the continent is certain. The Calvinists in the mid-sixties of the 16th-century,
and the French spoliators at the end of the 18th-century accounted for the
loss of vast numbers. Brasses are found in Switzerland, Finland, Poland,
Denmark, Sweden, and in small numbers in southern Europe.

The average European preferred stone-incised slabs, mainly as a matter
of tradition – not as a matter of cost, availability, or for aesthetic reasons.

Q

The search for brasses on the Continent reveals a few hitherto unknown
– more may yet be found. See Continental list at end.

COST OF BRASSES

We can obtain an idea of the approximate cost of brasses from existing
records. A few wills are extant by which certain memorials can be accurately
identified. Between 1465 and 1538 we find that in forty instances money was
left for brass memorials: twenty-seven ranged from £1 to £2 13s. 4d.,
sixteen were less than £1 13s. 4d.! It appears, however, that the earlier
brasses were more costly than the later ones, probably because for the early
brasses both a first-class artist was employed to design them and a first-class
craftsman to incise them. The later brasses were the products of men engaged on other works – not specialists as were the early craftsmen – and so
were less costly to purchase. In the will of Sir Thomas Ughtred (1398) £10
was left for a marble stone to be inlaid with two images in latten of his
father and mother and placed over their tomb at Catten, Yorkshire.

Sir John de St Quentin, in his will (1397) left 20 marks for a marble stone
to be placed over himself and his two wives, with three images of latten on it.

Thomas Graa left 100/- for a latten memorial for himself and his wife
Maud. Lady Manley left 20 marks in 1438 for a marble stone with her
portraiture thereon in copper and latten gilt. In 1509 Sir Thomas Marriot
directed the sum of 20/- or thereabouts to be expended on his tombstone,
inlaid with brass. These examples are taken from Haines, who lists a
few more and doubtless others could be found if a search were made, but it
is of small importance in the history of brasses. The brass of Duncan Liddel
(1613), measuring 5 ft 5 in by 2 ft 11 in, engraved at Antwerp, cost a total of
£121 (metal £31 0s. 6d., engraving £53, transport to Aberdeen £37 0s 6d.,
and there was also a bounty of salmon £3).

The cost of colouring brasses with enamel was an expensive item and
could only be for those with ample funds. In 1449 John Massingham was
paid £9 6s. 8d. for carving an image of the Virgin (Eton church), and Robert
Hickling was paid £6 13s. 4d. for colouring it.

SIGNED BRASSES

Most of the actual designers of brasses are unknown to us. We cannot
identify them as belonging to the school of a known master, because we
know only a few names of such. The brasses speak for themselves; close
study of them tells us more than any book. The mere handful of names that
are known are not of the early best period. I am doubtful regarding local
'schools of brasses' for reasons given earlier.

The brass of Sir John and Lady Creke at Westley Waterless (1325) has
a mark of the artist on the figure of Lady Creke. This consists of the letter N
reversed (И); above this is a mallet, on the left is a half-moon, and on the
right a star. (In Rheims Cathedral there are mason's marks in the form of a
crescent on some of the sculptural figures). A similar mark or design without
the letter is on a seal of a deed of Edward I's reign. The letter N in reverse
again appears on the canopy of the brass of Lord Camoys at Trotton (1419).
Metal smiths would have been responsible for a number of brasses, but here
again one is confronted with the same difficulty: even if we knew some of
their names, there is little or no evidence of which individual was responsible
for a certain brass or series of brasses. There are numerous signed inscriptions
on Yorkshire brasses of the 17th century. This is the best evidence.

The evidence of certain details common to sculptural effigies in either
metal, wood, or stone does not by any means prove conclusively that the same
craftsman was also responsible for brasses with similar details. These details
are largely impersonal, as was medieval art as a whole, and it is chiefly by
personal characteristics in the use of a particular medium that one can
trace the individual. As we know, medieval craftsmen worked from pattern

books which were available to all, so it is dangerous to assume that a craftsman working in a certain medium is the same one working in another simply because identical details appear in both mediums. Out of all the names of various architects and craftsmen known to us from the 14th century, only three are possible candidates for inclusion as designers of brasses. These are:

1. Henry Yevele, 1353-1400, a very famous London architect (mason), was responsible for designing the nave of Canterbury Cathedral, Westminster Hall, and other buildings. He was described as a 'latoner'.
2. Stephen Lote, 1381-1417, who worked under Yevele as an architect, was also described as a latoner.
3. John Orchard, 1376-95, described as a latoner, worked on the tomb of Queen Philippa of Hainault in Westminster Abbey.

Of 15th-century date there are:

1. William Hyndely, 1466-1505, who lived in York. His will states that he worked in brass.
2. John Forster, 1433-95, was a mason working in Suffolk and probably specializing in brass design.
3. John Wastell, 1485-1515, was responsible for the vaulting in Peterborough Cathedral and in the chapel of King's College, Cambridge. He also worked in metals.
4. Henry Harpur, 1510-?, made the brass image at St Mary's church, All Hallows, Chesterfield.

Robert Haydock was an artist who, we know, designed several brasses. Two are rectangular plates in Queen's College, Oxford: H. Robinson and H. Airay (both 1616) and another at Tingewick, Buckinghamshire of Erasmus Williams (1608); also the Sparke brass at Bletchley (1616).

Brayser of Norwich, an East Anglian engraver, may have produced several brasses in the Norwich area during the second quarter of the 16th-century.

A later brass to Sir Edward Filmer and family at East Sutton, Kent (1629) is signed by E. Marshall. The brothers Mann made some brasses in Yorkshire. Gerard Johnson made brasses in London (1567-1612), as did E. Evesham (1510-1624). The brass of Dorothy Williams at Pimperne, Dorset (1694) is signed 'Edmund Culpeper fecit'. Hilliger, a German, engraved designs by Gotting. Dürer designed for Vischer senior. Vischer the younger copied parts of Dürer woodcuts for use on brasses, such as that of Cardinal Frederick at Cracow (1510). Jacques de Gerines (died 1463), who designed various tombs, also probably designed brasses. It is clear that much more research is needed in an attempt to reveal the names of designers of the best brasses, as well as the sources of their inspiration.

A number of inscriptions also are signed by the engraver (see County Lists, page 111).

DESTRUCTION AND PRESERVATION

The dissolution of the monasteries from 1536-9 caused almost all monastic buildings with an income of less than £200 per annum to be closed. Valuable possessions which had adorned the buildings passed directly or indirectly into the outstretched hands of King Henry VIII. Shrines were destroyed, gold and valuable metals were taken away along with precious jewels that adorned many of the ornaments.

Brasses were taken up in addition to other useful materials, leaving the monasteries empty and devastated. Many of the buildings fell into disuse and soon became a mass of ruins. In churches and other edifices that were left intact, almost all the figures of saints and similar effigies in sculptural form, as well as stained-glass windows, were smashed or the heads were knocked off the effigies. Only a few escaped. A small number of beautifully illuminated service books – easier to hide – were preserved. The Dissolution was responsible for the ruin of a greater number of monumental brasses than was Oliver Cromwell's iconoclasm about 120 years later.

The commissioners of Edward VI caused additional destruction of brasses. Queen Elizabeth did not approve of destroying monuments and ordered many effigies to be restored, for she was interested in monumental works of art of earlier ages. It is recorded that she visited the small church at Aldworth in Berkshire to see the famous effigies of the de la Beche family. There are six of 13th-century date, known locally as 'the six giants'.

Theft and lack of attention in the fixing of loose portions of brasses were responsible for the further loss of a considerable number over the centuries. Even today we are not without blame, for loose plates are not fastened down and some are covered over with pews or other heavy church furniture. A few are situated under pulpits, and every time such brasses are rubbed, the heavy pulpit is dragged backwards and forwards, scratching the surfaces beneath. Others are concealed by the church organ. The Ansty brass at Stow-cum-Quy in Cambridgeshire was a recent case of the former treatment and an inscription at Cookham, Berkshire, an example of the latter which has now been rectified; the brass had been under the organ for about a hundred years and another was partly concealed by a heavy partition.

Some brasses are allowed to become corroded with verdigris. (The copper in the brass causes this corrosion). Others are being slowly worn away by well-meaning but misguided church polishers who keep them 'bright and shiny'. Most brasses in prominent places where they are liable to be walked on by the public are covered by carpets or rugs, but there are *still a number that are subject to wear by the passing of feet on their unprotected surfaces.*

It is not advisable to use carpets or rugs that let through grains of grit off people's shoes. A thick layer of felt placed between the brass and the top carpet is the best protection. Rubber mats make the brass 'sweat' and this causes corrosion on the surface of the brass.

There are still a few brasses or fragments locked in cupboards in the churches. One such piece was used as a poker for the church coal stove! The preservation of empty casements, too, is of great value to the archaeologist, for these contain the indent of brasses long since lost and much valuable information can be gained from a study of them. Casements exist which once held cross-legged knights of the late 13th-century, as well as bishops – two, for instance, at Salisbury, Bishop Bingham (c. 1247) and his successor Bishop William of York (c. 1256). Some casements are in excellent condition and should certainly be preserved, but others are almost beyond recognition, such as the one in St. Paul's church, Bedford, which dates from 1208.

In St Alban's Abbey over 270 empty casements remain today: there are a dozen with their original brasses in position! France, too, suffered great destruction during the Revolution, when innumerable brasses were melted down and the casements destroyed.

The two World Wars were responsible for the loss of a number of continental brasses. At Lübeck the large Clinghenberg brass (1356) and the Bercke brass (1521) were lost in the last war. Flemish brasses disappeared during the 1914-18 war. At Nieuport great destruction took place. London, too, suffered during the wars. Hitler's blitz accounted for the loss of several good brasses.

A few brasses of genuine ancestors have been restored – more often in the 17th and 18th centuries. A good example is that at Pluckley, Kent, of John Dering, in armour with inscription (1517).

Fortunately large collections of rubbings are preserved, some of which record lost brasses and are therefore of great value. Collections of incised stone slabs, however, are not numerous. These are just as important as the incised brass, and it is hoped that the omission will be remedied in the near future.

CHAPTER EIGHTEEN

Brass Rubbings and Reproductions

– upon the which, I trust,
Shall witness live in brass.

SHAKESPEARE, Henry V

EARLY RUBBINGS

A PAINTING by a Dutch artist of the 17th-century, Van der Vliet, shows children rubbing incised slabs. This was once thought to be the earliest record of rubbings being made from an incised memorial stone or plate! Far from this being the case, however, the simple technique of making rubbings from incised stones or metal plates dates from before the Christian era. In both China and Japan this method was used many centuries BC. According to Du Halde, a learned Jesuit priest of the 18th-century who travelled in China, the method of making rubbings was employed in the reign of Wu Wang about 1120 BC. He quotes from a Chinese manuscript of that date. 'As the stone me (Chinese for 'blacking') which is used to blacken the engraved characters can never become white, so a heart blackened by vices will always retain its blackness.' (*The Invention of Printing. T. L. de Vinne.*)

Inscriptions were incised on bronze long before stone (Ref. Peake 1935, citing Laufer and Yetts). The practice of cutting texts of Confucian classics dates from AD 175. 'Exact copies' were made – *these were rubbings.* Portions of a book of rubbings (Ou-yang Hsün AD 557-641) cut and mounted on leaves were found at Tun-huang.

The use of stones (similar to the lithographic lime stone) for preserving calligraphy as well as for printing autographs of famous men was a common practice.

Paper was invented in China about AD 105 though this is rather an arbitrary date. The oldest printed book in the world in existence is 'The Diamond of Sūtra' found in a Chinese temple and is dated AD 868. Johann Gutenberg or Peter Schoeffer invented the movable type faces in Europe in 1454.

The classics of the T'ang dynasty (AD 836-841) were cut on stone. The dynasty appointed certain officers whose duties were to make rubbings and issue them as authorised rubbings from the stone inscriptions. Part of these ancient stone inscriptions exists to-day. (*The Invention of Printing in China and its spread Westwards. Thomas F. Carter 1925.*)

Rubbings of ancient tomb inscriptions in Japan
In Japan, when an important person was buried, a grave stone or grave plate (Boshi, or if made of copper Boshi dōban) was incised with an inscription (Boshimei) in exactly the same manner as a European brass incised inscription and buried in the grave. It is for this latter reason that a few of these ancient funeral plates survive to-day. The number with epitaphs from the Asuka (AD 552-710) and Nara (AD 710-794) is fourteen altogether. Brief details of two of the most ancient are as follows:

1. Plate engraved with inscription of Senshi Ôgo. Asuka period bronze. Length 29.5 cm. Width 7 cm. (Mitsui Takanaru Tokyo). There are 162 characters in four vertical lines on obverse and reverse sides. The inscription is in formal script with some interspersion of Gyō (semi cursive script). The oldest existing grave plate in Japan dates in correspondence with AD 668 (see plate 268).

   The inscription states that man and wife were buried in the same tomb and the tombs of the brothers were built side by side. (This gives some idea of the funeral customs at that time). Ref. Kokuhō. *National Treasures of Japan.*

2. Plate engraved with epitaph of Ono-no-Emishi. Asuka period. Gilt-bronze. Length 58.8 cm. Width 6 cm. AD 667. Inscription gives full name and information in official Japanese chronicles. (His official rank etc).

(*There is a vast number of funeral inscriptions in other Asian countries – largely on stone. Their number is legion.*)

The Chinese Method of Making Rubbings

A sheet of thin tough paper is moistened and laid on the inscription. With a stiff brush the paper is forced into the incised lines. When the paper is dry a pad of silk is dipped in sized ink and passed lightly but evenly over the surface. When peeled off it is found to be imprinted with a perfect durable impression of the inscription – white on a black ground – the text is not reversed. (Thomas F. Carter 1925).

The Chinese and Japanese were far more advanced and civilized than our western civilizations in the early centuries. Printing from inked blocks to take impressions did not take place until the Middle Ages in Europe when patterns and designs were printed on materials. Printing as we know was a matter of demand, not a fortunate discovery. The ancient Egyptian printed on fabrics several centuries BC.

FORMING A COLLECTION

The study of monumental effigies as a whole sheds much light on the changing fashions of medieval art. This is reflected to a less extent in brasses, which however, give an excellent picture of the armour, costumes, and vestments worn by the aristocracy, the rich, the poor, ecclesiastics, professors, merchants, tradesmen, yeomen, mayors and aldermen, servants and others. The various types of ladies' head-dress worn through the 'brass era' make quite a remarkable record. Many brasses commemorate husband, wife and children also. The devices of heraldry, the development of armour and its decline, the history of the families represented are a fascinating study. Most of the brasses have dated inscriptions which open a field for further investigation, such as the type of lettering used and the language and its content – all matters of great interest, and each one a specialized study in itself.

Other subjects depicted are crosses, canopies, chalices, hearts, shrouds, coats-of-arms, tradesmen's marks, and various religious concepts such as Resurrection, Annunciation and Trinity – constituting a most formidable list.

In forming a collection it is best to adhere to an organized plan, bearing in mind the locality in which you live. If you desire to make rubbings of a mixed character rather than of one particular subject the task is easier, because in a limited area there may be several brasses of similar date and design, some of which will be in better condition than others, more suitable in size for your purpose and more convenient to rub. Therefore try to inspect the brasses before making an appointment to take rubbings. There are several good books available on the subject with county lists and illustrations (see Bibliography, page 12 and County List in this book). Another source which may be of great assistance is the local archaeological society or history society. Either of these, or your local county museum, will in all probability have a collection of rubbings of the county and permission can usually be obtained to view them. In addition there are large collections in the Victoria and Albert Museum, the British Museum, the Ashmolean in Oxford, the Society of Antiquaries in London and the Museum of Archaeology at Cambridge and numerous institutions elsewhere.

266B. CHINESE DRAGON, second century AD, Han Period.
Discovered in tomb wall, near Yi-Chou, Southern Shantung.

Obtaining permission to make rubbings
The next step is to obtain permission from the incumbents of the churches in which the brasses are situated. *It is absolutely essential to do this.* Remember that monumental brasses are funeral memorials, the church is the house of God, and the vicar is in charge and must be approached for his permission. Sometimes a fee is requested, which goes towards the maintenance of the fabric of the church, and nobody should object to giving a reasonable donation. When writing to the vicar you should enclose a stamped addressed postcard for reply, and when you go to make your rubbings take the card with you – the vicar may be away and the churchwarden may ask to see your written permission. If the living should be vacant, write to the churchwarden, and if you want to know the position of the brass – on the floor or a mural – ask for this information when you write. Mill Stephenson's *List of Monumental Brasses in the British Isles* gives the position of most of the brasses in the churches.

Sometimes a ladder is required for high mural brasses. This is usually available in churches where permission to rub is granted. Some brasses are not easily accessible, some are under large heavy carpets, some on top of altar tombs, some under pews, some under glass and locked in the frame, others behind canopied monuments.

A few brasses will be found in museums, cathedrals, and one or two in private hands, and there are a few outside the churches – on doors, walls or on slabs in cemeteries. From the brasses you contemplate choose those with the highest artistic merits rather than those of average archaeological interest, for your rubbings will then give you greater pleasure to look at from time to time and will help you to extend your aesthetic appreciation and give you a better understanding of medieval art and craftsmanship.

Equipment for making heel-ball rubbings
The equipment is simple – a large roll of suitable white paper, black heel-ball of the correct quality (as supplied by the Monumental Brass Society), some Scotch adhesive tape, some gum adhesive tape, a duster, a soft hand-brush, and a pair of scissors, while a few paper-weights are useful additions. A small soft cushion for kneeling when rubbing is usually available in the church.

'POSITIVE' RUBBINGS
You have the choice of making a positive or a negative rubbing. For the former, you require a roll of thin black paper and the 'gold' rubber now available for this purpose.* The black paper must not be too smooth otherwise your finished rubbing will look bitty owing to lack of 'tooth' on the paper. The tooth insures an even texture of the gold rubber deposit.

The gold rubber supplied commercially is perhaps a little too soft for certain fine work. To make a harder composition add some of the finest gold dust (Dutch metal) and a little shellac. Melt this together with the gold rubber and mix thoroughly as described for making black heel-ball composition. You can make a satisfactory gold composition if you use some large white or yellow wax crayons and melt them with shellac and finest gold dust. Manufacturers supply the latter in various tones – dull gold, bronze, light gold, etc. Always ask for the *finest* ground Dutch metal gold dust.† Experiment will prove the best way to determine the right quantity of the various items.

'NEGATIVE' RUBBINGS
Paper for Black Rubbings. This should be thin and strong with a fine but not smooth 'tooth'. If too thin the paper will tear and will be semi-transparent and lack whiteness. The detail paper obtained from artists' suppliers is satisfactory but is a little too hard for the best rubbings, and is inclined to pucker

Phillips & Page Ltd., 50 Kensington Church Street, W.8.

†Obtainable from G. M. Whiley Ltd., Whitfield Street, London W.1; Hopkins Purvis & Son, 20 Greek Street, London W.1, and elsewhere.

during the process of rubbing. Make sure that your paper is bone dry and is large enough for the job in hand. Most of these papers can be bought in various widths up to 60 in. The author has found a certain type of white lining paper the best.* Obtainable from some art shops and stationers, it is whiter than detail paper, softer and has a very fine 'tooth'.

Heel-ball for Brass Rubbings. It is essential for this to be of the correct type. Bought from the average shop, it is often too soft and lacks the blackness essential to a first-class rubbing. The Monumental Brass Society has prepared a formula for the best rubbing-ball, and prepared wax rubbers can be bought from a firm in London.† For those who prefer a matt black result, melt the MBS wax and add a little lamp black. Mix it well and cool down *slowly*, otherwise the cake will split. The author prefers to make his own rubbing wax and sometimes uses two or three different kinds on one rubbing. In cold weather use a softer wax, in hot weather a soft wax will become warm from use and make a poor rubbing, so always take the correct wax with you. If one wishes to rub an incised stone slab this requires a special technique and in the author's experience a slightly different wax rubber, though this may be a personal preference. For those who wish to make their own heel-ball wax the following ingredients are necessary:

> Russian tallow
> Beeswax
> Shellac: a natural resin, very hard but
>   easily melted by heat
> Household soap (very little)
> Lampblack

The addition of shellac and lampblack in greater quantities will ensure a harder and blacker wax heel-ball. The mixing quantities are largely a matter of experience. Melt the tallow, the beeswax and a *little* soap slowly in a tin, then add the shellac and lampblack and keep in a liquid form over the fire. Great care must be taken not to spill or let a flame near the composition. Mix well and when thoroughly melted and mixed pour into pre-heated china egg-cups, small coffee cups or similar utensils. Something slightly larger than the conventional egg-cup is desirable. This makes an excellently shaped cake of rubbing wax suitable for large rubbings. For smaller pieces, pour the mixture into an open 2 oz rectangular tobacco tin, and when cold cut it into strips. These are suitable for difficult corners when rubbing. Never use a plastic container – the hot wax will melt it – and never cool the wax composition quickly, for the centre will be the last part to cool off and as the composition shrinks a hollow or split will develop in the middle.

THE TECHNIQUE OF RUBBING

An experienced person will have developed his or her own method of rubbing, but for the beginner the following technique is suggested:

First thoroughly brush the face of the brass with a soft brush to remove all loose dirt. If the brass has been under a carpet or is in a position where people have walked, there are bound to be fine particles of grit or dirt on it, and if this is not removed it will ruin the rubbing. The particles of grit will tear your paper during the process of rubbing and will embed themselves in the rubbing wax and cause further damage to the paper as well as scratching the brass itself.

Now take a good look at the brass, try to memorize it for general shape and make a note of any loose or protecting parts. Sometimes the pins holding the brass in position project, or one of the plates of the brass projects, leaving an edge. If you rub over these you may tear your paper. If you have a small illustration of the brass keep it by you as you work.

*Raysol household paper. Winsor & Newton's fine detail paper is good.

†Phillips & Page Ltd., 50 Kensington Church Street, W.8.

267

267. From the brass of HENRY GIBBES, mayor, 1636, St James's, Bristol.

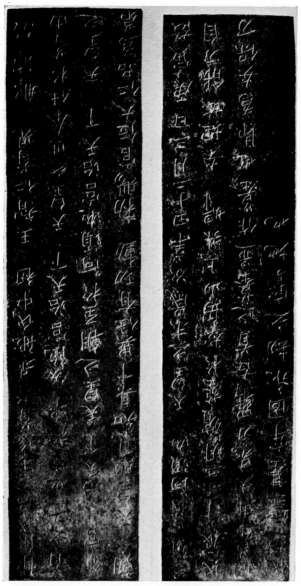

268. Japanese memorial inscription plate dated in correspondence with
AD 668 (see text).

268A. A partly-finished dabbing with equipment used. For finished
dabbing see plate 270.

269. The illustration shows the author making a rubbing. The paper has been held down firmly by pieces of adhesive tape. The three pieces at the top and two pieces on both sides were first stuck to the paper and floor after the paper had been drawn tight. When about 18″ of the rubbing was completed a piece of adhesive tape was fixed to both sides and more of the rubbing completed until the whole design was rubbed in a similar manner. Always dust and brush gently the face of the brass to remove grit and dirt prior to fixing the paper.

Next, lay your paper over the brass to make certain that it covers the entire surface; then cut off the required length from your roll. If the brass is a large one, larger than your paper, rub in sections of the same size as the brass plates. Large brasses are made up of several plates. 'Over-rub' the plate edges so that you can overlap. Keeping the paper in position, fix the top down with paper weights or with the adhesive tape. On a damp wall use a water gum tape; Scotch adhesive will not stick to a water-damp surface. It is advisable to use at least three fixing positions – one at each corner and another in the middle top. If the brass is a very wide one, use two fixing positions apart from the corners. Then roll up your paper to within about 18 in of the top and fix the two sides as in the sketch and place a weight in the middle:

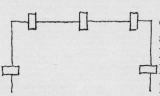

With your fingers now feel the shape of the top of the brass and press on to the paper to achieve a slightly embossed image. This has the effect of lowering the paper into the incised line and so keeping it clear of the black heel-ball when it passes over it. This also stretches the paper, which is a good thing, because unless you do this the paper will stretch as you rub and may cause a lack of definition – the paper will pucker within the rubbing area and so this may mean a slight closing up of your white lines, which must be avoided at all costs.

Some people take off their shoes and tread in stockinged feet on the part to be rubbed – then rub it – tread on the next part – rub – and so on. (It is a good idea to take off your shoes or wear rubber soles when brass-rubbing so as to avoid any damage by nails to the valuable brass).

When you have rubbed the first 18″ unroll more paper to the same extent and proceed as before. Avoid rubbing over the edges of the brass. If you have followed the above instructions closely you will be able to see the slight emboss of the brass as you proceed and so avoid going over the edges. A few people prefer to make a very quick, light, rough rubbing of the complete design, and have this in front of them as a guide when they make a second, good rubbing. Others use a dabbing pad with a very, very little dry graphite on it, and make a very slight impression in graphite of the design and proceed to rub over with the wax cake. As you proceed down the brass always fix two pieces of adhesive at either side every 18″ or so down the edges (or use paperweights). Work slowly and work for a *completely black and white* image. All flat surfaces of the brass should be completely black – incised lines completely white. On a few occasions grey can be permitted, as when rubbing over a garment where the craftsman has adopted a special method of cutting to express texture such as ermine, etc. The finer the detail, as in close-hatched work, the harder the wax required.

Rubbing a large brass can be quite exhausting. Place yourself in such a position that you can exert pressure when working without too much side or top rubbing movement. Get yourself well over the part you are rubbing. If you are dealing with a detailed area (such as chain-mail) do not rub heavily or too quickly, watch it build up – intelligently. Never rub mechanically, picture the design as it appears and *complete each part at one time.* Proceed downwards and never go back to 'blacken up'; it will probably not register! When rubbing large brasses with long perpendicular folds of drapery, run your rubbing wax in a downward or upward movement. This will give you a cleaner line. Rubbing against a perpendicular incised line will act as a blunt knife to your wax and thicken up the white slightly. Avoid getting flat pointed edges on your wax – they can dig in. As you rub slowly twist the wax in different directions in your hand and so keep a slightly convex surface. If part of the brass is in a difficult position, a piece of strip wax will be found useful to get into corners.

In general, there is no particular direction in which to rub a brass as long as you cover all the design uniformly with an even blackness. A circular movement, a top right to bottom left, or vice versa, or a horizontal or perpendicular action can all be satisfactory. Each person will find with experience which technique suits him or her best.

Never show the direction of your rubbing marks by not rubbing solid. The best rubbing is that which reproduces the original design absolutely accurately as a negative. Do not attempt to introduce 'effects' by 'tricky' rubbing. Remember that the medieval craftsman cut the brass in a certain way to give a certain result which is before you – do not attempt to improve on it!

When finished, but before you lift off your paper, check to see that you have completed all parts (shields etc). Take off the adhesive paper and dust the rubbing before rolling it up in a cardboard closed-end tube with fitting cap.* Replace everything as you found it; do not leave odd bits of paper or heel-ball lying about.

Polishing lightly will give the rubbing a shine (use a silk handkerchief). I prefer a matt finish – it has a better quality.

Some people rub the stone casement on which the brass is sunk to get a stone effect. Do this only slightly, otherwise the tonal value of the background will impose itself on the design. A grey wax is better for this purpose than black heel-ball. You can make this up by adding a white greasy crayon and a little yellow crayon to a small quantity of your black heel-ball, melt these together and finish by pouring into a china egg-cup as before. Check up the tonal value before using. Alternatively, a dabber with graphite can be used.

Sometimes it is attractive to add heraldic colours to the rubbing. If you wish to do this you must make the decision before you make the rubbing: you cannot very well add colour on top of black greasy heel-ball. Make sure of the correct heraldic colours. Only rub slightly where you want colour but make sure of all detail. Use poster colours with a little gum arabic. Add a little 'wetting' powder; this will enable you to paint over the parts you have rubbed without the colour forming globules. The wetting powder 'kills' the antipathy of fat for water (it can be bought from chemists). Use best sable brushes.

This colouring of rubbings must be approached with caution. Only an experienced person should attempt it, but even then it is something of a mixed accomplishment. Your rubbing is a negative – your colour a positive. You are really mixing your languages, which is not a good thing to do. If you obtain a positive by photographic methods from your negative rubbing, and colour this, you are then correct. Another method is to use coloured greasy crayons to rub the individual parts with the appropriate colour. When completed use a black heel-ball lightly over the colours to give them richness. This needs some thought and care as well as a sensitive judgement.

Finally, put the name of the effigy on the back of your rubbing, together with the date and other relevant details.

Cutting out the design to shape and mounting down is not recommended. If you want your rubbing mounted on linen it is best to take it to a competent picture-framer, who will make a first-class job of it. But if you do want to mount it yourself on linen, proceed as follows:

Make a wood stretcher the size you require for the rubbing. This stretcher should be similar to an artist's canvas stretcher, with wedges for tightening the the canvas. Stretch your linen over the frame, damp the linen and pull it tight. When dry, or nearly so, paste the back of your rubbing with a water paste, wait several minutes for the paper to stretch, paste again, and lay it down on the linen on the stretcher; two people are required for this operation. When it is in position, lay some white paper over the face of the rubbing and roll out any uneven surfaces with a small hand-roller, rolling from the middle outwards. Leave to dry, then trim off rough edges and your job is finished.

Storing the Rubbings
A dowel stick pasted at the top and another at the bottom of the rubbing is

a useful way to exhibit it. A picture-screw at either end of the top dowel with a length of black silk cord tied on makes an attractive scroll. Always wind up from the bottom when storing, and use two elastic bands to keep it in a rolled position. A large cardboard tube with one end closed and a movable cap for the other end (obtainable from some stationers) will take several rubbings and protect them from damage. Mark the contents on the outside, classifying them according to date, county, or type (military, ecclesiastic, etc).

Rubbing an incised stone slab (or casement)

Stone incised slabs are not usually in such good condition as incised brass slabs of the same age: dampness may have had a disastrous effect on the stone. Before you rub the stone inspect it closely; if the surface appears to be flaking, *leave it alone!* If it is damp you will be well advised to do the same. The action of rubbing on the paper on top of such slabs will only tend to remove a slight layer of the top surface and damage the slab still further. Soft sandstone and limestone slabs are some of the readiest to suffer in this way. Both these absorb moisture to a considerable extent.

Having found an incised slab that is suitable for rubbing and having obtained permission, proceed as for brass rubbing except for two important differences, that is to say, proceed much more slowly and use a gentle rhythmic action; and use a softer wax and build up your impression. There is no doubt that stone-slab rubbing is a more skilled technique than brass-slab rubbing. Brass is a much harder material and in general no damage can come from constant rubbing. This is not true of the stone slab. The softer edges of the incised line can suffer as well as the surface if not handled with great care and understanding. A few of the continental stone slabs are painted in various colours and the authorities concerned do not grant permission in the usual way except in very special circumstances, and then only to a person providing evidence of skill as a 'stone-slab rubber'.

THE DABBING TECHNIQUE

The next technique with which we are concerned is the dabbing technique, suitable for recording brasses, stone slabs and casements. Make a dabber of waste rags, felt and cotton-wool. This is done by taking a piece of chamois leather about 9 to 12 in square and placing the rags, felt, and cotton-wool in the middle, then securing the four corners tightly round the materials (see illustration). Make sure that the ball so formed is solid and that there are no corners or pieces of felt or rag making a ridge on the chamois leather. Then sew up the chamois leather round the material as firmly as possible (a dabber of this nature is used by etchers for spreading ink on the copper or zinc plate prior to wiping it).

Now use some finely powdered graphite mixed with a *little* linseed oil to which is added a pinch of carbon black powder to give greater tone value. This mixture should be of a fairly dry consistency. If too oily it will spread and ruin your efforts. Use the back of a tile with a slight 'tooth' to charge the dabber with the paste. This is done by rubbing the dabber up and down on the tile with the graphite paste. Use only a little at a time. Do not use a cardboard base; this tends to yield its surface and fine particles of cardboard will be found mixed with your paste so spoiling it. See that there is no surplus paste adhering to the dabber. Then apply it to the paper over your incised brass or slab.

The best action is a downward beating one – gently and smoothly and evenly. The use of a second dabber without any graphite on it, before using the graphite dabber, will give a better result. Do not attempt excessive rubbing action or your paper will tear and move, and the incised lines will take 'tone'. You can use an extremely thin paper for dabbing. The best paper for this purpose is grass-bleached 'Teapot' tissue.* The result is a dark grey tone, very smooth, but lacking the great contrast of the heel-ball rubbing. This method is best for the finest detail on brasses and slabs and for lightly incised brasses. The quality of a well-produced dabbing is superior to that of the finest rubbing.†

The author's technique for producing same-size 'positive' gilt facsimiles 'off the top of the brass' is, as explained elsewhere, not possible for the average person. It is the best technique available for reproducing brasses; it is as sharp as the conventional heel-ball rubbing in black and of course is better, in that it gives a 'positive' result.

REPRODUCTION OF BRASSES

The heel-ball rubbing is not a true rendering of the incised brass effigy or of the incised stone effigy. Since it is a negative, it is unsatisfactory as a record of individual brasses. It is a good substitute, nothing more. As every artist knows, a black line on white has a different significance from a white line on black (or gilt). The fact that all the major collections in the country consist of negative rubbings does not make them truer renderings of the original designs as conceived by medieval craftsmen. The heel-ball rubbing was used because no better method was known at the time. About the middle of last century attempts were made to produce a gilt positive by the use of a metallic rubbing compound. It was not satisfactory because it was too hard and damaged the brass. Now that means are available of obtaining an 'off the top of the brass' facsimile in gilt and black, museums and similar institutions are changing over to this technique.

The practice of employing an artist to redraw the brass design as a positive prior to reproduction is not really satisfactory. Those reproductions printed on a yellow base line-block are certainly nearer to the original idea, but unfortunately such drawings lack the feeling of the incised line. They are often 'slick', without sympathy for the true value of the engraved line. The burin (the tool used to cut the design in the brass) gives a very indivi-dual linear quality; the resistance of the metal as the engraver cuts into it produces a line of brittle quality which cannot be copied by a pen on a smooth white board. Many people accept as authentic the illustrations in various books written by experts on brasses. It is, however, clear to those familiar with the artistic quality of brasses that a considerable amount of bad art work has unfortunately been employed in retouching reduced photographs of original rubbings before the process of block making. Usually excessive reduction is used in illustrating brasses (say from 6 ft to 9 in) and the fine detail has been accentuated in order to obtain an open, sharp impression off the printing block. Often the brass has worn down through the ages and consequently the rubbing is not sharp, so the retoucher has been busy and completely 'restored' the detail! One writer, in trying to prove that the faces on three different brasses were stereotyped, attempted to illustrate his point with reproductions of negative rubbings about 3 to 4 in high which was about one-fifteenth of the size of the originals! How one was expected to identify similar features on a negative of a face measuring less than half an inch is beyond one's understanding.

The small Penguin book, *Monumental Brasses*, by the late Sir James Mann, is illustrated by a number of artist's drawings in line, showing the brass as a positive. A solid yellow is used behind the black line-block. This method is nearer the original and it is much easier to 'read'. Unfortunately these particular drawings, with a few exceptions, are not very good interpre-tations of the incised line.

The medieval artist conceived the design as an incised line which was filled in with a black compound enabling the design to be read as a positive.

Manufactured by Robert Fletcher & Sons Ltd., Columbia House, 69 Aldwych, London W.C.2.

†*The contrast of a black and white rubbing is in fact an overstatement. The tonal values in a first-class dabbing are nearer the craftsman's original conception.*

270

270. HENRY MORECOTE, rector, 1467, Ewelme, Oxon.
Demi-effigy in mass vestments. A finished dabbing.

271. THE RT HON GEORGE S. NOTTAGE, 1823-85, St Paul's Cathedral. Died in office. The only Lord Mayor to be buried in St Paul's Cathedral (crypt). Designed by Edward Onslow Ford, RA, 1852-1901. Engraved by Hart, Son, Peard & Co. Size 90″ x 35″. Reproduced by kind permission of the Dean and Chapter of St Paul's.

Though this brass is only 84 years old it cannot be called modern. Its design fits well with the Victorian conception of the best type of portrait memorials.

This brass is difficult to rub; working fast and concentrating hard, it took nearly three hours to complete. Most of the incised lines are filled in with a composition and many lines are lightly engraved. For rubbing I used three wax rubbers of varying hardness. On the fine, incised work I used a very hard wax and on the large, solid areas I used a soft wax. For the heraldic symbols I first used a medium wax to give a light impression and then finished with a hard wax.

The building up of a design as one rubs gives a special kind of experience which becomes more powerful on a first-class design.

An appreciation of monumental brasses requires comment on the visual quality of the surface of the casements. Various stones and materials were used – sandstone, limestone, Purbeck marble, Tournai stone, stone from quarries in the Midlands and Kent and even wood. The best casements are those which do not assert themselves and so detract from the brass design. A grey marble or buff limestone are most suitable though the latter is soft and wears unevenly. Some brasses which were relaid on floors during the 19th century and surrounded by tiles of coloured designs are not pleasing.

The famous photographer – the late Marcus Adams made many excellent photographs of brasses *in situ* – as positives. He did this by arranging special lighting on the brass in the church so that it read as a positive.

The new bright brass made this very clear. Modern methods of reproduction can produce an excellent black and gilt positive if only one takes the trouble to ensure that this is done. Now that the gilt rubbing technique is available to all, no doubt writers on brasses will adopt it in due course. Such illustrations can be shown with a stone casement surround similar to the black and gold frontispiece of this book.

MODERN BRASSES

In 1861 Haines listed over 150 brasses nearly all which were executed in the nineteenth century. These are chiefly inscriptions and crosses but a few effigies appear. A number have been executed since 1861, some of them of considerable merit: perhaps three hundred in all.

At the time of writing this I have heard of a brass that has been stolen from a Hertfordshire church. Photographs of a negative rubbing have been distributed to the Press for publication in the hope that this may lead to its recovery. Identification would be much easier if a positive photograph had been used. Lay a negative rubbing on one side of a brass and a positive rubbing on the other side and see which rubbing is the easier to identify with the brass effigy.

M + S
Sophiæ + Sheppard
hujus + Ecclesiæ + Fundatricis
Quæ + Obijt
Die + XXXI + July
A + S
MDCCCXLVIII.
Ætatis + suæ
LXXX.   272

SOPHIE SHEPPARD (widow), 1848, aged 80, Theale, Berks.
Canopy tomb. Brass engraved by John Hardmann.
Size of effigy 46″ deep.

A Select List of
Monumental Brasses
in the British Isles

The following list of brasses in the United Kingdom is not the one
usually given. It has been chosen for the unusual character of some
of the items. A number of inscriptions have been included for their
quaint or interesting details. A few well-known brasses have been
excluded. The list could be vast. To avoid this, in many instances
only selected brasses have been included here in an attempt to cover as
wide an area as possible under the limitation of space available.

The author has seen either the original brasses or rubbings of
the majority of the examples listed. There are numerous signed inscriptions (some shields and achievements, etc.) to be found in the
Yorkshire brasses of the 17th century (Briggs, Crosse, Fulmer,
Grigs, Hornbie, Mann and Raynold). Tom Mann signed several. A
few other signed inscriptions can be found in other counties.

As brasses are sometimes moved from one part of the church to
another part, the positions of a few listed may be incorrect.

The boundaries of London have greatly changed in recent times.
For our purpose, the context of monumental brasses, London as an
area has been included as part of Middlesex and Surrey.

ABBREVIATIONS

abp.	archbishop	knt.	knight
acad.	academical dress	Lat.	Latin
ach.	achievement	local	the work of a provincial school
arm.	armour		
A.T.	altar tomb	mar.	married
bart.	baronet	marg.	marginal
bp.	bishop	mcht.	merchant
br.	brass	mcht. mk.	merchant mark
C.	choir, chancel	mur.	mural, against wall
c.	circa, about	mutil.	mutilated
ch.	church	N.	nave
chil.	children	N.A.	north aisle
coh.	coheir	N.C.	north chapel
coll.	collection	N.Tr.	north transept
covd.	covered	obv.	obverse
dau.	daughter	orig.	original
dec.	deceased	palimp.	palimpsest
det.	detail	par.	parish
eff.	effigy	pos.	posuit, placed
Eng.	English	rect. pl.	rectangular plate
engr.	engraved	rel.	relaid
esq.	esquire	rev.	reverse
evang. symbols	evangelistic symbols	S.A.	south aisle
fem.	female	S.C.	south chapel
fig.	figure	S.Tr.	south transept
Fr.	French	sh.	shield
frag.	fragment	sm.	small
h.	heir	Trin.	Trinity
hf.	half	vests.	vestments
inscr.	inscription	vv.	verses
kng.	kneeling	w.	wife

BEDFORDSHIRE

Isherwood, Grace. 'Monumental Brasses in Bedfordshire Churches', 1906

AMPTHILL. I. Wm. Hicchecok, woolman, mcht., 'locum tenens' of the staple of Calais, 1450, in civil dress, mutil., and widow 'domina' Agnes. Sir Nich. Harve, 1532, in arm., marg. inscr. and 1 sh., mur., N.A.

ASPLEY GUISE. Priest in acad. kng., with St. John Bapt. standing, c. 1410; cross and marg. inscr. lost; rel., N.A. (Sir John Guise, 1501), in arm. with SS. collar, crest and 4 shs.; inscr. lost; N.A.

BARFORD, GREAT. Man in arm. and w., c. 1525; inscr. lost; mur., C.

BARFORD, LITTLE. Thos. Perys, 1535, in civil dress, and w. Agnes, local, N.

BARTON-IN-THE-CLAY. Rich. Brey, rector (1396), hf. eff. in mass vests.

BEDFORD, ST. MARY. Robt. Hawse, gent., thrice mayor, 1627, aged 52, in civil dress.

BEDFORD, ST. PAUL. Sir Wm. Harper, lord mayor of London (in 1561), founder of Bedford grammar school and almshouses, 1573, aged 77, in arm. with mantle, and 2nd w. Margt. (Leeder or Lethers), rel. and partly restored.

BIDDENHAM. Wm. Faldo and w. Agnes, also John Faldo, c. 1490, both in civil dress, rel. on vestry floor. Man and woman in shrouds, c. 1520; inscr. lost.

CARDINGTON. (Sir Wm. Gascoigne, comptroller of the household to cardinal Wolsey, 1540), in arm. with tabard, and 2 ws., both in heraldic dresses; children and inscr. lost; A.T.

COPLE. Nichol Roland, sergeant-at-law, in robes, and w. Pernel, c. 1410, Fr. inscr., C. Thos. Gray (1507), in arm., and w. Benet (Launcelyn), with 4 sons, 7 daus., 2 shs. and inscr. in 14 Eng. vv., local, A.T., S.C. Sir Walter Luke, justice of the pleas, 1544, in robes, and w. Anne, 'norysthe' (nurse) to Hen. VIII, dau. and h. of John Launceleyn, esq., in heraldic mantle, 1538, kng., 2 shs. on back and 1 on front of tomb; Trinity, scrolls and chamfer inscr. lost; mur., A.T., N.C.

DUNSTABLE. (Laur. Pygot, woolman, 1450), in civil dress, feet lost, and w. (Alice), also 2 mcht. marks, 3 sons, 6 daus., another son (?Laur. Cantelow, son-in-law), and inscr. lost; formerly in N. Rich. Fynche, citizen mcht.-tailor of London, 1640, aged about 81, in civil dress, and parents, Thos. Fynche, 1586, in civil dress, and Elizth. Fynche, 1607, marg. inscr. and arms of Mcht.-tailors' Co. S.A.

EATON BRAY. Jane, lady Bray, 1558, with 1 son, 10 daus, and arms on 2 lozenges, mur. A.T., C.

EYWORTH. Rich. Gadburye, gent., 1624, aged about 63, in civil dress, and 2nd w. Margt., with dau. Magdalenna (died 1618, aged 5); he left in trust 6 acres of arable land in Wrestlingworth and 8 acres at Dunton for the poor; 1 sh., C.

FLITTON. Harry, son and h. of Sir Harry Gray, 1545, in arm., 1 sh., N.C.

HATLEY COCKAYNE. Edm. Cokayne, esq., 1515, in arm., and w. Elizth. (Lock), with 12 sons and 4 daus., 1 sh.

HOUGHTON CONQUEST. Rich. Conquest, esq., 1500, in arm., and w. Elizth.; 6 sons, 2 daus, and Trinity lost; sm., C.

LEIGHTON BUZZARD. Wm. Jackmann of Billington, gent., 1597, in civil dress, and sons Wm. and Reginald, rect. pl. with inscr., mur., C.

LUTON. Lady in widow's dress, c. 1490, under mutil. triple canopy; chamfer inscr. lost; A.T., N.C. John Acworth, 1513, in arm., and ws. Alys and Amy, with 8 sons, 9 daus, mar. inscr. and 4 shs., repaired and rel. in 1911, mur., N. Edw. Sheffeld, LL.D, canon of Lichfield, vicar of Luton, rector of Camborne, Cornwall, and of Yate, Glouc. (died 1525), date not filled in, in cap and almuce, with scroll and 4 shs., now in S.Tr.

ROXTON. Inscr. John Fage senior of Chalvesterne, 1400

SHILLINGTON. Matthew de Asscheton, rector of (Shillington in the dioc. of Lincoln, and of Walpole in the dioc. of Norf., canon of York) and Lincoln, 1400, in cope, marg. inscr. mutil., large, N.C.

SUTTON. Cross fleury and inscr. to Thos. Burgoyn, 1516, and w. Elizth., N.A.

WILSHAMSTEAD. Wm. Carbrok, chaplain, C. 1450 or earlier (?), hf. eff. in mass vests, N.A.

WYMINGTON. John Curteys, lord of the manor, rebuilder of ch., mayor of the staple of Calais, 1391, in civil dress with anelace, and widow Aubrey in mantle, double canopy, 2 shs. and marg. inscr., A.T. Sir Thos. Brounflet, cupbearer to Ric. II, treasurer of household to Hen. IV, 1430, in arm., 2 shs., inscr. in 14 Lat. vv., large, S.C.

BERKSHIRE

Morley. Monumental Brasses of Berkshire, by T. H. Morley, 1924.

BINFIELD. Water de Annefordhe (rector, 1361), hf. eff. in mass vests., Fr. inscr., C.

BLEWBURY. Man in arm. (of the Latton? family), and 2 ws., each with 2 sons and 3 daus., of which only 3 daus. now remain, c. 1515; inscr. lost; now mur.

BRAY. Sir John de Foxle, 1378, in arm. with jupon, and ws. (Maud, and Joan), in heraldic dresses, on a bracket; double canopy nearly all gone, marg. inscr. lost; now mur. in original slab, N.A. Sir Wm. Laken, justice of the King's bench, 1475, in robes with rosary and anelace, and widow Sibil (eff. lost), 1 sh., now mur. S.C.

BRIGHTWELL. John Scolffyld, priest, 1507, in mass vests. with chalice and wafer, S.A.

BUCKLAND. John Yate, esq., 1578, aged 66, in civil dress, and w. Mary, dau. and h. of Wm. Justice of Reading, esq., with 5 sons and 7 daus., ach. and 4 shs., once on A.T., now mur., N.Tr.

CHILDREY. Wm. Fynderne, esq., 1444, in arm. with tabard, and w. Dame Elizth. in heraldic dress, fine double canopy mutil., foot inscr. and marg. inscr. in 20 Lat. vv., 2 shs. (another lost), large, C. Joan, dau. of Thos. Walrond, w. of Robt. Strangbon, 1477, recumbent on a tomb in shroud, large Trinity, inscr. in 7 Eng. vv., 6 shs. (one mutil. and palimp, but fastened down, and another lost), repaired in 1914, S.Tr.

CLEWER. Inscr. in 6 Eng. vv. Martine Expence (1600), who 'shott with a hundred men him selfe alone in the oulde felde at Bray', now mur., S.C.

COOKHAM. Margt. Andrew and her 2 husbands, John Monkeden and Wm. Andrew, 1503, both in civil dress, sm., N.A. Robt. Pecke, esq., 'master clerke of the spycerry' to Hen. VI, 1510, in arm., and w. Annes, Trinity, 2 shs., sm., A.T., C.

DENCHWORTH. Wm. Hyde, esq., 1557, in arm., and w. Margery, 1562, with 12 sons and 8 daus., 2 shs., 2 inscrs., one in 10 Eng. vv. and one with inscr. and 2 Lat. vv., the latter palimp., on rev. an inscr. in Fr. relating to the foundation of Bisham Abbey, 1333, 'Edward roy Danglet'e qe fist le siege deuant la cite de Berewyk et cõquyst la bataille illeoqz et la dite cite la veille seinte Margarete lan de g'ce MCCCXXXIII mist ceste pere a la requeste Sire William de Montagu foundour de ceste mesoun'.

HANNEY, WEST. (John) Seys, rector, c. 1370, in mass vests., lower part of eff. and bracket lost, marg. inscr. much mutil., large, C.

HENDRED, EAST. Inscr. Wm. Whitwey, clothier and woolman, 1479, now mur., N.Tr.

LAMBOURN. John de Estbury (1406), in civil dress, and w. Agnes, hf. effs.; inscr. in Fr. and 2 evang. symbols lost; rel., S.C.

MARCHAM. Edm. Fetyplace, esq., 1540, in arm., with 5 sons, and w. Margt. with 6 daus., all kng.; replaced in the ch. in 1911 and the inscr. and 4 shs. renewed; rel., mur., N.

NEWBURY. John Smalwode, *alias* Wynchcom, 1519, in civil dress, and w. Alice, with 2 sons and 1 dau., 2 roundels with monogram and 2 with St. John Bapt., rel., mur., Tower. John Winchcombe, clothier, better known as 'Jack of Newbury' built the greater part of the church.

READING, ST. LAURENCE. Walter Barton, gent., 1538, in civil dress, inscr. with 2 Lat. vv.; all palimp, on rev. of eff. are portions of the feet of a man in arm. and of a tabard with the arms of Popham; on rev. of inscr. is the complete inscr. to Sir John Popham, 'dñs de Turney in Normandia et dñs de Chardeford de Dene ac de Alvyntõn et alibi in Anglia', 1463. Edw. Butler, gent., five times mayor, 1584, aged 72, in civil dress, and w. Alce, 1583, aged 72, mar. 42 years and left 3 only daus. and heirs, Alce, w. of Wm. Buttell, esq., with 3 sons and 4 daus.; Mary, w. of Wm. Powell, D D, with 2 sons and 1 dau; Elizth., w. of Rich. Staverton, esq., with 2 daus.; eff. of w., the 2nd and 3rd daus., the grandchildren, shs., and marg. inscr. lost; tomb destroyed, slab in C., but remaining eff. and inscr. now mur., C.

SHOTTESBROOKE. Priest in mass vests. and a civilian with anelace, c. 1370, fine double canopy mutil.; inscr. lost; large. Thos. Noke, 'comenly called Father Noke', created esquire by Hen. VIII, and 'for his excellencie in artilarie made yeoman of the crowne of Englond', 1567, aged 87, in civil dress with badge on shoulder, and 3 ws., with 1 son and 3 daus. of 1st w. (now lost); 3 sons and 3 daus. of 2nd, and 1 dau. of 3rd w. (now lost); he left surviving his w. Julian, 2 brothers, 1 sister, 1 son and 2 daus.; inscr., 6 Lat. vv. by Dame Elizth. Hobbie, and ach., N.Tr.

SONNING. Laurence Fyton, esq., bailiff of Sonning, 1434, in arm., 4 shs. William Scott, Lord Stowell, 1836, Inscr. on rect. pl.

SPARSHOLT. Wm. de Herleston, rector (1353), in mass vests., in the head of a cross, which, together with the marg. inscr., is nearly all lost, 2 shs. (1 mutil.), C.

STANFORD-IN-THE-VALE. Roger Campedene, rector, 1398, large hf. eff. in mass vests., with evang. symbols on shs. (2 mutil.), C.

STREATLEY. Inscr. Elizth., dau. of Rich. Osbarn, esq., w. of John Prout, mcht. of the staple of Calais, 1440, 'que obiit in parturiendo in die Ephiphanie'.

THEALE. Sophie Sheppard, 1848. Canopy tomb. Brass engraved by John Hardmann.

TIDMARSH. (Hen. Leynham, esq., 1517), in arm. with tabard, head mutil., 4 shs.; inscr. lost; C.

WANTAGE. Priest, c. 1370, hf. eff. in mass vests.; inscr. lost; now mur., N.C. Sir Ivo Fitzwaryn, 1414, in arm., large, now mur., N.C.

WINDSOR, ST. GEORGE'S CHAPEL. Robt. Honywode, LL B, archdeacon of Taunton, canon of Windsor, 1522, in almuce, kng., under canopy with St. Kath. and B.V. Mary and Child, rect. pl. with diapered background, inscr. and sh., curious, mur., Rutland Chapel.

WITTENHAM, LITTLE. Cecily, w. of Geoff. Kydwelly, 1472, C. Geoff. Kidwelly, esq., 1483, in civil dress, 2 shs., C. Wm. Dunche, esq., auditor of the mints to Hen. VIII and Edw. VI, and 'esquier sworne extreordinairie for the body of our soveraigne lady Elizabeth', died 1597, in civil dress, and w. Marie Barnes, had 2 sons, Edm., Walter, all kng., engr. c. 1585, rect. pl. with inscr., 2 shs., and 4 crests.

BUCKINGHAMSHIRE

BLETCHLEY. Thos. Sparke, D D, rector, 1616, aged 68, a bust in an oval, with 3 sons and 2 daus., figures of death, fame, etc.; Thos. his son and h. pos.; rect. pl., very finely engr., mur., C.

CHALFONT ST. GILES. Priest, c. 1470, in mass vests., sm., mur., C. Thos. Fletewood, esq., born at Heskyn, Lancs., lord of the Vache, treasurer of the mint., M.P. for Bucks., late sheriff for Bucks and Beds., 1570, aged 52, in arm., and 2 ws., (1) Barbara (Francis) with 2 sons and 2 daus. (2) Brigett, dau. of Sir John Springe, with 8 sons and 6 daus., all kng., ach. and 4 shs., mur., A.T., C.

CHALFONT ST. PETER. Priest, c. 1440, in mass vests., sm.; a palimp. by appropriation, the figure slightly altered and an inscr. added to Robt. Hanson, vicar of Chalfont St. Peter and of Little Missenden, 1545.

CHENIES. Elizth., dau. of John Broughton, esq., 1524, with flowing hair, marg. inscr. and 2 shs. mur.

CLAYDON, MIDDLE. Roger Gyfford, esq., 1542, in arm., and w. Mary (Nansegles), with 13 sons, 7 daus., and 3 shs., large; the inscr. palimp., on rev. another inscr. to Walter Bellingham 'alias dicti Walteri Irelonde regis Armorum in hybernia', 1487, and w. Elizth.; one sh. in also palimp. by alteration; now mur., C., the palimp. fastened down.

DENHAM. Dame Agnes Jordan, abbess of Syon (died 1546), engr. c. 1540 (date of death erroneously filled in as 1544); marg. inscr. and shs. with the five wounds lost; rel., C.

DRAYTON BEAUCHAMP. Thos. Cheyne, esq., shield-bearer to Edw. III, 1368, in arm.; inscr. 2 shs. lost; large C. (Wm.) Cheyne, esq., 1375, in arm., marg. inscr. mutil., 4 shs. lost, large, C.

EDLESBOROUGH. John de Swynstede, rector of Edlesborough (prebendary of Lincoln), 1395, in mass vests., with scroll, large. Rose inscribed 'Ecce quod expendi habui' etc., and inscr. to John Killingworth, 1412.

ETON COLLEGE CHAPEL. Roger Lupton, provost of Eton, canon of Windsor (died 1540), in mantle with garter badge; inscr. lost; 1 sh., now filled in and mur., Lupton chapel.

HALTON. Hen. Bradschawe, esq., chief baron of the exchequer, 1553, in robes, and w. Joan (Hurst, see Noke, Oxon), with 4 sons and 4 daus., all kng., 1 sh., mur., C.

HAMBLEDEN. Robt. Scrop, esq., 1500, in arm. (eff. now lost), and widow Kath., in mantle once inlaid, kng., 4 shs. (2 not belonging), now on boards, mur., N.Tr.

HAMPDEN, GREAT. John Hampden, esq., 1496, in arm., and w. Elizth. (Sidney), engr. c. 1525, with 4 sons and 6 daus., 5 shs., C.

HITCHAM. Nich. Clarke, esq., son and h. to 'Syr John Clarke of Weston, knt., that tooke the duke of Longevyle prisoner' (see Thame, Oxon., 1539), 'dyed of the swett', 1551, in arm., with 4 children, Jane, Wm., Dorothy, John, the daus. lost; 1 sh., C. floor.

LECKHAMPSTEAD. Regenolde Tylney, gent., 2nd son of Ralph Tylney, citizen and alderman of London, and 'unus heres' of the manor, 1506, in civil dress, below are effs. of his 3 children, Elizth., Joan, Joan; 1 sh., N.A.

LILLINGSTONE DAYRELL. Paul Dayrell, esq., 1491, in arm., and w. Margt., A.T., C.

LILLINGSTONE LOVELL. Two hands issuing from clouds and holding a bleeding heart inscribed 'Ihc', John Merstun, rector, 1446, C.

MARSWORTH. Inscr. Wm. West, gent., 1583; palimp., made up of pieces of 3 different continental marg. inscrs., of one of which there are 5 other pieces at Walkerne, Herts., S.C., the palimp. fastened down. Nich. West, esq., one of the 6 clerks and afterwards a master in chancery, 1586, in arm. (legs only left), and w. Joan (Hawtrey), 1585 (eff. lost), with 4 sons (legs only left) and 2 daus., foot inscr., ach. and sh.; partly palimp., on rev. of legs of Nich. West, a frag. of a foreign br. with symbol of St. Luke and part of a marg. inscr.; on rev. of inscr., a portion of a priest, probably German, in diapered chasuble with large chalice on body, and maniple ornamented with sm. figures of prophets; S.C., the palimps, fastened down.

PENN. John Pen, esq., lord of the manor, 1597, aged 63, in arm., and w. Ursula, lower parts of effs. lost, with 6 sons, inscr. 4 Lat. vv. and sh., S.C. Wm. Pen, esq., 1638, in arm., and w. Martha, 1635, with 1 son and 2 daus., 1 sh., S.A. John Pen, esq., 1641, in arm., and w. Sarah, dau. of Sir Hen. Drury, with 5 sons and 5 daus., 1 sh., S.C.

QUAINTON. Margery, dau. and h. of Master John Iwarby, esq., w. of Sir Rauff Verney, 1509, with 1 son and 3 daus., 2 shs.

STOKE POGES. Sir Wm. Molyns, 1425, in arm., and widow Dame Margery 2 shs., C.

TAPLOW. Nichole de Aumberdene (Amerden in Taplow), 'iadis pessoner de Londres', *c.* 1350, sm. eff. in the head of a fine floriated cross with stem resting on dolphin; eff. and cross slightly mutil. Rich., son and h. of Robt. and Kath. Manfeld, 1455, aged 19 in civil dress with livery collar; his maiden sister Isabel, in mantle with flowing hair; and 'yong John his brother be the second wyfe', in shroud; inscr. in 8 Eng. vv., 1 sh. (others lost). Both N. floor.

TINGEWICK. Erasmus Williams, rector, 1608, aged 56, in ruff and gown, kng., rect. pl., with 14 Eng. vv., etc., curious, mur., C.

TWYFORD. John Everdon, rector, 1413, hf. eff. in mass vests., now mur., C.

UPTON. Edw. Bulstrod, esq., 1599, in arm., and w. Cecil, dau. of John Croke, esq., with 4 sons, Hen., Thos., Edw., Wm., and 6 daus., Elizth., Margt., Anne, Cecil, Magdalen, Dorothy, text in Hebrew on scroll.

WADDESDON. Hugh Brystowe, parson 'above the space of forty year elect unto the ffirst porcyon' of the rectory, 1548, in shroud, inscr. in 16 curious Eng. vv., C.

WINCHENDON, NETHER. Man in arm. (John Hampden), *c.* 1420; inscr. lost; C.

WINCHENDON, OVER. Inscr. with 4 Eng. vv., ach. and 2 shs. John Goodwyn, esq., 1558, and w. Kath. Bledlow, had 18 children, mur., C.

WOOBURN. John Godwyn, 1488, in civil dress, and w. Pernell (eff. lost), 'ffirst founders of the stepull of Obourne Deyncourt', N.A.

WYCOMBE, HIGH. Inscr. in 8 Eng. vv. Margery and Mary, ws. of John Lane, *c.* 1600, mur., S.C.

CAMBRIDGESHIRE

BALSHAM. I. John Sleford, rector, master of the wardrobe to Edw. III (chaplain to Queen Philippa, prebendary of St. Stephen's, Westminster, archdeacon of Wells), canon of Ripon and Wells, rebuilder of the ch. and erector of the stalls, 1401, in cope with SS., B.V. Mary and Child, John Evang., Kath., Paul, Mary Mag., John Bapt., Audrey, Peter, Margt., Wilfrid (bp.), triple canopy with Trinity, soul, seraphim, etc., arms of England and of Queen Philippa, marg. inscr. in 14 Lat. vv. mutil., very large, fine, C. Dr. John Blodwell, born in Wales, studied law in Bologna and practised in Rome, (prebendary of Lichfield and Hereford, canon of St. David's, dean of St. Asaph's, rector of Balsham), 'longo tempore cecus erat', 1462, in cap and cope with SS. Michael, Kath., Margt., single canopy with entablature and SS. John Bapt., 12 Lat. vv., marg. inscr. and 2 shs., large, worn, N.

CAMBRIDGE, KING'S COLLEGE. (Robt. Hacombleyn, provost, 1528), in almuce, marg. inscr. with text, sh. with the 5 wounds; a foot inscr. lost; S.C.

CAMBRIDGE, QUEENS' COLLEGE. Robt. Whalley, gent., born at Nottingham, fellow, 1591, aged 28, in civil dress, 10 Lat. vv., ach., and marg. inscr. with crests at the corners; one crest loose and palimp., on rev. a frag. of an inscr. to Thos. Cla–, 147–. On wall of old chapel.

CAMBRIDGE, ST. JOHN'S COLLEGE. Eudo de la Zouche, brother of Lord Zouche, canon of Sarum, chancellor of the University, archdeacon of Hunts., master of the suppressed hospital of St. John, 1414, in acad., head gone, triple canopy, 1 sh.; marg. inscr. lost; worn, large, mur. behind organ.

CAMBRIDGE, TRINITY HALL. I. Walter Hewke, DCL, master, died 1517, engr. *c.* 1510 (date not filled in), in cope with the twelve apostles on orphrey, head restored in 1895, foot inscr. with 3 Lat. vv. and another inscr. on scroll over head, large, Ante-chapel. Inscr. Laur. Moptyd, S.T.B, master of Corpus Christi Coll., founder of a scholarship, 1557, mur., Ante-chapel. Thos. Prestone, native of Lancashire, 'scholarem quem dixit princeps Elizabetha suum',

LL.D, master, 1598, aged 60, in civil dress; his w. Alice pos; inscr. in 8 Lat. vv., marg. inscr., and 3 shs., C.

ELY CATHEDRAL. Thos. Goodryke, bp. of Ely, often a foreign ambassador, a counsellor to Edw. VI, lord high chancellor, 1554, in episcopal vests. holding bible and great seal; canopy and foot inscr. lost; 2 scrolls (4 others lost), marg. inscr. with Evang. symbols on roses mutil.; large S.A. of C. Inscr. and arms Fishmongers' Co. Robt. Wagstave, fishmonger, 1616, and w. Mary, 1621; she mar. 2ndly Stephen Baetman; Lady Chapel.

FULBOURNE. Wm. de Fulburne, canon of St. Paul's London (1391), in cope, single canopy slightly mutil., foot inscr. in 2 Lat. vv., marg. inscr. mutil., large, C.

GIRTON. Wm. Malster, 'in decretis licenciatus', rector, canon of York, prebendary of Fenton, 1492, in cope, C.

HILDERSHAM. (Robt.) Parys (1408), in civil dress, and w. (Eleanor Busteler), kng. to a floriated cross with Trinity in the head, 2 shs.; inscr. lost C.

HORSEHEATH. (Wm. de Audeley, 1365), in arm., and frag. of canopy; marg. inscr. lost; large, C.

ISLEHAM. Thos. Peyton, esq., 1484, in arm., and ws., Margt., and Margt. (widow of Thos. Garnish, esq.), triple canopy mutil., foot inscr., A.T., C.

MILTON. Wm. Coke, esq., justice of the common pleas, 1553, in robes, and w. Alice (who pos.), with 2 sons and 3 daus., ach., 8 Lat. vv. and marg. inscr., C.

SAWSTON. Man in arm., *c.* 1480, with motto 'A dew en Blayne'; head, w. and marg. inscr. lost; nor mur., S.A.

SHELFORD, GREAT. Thos. Pattesle, rector, rebuilder and benefactor to the ch., prebendary of Southwell, (archdeacon of Ely), 1418, in cope with name on orphreys, lower part of eff. lost, single canopy much mutil., arms of see of Ely and of bp. Fordham; inscr. lost; C.

SHELFORD, LITTLE. (Robt. de Frevile, brother and h. of John de Frevile, 1393), in arm., and w. (Clarice, 1399), holding hands, engr. *c.* 1410; inscr. lost; S.C. Priest, *c.* 1480, in acad.; inscr. lost; C.

STOW-CUM-QUY. John Ansty, esq. (lord of the manor and founder of the chantry 'vocat Anstyes chantry', 1460), in arm., and w. Joan (eff. lost), with 12 sons in tabards and 4 daus. kng., marg. inscr. much mutil., N.

TRUMPINGTON. Sir Roger de Trumpington, a crusader in 1270, died 1289, in arm. with sh., large; marg. inscr. lost; A.T., N.C., now covered with glass.

WESTLEY WATERLESS. Sir John von Creke, *c.* 1325, in arm. with sh., and w. Alyne (Clopton or Chamberleyn), with maker's mark in lower dexter corner; double canopy, 6 shs., and marg. inscr. lost; large, S.A.

WESTON COLVILLE. Abraham Gates, S.T.B, rector, in gown, and w. Mary, 'forma satis speciosa sed speciosiori vita faeminae', 1636, kng.; they had 3 daus., Mary, Elizth., Margt.; rect. pl. with inscr. and 2 Lat. vv., archangel with trumpet, skulls, etc., and 4 Lat. vv. above effs.; mur. C.

WILBURTON. Rich. Bole, archdeacon of Ely, 1477, in cope, single canopy and marg. inscr., large rel. and restored, mur., C.

WISBECH. (Thos. de Braunstone), constable of the castle of Wisbech, 1401, in arm; canopy lost; marg. inscr. in Fr. Mutil., very large, worn, formerly in S.A., now in C.

WOOD DITTON. Hen. Englisshe, 1393, in arm., and w. Margt.; head of lady and canopy lost; large, S.A.

CHESHIRE

Thornely. 'Monumental Brasses of Lancashire and Cheshire', by J. L. Thornely, 1893.

CHESTER CATHEDRAL. Inscr. Elizth., dau. of Sir Thos. Aston, bart., by Magdalen, dau. of Sir John Pultney of Misterton, Leic., 1633, mur., S.Tr. Inscr. with angels and skeleton, Madock family, 1708-92, mur., S.Tr.

CHESTER, ST. PETER. Lawyer (cf. Rodmarton, Glouc.), c. 1460, in civil dress with curious cap over head, inscr. illegible; 2 shs. lost; worn, now mur., S.A.

MACCLESFIELD. Roger Legh, 1506, in civil dress, and w. Elizth. (Sutton), 1489, kng., with 6 sons and 7 daus., a representation of the mass of St. Gregory with a pardon inscr. below; eff. of w. and daus. lost; formerly in Legh chapel in S.A., now on a board in vestry.

TARVIN. Inscr. Hen. Hardware, alderman and twice mayor of Chester, 1584; arms of Chester and Mcht. Adventurers added later; mur., in wooden frame, C.

WILMSLOW. Sir Robt. del Bothe, lord of the manors of Bolyn, Thorneton, and Dunham, 1460, in arm., and w. Douce (Venables), 1453, with flowing hair, hands clasped, canopy and marg. inscr. much mutil., 3 shs., worn., C.

CORNWALL

Dunkin. 'The Monumental Brasses of Cornwall', by E. H. W. Dunkin, 1882.

ANTHONY, EAST. Margery, dau. of Sir Warin Erchedeken (w. of Thos. Arundell of Lanherne), 1420, single canopy, C.

BUDOCK. John Killigrew of Arwenack, esq., lord of the manor of Killigrew, made first captain of Pendennis Castle by Hen. VIII, and succeeded by his son Sir John at his death, 1567, in arm., and w. Elizth., dau. of (Jas). Trewinnard, ach. and 2 shs., C.

CONSTANTINE. Rich. Gerveys, esq., in civil dress, and w. Jane, dau. of Thos. Trefusis, esq., both buried 8 Oct., 1574, rect. pl. with 8 sons, 8 daus., and sh., detached marg. inscr., local; palimp. on rev. of larger pl. the upper portion of a man in arm. with armorial jupon, head resting on a diapered cushion supported by angels, also portions of canopy with saints; on rev. of children pinnacles of canopy and a portion of a marg. inscr. 'April bidt voer die ciel'; all foreign, c. 1375; rel. in a new slab and the palimp. fastened down, N.A.

FOWEY. Alice, dau. of Wm. Lanyon, esq., w. of no. III, died 20 Aug. 1591, and her husband 'who lieth buried under the monument neare adjoyninge 10 Aug., 1582, they left of their issue livinge one sonne and six daughters, which sonne caused this stone to be made in 1602'; sh. lost; N.

HELSTON. Inscr. Thos. Bougins of Helston, Mcht., 1602, mur. over door of S. porch.

LANDULPH. Inscr. with sh. Theodoro Paleologus of Pesaro in Italy, 'descended from ye Imperyall Lyne of ye last Christian Emperors of Greece', 1636, and (2nd) w. Mary, had 3 sons, Theodoro, John, Ferdinando, and 2 daus., Mary, Dorothy, mur.

LANTEGLOS-BY-FOWEY. Thos. de Mohun, c. 1440, in arm.; he was son of John, son and h. of Sir Reginald de Mohun by Elizth., dau. and h. of Sir John Fitzwilliam, and 2nd brother of John, last Lord Mohun; marg. inscr. 3 shs. (another lost), A.T., S.A.

LAUNCESTON. Lady, c. 1620, 'her age 65, married 47, children 15', lived 3 years at Launceston; inscr. lost; local and curious, N.A.

MAWGAN-IN-MENEAGE. Inscr. Hannibal Basset, 1709, aged 22, with 4 Eng. vv. 'shall we all dye' etc., mur., S.Tr.

MAWGAN-IN-PYDER. Cysselle Arundell, 1578, aged 52, 12 Eng. vv. commencing 'Though tyme that all devours' etc., and 2 shs., eff. rel., S.A., vv. and shs. on screen.

ST. COLUMB MAJOR. Sir John Arundell, 1590, aged 60, in arm., and w. Anne Stanley, dau. of the earl of Derby, 1602, aged 71, with 2 sons, John, Geo., and 5 daus., Dorothy, Elizth., Cecily, Margt., Gertrude, engr. 1633, ach. and 2 shs., formerly in S.C., now N.

ST. MELLION. Peter Coryton, esq., 1551, in arm., and w. Jane, dau. and h. of John Tregasso, with 17 sons and 7 daus., 3 shs., marg. inscr., mur., N.A.

TRURO CATHEDRAL. Cuthbert Sydnam, woollen-draper, mayor in 1627, died 1630, aged 54, in civil dress; he had 8 children, Humph., Cuthbert, Anne, Margt., Blanch (all dead), Wm., Cuthbert, Jane; his w. Jane pos. In choir vestry.

CUMBERLAND

BOOTLE. Sir Hugh Askew, 'late of the seller' to Edw. VI, 'made knight at Moskelbrough felde' in 1547, died 1562, in arm., now mur., C.

CARLISLE CATHEDRAL. Rich. Bell, bp., 1496, in full vests. with mitre and crosier, holding book, triple canopy mutil., 4 Lat. vv. and marg. inscr. mutil., large, C. Inscr. Thos. Musgrave, clerk, born 1618 Botchard, Cumb., 8 years at Queen's Coll., Oxford, 'archididascalus' of Carlisle school for some years, c. 1650, R. Preston sculpsit'. N.C.A.

CROSTHWAITE. Sir John Ratclif, 1527, in arm., and w. Alice, head of male eff. and 4 shs. restored in 18th cent.; A.T., C.

EDENHALL. Wm. Stapilton, esq., lord of Edenhall, 1458, in arm. with tabard, and w. Margt., dau. and h. of Nich. de Vipont and lady of 'Aldeston Mor', C.

GREYSTOKE. John Whelpdall, LL.D., master of the coll., rector of Caldbeck, 1526, hf. eff. in almuce, 2 shs. on inscr., very sm., S.A.

WESTWARD. Rich. Barwise of Ilekirke, esq., 1648, aged 47, rect. pl. with seated figs. of Truth and Fame, 14 Eng. vv. and sh., mur., N.

DERBYSHIRE

Field, H. E. 'The Monumental Brasses of Derbyshire', printed in Mon. Br. Soc. Trans. III, 194, 209, V, 1, 29, 101, 129, 171, 380.

ASHBOURNE. Inscr. Dedication and consecration of the ch. by Hugh de Pateshull, bp. of Coventry in 1241, sm., now mur., Vestry.

BAKEWELL. Latham Woodroofe, esq., servant to John, earl of Rutland, 1648, aged 40, in civil dress, rect. pl. with 2 Lat., 4 Eng. vv., and ach., very sm., mur., S.Tr.

CHESTERFIELD. Sir Godfrey Foljambe, one of the King's council, 1541, in arm. with tabard, and w. Kath., dau. of John Leake of Sutton, esq., 1529, in heraldic dress; children, shs., and marg. inscr. restored in 1879; S.C.

DERBY, ALL SAINTS. Inscr., John Walton, STB, rector of Breadsall and Gedling, benefactor to the ch., 1603, aged 57, mur., N.A.

DRONFIELD. Thos. Gomfrey of Wormehull, rector, 1399, and brother Rich., rector of Tadenhull, prebendary of Someschell in the King's chapel of Penkeriche, both in mass vests.; a hunting horn and bawdric between effs. lost; the inscr. states that Roger Braylisforde, rector of Dronfield, is buried under the stone; worn, C.

EDENSOR. John Beton, esq., son of John Beton of Authmuthy, Scotland, comptroller of the household of Mary, Queen of Scots, aider in her escape from Lochleven castle, and her ambassador to Chas. IX of France, and to Queen Elizth., died at Chatsworth, 1570, aged 32 years and 7 months, rect. pl. with recumbent eff. in arm., inscr., and ach.; his brothers, Jas., abp. of Glasgow, and Andrew pos.; mur., C.

HATHERSAGE. Robt. Eyre of Padley, in arm. with tabard, and w. Elizth., in heraldic mantle, c. 1500, with 7 sons, Thos., John, Christ., John, and 3 lost, and 2 daus., Elizth., Jane (now fixed in centre niche of sedilia), all kng.; inscr. lost; now fixed at back of A.T.

KEDLESTON. Rich. Curzon, lord of Kedleston, 1496, in arm., and w. Alice, with 4 sons (lost) and 8 daus., 2 shs., marg. inscr. much mutil.; another inscr. lost; C.

MORLEY. Sir Thos. Stathum, lord of this town, 1470, in arm., and 2 ws., (1) Elizth., dau. of Robt. Langley, esq., (2) Thomasine, dau. of John Curzon, esq., with SS. Anne, B.V. Mary and Child, and Christopher, 3 shs., A.T., S.C. John Sacheverell, esq., son and h. of Ralph Sacheverell, esq., lord of Snetherton and Hopwell, slain at

Bosworth Field in 1485, in arm., with 3 sons, and w. Joan, dau. and h. of Hen. Stathum, esq. with 5 daus., all kng., figure of St. Christopher above, engr. c. 1525, 3 shs., mur., S.C.

SAWLEY. Rich. Shylton, mcht. of the staple of Calais, 1510, in civil dress, mutil., and w. Alys, once on A.T., now in N.A.

STAVELEY. Peyrs Freychwell, 'squier' to Hen. VI, patron and benefactor to ch., 1503, in arm., with 8 sons, and w. Mawde, with 7 daus., all kng., B.V. Mary and Child above, mur., A.T., C.

TIDESWELL. Robt. Pursglove, born at Tideswell, educated by his uncle Wm. Bradshaw, prior of Gisburn, Yorks., suffragan bp. of Hull, archdeacon of Nottingham, provost of Rotherham college, endower of 2 grammar schools and a hospital, 1579, in episcopal vests., foot inscr. in 20 Eng. and 2 Lat. vv. renewed in 1705, also marg. inscr. with 4 Eng. vv., C.

WHITWELL. Inscr. with 4 Eng. vv. and sh. Tobie Waterhous, 1623, 'aged 4 yeares and 5 moneths, full of grace and truthe as a vessel not as ye fountaine', youngest son of Tobie Waterhous, D.D, by Elizth., dau. of Edw. Copley, esq., mur., C.

DEVONSHIRE

Rogers, Sep. Effs. 'Ancient Sepulchral Effigies and Monumental and Memorial Sculpture of Devonshire', by W. H. H. Rogers, 4to, 1877.

CLOVELLY. Robt. Cary, esq., son and h. of Sir Wm. Cary, 1540, in arm.; inlaid in an incised slab of earlier date; C.

COLYTON. Ach. Wm. Pole of Shute, esq., 1587, aged 72, and w. Kath., dau. of Alex. Popham of Huntworth, esq.; a long genealogical inscr. cut in stone; A.T., C.

COMBE-IN-TEIGNHEAD. Inscr. with 4 Eng. vv. and lozenge. Alice, w. of Gregory Hockmore, esq., 'to whome she brought forth fifteen children and lyved after his death a house-keeper and widow fortie yeares and one', 1613; her youngest son Philip pos.

DARTMOUTH, ST. SAVIOUR. John Hauley, founder of the chancel, died (1408), in arm., and 2 ws., Joan (whose hand he holds), 1394, and Alice (mutil.), 1403, triple canopy and foot inscr., both mutil., large, C.

EXETER CATHEDRAL. Sir Peter Courtenay, K.G., 'regis cognatus, camerarius intitulatus, Calesie gratus capitanius, ense probatus', 1409, in arm., nearly effaced, single canopy, 3 shs. (another lost), marg. inscr. (mutil.) with badges at the corners (2 lost), all much worn formerly in N., now in S.C.A.   Wm. Langeton, canon of Exeter, kinsman of Edw. Stafford, bp. of Exeter, 1413, in cope, kng., 1 sh. (others lost), chapel of St. Mary Mag.

FARWAY. Inscr. with 6 Eng. vv. stating he built the church. Rich. Bucknoll, 1632, aged 70, on a board, mur., N.A.

HARFORD. Thos. Williams, esq., twice appointed reader in court, speaker in parliament, 1566, aged 52, in arm., inscr., 8 Eng. vv. and sh., A.T., C.

HONITON. Inscr. Jas. Rodge of Honiton, 'bone lace-siller', benefactor to the poor, 1617, aged 50, in churchyard.

MONKLEIGH. Two angels holding a scroll with inscr. to Jas. Seyntleger, esq., 1509, S.C.

OTTERY ST. MARY. John Sherman, gent., 1542, Wm., his son, 1583, and Rich., his grandson, c. 1620 (?), all in civil dress, inscr. with 10 Lat. vv., S.A.

SHILLINGFORD. Sir Wm. Huddesfeld (attorney-general to Edw. IV, a justice of oyer and terminer, 1499), in arm. with tabard, and w. Kath., dau. of Sir Philip Courtenay (1516), in heraldic mantle, with 1 son and 2 daus., kng., rect. pl., with inscr. and sh. below; chamfer inscr. lost; sm., mur., A.T., C.

STOKE FLEMING. John Corp, 1361, in civil dress with anelace, and (grand-dau.) Eleanor, 1391, on pedestal, double canopy, Fr. inscr., curious, large, now mur., C.

STOKE-IN-TEIGNHEAD. Priest, c. 1370, in mass vests., once in a cross,

now rel. in a slab with incised inscr. to John Symon, rector canon of Exeter, 1497, C.

TIVERTON. John Greenway, mcht., in civil dress, and w. Joan, 1529, arms of mcht.-adventurers; Trinity, scrolls, 3 other shs., and marg. inscr. lost; large, S.C. (which he founded in 1517).

YEALMPTON. Sir John Crokker, cup and standard bearer to Edw. IV, 1508, in arm., rel., mur., N.A.

DORSETSHIRE

BRIDPORT. Inscr. with ach. Edw. Coker, gent., 2nd son of Capt. Robt. Coker of Mapowder, 1685, slain at the Bull Inn in Bridport by one Venner who was an officer under the late Duke of Monmouth in that rebellion, mur., S.C.

COMPTON VALENCE. Thos. Maldon, rector, rebuilder of ch., c. 1440, hf. eff. in mass vests., with 2 large scrolls with text from Psalm, LI, i, worn, N.

DORCHESTER, ST. PETER. Inscr. Oliver Hayne, 'one of ye capitall burgesses of this towne', 1622, aged 59, mur., S.A.

EVERSHOT. Wm. Grey, rector, 1524, in mass vests. with chalice and wafer, C.

LYTCHETT MATRAVERS. Thos. Pethyn, rector, c. 1470, in shroud, sm. now mur., C.

MELBURY SAMPFORD. Sir Gyles Strangwayes, 1562, in arm. with tabard, inscr., and 2 large shs. inscribed the arms of (1) Sir Gyles Strangwayes and Lady Joan his w., eld. dau. of John Wadham of Meryfylde, esq., (2) Hen. Strangwayes, esq., 'who dyed at the syege of Bolleyne', and Margt. his w., dau. of the Lord George Rosse; mur., S.Tr.

MILTON ABBEY. Sir John Tregonwell, knt., D.C.L, a master in chancery, 1565, in arm. with tabard, kng., ach. and 2 shs., mur., A.T., N.C.A.

PIDDLEHINTON. Mr. Thos. Browne, clerk, parson for 27 years, 1617, aged 67, in gown and hat, holding staff and book, sm. rect. pl. with inscr. and 12 Lat. vv., local, mur., C.

PIDDLETOWN. Christ. Martyn, esq., son and h. of Sir Wm. Martyn, 1524, in arm. with tabard, kng., rect., pl. with Trinity, 7 Eng. vv. and sh., mur., S.C.

PIMPERNE. Mrs. Dorothy Williams, 1694, rect. pl. with eff., recumbent skeleton, and inscr; her husband John Williams, clerk, pos.; 'Edmund Colepeper fecit'; mur., S.C.

POOLE, ST. JAMES. Inscr. Edw. Man, mcht., 1622, left 2 sons and 4 daus.; his w. Elinor pos. vestibule wall.

THORNCOMBE. Sir Thos. Brook, 1419, in civil dress, and w. Joan (dau. of Simon Hanap of Gloucester, widow of Robt. Chedder of Bristol), 1437, both with SS. collars; marg. inscr. restored, also 4 shs. blank; large, rel. in new ch.

WHITCHURCH CANONICORUM. Inscr. John Wadham of Catherston, esq., 'captayne of the castell of Sandesfote besides Waymouth', recorder of Lyme Regis, 1584; sh. lost; A.T., C.

WIMBORNE MINSTER. St. Ethelred, King of the West Saxons, martyr, 'anno dn̄i 873 (error for 871) 23 die Aprilis per manus dacorum paganorum occubuit', hf. eff. in regal robes with crown and sceptre, engr. c. 1440, inscr. restored in 17th cent., now in C.

YETMINSTER. John Horsey, esquire for the body of Hen. VIII, lord of Clifton, 1531, in arm., and w. Elizth., lady of Turges Melcombe, sister and h. of Robt. Turges, esq., son and h. of Rich. Turges, esq., scrolls and 2 shs., rel., mur., S.A.

DURHAM

AUCKLAND ST. ANDREW. Fridesmond (Giffard), w. of Rich. Barnes, bp. of Durham, 1581, rect. pl. with cross, floral emblems, scrolls, etc., the work of a York goldsmith, sm., now mur., C.

DURHAM CATHEDRAL. Large indent, 16 by 10 feet, for the br. to bp. Lewis de Beaumont, 1333.

HAUGHTON-LE-SKERNE. Dorothy, w. of Robt. Parkinson of Whessey, gent., 1592, holding her twins, Rich., Marmaduke, in swaddling clothes, inscr., 6 Eng. vv., and sh.; her husband pos.; rel., mur., C.

SEDGEFIELD. Inscr. with helmet and crest. Wm. Hoton, esq., 1445. Man and woman as skeletons in shrouds, c. 1500; inscr. lost; N.A.

ESSEX (LONDON)

AVELEY. Ralph de Knevynton, 1370, in arm., under canopy, sm. rect. pl. and inscr., C.

BARKING. Inscr. and sh. Christ. Merell, citizen and goldsmith of London, 1593, aged 60; also his sister Anne Yardlye, widow, 1579, N. John Tedcastell, gent., in civil dress, and w. Elizth., dau. of Wm. Mey, LL.D, 1596, aged 43, with 9 sons (5 in swaddling clothes); 7 daus. lost; inscr. and ach., C.

BARNSTON. Inscr. Petyr Wood, 'departyd the xxx day of maye beseching Ihu yt was crucifid on the rood to bryng hys sowle to ye blyths yt schall last ays'; 1525, local, mur., N.

BOWERS GIFFORD. Sir John Gifford, c. 1348, in arm. with sh.; head and marg. inscr. lost; large, rel., C.

BRAINTREE. Inscr. Sam Collins, M.D, 'who served about 9 years as principal physician to ye great Czar or Emperor of Russia and afterwards returning from thence taking a journey into France dyed at Paris', 1670, aged 51, mur.

BROMLEY, GREAT. (Wm. Byschopton, rector, 1432), in mass vests., single canopy mutil., foot inscr. in 4 Lat. vv. also mutil., formerly in C., now in S.A.

CANFIELD, GREAT. John Wyseman, Esq., auditor to Hen. VIII, 'of ye revenues of his crown', 1558, in arm., and w. Agnes (Jocelyne), with 4 sons and 6 daus., all kng., 4 shs., C.

CHIGWELL. Sam. Harsnett, 1631, in cope with mitre and crosier, marg. inscr., 4 shs., large, now mur., C.

CHRISHALL. Sir John de la Pole, in arm., and w. Joan, dau. of Sir John de Cobham by Margt., dau. of Hugh Courtenay, earl of Devon, c. 1380, holding hands, triple canopy, 3 shs., marg. inscr. in Fr.; restored by Messrs. Waller; S.A.

COGGESHALL. John Paycock, 1533, in civil dress, and w. Joan; children, scrolls, device, foot and marg. inscr. lost; local, N.C.

COLCHESTER, ST. PETER. John Saye, alderman, 1509, in civic mantle inlaid red, and w. Elizth., 1530, with 4 sons and 1 dau., all kng., rect. pl. with inscr., mur., S.A.

DAGENHAM. Sir Thos. Urswyk, recorder of London, chief baron of the exchequer, 1479, in mantle without coif and hood, and w. in mantle, with 4 sons (stolen) and 9 daus. (the eldest a nun), 2 shs.; 2 other shs. and chamfer inscr. lost; A.T., C.

EAST HAM. Hester, 'the vartuous loveing and obedyent wife' of Frances Neve, citizen and mcht.-tailor of London, 1610, aged about 58, 1 sh., C.

EASTON, LITTLE. Hen. Bourchier, K.G, first earl of Essex, lord treasurer, 1483, in arm., with garter and mantle, crest lost, and his countess Isabel, both with collars of suns and roses, coloured, fine; inscr. lost; A.T., C.

ELMSTEAD. Two hands issuing from clouds and supporting a heart, scroll above, c. 1500; inscr. lost; C.

FAULKBOURNE. Hen. Fortescue, 'one of the fower esquires for the bodie' to Queen Elizth., 'lorde and patron of Falkborne', 1576, in arm., with 4 sons and 5 daus. by his 1st w. Elizth. Stafford, and 1 son by his 2nd w. Dame Mary Darrell, 4 shs., marg., inscr., C.

GOSFIELD. Thos. Rolf, sergeant-at-law, 1440, in robes with coif, inscr. in 10 Lat. vv., A.T., C.

HARLOW. John Gladwin the elder, 1615, aged 95, in civil dress, who 'with longe and tedious sutes in lawe with ye lord of ye mannor of Harlowe did prove the custome for the copieholds to ye great benifitt of posteritie for ever', sm. West wall. N. Tr.

HORKESLEY, LITTLE. Sir Robt. Swynborne, lord of the manor, 1391, in arm., and his son Sir Thos., lord of Hammys, mayor of Bordeaux, captain of the castle of Fronsac, 1412, in arm. with collar of SS., each under triple canopy, 5 shs. (another lost), marg. inscr. in Fr., large, very fine, A.T., S.C. Dame Brygete Marnay, 1549, heraldic mantle, and her 2 husbands, Thos. Fyndorne, esq., and John, lord Marnay, (1524), both in arm. with tabards, 2 shs., A.T., C.

HORNCHURCH. Thos. Hone of Garolens, gent., 1604, aged 63, in civil dress, and w., with 6 sons and 6 daus., 1 sh., sm.; inscr. and children now mur., N.C., effs. rel. in another stone, C.

INGRAVE. Sir Rich. Fitzlewes, 1528, in arm., with tabard, and 4 ws., (1) Alice, (2) unknown, (3) Elizth., (4) Joan, all except no. 2 in heraldic mantles; children, device and inscr. lost; C.

KELVEDON HATCH. Inscr. and sh. Abigail, eld. dau. of Andrew Hawes of London, fishmonger, w. of Robt. Thurkettle, grocer, 1656, had 5 sons and 6 daus., 'whereof 2 sons and 1 dau. lie with her', N.

LAMBOURNE. Robt. Barfott, citizen and mercer of London, 1546, in civil dress, and w. Kath., with 2 groups of children, 4 sons and 1 dau., and 4 sons and 10 daus., mcht. mark and arms of Mercers' Co., C.

LATTON. Sir Peter Arderne, chief baron of the exchequer and a justice of the common pleas, 1467, in robes with coif, and w. Kath. (Bohun), 4 shs.; inscr. lost; A.T., C.

LEYTON, LOW. Inscr. in 15 Eng. vv. 'Good' Lady Mary Kyngestone, died 1548, 'whose yerly obyte and annuversy ys determined to be kept at the cost of her son Sir Hen. Jerninghame of the Queenes garde cheffe capteyn', who pos. 1557, mur., S.A.

LOUGHTON. Abel Guilliams, gent., mcht. of London, 1637, aged 42, in civil dress, and w., with 6 sons and 4 daus., all kng., rect. pl.; inscr. and sh. lost, on floor, church rebuilt in 1877.

NEWPORT. Inscr. Wm. Nightingale, citizen and mcht. of London, 'who after 3 jorneys out of Turkey from Egipte and Sydon departed this life', 1609, aged 30, Tower.

PEBMARSH. Sir Wm. Fitzralph, c. 1323, in arm., cross-legged, with sh., mutil., fine, large; canopy lost; C.

SAFFRON WALDEN. Priest, c. 1430, in mass vests.; inscr. lost; device of pelican in piety renewed; mur. N.A.

SANDON. Two scrolls, arms of Lathum and Goldsmiths' Co., c. 1510; effs. and inscr. lost; C.

SHELLEY. Inscr. John Greene, 1595, aged 89, and w. Kathc., dau. of John Wright, aged 71, had 13 children, 'and the issue of there two bodyes weare one hundred and a leaven in there lyves tyme,' mur., Tower.

SPRINGFIELD. Thos. Coggeshall, esq., 1421, in arm., 1 scroll; inscr., sh., and 3 scrolls lost; C.

STANFORD RIVERS. Inscr. Thos. Grene, 'bayle of this towne', 1535, and ws. Margt. and Margt., 'wylled a prest to syng for 20 yeres for hym, his wyves, chyldren, and all xten soules', and 'an obyte to be kept ye viii day of July for ye soules above sayd', at which 20s. to be bestowed, etc., mur., C.

STEEPLE BUMPSTEAD. Inscr. Sir Thos. Bendishe, bart., ambassador of Chas. I, to the Sultan of Turkey, where he resided 14 years, 1672, aged 65, very lightly engr., mur., N.A.

STONDON MASSEY. John Carre, citizen of London, ironmonger and mcht.-adventurer, 1570, in civil dress, and 2 ws., children lost., inscr. in 8 Eng. vv., mcht. mark, arms of London, Ironmonger's Co., and mcht.-adventurers, C.

THEYDON GARNON. Man in arm. with 2 sons, and w. with 3 daus., c. 1520, kng.; inscr. lost; mur., A.T., C.

TILTY. Gerard Danet of Bronkynsthorp, Leics., esq., councillor to Hen. VIII, 1520, in arm., and w. Mary (Belknap), with 5 sons and 6 daus., 4 shs., marg. inscr., large, C.

TOLLESHUNT D'ARCY. Lady, *c.* 1535, inscr. lost; palimp., on rev. a portion of an abbot or bp., *c.* 1400.

UPMINSTER. Nich. Wayte, citizen and mercer of London, lord of the manor of Geynes, in civil dress, and w. Ellyn, 1545. Lady holding a book, *c.* 1560; inscr. lost; now mur., N.A.

WALTHAM, GREAT. Rich. Everard, esq., 1617, aged 78, in civil dress, and w. Clemence (Wyseman), 1611, mar. 53 years, ach. and 4 shs., N.

WALTHAMSTOW. Sir Geo. Monox, lord mayor of London, died 1543, in civil dress, and w. Dame Ann, died 1500, kng., 3 original shs., London, Bristol, and Drapers' Co.; rel., modern inscr. and 2 other shs. cut in stone; mur., N.A.

WEST HAM. Thos. Staples of West Ham, tanner, who left 20s. yearly to the poor, 1592, in civil dress, and 4 wives, Anne, Margt., Denis, Alice, rect. pl. with 20 Eng. vv. and sh., mur., N.

WIMBISH. Sir John de Wautone, 1347, in arm., feet lost, and w. Ellen, sm., in the head of a cross nearly all lost, as is also the marg. inscr. N.C.

WIVENHOE. Wm., viscount Beaumont and lord Bardolf, 1507, in arm., triple canopy and super-canopy, the side shafts and an Annunciation lost, marg. inscr. mutil., 1 sh., large, C.

WOODHAM WALTER. Death's head inscribed 'Ecce quod eris', *c.* 1650; inscr. lost; C.

WRITTLE. Constans. 'meyden doughter' of John Berners, esq., 1524, with flowing hair, 2 shs. (2 others lost), sm., now mur., S.C.

GLOUCESTERSHIRE
Davis. 'Monumental Brasses of Gloucestershire', by C. T. Davis, 1899. Originally published as a supplement to 'Gloucestershire Notes and Queries'.

BRISTOL, ST. JAMES. Hen. Gibbes, 'sometime mayer and allderman of this citty', 1636, aged 73, in civil dress with 4 sons, and w. Anne, 1631, aged 70, with 4 daus., all kng., rect. pl. with inscr., mur., S.A.

BRISTOL, ST. JOHN. Thos Rowley, mcht., sheriff (in 1475), died 1478, in civil dress, and w. Margt., 1470, mcht. mark and rebus, mur., C.

BRISTOL, ST. MARY REDCLIFF. Sir John Juyn, recorder of Bristol, baron of the exchequer, chief justice of the king's bench, 1439, in robes with coif, inscr. in 8 Lat. vv. and marg. inscr., 2 shs., Lady Chapel. John Brook, serjeant-at-law, justice of assize in west of England, chief steward of the monastery of Glastonbury, 1522, in robes with coif, and w. Joan, dau. and coh. of Rich. Amerike, 1 sh. (others lost), C.

BRISTOL, TEMPLE CHURCH. Priest in cope, *c.* 1460, inscr. lost; palimp., on rev. a lady in mantle, of about same date; rel., mur., C., the palimp. fastened down.

CHELTENHAM, ST. MARY. Wm. Greville of Arle Court, esq., justice of the common pleas, 1513, in robes with coif, and w. with 3 sons and 8 daus., marg. inscr. mutil., much worn, rel., now mur., C.

CHIPPING CAMPDEN. Wm. Grevel, citizen of London, 'flos mercatorum lanar tocius Anglie', 1401, in civil dress with anelace, and w. Marion, 1386, double canopy, slightly mutil., with mcht. marks in the pediments, 4 shs., marg. inscr., very large, C.

CIRENCESTER. Robt. Pagge, wool-mcht., 1440, in civil dress standing on a wool pack bearing his mark, and w. Margt., with 6 sons and 8 daus. (mutil.), double canopy, mcht. marks, and 6 Lat. vv. stating he repaired churches and roads; inscr. lost; Trinity Chapel. Reginald Spycer, mcht. 1442, in civil dress, and 4 ws., Margt., Julian, Margt., Joan, mcht. mark, Trinity Chapel. Phillip Marner (clothier), 1587, in civil dress, standing with staff in hand, shears by head, and dog at feet, inscr. in 6 Eng. vv. stating he left a noble yearly for a sermon in Lent, 7 nobles to the poor, and the interest on £80 to 16 men in Cirencester, Burford, Abingdon and Tetbury, mur., S.A.

DEERHURST. Sir John Cassy, chief baron of the exchequer, 1400, in robes, with coif, lion at feet, and w. Alice (Giffard), with dog named

'Terri' at feet, double canopy with SS. Anne and John Bapt. (the latter stolen about 1860), 4 shs. (2 others lost), marg. inscr., fine, large, N.A.

EASTINGTON. Elizth. (dau. of Sir Wm.) Knevet, (1518), in heraldic mantle, 2 shs. and 2 lozenges, marg. inscr. mutil., now mur., N.C.

FAIRFORD. John Tame, esq., 1500, in arm., and w. Alice (Twynihoe), 1471, 3 shs., chamfer inscr., A.T., C.

GLOUCESTER CATHEDRAL. In N.Tr. is a br. to Rev. Herbert Haines, M.A, master in the cathedral school for 23 years, died 1872, aged 46. He was the author of the well-known 'Manual of Monumental Brasses', published in 1861.

GLOUCESTER, ST. MICHAEL. Wm. Henshawe, bell-founder, 'late maire of this towne', and ws. Alys, 1519, and Agnes; male eff., about 3 sons and 3 daus., lost; formerly N., mur., S.A.

LECHLADE. Wool-mcht. and w., *c.* 1450; children, shs. and marg. inscr. lost; N.

NORTHLEACH. Wool-merchant, in civil dress with anelace and the letter T on girdle, and w., *c.* 1400; inscr. lost; once in N.A., now N. Agnes Fortey (head lost) and her 2 husbands, Wm. Scors, tailor, died 1420, and Thos. Fortey (head lost), woolman, repaired churches and roads, 1447 in arabic numerals, both in civil dress, 2 groups of children, 2 daus. (3 ? other children lost) and 2 sons and 4 daus., canopy and marg. inscr. mutil., worn, N.A. John Fortey, woolman, erector of the roof, 1458, in civil dress, single canopy 6 mcht. marks, marg. inscr. mutil., large, N. Woolman and w. (mutil.), *c.* 1485, with 2 sons and 2 daus., mcht. mark and marg. inscr. in 6 Eng. vv., N.A. John Taylour, woolman, civil dress, and w. Joan, *c.* 1490, with 8 sons and 7 daus., device of sheep on woolpack, marg. inscr. mutil.; Trinity lost; S.C. Thos. Bushe, woolman, mcht. of the staple of Calais, 1525, in civil dress, and w. Joan, 1526, double canopy, slightly mutil., with devices and arms of the staple in the pediments, mcht. mk., marg. inscr.; children lost; N. W. Lawnder, priest, *c.* 1530, in surplice, kng. marg. inscr. mutil.; Trinity and B.V. Mary lost; C.

WESTON-UPON-AVON. Sir John Greville, lord of the manor of Milcot, 1546 in arm. with tabard; 2 shs. lost; C.

WINTERBOURNE. Lady, *c.* 1370; canopy, shs., marg. inscr. lost; N.A.

WORMINGTON. Anne, eld. dau. of Rich. Daston, w. of John Savage of Norbury, Worc., 1605, aged 23, died in childbirth and represented in bed with infant in swaddling clothes, inscr. in 6 Lat. vv., marg. inscr. mutil., 2 shs.; mur., C.

WOTTON-UNDER-EDGE. Thos. lord Berkeley, 1417, in arm. with collar of mermaids, and w. Margt., dau. and h. of Gerard Warren, lord Lisle, 1392; marg. inscr. lost; large, A.T., N.A.

HAMPSHIRE
Cave, C. J. P. List of Hampshire Brasses, printed in Mon. Br. Soc. Trans., V, 247, 295, 343, VI, 1, 21.

ALTON. Inscr. with rebus. Christ. Walaston, groom of the chamber and 'on of ye yostregere (keeper of the goshawks) unto ye late kynges and quenes of famous memorye', 1563 (date added), mur., N.

BRAMLEY. Wm. Joye, yeoman, 1452, in civil dress, with 6 sons standing by his side, much worn, Tower.

CANDOVER, BROWN. Civilian and lady, arm in arm, *c.* 1490; inscr. lost; mur., C.

CRONDALL. (Nich. Kaerwent, rector, 1381), in mass vests.; canopy and inscr. lost; large, rel., C. John Gyfford, heir apparent to Sir Wm. Gyfford, 1563, in arm., kng., and w. Elizth. (eff. lost), with 5 sons (lost) and 8 daus., ach., mur., A.T., C.

HAVANT. Thos. Aileward, rector, 1412, in cope, inscr. with 2 Lat. vv. sh., C.

HEADBOURNE WORTHY. John, son of Simon Kent of Reading, a scholar of Winchester (died 1434), in civil dress, sm., now mur., C.

HECKFIELD. Inscr., 2 Evang. symbols and rebus. John Creswell 'lorde of this towne at the tyme of the byldyng of thys stepyll and the newe yle and chapell in this cherche', 1518, and w. Isabel, now mur., N.

HINTON AMPNER. Inscr. and ach. Sir Hugh Stewkeley, knt. and bart., 1642; 'Thos. Brome fecit', mur., C.

SOMBORNE, KING'S. Two civilians, c. 1380; inscr. lost; rel., C.

ODIHAM. Civilian with pouch and dagger and w., c. 1480; inscr. lost; now mur., N.   Thos. Chapman, 1522 (eff. in civil dress lost), w. Agnes, with 9 daus., device of a crossbow on inscr., now mur., N.C.

PETERSFIELD. Inscr. with ach. Thos. Aylwyn, M.D, 1704, mur., N.A.

RINGWOOD. John Prophete, prebendary of Lincoln, dean of Hereford and York, 1416, in cope, single canopy much mutil.; marg. inscr. and 6 shs. lost; large, C.

SHERBORNE ST. JOHN. Raulin Brocas, in civil dress, and his sister Margt., c. 1360, hf. effs. Fr. inscr., sm., mur., N.C.   Bernard Brocas, esq., 1488, in arm. with tabard, kng. to a cross now lost, below is a skeleton in shroud, marg. inscr. in 8 Lat. vv. mutil., ach. and 2 shs., N.C.

SHERFIELD-ON-LODDON. Stephen Hadnall, esq., born in Salop, one of the privy chamber to Queen Mary, died at Launcelevye in 1590, in civil dress, kng.; mar. Margt., dau. of Thos. Atkins, esq., had 2 daus. and cohs., ach., mur., C.

STOKE CHARITY. Thos. Wayte, esq., 1482, in arm., with fig. of Our Lord in Pity, 1 sh. (3 others lost), A.T., N.

THRUXTON. Sir John Lysle, lord of Wodynton in the Isle of Wight, husband of lady Elizth. Lysle, died 1407, engr. c. 1425, in arm., triple canopy, marg. inscr. and 4 shs., large, C.

WALLOP, NETHER. Dame Mary Gore, prioress (of Amesbury), 1436, in kirtle, veil head-dress, barbe and mantle, N.

WEEKE. Figure of St. Christopher and inscr. to Wm. Complyn, 1498 (date added), and w. Annes, sm. mur., N.

WINCHESTER CATHEDRAL. Inscr. Rich. Boles, killed at Alton in 1641; 'Ric. Boles, M.A, composuit posuitque An. Dom. 1689', mur., N.

WINCHESTER COLLEGE CHAPEL AND CLOISTERS. Edw. Tacham, fellow, 1473, hf. eff. in cope, mur., W. cloister.   John Gylbert, fellow, 1514, three-quarter eff. in mass vests., mur., E. cloister.

WINCHESTER, ST. CROSS. John de Campeden, warden of the hospital (canon of Southwell, 1382), in cope, with inscr., marg. inscr. with text from Job, and shs. of the Passion and Trinity, very large, rel., C. Rich. Harward, 'decretorum doctor', warden, 1493, in cap and almuce, inscr. restored, rel., C.

ISLE OF WIGHT

CALBOURNE. Man in arm., c. 1380; canopy and inscr. lost; once on A.T., slab and tomb destroyed, rel., S.A.

FRESHWATER. Man in arm., of the Compton family, c. 1365, with sh. on jupon, scroll in Fr. from hands; inscr. lost; on a board in Vestry.

HEREFORDSHIRE

B. and M. Instit. 'The Monumental Brasses of Herefordshire and Worcestershire', by C. T. Davis, printed in the Transactions of the Birmingham and Midland Institute (Archaeological Section), vol. for 1884-5, p. 62.

CLEHONGER. Man in arm. and w., c. 1470; inscr. lost; N.C.

HEREFORD CATHEDRAL. St. Ethelbert, king and martyr, a sm. seated fig. holding his crowned head in his left hand; from the brass to bp. Thos. de Cantilupe, died 1282, engr. c. 1290; now in a glass case in canons' vestry.   John Trilleck, bp., 1360, in episcopal vests. with mitre and crosier, single canopy with super-canopy, marg. inscr. 2 shs.; canopy, inscr. and shs. restored; large, C.   John

Stockton, mayor of Hereford, 1480, in civil dress with ton or cask underfeet, much worn; inscr. lost; formerly in N., now mur., N.E. Tr. Many other brasses.

LEDBURY. Thos. Caple, esq., 1490, in arm. with livery collar, now mur., C.

HERTFORDSHIRE

Andrews. 'Memorial Brasses in Hertfordshire Churches', by W. F. Andrews, 1st ed., 1886, 2nd ed., 1903.

ALBURY. Hen. Barley, in arm. with salade, and w., c. 1475, with 4 daus., ach.; sons and inscr. lost; N.

ALDBURY. Sir Ralph Verney, 1547, in arm. with tabard, and w. Elizth., in heraldic mantle, with 9 sons and 3 daus., 4 shs.; chamfer inscr. and 6 shs. on side of tomb lost; A.T., N.C.

ALDENHAM. Civilian and w., c. 1520; children and inscr. lost; S.C.

AMWELL, GREAT. Friar in gown and hood, c. 1440; inscr. lost; sm., now mur., N.

ASTON. John Kent, servant to Edw. VI, Queens Mary and Elizth., 1592, aged 72, in habit of yeoman of the guard, and w. Mary, dau. of Thos. Saunders, had 5 sons and 5 daus., N.

BARLEY. Inscr. Robt. Bryckett, gent., 1566, aged 49; palimp., on rev. a portion of another inscr. to Rich. Pecok, citizen and armourer of London, and ws., 15th cent., now mur., S.C.

BERKHAMPSTEAD, GREAT. (Rich. Torryngton, 1356), in civil dress, and w. Margt. (1349), holding hands; double canopy and nearly all marg. inscr. lost; 2 shs., mur., C.   Man in arm., c. 1335; inscr. lost; rel., S.C.   Lady, c. 1370; canopy and inscr. lost; rel., N.Tr.

BROXBOURNE. Sir John Say, 1478, in arm. with tabard and collar of suns and roses, head lost, and w. Elizth. (dau. of Laur. Cheyne) of Cambs., esq., 1473, in heraldic mantle, enamelled, marg. inscr. mutil., ach. and 2 shs. A.T., C.   John Borrell, serjeant-at-arms to Hen. VIII, 1531, in arm. holding mace, legs lost, 2 scrolls bearing 'espoier en dieu'; w. Elizth., 8 sons, 3 daus., and inscr. lost; N.A.

DIGSWELL. John Peryent, esquire for the body and (pennon-bearer) to Rich. II, esquire to (Hen. IV) and Hen. V, master of the horse to Joan (of Navarre, Queen of England), in arm. with leopard at feet, and w. Joan, (dau. of Sir John Risain, chief lady in waiting to the said Queen), 1415, with hedgehog at feet and swan on collar of dress, both with SS. collars, marg. inscr. much mutil., 2 shs. (other lost) large, C.   Thos. Hoore, citizen and mercer of London, 1495, civil dress, and w. Alice, with 4 sons and 8 daus., scrolls, 4 shs. including 2 of Mercers' Co.; Trinity lost; C.

HADHAM, MUCH. Clement Newce, esq., citizen and mercer of London, 1579, in civil dress, and w. Mary, 1582, with 8 sons and 9 daus., 4 shs. including London and Mercers' Co., and crest, N.

HADHAM, LITTLE. Man in arm. and w., c. 1485, with 4 daus.; inscr. lost; now mur., C.

HEMEL HEMPSTEAD. Robert Albyn, in arm., and w. Margt. (1390), Fr. inscr. mutil., 2 shs., once on A.T., now mur., S.A.

HITCHIN. Mcht. of the staple of Calais, 1452, and w. Alice, with 4 sons and 6 daus., inscr. mutil., 6 scrolls lost; 1 sh. remains but illegible, C.   Female in shroud, mutil.; remains of the br. to Nich. Mattock, mcht. of the staple, citizen and fishmonger of London, and w. Elizth., 1485, with 2 sons and 1 dau., all in shrouds, a religious device, scrolls, shs. and inscr.; N.C.   Jas. Hert, D.D, vicar, 1489, in cope without almuce, a wounded and bleeding heart above, another lost as is also the inscr., some device and 2 shs., C.

HOLWELL. Chalice and wafer, two woodhouses or wild men, and inscr. Robt. Wodehouse, rector, 1515, benefactor to ch. N.

HUNSDON. Jas. Gray, 35 years park and housekeeper at Hunsdon, 1591, aged 69, in hunting dress shooting at a stag while Death strikes him with a dart, rect. pl. with inscr. and 6 Eng. vv., mur., N.

IPPOLLITTS. Ryce Hughes, citizen and haberdasher of London, in civil dress, with 1 son, and w. Alice, 1594, aged 29, with 2 daus. 'all deceased and lye buried lykewyse in this church at ye chauncell dore', all kng., rect. pl. with inscr. and 4 Eng. vv., mur., C.

KNEBWORTH. Simon Bache, treasurer of the household to Hen. V, canon of St. Paul's London, 1414, in rich cope with B.V. Mary, SS. Peter, Nicholas, Andrew, John Bapt., Paul, Thos. of Canterbury, Jas. the Great, on orphreys, head of Our Lord on morse, 2 shs., C.

MIMMS, NORTH. Priest, c. 1370-80, in mass vests. with chalice covered by paten on breast, feet on stag, under canopy with God the Father, censing angels, and SS. Peter, John Evang., Barth., — Paul, Jas. the Great, Andrew, resting on a bracket composed of a sh. betw. 2 lions, the stem. and inscr. lost, ; original stone destroyed, now mur. and inaccurately rel., C.

NORTHAW. Inscr. and 2 shs. Geo. Sowthaik, citizen and grocer of London, 1606, aged 86; mar. Elizth., dau. of Philip Gunter, alderman of London, had 5 sons and 5 daus.; his son Thos., grocer of London pos., N.

PELHAM, FURNEUX. Robt. Newport, esq., founder of a chapel, 1518, in arm., and w. Mary, with 2 sons and 3 daus., all kng., 1 sh.; inscr., Trinity, scrolls and 2 other shs. lost; sm., mur., N.A.

PELHAM, STOCKING. Sh., with rebus, letter H. on a heart, c. 1440, inscr. lost; N.

RICKMANSWORTH. Thos. Day, 1613, in civil dress with staff and book, and 2 ws., Alice, 1585, and Joan, 1598, N.A.

ROYSTON. Cross with the five wounds, c. 1500; inscr. lost; C. under altar.

ST. ALBAN'S ABBEY. Thos. de la Mare, abbot 1349-96, brass engr. c. 1370-80, eff. in rich vests. with hands folded, very fine canopy with God the Father and censing angels, SS. Peter, Paul, Alban, and Offa, King of Mercia, founder of the monastery, in the upper part; below them SS. John Evang., Andrew, Thos., — Jas. the Great, Barth., Philip, with attendant prophets, marg. inscr. unfinished, rect. pl. in Abbot Wheathampstede's Chantry.

Thos. Fayreman, mcht. of the staple of Calais (bailiff of St. Alban's), 1411, in civil dress, and w. (Alice), inscr. mutil., very much worn, N.C.A.   Robt. Beauner (or Beauver), monk, held various offices for more than 40 years, c. 1460, holding a bleeding heart, Presbytery. Sir Anth. Grey, son and h. of Edm., earl of Kent, 1480, in arm. with collar of suns and roses, 1 sh.; inscr. and 3 other shs. lost; Presbytery.

ST. ALBANS, ST. MICHAEL. John Pecok, in civil dress, and w. Maud (Weyland), c. 1380, inscr. in Fr., 2 shs., S.A.   Man in arm. of the Peacock family, c. 1380, 1 sh., Peacock with a label; inscr. lost; N.

ST. ALBAN'S, ST. STEPHENS. Wm. Robins, esq., clerk of the signet to Edw. IV, 1482, in arm., and w. Kath., with 4 sons and 5 daus.; inscr. lost; now mur. on a board, S.C.

SAWBRIDGEWORTH. John Leventhorpe, esq., 1433, in arm. with Lancastrian livery collar, and widow Kath. (Twychet), 1437; 2 shs., Royal and Duchy of Lancaster; inscr. and other shs. lost; large S.A. John Leventhorpe, esq., 1484, and w. Joan Barrington, 1448, in shrouds holding inscribed hearts, 2 shs., both Royal, 6 Lat. vv.; inscr. and other shs. lost; slab removed from S.A. to W. end of Nave, verses now mur., S.A.

STANDON. John Feld, alderman of London, mcht. of the staple of Calais, 1474, in civil dress with mantle, with 2 sons and 1 dau., also John Feld, esq. (1477), his son, in arm. with tabard, with 2 sons and 2 daus., 4 shs., Feld, London, the Staple, and mcht. mark, marg. inscr. mutil., A.T., N.A.

STANSTEAD ABBOTS. Wm. Saxaye of Gray's Inn, gent., son of Hen. Saxaye, citizen and mcht.-venturer of London, by Joyce, dau. of Robt. Trappes of London, goldsmith, 1581, aged 23, in civil dress, ach., C.

TEWIN. Thos. Pygott, gent., whose ancestors lived here upwards of 300 years, 1610, aged 70, in civil dress.

WALKERN. Inscr. Rich., son of John Humberstone, 1581; palimp., on rev. a portion of an inscr. to John Lovekyn, 4 times mayor of London, 'bis fuit hic maior, iterum bis rege jubente', died 1370, buried in St. Michael's, Crooked Lane, London, plate engr. later; mur., Vestry.

WARE. Wm. Pyrry, in civil dress, and ws. Agnes and Alice, each with 5 sons and 5 daus., engr. c. 1470 (date not filled in), rel., mur., N.

WATFORD. Sir Hugh de Holes, justice of the king's bench, 1415, in judicial robes with coif, large, mutil.; marg. inscr. lost; now mur., C. Hen. Dickson, 1610, Geo. Miller, 1613, and Anth. Cooper, all in civil dress, servants to Sir Chas. Morrison, his widow Dorothy, (who pos.), and their son Sir Chas., rect. pl. with inscr., N.C.

WATTON-AT-STONE. Sir Philip Peletoot, 1361, in arm.; legs, canopy, and inscr. restored in 1851; large, N.C.   Priest, c. 1370, in choir cope, lion at feet, large; canopy and inscr. lost; rel., C.

WEATHAMPSTEAD. Civilian, c. 1510; a lady, sideface, c. 1510; 2 sons, 6 daus., and 3 shs.; frags. found in different parts of the ch. during a restoration and now on one slab in N.Tr.

WORMLEY. Walter Tooke of Popes in Bishop Hatfield, esq., in civil dress, and w. Angelett, 1598, with 8 sons and 4 daus., 4 Eng. vv., 1 sh.; C.

HUNTINGDONSHIRE

Macklin, Rev. H. W. 'The Brasses of Huntingdonshire', published in Trans. Mon. Brass Soc., III, 144, 167.

DIDDINGTON. Wm. Taylard, 1505, in arm. with tabard (upper hf. lost), and w. Elizth., in heraldic mantle, kng., square headed canopy, (mutil.) with SS. in the side shafts, Our Lord, SS. John Bapt., John Evang., — B.V. Mary and Child, Mary Mag., Kath., Inscr. in 6 Lat. vv.; 5 sons, 7 daus., Trinity, and 2 shs. lost; local, mur., A.T.

GIDDING, LITTLE. Inscr. with lozenge. Eleanor, dau. of Geo. Long of London, mcht., relict of Jas. Goddard of Marston, Wilts., gent., 1717.

OFFORD DARCY. Wm. Taylard, LL.D, rector, c. 1530, in cap and acad., kng.; inscr., etc. lost; local, C.

SAWTRY ALL SAINTS. (Sir Wm.) Moyne, 1404, in arm., and w. Mary, marg. inscr. nearly all lost, large, mur. C. in new ch., A.T. destroyed.

WINWICK. Inscr. Edw., son of Edw. Collins, gent., 1685, aged 49, left an only son Edm., Tower.

KENT

Belcher. Kentish Brasses', by W. D. Belcher, 2 vols., 1888, 1905. G. and S. 'List of Monumental Brasses remaining in the county of Kent in 1922, with notes of some lost examples', by Ralph Griffin and Mill Stephenson.

ADDINGTON. Wm. Snayth, esq., lord of the manor, sheriff of Kent (in 1407), died 1409, in arm., and w. Alice, double canopy slightly mutil.; 5 shs. lost; mur. in original slab, S.C.

ASH-NEXT-SANDWICH. Christ. Septvans *alias* Harflete of Moland in Ash, esq. (1575), in arm., and w. Mercy, born 1530, died 1602, 6 Lat. vv., marg. inscr. mutil., ach. and 2 shs.; children lost; N.C. Walter Septvans *alias* Harflet of Checker in Ash, esq., born 1567, died 1642, in civil dress with cloak, and w. Jane, born 1576, died 1626, with 3 sons, Thos., Wm., John, and 3 daus., Jane, Mercy, Jone, 6 Lat. vv., marg. inscr., ach. and 2 shs., N.C.

ASHFORD. Head of a priest, c. 1320, rel., C.   Elizth., countess of Athol, dau. of Hen., lord Ferrers of Groby, w. of David de Strabolgi, earl of Athol, 1375, arms and feet lost, pediment of round headed canopy, 2 banners, royal arms and Ferrers, marg. inscr. in Fr. much mutil., rel., C.

BECKENHAM. Sir Humf. Style, 1552, in arm. with tabard, and 2 ws. in heraldic mantles, (1) Brydgett, with 6 sons and 3 daus., (2) Elizth., with 1 son and 1 dau., all kng., 4 shs., mur., S.C.

BEXLEY. Hunting horn with bawdrick enclosing a sh. with arms of Castelyn; inscr. and 2 other shs. lost; 15th cent., N.C.

BIDDENDEN. Rich. Allarde, alderman of Rochester, 1593, aged 60, in civil dress, and 3 ws., (1) Helen, with 3 sons, Hen., Rich., John, and 3 daus., Anne, Mary, Elizth., effs. lost, (2) Joan, with 1 son Francis, and 2 daus., Susan, Phoebe, (3) Thomasin, S.C. Inscr. with sh. Elizth., eld. dau. of Anth. Nowers, gent., w. of Francis Taylor, gent., 1700, had 6 children, N.A.

BOBBING. Sir Arnold Savage, 1410, in arm., and widow Dame Joan, (1413), double canopy all lost but portions of the shafts, engr. c. 1420, now mur. in original slab, N.

BOUGHTON-UNDER-BLEAN. Thos. Hawkins, servant to Hen. VIII, 1587, aged 101, in arm., inscr. in 12 Eng. vv., ach., N.C.

BROMLEY. Inscr. Mr. John King of London, draper, free of the Clothworkers' Co., 1603, aged 51; mar. Susan Woodwarde and left issue then living Hen., Jas., John and Elizth., N.

CANTERBURY, ST. MARGARET. John Wynter, twice mayor, 1470, ordained a light for the altar, recut and filled in, C.

CANTERBURY, ST. MARTIN. Mich. Fraunces, gent., in civil dress, and w. Jane, dau. of Wm. Quilter, esq., she died 4 and he 10 Jan., 1587, with 1 son and 5 daus., ach. and sh., C.

CANTERBURY, ST. MARY NORTHGATE. Raff Brown, alderman and mayor (in 1507 and 1510, died 1522), in civil dress, kng., arms of city on front of desk, inscr. in 4 Eng. vv., rect. pl., local, mur., S.A.

CHART, GREAT. Notary, c. 1470, in civil dress with ink horn and penner; inscr. lost; mur., S.A. Wm. Goldwell, 1485, in civil dress, and w. Alice; children, Trinity, marg. inscr. with rebus lost; A.T., N.C.

✓ CHARTHAM. Sir Robt., son of Sir Robt. de Setvans, 1306, in arm., cross-legged, surcoat, ailettes, and sh. charged with winnowing fans; marg. inscr. in Lombardics and 2 shs. lost; formerly in C., now in N.Tr.

CHATHAM. Inscr. (sh. lost). Steven Borough, born at Northam, Devon, 25 Sept., 1525, died 1584, 'in his lifetime discovered Muscovia by ye northerne sea passage to St. Nicholas in the yere 1553', when Sir Hugh Willoughby and the crews of two other ships were frozen to death in Lappia the same winter, afterwards he was one of the 4 principal masters in ordinary to the royal navy, N.

CHISLEHURST. Alan Porter, rector, 1482, hf. eff. in mass vests., rel., A.T., C. Rich. Carmarden, esq., supervisor of customs and subsidies in the port of London, 1603, aged 76, rel., C.

COBHAM. Dame Jone de Kobeham, single canopy, engr. c. 1310-20; marg. inscr. in Fr. in Lombardics, and 4 shs. restored; large, C.
Sir John de Cobham (2nd baron Cobham), 1354, in arm., single canopy, 2 shs., marg. inscr. in Fr.; head, portions of canopy, parts of inscr., 1 sh. restored; large, C. Sir John de Cobham (3rd baron Cobham), died 10 Jan., 1407-8, founder of the college in 1362, brass engr. c. 1365, in arm. holding a church, single canopy, 2 shs., marg. inscr. in Fr.; parts of the canopy, 2 shs., and a greater portion of marg. inscr. restored; large, C. Sir Thos. de Cobham, 1367, in arm., single canopy, 2 shs., marg. inscr. in Fr.; portions of canopy, the 2 shs., and most of marg. inscr. restored; large, C. Dame Maude de Cobeham, (sister or dau. of Sir Wm. Pympe), w. of Sir Thos. de Cobeham (of Roundall), 1380, single canopy, 2 shs., marg. inscr. in Fr.,; portions of canopy, the 2 shs., and greater part of marg. inscr. restored; large, C. Dame Margt. de Cobeham (dau. of Hugh Courtenay, 2nd earl of Devon), w. of Sir John de Cobham the founder, 1395, single canopy with B.V. Mary and Child above centre finial, 2 shs., marg. inscr. in Fr.; slight restorations canopy and inscr.; large. C. Sir Nicholas Hawberk, (3rd)

husband of Dame Joan, lady of Cobham, died at Cowling Castle, 1407, in arm., with son John standing on a pedestal, triple canopy with Trinity, B.V. Mary and child, and St. George, each under a sm. canopy, 2 shs., marg. inscr.; helmet under head and crest, dexter sh. and hf. sinister, sm. details of canopy and a few words of inscr. restored; large, C.

Joan, lady of Cobham, formerly w. of Sir Reginald Braybrook, 1433, in mantle, with 6 sons and 4 daus., 3 scrolls, 6 shs., and inscr., large, C. Joan, lady Cobham, only dau. and h. of Sir John de la Pole by Joan, only dau. and h. of Sir John de Cobham the founder, succeeded her grandfather in 1408. She had 5 husbands, (1) Sir Robt. de Hemenhale, who died in 1391, and was buried in Westminster Abbey: (2) Sir Reginald Braybrook: (3) Sir. Nich. Hawberk: (4) Sir John Oldcastle, burnt as a Lollard in 1417: and (5) Sir John Harpeden, who survived her and was buried in Westminster Abbey in 1438, where his brass still remains. Sir Thos. Brooke, (8th) baron Cobham, kinsman and h. of Sir Richard Beauchamp, 1529, in arm., and (1st) w. Dorothy, dau. of Sir Hen. Haydon, with 7 sons and 6 daus., 4 shs., marg. inscr.; C.

CRANBROOK. Civilian, c. 1520, with a child in swaddling clothes, mcht. mark with initials T.S.; inscr. lost; S.C.

CRAY, ST. MARY. Benj. Greenwood, esq., son of Augustine Greenwood of Lancaster, mcht., 1773, aged 81, rec. pl. with inscr., C.

DARTFORD. Rich. Martyn of Dartford, in civil dress with mantle, and w. — , 1402, double canopy, marg. inscr., repaired and rel., large, C. W. Death, gent., principal of Staple Inn, one of the attorneys of the common pleas at Westminster, 1590, aged 63, in civil dress, and 2 ws., Elizth., holding an infant in swaddling clothes, she had 10 sons and 6 daus., and died in 1582, aged 40, and Anne, 1 sh., rel., N.

DEAL, UPPER. Thos. Boys, esq., 'in his youthe a gentleman at armes at Calles and mayor for two years together of Calles', attended Hen. VIII at the siege of Boulogne, receiver of Guisnes, made captain of Deal Castle in 1551, died 1562, aged 60, in arm., kng., ach. and motto, mur., S.C.

DOVER, ST. MARY. Wm. Jones, gent., 1638, aged 75, in civil dress, and w. Kath., 1636, aged 72, mar. 49 years, had 1 son and 9 daus., 'he was married on a Saboth day and buried on a Saboth day, both in this church', 2 shs., now mur., N.C.

DOWNE. Jacob Verzelini, esq., born in Venice, died 1606, aged 84, in civil dress, and w. Elizth., born in Antwerp, of the ancient house of Vandburen and Mace, died 1607, aged 73, mar. 49 years and 4 months, with 6 sons and 3 daus., 3 shs., large, C.

ERITH. Emme, w. of John Wode, citizen of London, merchant of the staple, 1471, 1 sh., S.C.

FAVERSHAM. Hen. Hatche, mcht.-adventurer jurat and one of the barons of the five ports, a great benefactor to the ch. and town, 1533, in civil dress, and w. Joan, large double canopy, arms of the 5 ports and mcht.-adventurers, mcht. mark and device of a dolphin, marg. inscr., large, N. Rich. Colwell, mayor of Faversham in 1533, in civil dress, and 2 ws., Agnes (with 2 sons and 3 daus.) and Agnes (with 3 sons and 1 dau.), 8 Eng. vv., marg. inscr. with rebus and shs. at corners, the latter lost, worn, S.A.

FAWKHAM. Inscr. and sh. Rich. Meredyth, esq., 'clarke of the catrye' to Queen Elizth. and Jas. I, 1607; mar. Elizth., dau. of Humf. Mitchell, esq., had 4 sons, Humf., Rich., Edm., John, N.

FOLKESTONE. Inscr. Joan, w. of Thos. Harvey, 1605, aged 50, had 7 sons and 3 daus., restored, mur., C. One of her sons was the celebrated Wm. Harvey, discoverer of the circulation of the blood.

GILLINGHAM. Inscr. John Bregge, vicar (1416-1425), rel., N.

GRAVENEY. John Martyn, justice of the common pleas, 1436, in robes with coif, holding a heart inscribed 'Ihu-m'ey', and w. Anne (Botiler), double canopy slightly mutil., 12 Lat. vv. and marg. inscr.; 5 shs. lost; very large, N.C.

HARDRES, UPPER. John Strete, rector, 1405, in acad. with cap, kng. to a bracket on which stand figs. of SS. Peter and Paul, fine, C.

HERNE. Peter Halle, esq., in arm., and w. Elizth., dau. of Sir Wm. Waleys by Dame Margt., dau. of Sir John Seynclere, c. 1430, with clasped hands, 1 sh., N.C. Inscr. W. Bysmare, citizen and goldsmith of London, 1456, date added, and ws. Elizth., Agnes, and Margt., mutil., mur., N.C. Dame Christine, w. of Sir Matthew Phelip, citizen and goldsmith, mayor of London (in 1464), 'que migravit ab hac valle miserie' 25 May, 1470, in mantle with hands apart, 2 shs. (2 others lost), N.C. Inscr. John Fyneaux of Herne, esq., 1592, and w. Margt., leaving an only dau. and h. Elizth., mar. to John Smith, esq., mur., C.

HEVER. Margt., w. of Wm. Cheyne, 1419, in mantle, head on cushion supported by angels, 1 sh. (another lost), C. Sir Thos. Bullen, K.G, earl of Wiltshire and Ormond, 1538, in arm. with collar, mantle and hood of the Order, large, A.T.

HORSMONDEN. (John de Grofhurst), priest, in mass vests. with inscr. on breast stating he gave in 1338 the manor of Leveshothe to the abbot and convent of Beghame (Bayham) for a chaplain for the church of Horsmonden and chapel of Leveshothe, engr. c. 1340, under single canopy, rel. and restored in 1867 and a new marg. inscr. added recording the same, C.

HYTHE. Inscr. with 4 Eng. vv. John Bredgman, 'jurat of this towne and porte of Heythe ye laste bayly and fyrste mayer of ye same', 1581, mur., S.A.

IGHTHAM. Sir Rich. Clement, in arm. with tabard, and 1st w. Anne, 1528, inscr. and 1 sh; w., lower part of man and other shs. lost; rel., C.

KEMSING. Thos. de Hop (rector 1341-47), hf. eff. in mass vests., rel., C.

LEIGH. Shrouded fig. in a tomb and kng. eff. of a lady summoned by an angel, c. 1580, rect. pl; inscr. lost; sm., N.

LENHAM. Inscr. and sh. Robt. Thompson, 1642, aged 47; mar. (1) Dorothy, by whom 2 sons and 6 daus., (2) Sarah, by whom 6 sons and 2 daus., and died 'great of the ninth'; Robt. was grandchild of Mary, w. of Robt. Honywood of Charing, esq., 'who had at her decease lawfully descended 367 children, 16 of her own body, 114 grandchildren, 228 in the third generation and 9 in the fourth', C.

LULLINGSTONE. Sir Wm. Pecche, 1487, in arm., inscr. in 6 Lat. vv., 4 shs., C.

LYDD. Thos. Harte, yeoman, sometime baylye of Lydd, 1557, in civil dress, and w. Malyn, mur., S.A.

MAIDSTONE, ALL SAINTS. Thos. Beale, twice mayor, 1593, in civil dress, and 2 ws., Joan and Alice, with 6 sons and 2 daus. surviving of 21 children; also his ancestors, Wm. Beale, 1534, and w. Joan, with 4 sons and 3 daus.; Robt., 1490, and w. Agnes, with 2 sons and 1 dau.; John, 1461, and ws. Agnes and Alice, with 2 sons; Wm., 1429, and w. Kath., with 2 sons and 2 daus.; and John 1399, and w. —, with 1 son; sm. kng. effs. in 6 tiers each of 3 divisions, rect. pl. with inscr., S.C.

MALLING, WEST. Elizth., w. of Geo. Perepoynt, esq., 1543, 2 shs., one palimp, on rev. canopy work, 15th cent., lower part of eff., children, another sh. and marg. inscr. lost; C.

MARGATE. Nich. Canteys, 1431, in civil dress with long beard, anelace, ornamented shoes, C. Man in arm., c. 1590, and ach.; a modern inscr. ascribed to Wm. Cleaybroke of Nash Court, 1638, C. Ship of war under full sail and inscr. Roger Morris, one of the 6 principal masters of attendance of his Majesty's navy royal, 1615, rect. pl., C.

MEREWORTH. Wm. Shosmyth, citizen and skinner of London, 1479, in civil dress, and w. Julian, arms of Skinners' Co.; children and inscr. lost; sm., vestry, N.A.

MINSTER, ISLE OF SHEPPEY. Man in arm. of the Northwood family, in cyclas with sh. on thigh, c. 1330. Lady, c. 1335, with plaited hair, large gorget, sleeveless cote-hardie, and curious hood, head on cushion. *The two figures, although now relaid in one stone on C. floor, belonged to two separate monuments. They are usually assigned to Sir John de Northwood who died in 1320, and his wife Joan, dau. of Barth. de Badlesmere, who also died in 1320.*

MONKTON, ISLE OF THANET. Priest, c. 1460, in mass vests.; inscr. lost; N.

NEWINGTON-NEXT-HYTHE. John Clerk, vicar, 1501, in mass vests. with chalice and wafer, sm., mur., C.

NEWINGTON-NEXT-SITTINGBOUTNE. Wm. Monde, 1488, and John Sayer, both in civil dress, N.A.

NORTHFLEET. Peter de Lacy, rector, prebendary of Swerdes in Dublin Cath., 1375, in mass vests.; canopy lost; rel. and marg. inscr. restored, large, C.

ORPINGTON. Thos. Wilkynson, M.A., prebendary of Ripon, rector of Harrow-on-the-Hill and of Orpington, 1511, in cope, rel., now mur., C.

OTTERDEN. Thos. Seintlegier, esq., 1408, in arm., marg. inscr. mutil.; 2 shs. lost; N.

PENSHURST. Inscr., ach. and sh. John Paswater, gent., servant and steward to Sir Thos. Cheyney, K.G, lord warden of the cinque ports, and then to Sir Hen. Sydney, K.G, lord president of Wales and lord deputy of Ireland, 1577, and w. Elizth., mur., C.

PRESTON-NEXT-FAVERSHAM. Valentine Baret, esq., 1440, in arm., and w. Cecily, 1442; shs. lost; C.

RAINHAM. Inscr. (sm. floriated cross lost), Jas. Donet, esq., 1409, C.

ROCHESTER, ST. MARGARET. Thos. Cod, vicar, 1465, hf. eff. in surplice, cope, and amice; palimp., on rev. a similar eff. but wearing almuce; inscr. in 9 Lat. vv.; inlaid in a copper plate and now mur., N.A.

SALTWOOD. Angel issuing from clouds and holding a heart, sh. and inscr. 'Here lieth the bowells' of Dame Anne, w. of Wm. Muston, 1496, C.

SANDWICH, ST. CLEMENT. Inscr. and ach. Geo. Rawe, gent., mayor and customer of the town, Mcht.-Adventurer and haberdasher of London, and w. Sara, both died 1583, had 7 sons and 5 daus.; a marg. inscr. and 4 shs. incised in slab; C.

SEAL. Sir Wm. de Bryene, lord of Kensing and Sele, 1395, in arm., 2 shs., marg. inscr., large, C.

SHELDWICH. Sir Rich. Attelese, 1394, in arm., and w. Dennis, lower hf. of eff. gone, fine double canopy slightly mutil., inscr. also mutil., several shs. lost; N.C. Joan, w. of Wm. Mareys, 1431, hf. eff. in shroud holding inscribed heart, 2 shs., one loose, C.

SOUTHFLEET. John Urban, esq., 1420, in civil dress, and w. Joan dau. of Sir John Reskemer; a bracket with fig. between the effs. lost; partly covered, C. John Sedley, an auditor of the king's exchequer, in civil dress, and w. Elizth., c. 1520, with 4 sons and 2 daus., marg. inscr. mutil., on a sm. pl. 'Dyg not wtyn too ffote of this tombe'; Trinity lost; A.T., S.A.

STONE. Inscr. in 8 Eng. vv., and 4 shs., including the Mcht.- Adventurers and Drapers' Co. Robt. Chapman, esq., mcht.-adventurer and draper of London, owner of Stone Castle, 1574, C.

TEYNHAM. John Frogenhall, esq., 1444, in arm. with SS. collar; inscr. lost; S.Tr.

ULCOMBE. Ralph St. Leger, esq., 1470, in arm., and w. Anne; 2 shs. lost; N.A.

WESTERHAM. Rich. Hayward, 1529, in civil dress, and w. Anne (eff. lost), rel., mur., S.A. Thos., son of John Potter, 1531, in civil dress, S.A. Inscr. Rich. Potter, esq., 1563, had by his 3 ws., Elizth., Anne, and Alice, 20 children, whereof 3 sons and 7 daus. survived him; palimp., on rev. a portion of a column with sh. on base, Flemish, 16th cent., fastened down; rel., mur. Another piece of the Flemish brass has been reused at Broadway, Worc. (q.v.).

WICKHAM, EAST. John de Bladigdone, in civil dress, and w. Maud, sm. hf. effs. in the head of a cross with Fr. inscr. in Lombardics on stem, c. 1325, restored and rel. in a new stone in 1887, now mur., N.

WICKHAM, WEST. Wm. de Thorp, rector, 1407, in mass vests., sm., C.

WOODCHURCH. Nichol de Gore, priest, c. 1330, sm. eff. in mass vests. in head of a cross encircled by Fr. rhyming inscr. in Lombardics; stem, 1 finial and marg. inscr. lost; C.

WROTHAM. Reynold Pekham the elder, esq. for the body of Hen. VIII, 1525, in arm., with tabard, and w. Joyce (Colepeper), 1523, in heraldic mantle, 1 sh., 2 sons and 3 other shs. lost; N.

LANCASHIRE

Thornely, 'The Monumental Brasses of Lancashire and Cheshire', by J. L. Thornely, 1893.

CHILDWALL. Hen. Norris of Speke, esq., 1524, in arm. with tabard, and w. Clemence, dau. of Sir Jas. Harrington, in heraldic mantle; inscr. restored; now mur., S.A.

LANCASTER, ST. MARY. Thos Covell, esq., J.P, 6 times mayor, 48 years keeper of the castle, 46 years one of the coroners for the county palatine, captain of the freehold band of the hundred of Loinsdall, 1639, aged 78, in civil dress, inscr. with 10 Eng. vv., now on screen.

MANCHESTER CATHEDRAL. John Huntingdon, 1st warden of the college and builder of the choir, 1458, in surplice and almuce, single canopy, marg. inscr., restored and rel. in 1907, Presbytery. Anth. Mosley, mcht., 1607, aged 70, in civil dress, with 5 sons, Oswald, Francis, Edw., Rich., Rowland, and w. Alice with 3 daus., Helen, Alice, Ann, all kng., rect. pl. with inscr. and ach., on stalls in N.C.A. Oswald Mosley of Ancoats, esq., 1630, aged 47, civil dress, with 5 sons, Nich., Edw., Oswald, Sam., Francis, and w. Anne with 3 daus., Anne, Margt., Mary, all kng., rect. pl. with inscr. and ach., on stalls in N.C.A.

MIDDLETON. Edm. Assheton, rector, 1522, in mass vests, without stole and maniple, holding chalice and wafer, local, C.

ORMSKIRK. Man in arm. with tabard bearing the Scarisbrick arms, c. 1500; inscr. lost; large, rel. and floral border added in 1878, mur., St. Nich. chapel.

PRESTON. Seath Bushell, woollen draper, bailiff and a brother of Preston, 1623, aged 53, in civil dress, benefactor to the poor, etc., rect. pl. and inscr., local, rel., mur., N.A.

SEFTON. Sir Wm. Molineux, lord of the manor, died 1548, aged 65, in arm. with mail coif and SS. collar, and 2 ws., (1) Jane, had 1 son Rich., and 2 daus., Jane, Anne, (2) Elizth., had 2 sons, Wm., Thos., and 1 dau. Anne, inscr., 2 achs. (1 showing the captured banners mutil.), 1 lozenge (another lost), brass eng. c. 1570, C.

WALTON-ON-THE-HILL. Thos. Beri, 1586, in civil dress, he 'xii penie loaves to xii poore foulkes geve everie sabathe day for aye', rect. pl. with inscr. in 12 Eng. vv. and mcht. mark, Vestry.

WINWICK. Peers Gerard, esq., son and h. of Sir Thos. Gerard of the Bryne, 1492, in arm. with tabard, and 1 son, triple canopy mutil., 2 shs. (others lost), large, worn, N.C.

LEICESTERSHIRE

AYLESTONE. Wm. Heathcott, parson, 1594, in gown holding book, inscr. with 12 Lat. vv., marg. inscr. nearly all lost, large, now mur., C.

BOTTESFORD. (Hen). de Codyngtoun, rector, prebendary of Oxtoun and Crophill in the coll. ch. of Southwell, 1404, in cope with SS. Peter, John Evang., John Bapt., Kath., — Paul, Jas. the Great, a bp., Margt. on orphreys and Trinity on morse, fine triple canopy with B.V. Mary and Child in centre pediment, 2 shs., marg. inscr. mutil., large, C.

CASTLE DONINGTON. (Robt.) Staunton, esq., in arm. with salade, and 4 sons standing beside him, and w. Agnes with 3 daus., 1458, fine groined double canopy, and marg. inscr., both mutil.; shs. lost; A.T., S.C.

LEICESTER, WIGSTON'S HOSPITAL. Wm. Fyssher, 1st master of the hospital founded by Wm. Wigston, mcht., 4 times mayor of the staple of Calais, c. 1540, in shroud, marg. inscr., in chapel of new hospital.

LOUGHBOROUGH. Thos. Marshall, mcht., 1480, in civil dress, and w. Agnes, with 6 sons and 6 daus., local, mur., Tower.

LUTTERWORTH. Civilian with pouch and dagger, and w., c. 1470, local; inscr. lost; repaired and rel., mur., N.

QUEENIBOROUGH. Margt., dau. of Anth. Cave, esq., w. of Gilbert Bury, gent., 1633, rect. pl. with recumbent eff. on a tomb, inscr. and 6 Eng. vv.; 'G.B. pos. and C.B. pinxit November 1634'; very lightly engr. and gilded, mur., in wooden frame, C.

SIBSTONE. John Moore, M.A, rector, prebendary of Osmonderley (Osmotherly, Yorks), 1532, in almuce, with scrolls from hands to figure of Our Lord seated on a rainbow above, mur., C.

STAPLEFORD. Geoffrey Sherard, esq., in arm., and w. Joyce, dau. of Thos. Assheby of Lovesby, esq., 1492, with 7 sons and 7 daus., 4 shs., N.

STOKERSTON. John Boville, esq., 1467, in arm., head gone, and w. Isabel (Cheyne?) in mantle, clasping hands, 2 shs.; inscr. and other shs. lost; local, large, now mur., N.

WANLIP. Sir Thos. Walsch, lord of Anlep, in arm., and w. Dame Kath., 'whiche in her tyme made the kirke of Anlep and halud the the kirkyerd in wurchip of god and oure lady and seynt Nicholas', 1393, marg. inscr. in English; 2 achs. lost; C.

LINCOLNSHIRE

Jeans, G. E. 'A list of the existing brasses in Lincolnshire,' 1895. Published as a supplement to Lincolnshire Notes and Queries.

ALGARKIRK. Nich. Robertson, mcht. of the staple of Calais, 1498, in civil dress, and 2 ws., Isabel and Alice (1458, buried at St. Botolph's, Boston), hf. eff. of B.V. Mary and Child, 4 Lat. vv.; children, shs., scrolls, and marg. inscr. lost; local, N.

ALTHORPE. Wm. de Lound (rector), c. 1360, hf. eff. in mass vests., mur., Sedilia.

BARTON-ON-HUMBER. Simon Seman, citizen, vintner and alderman of London, 1433, in civil dress standing on wine casks, marg. inscr. and 2 mcht. marks (2 others lost), large, C.

BOSTON, ST. BOTOLPH. Walter Pescod, mcht., benefactor to the guild of St. Peter, 1398, in civil dress with mantle (lower part of eff. gone), and w. (eff. lost), each under triple canopy, with apostles in the side shafts, John Evang., Jas. the Great, Matthew, Philip, Simon, — lost (? Andrew), Thos., Barth, Jas. the Less, Jude, super-canopy with device (now lost) between the figs. of SS. Peter and (? Paul, lost); marg. inscr. lost; large, now partly covered, C.

Inscr. and ach. Rich. Bolle of Haugh, esq., 1591, aged 85, had 3 ws., 'after he had sundrie tymes had charge in France Scotland and ys realme & had bene twise sheriff of the said countie'; mur., S.A.

BUSLINGTHORPE. Sir Rich., son of Sir John de Boselyngthorpe, c. 1310 (or earlier?), hf. eff. in mail with ailettes and surcoat, holding a heart; marg. inscr. in single Lombardic letters and sh. below eff. lost; mur., N.

CROFT. Man in arm., c. 1300, hf. eff. in mail and surcoat; marg. inscr. in Lombardics lost; S.A.

EDENHAM. Sm. fig. of St. Thos. of Canterbury in full vests. with mitre and cross, c. 1500, mur., N.

GEDNEY. Lady, c. 1390, in mantle; triple canopy with Annunciation and saints in side shafts, super-canopy also with saints in niches, shs., and marg. inscr. lost; large, S.A.

GRAINTHORPE. Fine and large floriated cross, c. 1380, stem and marg. inscr. nearly all lost, C.

GUNBY. Man in arm., of the Massingberd family, and w. in mantle, c. 1400, both with SS. collars, double canopy much mutil., 2 shs.; appropriated to Sir Thos. Massyngberde, 1552, and w. Joan Bratoft, by beating up the original marg. inscr. which was in incised lettering and cutting a fresh one in raised letters; this marg. inscr. is now much mutil., partly covered, N.   Wm. de Lodyngton, justice of the common pleas to Hen. V, 1419, in robes with coif and anelace, leopard at feet, single canopy mutil., inscr., and 2 Lat. vv., 1 sh. (another lost), N. floor.

HORNCASTLE. Sir Lionel Dymoke, 1519, in arm. kng., with 2 sons (now lost), 3 daus., 3 shs., and inscr. with rebus; partly palimp., on rev. of sons a portion of a marg. inscr., on rev. of one of the shs. a fig. playing on a violin, also Flemish; Trinity lost, and a sh. now painted in the indent; local, mur., N.A.

INGOLDMELLS. Wm. Palmer 'with ye stylt', died 'on holy rode day', 1520, in civil dress with stilt or crutch beside him, local, S.A.

IRNHAM. Sir Andrew Loutterell, lord of Irnham, 1390, in arm., single canopy slightly mutil., large, N.C.

KELSEY, SOUTH. Rich. Hansard, in arm., and w. (Joan, dau. of John Aske of Aughton, Yorks.), in mantle with head on cushion, c. 1410, marg. inscr. nearly all lost, 1 sh. (3 others lost), local, mur. in orig. slab, C.

LAUGHTON. Man in arm. (probably of the Dalison family), c. 1400, and fine triple canopy, large; repaired and appropriated by the insertion of a new foot inscrip. to Wm. Dalison, esq., sheriff, escheator and JP for the county, 1546, and his son and h. Geo. 1549; A.T., S.A.

LINCOLN MINSTER. Sh., Russell, 2 chevrons between 3 roses, on tomb of John Russell, bp. 1480-1494. Sh., Russell, a chevron between 3 crosslets fitchy, with motto surmounted by a mitre, from tomb of bp. Russell (was loose – position now not known).

LINCOLN, ST. PETER-AT-ARCHES. John Becke, twice mayor, 1620, in civil dress, with 7 sons, Robt., John, Thos., Edw., Roger, Augustine, Geo., and w. Mary, 1617, with 3 daus. Mary, Martha, Mary, all kng., rect. pl. with inscr. and arms of Drapers' Co., mur., Vestry.

LINWOOD. John Lyndewode, woolman, 1419, in civil dress with mantle, standing on woolpack, and w. Alice in mantle, mar. 43 years, double canopy with entablature, 4 sons and 3 daus. also under canopies, inscr. in 10 Lat. vv., 1 sh. (3 others lost), large, now in N.A.

ORMSBY, SOUTH. Sir Wm. Skypwyth, 1482, in arm., and widow Agnes, with 1 son and 2 daus., double canopy slightly mutil.; 2 shs. lost; chapel.

SCRIVELSBY. Sir Robt. Demoke, 'knyght and baronet' (engraver's error for banneret, 1545, in arm. with beard, 1 sh., local, A.T., N.A. Sir Robt. was champion at the coronations of Rich. III, Hen.VII, and Hen. VIII.

SLEAFORD. Inscr. Rich. Warsope, woollen-draper, 1609, aged 52; his friend Robt. Camock pos.; C.

SPALDING, JOHNSON HOSPITAL. Thos. Lovell, esq., in civil dress, with 4 sons, 1597, aged 61, with 5 daus., mar. 33 years and 2 days, all kng., rect. pl. with inscr. and sh. This br. is the property of the Spalding Gentlemen's Society and is preserved in the board room of the hospital.

SPILSBY. Margery (dau. of Wm., lord Zouch of Harringworth, 2nd w.) of Robt. de Wylughby, lord of Eresby, 1391, in mantle, head on cushion, 7 shs. (another lost), marg. inscr. mutil., fine, large, N.C. (Wm., 5th baron Willoughby d'Eresby), in arm., and (1st) w. (Lucy, dau. of Roger, lord Strange of Knokyn), c. 1400, each under a triple canopy, the side shafts lost, as is also the inscr., 2 shs. on base of canopy, local, N.C.

STAMFORD, ALL SAINTS. John Brown, mcht. of the staple of Calais,

1442, in mantle, standing on wool packs, and w. Margery, 1460, inscr. 2 mcht. marks, mur., N.A.   Wm. Browne, son of John Browne, founder of the bedehouse and builder of the steeple, died 1489, in mantle, standing on wool-packs, and w. Margt., dau. of John Stokke of Warmington, Northants, esq., double canopy (hf. gone), inscr. in 12 Lat. vv. with devices of stork on wool-pack; marg. inscr. lost; engr. c. 1465, large, S.C.

STAMFORD, ST. GEORGE. Inscr. Tobie Norris, bellfounder, 1626, N.A. Probably cast in the foundry.

TATTERSHALL. Ralph, baron Cromwell, lord high treasurer, founder of the college, died 1455, in arm. with mantle, head and right shoulder lost, and w. Margt. (eff. lost), died 1454, br. engr. c.1470, each under triple canopy with entablature above, nearly all lost now, inscr. mutil.; shs. lost; large, N.Tr.   Priest, c. 1510, in cap and cope with the 12 Apostles on orphrey, and morse with demi-fig. of Our Lord in glory; inscr. lost; large, N.Tr.

THEDDLETHORPE, ALL SAINTS. Robt. Hayton, esq., 1424, in arm., 2 shs. local, S.C.

WINTERTON. John Rudd, mcht. of the staple of Calais, 1504 (eff. in civil dress lost), and 2 ws., marg. inscr. mutil.; children and shs. lost; much worn, partly covered, C.

WINTHORPE. Rich. Barowe, mcht. of the staple of Calais, 1505, in civil dress, and w. Baterich, with 4 daus.; sons and 2 shs., lost; N.

WRANGLE. John Reed, mcht. of the staple of Calais, in civil dress, and w. Margt., both died 1503, with 8 sons and 5 daus., 2 mcht. marks and 2 arms of the Staple, 12 Lat. vv., and marg. inscr. in Eng. partly in vv., mutil., C.

MIDDLESEX (LONDON)

BRENTFORD. Hen. Redmayne, chief mason of the king's works, a special benefactor to the ch., 1528, in civil dress, and w. Joan, with 2 daus., kng.; Trinity lost; N., Tower.

CHELSEA. Lady Jane Guyldeford, 'late dvches of Northvmberland', dau. and h. of Sir Edw. Guyldeford, knt., lord warden of the 'fyve ports', w. of John Dudley, 'late dvke of Northvmberland', died 'at her maner of Chelse', 1555, aged 46, a heraldic mantle, kng., with 8 sons (effs. lost) and 5 daus. also kng., 2 shs.; a lozenge lost; inscr. in marble; mur., A.T., S.C.   Sir Arthur Gorges, 1625, in arm., and 2nd w. Elizth., with 6 sons (the eld. in arm.) and 5 daus., all kng., rect. pl. and ach.; inscr. lost; mur., S.A.

CLERKENWELL, ST. JAMES. John Bell, bp. of Worcester, 1556, in episcopal vests. with mitre and crosier; lower part of eff. and inscr. lost; rel., mur., N.A., with an inscr. stating it to have been replaced by Stephen Tucker, Somerset Herald, in 1884.

DRAYTON, WEST. Margt., dau. of Roger North, haberdasher of London, w. of Thos. Burnell, mercer of London, 1529, with 2 sons and 1 dau., 4 shs. including Mercers' Co. and Staple of Calais, S.A. Inscr. John Burnell, gent., 'sometyme officer of the seller' to Hen. VIII, 1551, mur., S.A.

EALING. Rich. Amondesham 'otherwise called Awnsham', mercer, mcht. of the staple of Calais, in civil dress, and w. Kath., c. 1490, with 3 sons and 6 daus., all kng., 1 sh., mur., N.C.

EDGWARE. Inscr. Sir Rich. Chau(m)berlayn, 1532, mur., C. II. Anth., 'the first borne sonne' of John Childe, goldsmith of London and 'the first fruits of Elizth. Childe his wife', 1599, in swaddling clothes, mur., C.

EDMONTON. John Asplyn and Godfrey Askew, both in civil dress, and Elizth. 'the wyfe of them bothe', c. 1500, sm. mur. N.

ENFIELD. Joyce, dau. and coh. of (Sir Edw.) Charlton, lord Powys, by his w. (Eleanor, dau. of Thos. Holland, earl of Kent, widow of Roger Mortimer, earl of March), w. of Sir John Tiptoft, baron Tiptoft, died 1446, br. engr. later, c. 1470 (?) in heraldic mantle and coronet, fine triple canopy with 6 shs. on side shafts, marg. inscr., partly covered, large, A.T., N.C.

FINCHLEY. Simon Skudemore, gent., 1609, aged 83, in civil dress, and w. Jeane (Edwards) had an only dau. Elizth., I ach., mur., N.C. Thos. White, citizen and grocer of London, 1610, in civil dress, and 3 ws., (1) Mary with 3 sons, and 2 daus. (2) Mary with 2 sons, and 3 daus., (3) Honor with 3 sons Thos., Nathaniel, Sam (dec.), and I dau. Hanna, all kng., rect. pl. with inscr., arms of London and Grocer's Co., mur., N.C.

FULHAM. Margt. Svanders (de Vandere or des Vanders), a native of Ghent, w. of Gerard Hornebolt (Horenbault), the celebrated painter, and mother of Susan, w. of John Parcker, the King's bowyer (archarius regis), 1529, a lozenge-shaped plate with hf. eff. in shroud, inscr. held by angels, sh., and initials, Flemish, mur., S.A.

GREENFORD, GREAT. Thos. Symons, rector (1521), in mass vests., inscr. in 2 Lat. vv., mur., C.

HACKNEY. Christ. Urswic (D.C.L, rector), almoner to Hen. VII, eleven times an ambassador, dean of York and of Windsor, archdeacon of Richmond, the inscr. also states he refused the bishopric of Norwich, 1521, aged 74, cap and cope, I sh., A.T. Arthur Dericote, esq., 'of London somtyme citizen and of esquiers state, of Drapers whilome companie but laste of Hackneie towne', 1562, in arm., and 4 ws., Marie, Eme, Margt., and Jane (with 2 sons), all kng., inscr. in 12 Eng. vv.

HADLEY or MONKEN HADLEY. Wm. Turnour, 1500, in civil dress, and w. Joan, with 4 daus., mur., S.A. (Thos. Goodyere, 1518), in civil dress, and w. (Joan Hawte); inscr. and shs. lost; now mur., C.

HAREFIELD. John Newdegate, serjeant-at-law, 1528, in robes with coif, holding scroll, and w. Amphelice, 1544 (date added), in heraldic mantle, with 10 sons and 7 daus.; Trinity lost; A.T., S.A.

HARROW. John Flambard, c. 1390, in arm., inscr. in 2 Lat. vv., large, worn, C. John Byrkhed (rector) 1468, cope, head lost, single canopy mutil., as is also the marg. inscr. with shs. at the corners, C. John Lyon of Preston in par. Harrow, yeoman, left lands to a corporation for a free grammar school for the poor, for poor scholars at the universities, repairing highways, etc., 1592, in civil dress, and w. effs. mutil., a child lost; now mur., N.

HAYES. Robt. Levee or Lenee, rector, c. 1370, hf. eff. in mass vests., rel., C. Walter Grene, 14(56), in arm., 4 shs., marg. inscr. mutil., A.T., N.A.

HENDON. Rich. March, yeoman, 1615, aged 37; mar. Alice, dau. of John Oxton, had 2 children, now mur., N.C.

HILLINGDON. (John le Strange, lord Strange of Knockyn, Mohun, Wassett, Warnell, Lacy, and Colham, died 1479), in arm., and w. (Jacquette, sister of Elizth. Widville, Queen of England), and only child Joan, who pos. 1509, under double canopy; inscr. lost; mur., S.A. (Hen. Stanley, son of Thos., 'late erle of Derby and of Anne countess of Derby, brother to Edward erle of Derby', 1528), in arm., 2 shs.; inscr. lost; slab mur., C. Device with initials I.M., arms of Marsh, Mcht.-Adventurers and Mercers' Co. (John Marsh, mercer, 1561), rel., S.A. Drew Saunders, mcht. of the 'estaple of England', 1579, in civil dress, and w., with 1 son (lost) and I dau. (mutil.), inscr. and mcht. mark, slab now mur., N.

HORNSEY (old church). John Skevington, c. 1520, a chrysom, inscr. in 2 Eng. vv.; sh. lost; sm., rel., Porch.

ISLEWORTH. Inscr. Wm. Chase, esq., serjeant to Hen. VIII, and of his hall and woodyard, 1544; palimp., on rev. a saint under a canopy, 14th-cent., N.

ISLINGTON, ST. MARY. Hen. Savill, esq., in arm., and w. Margt., dau. of Thos. Fowler, esq., died in childbirth, 1546, aged 19, 2 shs.; eff. of child and 2 foundels lost; all palimp., C.

KILBURN, ST. MARY. Head of a nun, 15th-cent., found on the site of the priory, mur., S.C.

LONDON, ALL HALLOWS BARKING, GT. TOWER STREET. John Bacon, citizen and woolman of London, 1437, in civil dress standing on woolpack, and w. Joan, scrolls encircling a heart, N.A. (John Croke, citizen, skinner, and alderman of London, 1477), in civil dress with mantle and 7 sons, and widow (Margt.), with 5 daus., all kng., I sh.; inscr. lost; finely engr., now much corroded, mur., A.T., N.A. A. Evyngar, citizen and salter of London (1533), in civil dress, and w. Ellyn, with I son and 6 daus., under double canopy with fig. of Our Lady of Pity, mcht. mark, arms of the Mcht.-Adventurers and Salters' Co., rect. pl., Foreign, N. Wm. Thynne, esq., master of household to Hen. VIII, 1546, in arm., and w. Anne, dau. of Wm. Bonde, with marg. inscr.; all palimp., c. 1530; rel. and restored by Messrs. Waller in 1861, the palimps. fastened down, S.A. Inscr. with sh. Geo. Snaythe, auditor to Wm. Laud, late abp. of Cant., born at Durham 1602, died 1651, N.A.

LONDON, ST. HELEN, BISHOPSGATE. John Le(v)enthorp, esq., one of 4 ushers of the chamber to Hen. VII, 1510, in arm., N.C. Robt. Rochester, esq., serjeant of the pantry to Hen. VIII, 1514, in arm. with SS. collar, S.C. Lady in heraldic mantle, c. 1535, inscr. lost; rel., S.C.

LONDON, ST. PAUL'S CATHEDRAL. Rt. Hon. George S. Nottage, mayor, 1823-85. The only Lord Mayor to be buried in St. Paul's; crypt.

LONDON, WESTMINSTER ABBEY. Base and about 20 inches of stem of cross, also 8 Lombardic letters of marg. inscr. to Margt., dau. of Wm. de Valence, c. 1270. Eleanor de Bohun, eld. dau. coh. of Humphrey de Bohun, earl of Hereford, Essex, Northampton, and constable of England, w. of Thos. of Woodstock, youngest son of Edw. III, duke of Gloucester, earl of Essex and Buckingham, constable of England, 1399, in widow's dress, fine triple canopy with 5 shs. (another lost) on the side shafts, chamfer inscr. in Fr. mutil., large A.T., Chapel of St. Edmund. Sir John Harpeden, 1438, in arm., 4 shs.; chamfer inscr. lost; now on A.T., N.A. of C. Sir Humfrey Bourgchier, descended from Edw. III, son and h. of John, lord Barnes (Berners), chief carver to Elizth., Queen of Edw. IV, slain on Easter-day at the battle of Barnet (1471) whilst fighting for Edw. IV, eff. in arm. lost; inscr. in 14 Lat. vv., helmet with crest, 4 shs. and 6 badges, large, A.T. Chapel of St. Edmund. John Estney, abbot, 1498, in full vests. with mitre and crosier, fine triple canopy slightly mutil.; marg. inscr. and 2 shs. lost; now on A.T., N.A. of C. Sir. Humph Stanley, of the bodyguard to Hen. VII, 1505, in arm., 5 shs. (2 lost), Chapel of St. Nicholas.

LONDON, WESTMINSTER, ST. MARGARET. (Thos.) Cole, a burgess in parliament, 1597, in civil dress, and w. Margt. (who pos.) with I son and 2 daus., all kng., rect. pl. with inscr. in 47 Eng. and 2 Lat. vv., I sh. mur., S.A.

MIMMS, SOUTH. Two shs., Haberdashers Co., and East Lands Co., 16th.-cent., the former rel. on N. floor, the latter rel. on floor of N.C.

NORTHOLT. Hen. Rowdell, esq., 1452, in arm. with livery collar, sm., S.A.

PINNER. Anne, dau. of Eustace Bedingfeld, gent., 1580, in swaddling clothes, buried by her grandmother Margery, widow of John Draper, citizen and 'bere' brewer of London; palimp., Vestry.

RUISLIP. John Hawtrey, esq., JP, 1593, aged 68, in civil dress, and w. Bregget (Lovett, widow of Gabriel Dormer), 4 shs.; an ach. lost; C.

STANMORE. Inscr. John Burnell, mcht., free of the Clothworkers' Co., 1605, aged 78; left issue by his w. Barbara 3 sons and 2 daus., mur., N.A.

STANWELL. Rich. de Thorp, rector, 1408, hf. eff. in mass vests., C.

TOTTENHAM. Inscr. Jeffrye Walkdine, citizen and skinner of London, free of the Mcht.-Adventurers and Muscovia Cos., 1599, now mur., S.A. John Burrough of Tottenham High Cross, in civil dress, and w. Elizth., 1616, with 2 sons and I dau., rel., N.

WILLESDEN. Barth. Willesden, comptroller of the great roll of pipe, 1492, in civil dress, and ws. Margt. and Margt.; one w., 4 daus., and inscr. lost; rel., C.   Edm. Roberts of Neasdon, 1585, in arm., and 2 ws., (1) Frauncys, with 2 sons and 4 daus., (2) Fayth, with 2 sons and 1 dau., 16 Eng. and 2 Lat. vv., inscr. and 3 shs.; C.

MONMOUTHSHIRE

ABERGAVENNY. Inscr. with arms of Mercer's Co. John Morgon, gent., son of Evan Morgon, 1587, aged 42, on stalls.   Maurice Hughes, vicar, master of the free school, 1631, in gown; he left surviving by his w. Joan, 1 son Robt., a clerk, and a dau., Cath.; under wooden floor, C.

LLANOVER. Wm. Prichard of Llanover, esq., and his son and h. Math., (1610), 'lineally descended from the bodye of Cradocke Vraichvras Earle of Hereford and Prince betweene Wye and Seaverne', rect. pl. with 2 effs. in arm., ach. and inscr., on a pew.

USK. Inscr. in 8 Welsh vv. Adam de Usk (1421).

NORFOLK

Cotman. 'Engravings of Sepulchral Brasses in Norfolk and Suffolk', by J. S. Cotman, 2nd ed., 2 vols., 4to, 1839.
Farrer. 'Brasses. A List of Monumental Brasses remaining in the county of Norfolk in 1890', by E. Farrer, 8vo, 1890. (N.B. - illustrations in the large paper or 4to copies only.)

ANTINGHAM. Rich. Calthorp, esq., son of John Calthorp of Cokthorp, esq., 1554, in arm., and w. Anne, with 19 children, 11 sons, Hen., Geo., John, Anth., John, Thos., Edm., Wm., Geo., Martyn, Bartram (names mutil.), and 5 daus., Mary, Elizth., Anne, Alice, Fraunces, and 2 sons and 1 dau. unnamed by her 1st husband, 4 shs. including the Mcht.-Adventurers and Mercers' Co.; a sm. pl. bearing 'Anthony Calthorp mercer' who probably pos. lost; N.

AYLSHAM. Robt. Farman, in civil dress, and w. Kath., c. 1490, local, sm., rel., C.   Rich. Howard, citizen and sheriff of Norwich, 1499, and w. Cecily, skeletons in shrouds, local, rel., C.

BLICKLING. Sir Nich. Dagworth, lord of Blickling, 1401, in arm., 4 shs., marg. inscr. mutil., large, S.A.   Roger Felthorp, 1454, civil dress, and w. Cecilie, with 11 sons and 5 daus. standing before their parents, an early instance of this, sm., N.   Isabel (Boleyn), w. of Wm. Cheyne of the Isle of Sheppey, Kent, esq., 1485, 1 sh., C.

BRAMPTON. Edw. Brampton, esq., in civil dress, and w. Jone, dau. of Christ. Daubene of Sharington, Norf., esq., both died 1622, mar. 48 years, with 6 sons and 3 daus. (lost), 1 sh., effs. mutil., C.

BUCKENHAM, OLD. Stork with scroll 'deo gracias', and inscr. Thos. Browne, c. 1500, N.

BURLINGHAM, SOUTH. (St. Edmund). Chalice and wafer for Wm. Curtes, priest, 1540, C. under altar.

BURNHAM THORPE. Sir Wm. Calthorp, lord of the manor and patron of the ch., 1420, in arm. with SS. collar, single canopy with entablature, marg. inscr., 2 shs. and 2 badges, large, partly restored, C.

CLEY. John Symondes, mcht., 1508, and w. Agnes, 1512, in shrouds, with 8 children in ordinary dress detached, 4 sons, and 4 daus., 9 scrolls (2 lost) inscribed 'now thus', inscr., etc., reversed, S.C.   John Yslyngton, S.T.P, c. 1520, in cassock, scarf and cap. holding chalice, sm., N.A.

CREAKE, NORTH. Civilian, c. 1500, holding church on arm., triple canopy slightly mutil., 2 Lat. vv. at base; marg. inscr. lost; C.

CROMER. Margt. Counforth, 1518, sm., local, mur., S.A.

ELSING. Sir Hugh Hastings, builder of the ch., 1347, in arm. with arms on jupon and sh. on arm, head on cushion, legs lost, fine but mutil. single canopy, with St. George in pediment, 2 figs. on brackets representing the coronation of the Virgin, and in the side shafts 8 weepers (2 lost), Edw. III, Thos. Beauchamp, earl of Warwick, Despencer (lost), Roger, lord Grey of Ruthyn – Hen. Plantagenet,

earl of Lancaster, Laurence Hastings, earl of Pembroke (lost), Ralph, lord Stafford, and Almaric, lord St. Amand, all in arm. with armorial bearings on their jupons; inscr. lost; large, C.

FAKENHAM. Hen. Keys, rector, archdeacon of Norwich (1428), in cope, lower part of eff. gone, much worn; canopy and marg. inscr. lost; in orig. stone, mur., C.

FELBRIGG. Symond de Felbrig (died c. 1351), in civil dress with anelace, and w. Alice (Thorpe) buried at Harling (lower part of eff. lost); also Roger de Felbrig, his son, died and buried in Prussia, in arm., and his w. Elizth., engr. c. 1380, Fr. inscr., 1 sh. (2 others lost), C.   Sir Symon Felbrygge, K.G, banner bearer to Rich. II (died 1443), in arm. with banner, and 1st w. Margt., and nephew of Winceslaus V, King of Bohemia, lady in waiting to Anne of Bohemia, Queen of Rich. II, 1416, in mantle, double canopy slightly mutil., 3 shs., and 2 badges, foot inscr.; 2 achs. lost; large, N.

FRENZE. Ralph Blenerhaysett, esq., 'venerabilis vir', 1475, in arm., 4 shs. (1 mutil.), local, C.   Jane, widow of John Blenerhaysett, 1521, in ordinary dress, 2 shs., N.   Inscr., lozenge, 4 shs. crest. Mary, dau. and sole h. of Geo. Blenerhaiset, esq., w. (1) of Thos. Culpeper, esq., (2) of Francis Bacon, esq., buried at Petistree, Suff., 1587, aged 70; C.

HELLESDON. Rich. de Heylesdone, in civil dress, and w. Beatrice, c. 1370, hf. effs., Fr. inscr., N.C.   Inscr. John de Heylesdon, 1384, and w. Joan, patrons of the ch. and founders of a chantry, engr. c. 1420, N.C.

HOLME-NEXT-THE-SEA. Herry Notingham, in civil dress with livery collar and anelace, and w., c. 1405, 'yat maden this chirche stepull and quere, two vestments & belles they made also', inscr. in 6 Eng. vv., sm., mur., N.

HUNSTANTON. Sir Roger le Strange, one of the body guard to Hen. VII, son and h. of Hen. le Strange, esq., 1506, in arm. with tabard, hands uplifted, fine ach. above head, standing on a bracket under triple canopy with sm. effs. of himself and 7 of his ancestors, in the side shafts, all in arm. with tabards, marg. inscr. (mutil.) gives genealogy from Haymo le Strange, 14th-cent., 4 shs. (2 lost) on slab, and 4 shs. and 4 badges on sides of tomb, A.T., C.

INGHAM. The remains of the br. to Sir Brian de Stapleton, son of Sir Miles, son of the founder Sir Miles, 1438, in arm. with lion and dog named 'Jakke' at feet, and w. Cecily, dau. of lord Bardolf; 1432, in mantle, double canopy, marg. inscr. and 5 shs.; C.

KETTERINGHAM. Lady. c. 1470; the remains of the br. to Sir Hen. Grey 'that dyed at Venys', in arm., and w. Emma, foot inscr. in Eng. and 1 sh., engr. c. 1470; local, mur., C.   Thos. Hevenyngham, esq., son and h. of Sir John Hevenyngham, knt. and baronet (? engraver's error for banneret), 1499, in arm. with tabard and 5 sons, and w. Anne, in heraldic dress with 5 daus., all kng., coloured, inscrs. on 2 large scrolls, 2 shs., mur., A.T., C.

KING'S LYNN, ST. MARGARET. Adam de Walsokne, burgess of Lynn, 1349, in civil dress, and w. Margt., born at Cley, under rich canopies, the 12 apostles with attendant prophets beside and between the effs., and a rustic scene below, marg. inscr. in Lombardics, Royal arms and mcht. mark, very large, 118 in. by 68 in., rect. pl., foreign, formerly in C., now west end of S.A.   Robt. Braunche, 1364, in civil dress, and 2 ws., Letice and Margt., under rich canopy 'Peacock feast' below, marg. inscr. in Lombardics, Royal arms and arms of Braunche, very large, 107 in. by 61 in., rect. pl., Foreign, formerly in C., now at west end of S.A.

LODDON. Two hands, issuing from clouds, holding a heart with 3 scrolls (1 lost), sh. with monogram (3 others lost). Denis Willys, 1462, local, N.A.   Hen. Hobert, esq., 1561, arm. with tabard, head restored; eff. of w. lost; local, A.T., N.C.

LUDHAM. Inscr. in 2 Lat. vv. John Colman, c. 1450, S.A.

MERTON. Wm. de Grey, esq. (1495), in arm. with tabard and 5 sons, and 2 ws. (1) Mary, with 3 daus., and (2) Grace, with 2 daus., all kng., 3 shs.; inscr., 4 scrolls and ach. lost; local, mur., N.

METHWOLD. Sir Adam de Clyfton, 1367, in arm. with arms on jupon, single canopy much mutil. as is also the eff.; inscr. lost; mur., N.A.

MULBARTON. Inscr. composed of 2 hinged copper plates in the form of a book which open, on the lower pl. is the inscr. and a sh. of arms, on the upper a hand issuing from clouds and 16 Eng. vv. by her husband. Sarah, dau. of Thos. le Neve of Aslacton, w. of Dan. Scargill, rector, mar. near 7 years, 1680, aged 30, mur., C., resting on a painted iron shelf in the form of a bible.

NARBOROUGH. Hen. Spelman, 'juris peritus', recorder of Norwich, 1496, in civil dress with mantle, and w. Ele (dau. and h. of Wm. Narburgh), inscr. mutil.; 6 shs. lost; local, C.

NECTON. Ismayne, w. of Wm. de Wynston, died on Innocents' day, 1372; Fr. inscr. and 2 shs. lost; N.   Wm. Curteys, notary, in civil dress with penner and inkhorn, and w. Alice, both died 'v° kalendas marcii a° ihū' 1499, local, N.   Robt. Goodwyn, in civil dress, and w. Sabine, 1532, with 7 sons; 4 daus. lost; local, N.

NORWICH CATHEDRAL. Inscr. in 9 Lat. vv. Ralph Pulvertoft, 'custos caronelle' (charnel-house), c. 1500, mur., Jesus chapel. Inscr. Edw., youngest son of Joseph Hall (bp. of Norwich), 1642, aged 23, mur., Presbytery.

NORWICH, ST. ANDREW. Civilian in mantle, and w. c. 1500; inscr., 2 shs. and another plate lost; local, C.

NORWICH, ST. CLEMENT. Margt. Pettwode, widow, 1514, in ordinary dress, local, N.

NORWICH, ST. GEORGE COLEGATE. Wm. Norwiche, mayor (in 1461), founder of the chantry of the B.V.M. and All Saints, died 1468, in civil dress with mantle, and w. Alice, 1472, with 1 son between them, all standing on a bracket rising from inscr., local., N.C.

NORWICH, ST. GILES. Robt. Baxter, mayor (in 1424, 1429), died 1432, in civil dress with mantle, and widow Cristine, N.

NORWICH, ST. JOHN MADDERMARKET. John Todenham, c. 1450, in civil dress, with long scroll from hands; the inscr. mentions his w. Joan; sm., mur., N.   John Terry, mcht., mayor (1523), left £200 for loans to citizens and £200 to be invested in land for the discharge of taxes, 1524, in civil dress with mantle, and w. Lettys, with 2 sons and 2 daus., all standing on brackets springing from the trunk of a tree, between them 2 shs., one with arms of Norwich, the other with Mcht.-Adventurers, Mercers' Co and mcht. mark combined, inscr. in 20 Eng. vv. orig.-above effs., mur., N. John Marsham, mayor (1518), died 1525, civil dress with mantle, and w. Elizth. with crucifix at end of rosary, standing on a bracket; 5 sons, 8 daus., 3 shs., and inscr. lost; local, now mur. on a board, N.

NORWICH, ST. LAURENCE. (John Asger, mcht. of Bruges, mayor of Norwich in 1426, died 1436), in civil dress with mantle, feet and inscr. lost, 8 Lat. vv. on semi-circular plate above head, mcht. mark and 1 scroll, N.   John Stylle, chaplain, 1483, in mass vests. without stole and maniple, N.

NORWICH, ST. MARTIN-AT-PALACE. Inscr. John Powl, 'innholder', 1620, local, S.C.

NORWICH, ST. MICHAEL-AT-PLEA. Inscr. with skeleton rising from a tomb, thereon a mcht. mark. Barbara, w. of Wm. Ferrer, alderman and twice mayor, 1588, C.

NORWICH, ST. MICHAEL-AT-THORNE. Wm. Frederick Creeny, M.A., vicar for 21 years, born at Portaferry, Ireland, 1825, died Easter-day, 1897, rect. pl. with bust, canopy work, etc., 'erected by his many friends' in 1898, mur., C. Mr. Creeny was the author of 'A book of fascimiles of Monumental Brasses on the Continent of Europe', and of 'Illustrations of Incised Slabs on the Continent of Europe'.

NORWICH, ST. PETER MANCROFT. Peter Rede, esq., 'who hath worthely served not only hys prynce and cuntrey but also the emperour Charles the 5 bothe at the conqueste of Barbaria and at the siege of Tunis as also in other places who had geven hym by the sayd emperour for hys valiaunt dedes the order of Barbaria', 1568, in arm. with salade; palimp., rel., C.

ORMESBY, GREAT. Lady, c. 1440, hf. eff. holding a heart inscribed 'Erth my bodye I give to the, on my soule Ihū have m'cy'; altered by the addition of an inscr. and 2 shs., both now lost. Dame Alice, dau. of Sir Wm. Boleyn, 2nd w. of Sir Robt. Clere, 1538, N.

REEPHAM. Sir Wm. de Kerdeston, 1391, in arm., legs mutil., and w. Cecily (Brewes) in mantle, double canopy much mutil., marg. inscr. nearly all lost, large, C.

ROUGHAM. Sir Wm. Yelverton, justice of the king's bench (1472), in arm. with coif, judicial mantle, and collar of suns and roses, and 2nd w. Agnes, in mantle; inscr. lost; once on A.T., now mur., C.

SALL. Two ladies, 1 scroll and inscr.; the remains of the br. to John Funteyn, 1453, and 3 ws., Alice, Joan, Agnes, with 2 sons and 1 dau.; sm., N.Tr.

SANDRINGHAM. Inscr. and sh. (2 others lost). Wm. Cobbis of Sandringham, esq., 1546; mar. Dorothy, dau. of Sir John Spelman, had 4 sons and 8 daus., mur., E. wall of S. porch.

SCULTHORPE. Hen. Unton, 'gentilman, cirographorius' of the court of common pleas, 1470, in arm., kng.; Trin. and 4 shs. lost; restored and filled in, N.

SHERNBOURNE. Thos. Shernborne, esq., chamberlain to Queen Margt. of Anjou, 1458, in arm., and w. Jamon de Cherneys, maid of honour to the Queen, in mantle; marg. inscr. and 4 shs. lost; mur., in orig. stone, C.

SHERINGHAM. John Hook, 1513, in civil dress, and w. Magdalen; children lost; S.A.

SNORING, GREAT. Sir Ralph Shelton (1424), in arm. with tabard, all now lost but head, and w. Alice, dau. of Sir Thos. Uvedale, in mantle with arms on kirtle; marg. inscr., foot inscr. and 4 shs. lost; C.

SOUTH ACRE. Sir John Harsick, 1384, in arm. with arms on jupon, and w. Kath., dau. of Sir Bartholomew Calthorpe, in mantle with arms on kirtle, holding hands, ach. above, marg. inscr. mutil., large, N.C.

SWAFFHAM. Man in arm., c. 1480, worn; w., inscr. and 2 shs. lost; local, N.

THORNHAM. Scroll, 'Jesu mercy, Lady helppe', c. 1460, N.

UPWELL. Hen. Martyn, rector of Yaxham, 1435, in amice, albe crossed stole and cope; 2 scrolls and 2 shs. lost; now mur., C.

WALSHAM, NORTH. Inscr. and sh. of Grocers' Co. Robt. Raunt, chief constable of the hundred of Tunstead, 1625, aged 60; N.

WALSINGHAM, NEW, OR LITTLE. Hen. Clederow, 1509 in arabics, in civil dress, and w. Joan, local, N.

WHISSONSETT. Wm. Bozon, esq., died 1460, engr. c. 1485, in arm. without sword; inscr. and sh. lost; Tower.   Thos. Gyhon, gent., 1484, in arm. without sword; sh. lost; Tower.

WITTON (Blofield). Dame Julian Anyell, vowess, c. 1500, sm., local, N.

WORSTEAD. John Yop, rector of Boton (1404 ?), hf. eff. in mass vests., C.   Inscr. Thos. Whatt, 'wursted wever, 1506, local, N. Inscr. and sh. with mcht. mark imp. Mercers' Co. John Carman, 1508, local, N.

NORTHAMPTONSHIRE

Hudson. 'The Brasses of Northamptonshire', by F. Hudson, 1852.

ALDWINKLE ALL SAINTS. Inscr. with ach. John Pykering, 'physitian', 1659, with 8 Eng. vv. written by himself in 1652 at the age of 56, mur., N.A.

ASHBY, CANONS. John Dryden, gent., 1584, in civil dress, ach.; inscr. lost; N.

ASHBY ST. LEGERS. Thos. Stokes, esq., 1416, in civil dress, and w. Ellen, single canopy with sm. super-canopy containing Trinity (now lost), kng. effs. of 4 sons, 12 daus., S.A.   Wm. Catisby, esq., died

20 Aug. 1485, in arm. with tabard, and w. Margt., 1494, in heraldic mantle, with 3 sons and 2 daus., double canopy, earlier, *c.* 1430, appropriated, ach. and 2 shs., local, C.

BLAKESLEY. Matthew Swetenham, 'portitor arcus' and esquier to Hen. IV, 1416, in arm. with SS. collar, mur., S.A.

BRINGTON, GREAT. Priest, *c.* 1340, hf. eff. in mass vests, with cap, on a bracket; stem and marg. inscr. lost; rel., C.

CHACOMBE. Trinity, arms of London, Grocers' Co., Mcht.-Adventurers, mcht.-mark and inscr. Myghell Fox, citizen and grocer of London, patron of the ch. (died 1579), engr. *c.* 1545, and 2 ws., Mary (Eddes) and Clemence (Hawtyn), and children Rich., Anth., John, Anne, Alice, Jone, and Alys, C.

CHARWELTON. Thos. Andrewe, gent., mcht. (died 1496), in civil dress, and w. Margery, double canopy with 4 pediments, 5 sons and 3 daus. under sm. canopies, 6 Lat. vv., marg. inscr., ach. and sh., engr. *c.* 1490, large, rel. and repaired in 1904, N.

COTTERSTOCK. Robt. Wyntryngham, canon of Lincoln, prebendary of Ledyngton (Rutland), provost of the chantry of Cotterstock, 1420, in cope, on a bracket under single canopy, marg. inscr. slightly mutil., C.

DENE. Sir Thos. Brudenell, justice of the common pleas, 1549, in arm., and w. Elizth., inscr. with 12 Lat. vv., ach. and sh.; their son Thos. pos. 1586; A.T., S.C.

DINGLEY. Anne, 2nd dau. of Nich. Boroeghe of Stanmer, Middx., esq., 'sometyme professed in Clerkenwell nere London', 1577, aged 75, 'to the greate losse of ye poore who dyverse wayes were by her relieved', in widows dress, kng., rect. pl. with inscr. and sh., mur. C.

EARL'S BARTON. John Muscote, gent., a prothonotary of the court of common pleas, 1512, in civil dress, and w. Alice; 4 sons, 2 daus., Trinity, inscr. and 3 evang. symbols lost; N.

EASTON NESTON. Rich. Fermer, esq., mcht. of the staple of Calais, 1552, in arm., and w. Anne, dau. of Sir Wm. Browne, knt., (mayor of London in 1513), marg. inscr. and 8 shs., A.T., C.

FAWSLEY. Sir Edm. Knyghtleye, 1542, in arm., and w. Ursula, (dau. of Sir Geo. Vere), sister of John, earl of Oxford, 1557, with 6 daus., Jane, Isabell, Jane, Joan, Jane, Joan, 18 Lat. vv., marg. inscr., and 4 shs., N.

GREENS NORTON. Sir Thos. Grene, lord of Norton, 1462, in arm., and widow, Maud, with 3 sons (lost), Thos., —, John, and 1 dau. Elizth., 2 shs. (2 others lost), marg. inscr., large, A.T., N.A.

HEYFORD, NETHER. Sir Walter Mauntell, 1487, in arm., and w. Elizth., holding hands, chamfer inscr. and 5 shs., large, A.T., C.

HIGHAM FERRERS. Laurence de St. Maur (Seymour), rector, (1337), in mass vests., single canopy with SS. in side shafts, John Evang., an angel, John Bapt., Stephen, an abbot (?), Luke – Mark, 4 gone (the 4th was Christopher), Matthew, super-canopy with the Deity with soul, SS. Peter, Andrew, Paul and Thos., inscr. on base and arch of canopy and on breast of eff.; 4 shs. lost; A.T., C.   Large cross with Deity at intersection and evang. symbols at extremities (St. Mark restored), and inscr. Thos. Chichele, 1400, and w. Agnes, N.C. W. Chichele, sheriff and alderman of London, 1425), civil dress with mantle, and w. Beatrice, in mantle, double canopy, marg. inscr. in 12 Eng. vv., 2 shs., and 2 roundels; foot inscr. lost; repaired, 1 sh. renewed, and a new inscr. added in 1923; large, N.C. Wm. Thorpe, mercer, 1504, and widow Marion, with 6 sons and 6 daus., arms of Mercers' Co., N.C.

IRCHESTER. John Glynton, mcht. of the staple of Calais, 1510, in civil dress (eff. lost), and w.; sh. and children lost; inscr. mutil., N.

KETTERING. Edm. Sawyer, esq., 1630, aged 69, in arm., and w. Anne, kng., had 15 children, rect. pl. with inscr. and ach., mur., S.C.

LAMPORT. Inscr., ach. and arms of London and Mercers' Co. John Isham, one of the 20 children of Euseby Isham of Picheley and his w. Anne Palton of Desborough, once governor of the English mcht.-

adventurers in Flanders and thrice warden of the Mercers' Co., purchased the manor and patronage of Lamport, 22 years a J.P, and once sheriff of Northants, 1595, aged 70; mar. Elizth., dau. of Nich. Barker, citizen of London, 1594, left 3 sons, Thos., Hen., Rich.; C.

MARHOLM. Sir Wm. Fitzwilliams, knt., 1534, in arm. with tabard, and 1st w. Anne, in heraldic mantle, kng., 11 shs. including 1 on inscr.; upper hf. of man and 2 shs. renewed and an inscr. and 2 shs. added stating 'these monuments were repaired and beautified by ye Rt. Honble William, Lord Fitzwilliams anno 1674', mur., A.T., C.

NEWNHAM. Lady, and 1 sh. encircled by mottoes 'God send gud ende'; the remains of the br. to Rich. Catesby, esq., 1467, in arm., and w. Lettice in mantle, holding hands; rel., now mur., S.A.

NEWTON-BY-GEDDINGTON. John Mulsho, esq., in civil dress, and w. Joan, 1400, sm. effs. kng. to a cross with St. Faith in the head, marg. inscr.; rel. and restored in 1858; N.

NORTHAMPTON, ST. SEPULCHRE. Geo. Coles, left £11 yearly to the town for pious uses, 1640, in civil dress, and 2 ws., Sarah with 2 sons and 1 dau., and Eleanor with 7 sons and 2 daus., holding hands, also a device of 2 clasped hands and 8 Eng. vv. referring to this emblem of firm friendship, marg. inscr., large., rel., mur., N.

OUNDLE. Inscr. Kath., dau. of Edw. Cuthbert of Oundle, w. of Peter Dayrell, 2nd son of Sir Thos. Dayrell of Lillingstone Dayrell, Bucks., knt., 1615, N.A.

ROTHWELL. Wm. de Rothewelle, archdeacon of Essex, prebendary of Croprych (Croperdy, a prebend of Lincoln), Ferryng and Yalmerton, (1361), in cope, head on cushion supported by angels, inscr. in Fr. with text in Lat., rel., C.

SULGRAVE. Laur. Wasshington, gent. (1584), in civil dress, head gone, and w. Amy (dau. of Robert. Pargiter), 1564, eff. lost, with 4 sons and 7 daus., inscr. and 1 sh., N. *They were ancestors of Geo. Washington, first president of the United States of America.*

WAPPENHAM. Thos., son of Thos. Lovett, esq. (died 1542), in arm., and w. Elizth., dau. of John Butler, *c.* 1500, 3 shs. (another lost), sm., S.A.

WARKWORTH. Wm. Ludsthorp, esq., 1454, in arm; mar. Elizth., dau. of Sir John Chetwode and lady of Wodehill and Warkworth; S.Tr.

NORTHUMBERLAND

HEXHAM. Inscr. and 3 shs. (eff., canopy and another sh. lost). Robt. Ogle, son of Ellen, dau. of Sir Robt. Bertram, 1410, S.C.A.

NEWCASTLE-UPON-TYNE, ALL SAINTS. Roger Thornton, mcht., 1429 (date added), in civil dress, and w. 'domicella' Agnes (Wanton), 1411, in mantle, with 7 sons and 7 daus., fine triple canopies with the Deity, souls, angels, etc. in the upper parts, the 12 Apostles in the outer shafts and saints in the centre shaft, marg. inscr. with evang. symbols and shs., rect. pl., large, 80 in by 52 in. Foreign, now mur. in Vestry, and covered with glass.

NOTTINGHAMSHIRE

ANNESLEY. Wm. Breton of Ansley, 1595, in hunting dress with bow, arrows, and hound, sm. rect. pl. with inscr. Church disused, br. now at the Hall.

CLIFTON. Sir Gervis Clifton, died in London at the house of the preaching (black) friars, when his body was removed by his 2nd w. Agnes, and buried in the college of Flicton, which he had completed, 1491, in arm., 2 shs., N.C.

MARKHAM, EAST. Dame Millicent, w. of Sir Wm. Meryng, 1419, marg. inscr., S.A.

NEWARK. Alan Fleming, mcht., 1361, in civil dress, fine groined triple canopy with Deity, soul, etc., St. Peter and other figures (39 in all including male and female weepers in the side shafts), marg. inscr. with evang. symbols and mcht. marks, large rect. pl., 112 in by 68 in. Foreign, worn, mur., S.Tr.   Inscr. (chamfer). Robt. Browne, esq., alderman of the guild of Hy. Trin. in the ch., constable of the castle, receiver for cardinal Wolsey and for John Longland, bp. of Lincoln, sheriff of Notts. and Derby, keeper of the rolls in Notts. and the district of Kesteven, Lincs., 1532, and w. Agnes, A.T., with shs. on sides, C. Civilian, *c.* 1540, arms of Drapers' Co.; inscr. lost; rel., N.Tr. Inscr. Thos. Hobman the younger, ironmonger, 1653, S.Tr.

SOUTHWELL MINSTER. Six inscriptions.

STRELLEY. Sir Robt. Strelley, 1487, in arm., and w. Isabel, 1458, in mantle, ach. mutil.; 5 shs. lost; 1 roundel with badge (8 others lost); C.

WHEATLEY, NORTH. Inscr. and mcht. mark. Edm. Sheffield, citizen and vintner of London, 1445; inscr. palimp., on rev. another inscr. to Dame Joan, fastened down; mur., N.

WILLOUGHBY-ON-THE-WOLDS. Inscr. Col. Michael Stanhope, 'slayne in Willoughby Field', 1648, worn, N.A.

WOLLATON. Rich. Wylloughby, esq., 1471, in arm. standing on a large whelk shell, and w. Anne (dau. of Simon Leek), 1467, in mantle, 3 shs. and slab powdered with whelk shells, chamfer inscr. mutil., A.T., C.

OXFORDSHIRE (Numerous Publications, see bibliography)

ADDERBURY. Man in arm. with livery collar, and w., *c.* 1460; inscr. lost; rel., S.Tr.

BICESTER. Inscr. Rafe Hunte, born at 'Chilve in Lankeyshere, longe dweller in this towne of Bisseter', benefactor to the poor, 1602, had 2 ws. Ellen and Math. (who had 1 dau. Anne), mur., S.C. Inscr. John Lewes, gent., 'born in Lyn̄ in the county of Carnarvon, who for the love he bare to the said John Coker desired by his will to be buried neere him', died in Oxford, 1612, mur., N. Inscr. John Coker, 1606, and w. Joan, 1618; Anne, w. of Cadwallader Coker, eld. son of John and Joan, 1625; Cadwallader Coker, 1653, aged 82, and 2nd w. Cath., 1635, aged 36, had issue John, Cadwallader, Frances, Wm., Cath., Joan and Elizth., mur., N.

BRIGHTWELL BALDWIN. Inscr. in 7 Eng. vv. John the smith, *c.* 1370, N.A. John Cottusmore, chief justice of common pleas, 1439, in coif and robes, and w. Amice (Bruley), kng., very sm., inscr. in 26 Lat. vv., each couplet on a separate plate, 2 shs.; Trinity on a bracket between effs. lost; mur., C. The same persons standing under fine double canopy (slightly mutil.), with kng. figs. of 5 sons and 13 daus. below, 4 shs., no inscr., large, C.

BURFORD. John Spycer, 1437, in civil dress, and w. Alys, kng. to a bracket (with B.V.M. and Child under a sm. canopy now lost), 12 Eng. vv. recording their benefactions to the ch., marg. inscr. mutil., C.

CASSINGTON. Cross fleury (one arm mutil.), 2 shs. and inscr. Roger Cheyne, esq. to the king (1414), N.

CHECKENDON. Soul borne by 2 angels, inscr. and sh. Walter, son of Sir Wm. Beauchamp, *c.* 1430, C. Anne, dau. of John and Kath. Gaynesford of Crowhurst, Surrey, w. of Rich. Bowett, esq., 1490, eff. on C. floor, inscr. on wall above.

CHINNOR. Floriated cross with head of a priest in centre, *c.* 1320; stem and marg. inscr. lost; mur., C. John Hotham, 'Magister in theologia', rector (provost of Queen's Coll., Oxford), 1361, large hf. eff. in cap, acad., mur., C. 'Mons' Reynald de Malyns' (1385), in arm., and 2 ws., foot inscr. in Fr. mutil.; shs. lost; large, Vestry. 'Mouns' Esmoun de Malyns', son of Sir Renald de Malyns, in arm., and w. Isabel, *c.* 1385, hf. effs., inscr. in Fr., Vestry.

CHIPPING NORTON. John Yonge, woolman, 1451, in civil dress, standing on a woolpack, and w. Isabel, inscr. mutil.; children lost; large. John Pergetter, ironmonger, 1484, in civil dress, feet gone, and w. Agnes with 7 daus.; 5 sons and 4 mcht. marks lost; N.A. in orig. stone now upright.

DEDDINGTON. Inscr. (kng. effs., crucifix and shs., lost). Wm. Byllyng, mcht. of the staple of Calais, 1533 (date added), and w. Elizth., 1522, mur., A.T., N.C. Inscr. Thos. Higgins, 1660; 'George Harris fecit'; S.C.

DORCHESTER. Sir John Drayton (1417), in arm. with SS. collar, legs mutil.; eff. of w. Alice, double canopy, shs. and foot inscr. in 10 Lat. vv. lost: large, S.C.A. Rich. Bewfforeste (abbot of Dorchester), *c.* 1510, in surplice, almuce, and mantle of an Austin canon with crosier, inscr. in 2 Eng. vv., C.

EWELME. Thos. Chaucer, esq., lord of the manor and patron of the ch., 1434, in arm., and widow Maud, 1436, in mantle; chamfer inscr. shs. restored; A.T., S.C. Hen. Morecote, rector, 1467, hf. eff. in mass vests., N. Wm. Branwhait, master of hospital, 1498, hf. eff. (? engr. earlier, *c.* 1470) mass vests., S.A. Thos. Broke, esq., serjeant-at-arms to Hen. VIII, 1518, in arm., and w. Anne (Bulstrode), 4 shs.; N.

LEWKNOR. John Aldebourne, rector, *c.* 1380, hf. eff. in mass vests. with fylfot ornament, inscr. mutil., mur., C.

ODDINGTON. Ralph Hamsterley, rector, fellow of Merton Coll., Oxford (died 1518), engr. *c.* 1510, a skeleton in shroud eaten by worms, scroll with vv. 'vermibus hic donor', etc., and foot inscr., N. *See Queen's College, Oxford.*

OXFORD, ALL SOULS' COLLEGE. David Lloyde, in acad. with tonsure, and Thos. Baker, in civil dress with scholar's gown and without tonsure, both died 24 Dec., 1510, hf. effs. All in Ante-chapel.

OXFORD, CHRIST CHURCH. Edw., son of Hugh Courtenay, brother of the earl of Devon, *c.* 1450, in civil dress with anelace, 1 sh., sm., Lady Chapel. J. Coorthopp (canon of Christ Church, dean of Peterborough), 1557, in almuce, foot inscr. in 12 Lat. vv., marg. Inscr. mutil., N.C.A. John, son of Geo. Bisshop, citizen, bookseller of London, 1588, aged 18, in civil dress, kng., rect. pl. with inscr. and 8 Lat. vv., mur., Lady Chapel. Thos. Thornton, M.A, educated Westminster and Christ Church, 1613, aged 37, in gown and hood, kng., rect. pl. with inscr. and 2 Lat. vv.; his brother Geo. pos.; mur., Lady Chapel.

OXFORD, CORPUS CHRISTIE COLLEGE. Francis Colthurst, gent., citizen and mcht. of London, commoner of Christ Church, 1602, aged 26, civil dress, inscr. 10 Lat. vv.; his brother Hen. pos. Anti-chapel.

OXFORD, MAGDALEN COLLEGE. Ralph Vawdrey, M.A, chaplain, 1478, hf. eff. in acad. with scroll, Ante-chapel. Arthur Cole, S.T.B, president, canon of Windsor, 1558, almuce, garter mantle; palimp.

OXFORD, MERTON COLLEGE. (Rich. de Hakeborne), rector of Wolford, Warw. (died *c.* 1311), large hf. eff. in mass vests. on the head of a floriated cross; cross and marg. inscr. in single Lombardic letters lost; N.Tr. John Bloxham, warden (died 1387), gown and hood, and John Whytton, rector of Wodeton (Wood Eaton, Oxon.), benefactor to the coll., who pos. *c.* 1420, in cassock and hood, under sm. double canopy supported on a bracket with long shaft with Holy Lamb at base, rel., C. Hen. Sever, 'sacre theologie professor', warden and a special benefactor to the coll., also of kin to the founder, 1471, in cope with a bp. (probably the founder, Walter of Merton, bp. of Rochester), and SS. Jas. the Great, Jas. the Less, Paul — John Bapt., John Evang., Barth., Thos., on orphreys, triple canopy, foot inscr. and 2 shs., rel. and partly restored, C.

OXFORD, NEW COLLEGE. (Thos. Cranley, warden, abp. of Dublin, 1417), in archiepiscopal vests. with mitre and cross, triple canopy with embattled entablature, 8 Latin vv. and 2 shs., marg., inscr. also in 8 Lat. vv. nearly all lost, large, Ante-chapel. T. Hylle, 'professor sacre theologie', fellow, benefactor to the coll., 1468, in cap and acad., holding cross with 5 wounds, inscr. with 2 Lat. vv., Ante-chapel. John Frye, 'sacre theologie scolaris', fellow, 1507, hf. eff. in mass vests., chalice and wafer, Ante-chapel. John Young, bp. of Callipolis, Thrace, suffragan of London, warden (died 1526), br.

engr. *c.* 1525, date not filled in, in episcopal vests. with mitre and crosier, head of eff. and crosier lost, large, Ante-chapel.   Hugh Lloyd, D.C.L, fellow, chancellor to bp. of Rochester, master of Winchester Coll., 1601, in gown and hood, kng., rect. pl. with inscr. 10 Lat. vv. and sh., mur., Ante-chapel.

OXFORD, QUEEN'S COLLEGE. Inscr. (eff. lost), Ralph Hamsterley, master of University Coll. (died 1518), see Oddington, Oxon. H Robinson, 18 years provost, restorer of coll., 18 years bp. of Carlisle, 1616, aged 63, in rochet and cap, with crosier, kng., rect. pl. with inscr., views of the coll., Carlisle Cath., and other subjects. There is a duplicate plate in Carlisle Cath.

OXFORD, ST. ALDATE. Arthur Strode of Devon, a member of the Middle Temple and of Broadgates Hall (now Pembroke Coll.), 1612, aged 23, in civil dress, kng., rect. pl. with inscr., 4 Lat. vv. and sh., mur., S.A.

OXFORD, ST. JOHN'S COLLEGE. Hen., eld. son of John Huchenson, born in London, fellow, 1573, aged 23, in gown and hood, kng., inscr. and 2 Lat. vv.; Ralph Hucheson pos., mur., Baylie Chapel.   John Glover, M.A, fellow, student of medicine, senior proctor, 1578, aged 35, in gown and hood, kng., inscr. and 2 Lat. vv.; his friends Ralph Huchenson and Thos. Mainwaring pos.; mur., Ante-chapel.

OXFORD, ST. CROSS, HOLYWELL. Eliza, 3rd w. of Thos. Franklin, 'who dangerously escaping death at 3 severall travells in childbed, died together with the fourth, 1622, aged 35, in bed with 3 children in shrouds, and 1 in swaddling clothes on coverlet, rect. pl. with inscr. and 6 Eng. vv., mur., S.A.

OXFORD, ST. MARY MAGDALEN. Wm. Smith, M.A, fellow of Merton Coll., a very skilful physician, 1580, aged 58, in gown and hood, kng., inscr. with 16 Lat. vv., mur., S.A.

OXFORD, ST. MARY-THE-VIRGIN. Edw. Chernock of Brasenose Coll., son and h. of Robt. Chernock of Chernock, Lancs., esq., 1581, in civil dress, kng., rect. pl. with inscr., 14 Lat. vv. and sh., mur., N.A.

OXFORD, ST. MICHAEL. Ralph Flexney, alderman, 1578, in civil dress, and 2nd w. Cath., 1567, kng., had 2 sons, Thos. (who pos.), Rich., and 7 daus., rect. pl. with inscr., 4 Lat. vv. and ach., mur., S.A.

PYRTON. An incised slab to a priest, 14th-cent., with marg. inscr. in Lombardics (1 brass stop remaining), C., under altar.

ROTHERFIELD GREYS. Sir Robt. de Grey, lord of Rotherfield, 1387, in arm., single canopy, marg. inscr.; shs. lost; large, C., under altar.

SHIPTON-UNDER-WYCHWOOD. Elizth., w. of Edm. Horne, esq., 1548, recumbent in shroud, rect. pl. with inscr. in 12 Eng. vv. and sh; palimp., on rev. a confirmation of a grant in Eng. (in 1494) by John Stone and his w. Alice to the wardens of the guild of St. Mary at Aylesbury of a messuage in Aylesbury on condition of dirges and masses being sung on 23 April for the souls of the said John and Alice; now on a bracket, N.C.

SOMERTON. Mr. Wm. Fermoure, esq., lord of the town, patron of the ch., 'clarke of the crowne in the kyngs benche' under Hen. VII, VIII, 1552, in arm., and 'last' w. Elizth., 3 shs., the inscr. ends 'upon whose soulles and all crysten soulles Jesu have mercy', A.T., S.C.

STANTON HARCOURT. Thos. Harecourt, esq., 1460, and Nich. Atherton, esq., 1454, both in civil dress, below are 3 very sm. effs. (Geo., Alys, and Isabel Harcourt), 1 sh. (others lost), sm., S.C.

SWALECLIFFE. Inscr. Joyce, dau. and coh. of John Hawlthen of Swalecliffe, gent., w. of Rich. Newman of Eppwell, gent., 1584, S.A.

SWINBROOK. Anth. Fetyplace, esq., 1510, in arm. with tabard, 4 shs. C.

TEW, GREAT. (John Wylcotes, died 1422), in arm. with livery collar, and w. Alice (dau. of Thos. Wylcotes by Elizth., dau. and h. of Edw. Hall, 1410), in mantle, double canopy mutil. as is also the marg. inscr. in 8 Lat. vv., 3 shs. (2 others lost), badges in pediments of canopy and between each word of the inscr., large, worn, C.

THAME. Thos. Quatremayn of North Weston, in arm., and w. Kath., dau. of Guy Breton by Joan, dau. and coh. of Thos. de Grey, son of Sir Robt. Grey of Rotherfield, both died 1342, also their son Thos. Quatremayn, died 1396, in arm., lower part of eff. lost, and his widow Joan, on brackets (mutil.), engr. *c.* 1420, chamfer inscr. much mutil.; 7 shs. lost; A.T., S.Tr.   Rich. Quatremayns, councillor to Rich., duke of York, and to Edw. IV, founder of a 'chauntrie vi pore men and a fraternite in the worshipp of Seynt Cristofere to be relevid in perpetuyte' (died 1478), in arm., and w. Sibil (dau. of Nich. Englefeld, died 1483), in mantle, head gone, with 1 son in arm., engr. *c.* 1460, chamfer inscr. in 10 Eng. vv., 1 sh. (4 others lost), A.T., S.Tr.   Geoff. Dormer, mcht. of staple of Calais, 1502, in civil dress, and 2 ws., (1) Margery with 5 sons (lost) and 8 daus., (2) Alice (Collingridge) with 7 sons and 5 daus., sh. and mcht. mark, 2 other shs. lost, chamfer inscr., A.T., N.Tr.

WATERPERRY. Isabel Beaufo, *c.* 1370, sm., mutil.; inscr. in Fr. lost; rel., N.   Walter Curson, esq., died 1527, br. engr. later *c.* 1540, in arm., and w. Isabel, both buried in the church of the Augustine Friars at Oxford, with 8 sons and 7 daus., 4 shs., marg. inscr. with text from Job xix; foot inscr. and group of daus. lost; palimp., the effs. *c.* 1440, altered and adapted to the later date; large, N.

WHITCHURCH. Roger Gery, vicar, who in 1455 procured the sanction of John bp. of Lincoln, to the union of the rectory and vicarage of the ch., engr. *c.* 1455, in mass vests. with chalice and wafer, 1 sh., C. floor.

WOODSTOCK. Jerome Keys, LL.B, fellow of St. John's Coll., Oxford, 1631, aged 71, in gown and hood, kng., rect. pl. with inscr. and sh., mur., S.A.

RUTLAND

BRAUNSTON. Kenelme Cheseldyn of Uppingham, esq., 'linally descended from Anne Broogh, dau. and h. to ye Lord Broogh', 1596, in civil dress, and w. Winefrid, dau. of Francis Say of Wilby, Northants, gent., had 11 sons and 3 daus. and left a son Edw. his heir, effs. mutil., 1 ach., N.

CASTERTON, LITTLE. Sir Thos. Burton, lord of Tolthorp, patron of the ch., (died 1381), in arm. with SS. collar, and w. Margery (Greenham (?)), in mantle, engr. *c.* 1410, marg. inscr. mutil., 1 sh. (ach. and 3 others lost), C.

SHROPSHIRE

ACTON BURNELL. Sir Nich. Burnell, lord of Holgot, 1382, in arm., single canopy slightly mutil.; shs. lost; large, A.T., N.Tr.

ADDERLEY. Abbot or bp., *c.* 1390, in full vests., holding crosier and book; head and inscr. lost; large, C.

DITTON PRIORS. Inscr. Thos. Jencks, pastor, 1648, aged 49; mar. Dorothy, dau. of Nich. Clark of Lichfield, had 6 sons; Thos. Jencks of Shrewsbury, goldsmith, pos. in 1667; local, mur., S.A.

GLAZELEY. Thos. Wylde, esq., 1599, in civil dress, and w. Elizth., dau. and h. of Rich. Cooke, esq., with 4 sons and 2 daus., ach., and 2 shs., mur., C.

IGHTFIELD. Dame Margery Calveley, dau. of Wm. Maynwaryng of Ightfield, sometime w. of Philip Egerton of Egerton, esq. (died 1509), br. eng. *c.* 1495 (date not filled in), with 4 sons and 4 daus., triple canopy with St. John Bapt. on centre finial mutil., marg. inscr. with shs. at corners, large, N.

LUDLOW. Inscr. in 4 Lat. vv. Dorothy Wogan, 1632, mur., C.

SHIPTON. Inscr. 'This chauncell was reedified and builded of newe from the foundacion and glazed' by John, youngest son of Rich. Lutwich, 1589, mur., C.

TONG. Sir Wm. Vernon, knight constable of England, son and h. of Sir Rich. Vernon, treasurer of Calais, 1467, in arm., and widow

Margt., dau. and h. of (Sir Wm. Swynfen), with 7 sons and 5 daus. (2 lost), marg. inscr. and 8 shs., A.T., N.

Ralph Elcok, 'cel're', a brother of the college, born at Stopford (Stockport), Ches., died 1510, in surplice and almuce, local, worn, now mur., S.A.

WENLOCK, MUCH. Rich. Ridley, son and h. of Raynold Ridley of Lynley, gent., by Alice Leighton who before was the w. of Thos. Mownsloe of Caughley, gent., and had by him 1 son and 5 daus., twice bayly, 1592, in civil dress, and w. Eleanor (who pos.), dau. of John Sydenham of Chilworthy, Somerset, kng., 3 shs., mur., C.

WROXETER. Inscr. Thos. Alcocke, yeoman, gave 20 marks yearly for maintenance of a free grammar school, and a bell to the ch. of Wroxeter, also £10 to the poor, 1627, mur., N.

SOMERSET

BATH ABBEY. Sir Geo. Ivy of West Kington, Wilts., knt. (1639), in arm., and w. Susanna, with 4 sons. Thos., Palmer (in arm.), 'slaine in ye Venetian warrs in ye Ile of Corffue', Geo., clerk, Robt. (in arm.), 'died in ye Netherlands at ye seige of Bredah', and 4 daus., Elizth. (dec.), Anne (dec.), Avis, Barbara, all kng., rect., pl. with inscr. and 2 shs., mur., C.

CHEDDAR. (Sir Thos. Cheddar, 1442), in arm.; marg. inscr. and 4 shs. lost; A.T., C.

CREWKERNE. Thos. Golde, esq., 1525, in arm., kng., sm., rel., mur., C.   Inscr. Edw., son of Edw. Sweet, goldsmith, born 1679, died 1683, mur., N.C.

DUNSTER. John Wyther, in civil dress, and w. Agnes, their eld. son John bur. with them 1497, engr. c. 1520, rel., N.

GLASTONBURY, ST. JOHN. Inscr. with 4 Eng. vv. and ach. Alex. Dyer, son and h. of Thos. Dyer of Street, 1633, and w. Kath., dau. of John Thornburgh of Shaddsdon, Hants, 1650, also Capt. John Dyer, 1670, with 4 Eng. vv., mur., S.C.

ILMINSTER. Sir Wm. Wadham (died 1452), in arm., and mother (Joan, widow of Sir John Wadham, justice of the common pleas), in widow's dress, each under triple canopy with super-canopy, engr. c. 1440, foot inscr. in 8 Lat. vv., marg. inscr. much mutil.; shs. lost; large, A.T., N.Tr.   Nich. Wadham of Merefield, founder of Wadham Coll., Oxford, died 1609, in arm., and w. Dorothy (dau. of Sir Wm. Petre), 1618, aged 84, inscr., ach. and 4 shs., very large, A.T., N.Tr.

PETHERTON, SOUTH. Sir Giles Daubeney (died 1445), and 1st w. Joan, dau. of John, lord Darcy and Meinell, in mantle, engr. c. 1430, double canopy, foot inscr. in 4 Lat. vv., 1 sh. (other lost), marg. inscr. restored in 1883, A.T.

SHEPTON MALLET. Wm. Strode of Barington, esq., in arm., with 6 sons, Wm., Edw., John, Geo., Essex, Barnard, and w. Joan, 1649, aged 42, with 3 daus., Jane, Elizth., Joan, mar. 28 years, 6 other sons and 1 dau. dec., all kng., large rect. pl. with figure of Death, etc., inscr. and 5 shs., mur., Tower.

TAUNTON, ST. MARY. Inscr. with emblems of mortality, etc. Bernard Smith, twice mayor, 1696, aged 52; also Charity his w., dau. of Emanuel Sharp, vicar, 1716, and their dau. Mary, 1714, aged 37, both added to original plate, mur., S.C.

WEDMORE. Inscr. with heart, ensigns, etc., and 4 Eng. vv. Capt. Thos. Hodges, slain at the siege of Antwerp about 1583, 'wonne two ensigns from the enemy', left 3 legacies, 'his soule to his Lord Jesus, his body to be lodged in Flemish earth, his heart to be sent to his deare wife in England', engr. c. 1630, mur., N.C.

Geo. Hodges, esq., c. 1630, in buff coat with pike and sword, rect. pl. and inscr., mur., N.C.

WELLS CATHEDRAL. Priest, c. 1460, hf. eff. in cope; inscr. lost; N.E.Tr. Inscr. Wm. Powell, S.T.D, archdeacon of Bath, canon of Wells, 1613, N.C.A.   Humf., son of Humf. Willis, 1618, aged 28, civil dress,

kng., rect. pl. with allegorical subjects, inscr., 4 Lat. vv. and sh.; his w. pos., very lightly engr., mur., S.E.Tr.

YEOVIL. Martin Forester, friar, c. 1460, hf. eff. in gown and hood, inscr. in 2 Lat. vv. on a scroll, on lectern.

STAFFORDSHIRE

AUDLEY. Sir Thos. de Audeley, son of Jas. de Audele, 'seignour de Helegh de rouge chastell', 1385, in arm.; single canopy all lost but pediment, inscr. in Fr.; repaired and a new head added in 1914; large, C.

BROUGHTON. Inscr. Elizth., dau. of Thos. Broughton, esq., 1681, aged 64. 'desired all persons to forbeare to stirr her bones', C.

CLIFTON CAMPVILLE. Lady, c. 1360, hf. eff. on a bracket; stem, canopy, shs., and marg. inscr. lost; palimp, on rev. a portion of a cross-legged eff. in mail with surcoat, c. 1300; rel. in orig. slab in 1914, S.C.

HANBURY. Priest, c. 1480, in cope; inscr. lost; worn, rel., C.

NORBURY. Hawise Botiller (1360), in widow's dress, single canopy much mutil., frag. of marg. inscr. in Fr. rel. and repaired in 1914.

OKEOVER. Wm., 5th Lord Zouch of Harringworth (died 1462), in arm., and 2 ws., Alice, 1447, in mantle, and Elizth., with flowing hair, triple canopy with shs. on finials, marg. inscr.; appropriated and altered as a memorial to Humf. Oker, esq. (1538), his w. Isabel and their 13 children. About the year 1857, the whole brass was stolen from the ch. and the frags. recovered were mostly broken into pieces ready for the melting pot. These frags., 55 in all, were arranged on a board and replaced in the ch. in 1898.

TRENTHAM. Sir Rich. Leveson of Lylieshall, Salop, knt., 1559, in arm., and w. Mary, spent her widowhood and was buried at Trentham, died at Battersea, Surrey, 1591, with 1 son Sir Walter, in arm., all kng., ach., mur., S.C.

WOLVERHAMPTON. Inscr. Sir Rich. Leveson, vice-admiral of England, died 1605, on base of statue by Lesueur erected in 1634.

SUFFOLK

Cotman. 'Engravings of Sepulchral Brasses in Suffolk', by J. S. Cotman, 1838.

Farrer. 'A List of Monumental Brasses remaining in the county of Suffolk', by E. Farrer, 1903.

ACTON. Sir Robt. de Bures, 1302, cross-legged, in mail and surcoat, with sh. on arm; Fr. marg. inscr. in single Lombardic letters lost; large, N.C.   (Alice, dau, h. of Sir Robt. de Bures, widow of Sir Guy Bryan, 1435), in widow's dress, triple canopy much mutil. with 4 shs. (2 lost) on finials; marg. inscr. lost; large, N.C.

BARROW. Sir Clement Heigham, twice reader at Lincoln's Inn, speaker (in 1554), chief baron of the exchequer, to Queen Mary, 1570, in arm., with 1 son in shroud, and 2 ws., (1) Anne, with 5 daus., (2) Anne, with 3 sons (lost) and 2 daus., all kng., inscr. in 44 Eng. vv., ach. and 2 shs., mur., A.T., C.

BARSHAM. Man in arm., c. 1415, with SS. collar, initials R.S. on sword hilt; marg. inscr. lost; large, C.

BOXFORD. Inscr. and 4 shs., London, Mercers' Co., Mcht-Adventurers, and East India Co. Wm. Doggett, mcht-adventurer, citizen and mercer of London, free of East India Co., 1610, aged 53; mar. Avis, dau. of Thos. Lappadge of Boxford, gent., mar. 19 years, had 6 sons and 6 daus.; N.C.A.

BURGATE. Sir Wm. de Burgate, 1409, in arm., and w. Eleanor, in mantle, double canopy and marg. inscr. both slightly mutil.; shs. lost; large, A.T., C.

BURY ST. EDMUND'S, ST. MARY. Civilian with Yorkist collar, and w. c. 1480, kng.; inscr., scrolls, and shs. lost; S.C.   John Fynexs, archdeacon of Sudbury (1497-1514), in almuce, insc. in 2 Lat. vv., local, N.C.

DENHAM near EYE. Anth., 3rd son of Sir Edm. Bedingfeld, 1574, in civil dress, and inscr.; eff. palimp., on rev. the feet of 3 persons with a portion of an inscr., and 2 shs., Flemish, c. 1500, C.

DENSTON. Hen. Everard, esq., in arm. with tabard, and w. Margt., dau. of Sir Robt. Broughton, 1524, in heraldic mantle, 4 shs.; inscr. lost: local, C.

EASTON. Man in arm., c. 1425; inscr. lost; C.   John Brook? 1426.

FORNHAM. Thos. Manock, gent., 1656, aged about 64, 'a person of open house and harte', left monuments to his mother Mary, his w. Dorothy, and his brother John, and 'for all deserves this monument for him selfe'; the vv. read 'Let noe man steale away this brasse but he whoe knowes himselfe unworthie memorye'. mur. N.T.

GORLESTON. Man in arm. of the Bacon family, c. 1320, cross-legged, with surcoat, ailettes, and sh. on arm.; legs of eff., canopy, and marg. inscr. lost; now mur., N.C.

HADLEIGH. John Alabaster, clothier, twice mayor, 1637, aged 76, in civil dress, kng. under arch; he was mar. 52 years to his w. Mary and had 2 sons and 9 daus., mur., S.C.A.

HALESWORTH. John Browne (1581), aged 80 years and 25 weeks (eff. lost), had 65 grandchildren, left 54 surviving, and 'onely' w. (lower hf. lost), with 6 sons and 10 daus. (mutil).; the inscr. (mutil.) is palimp., on rev. a sm. portion of a Flemish br., 16th century; now mur., S.A., the palimp. on hinges.

IPSWICH, ST. MARY QUAY. Thos. Pownder, mcht., bayly of Ipswich, 1525, in civil dress, and w. Emme, standing, with 2 sons and 6 daus. kng., rect. pl. with diapered background, mcht. mark, arms of Ipswich, Mcht.-Adventurers, and marg. inscr., Flemish, C. Inscr., mcht. mark and arms of Mcht.-Adventurers. Augustine Parker, 1599, aged 63, C.

IPSWICH, ST. MARY TOWER. Notary, c. 1475, in civil dress with penner and inkhorn; canopy and inscr. lost; large, rel., C.   Alys Baldry, 1506, and her 2 husbands, Robt. Wymbyll, notary, in civil dress with penner and inkhorn, and Thos. Baldry, in civil dress with pouch, 4 sons, 5 daus., arms of Mercer's Co. imp. mcht. mark of Baldry, C.

IPSWICH, ST. NICHOLAS. Inscr. and mcht. mark, arms of Grocers' Co. and Mcht.-Adventurers. Susan, w. of Augustine Parker, mcht., 1604, aged 24, C.

KENTON. John Garneys, esq., 1524, in arm. with tabard and 6 sons, and w. Elizth. (Sulyard), in heraldic mantle, with 9 daus., all kng., rect. pl. with crucifix, ach. and sh., slightly mutil., mur., S.A.

LAVENHAM. Clopton, son and h. of Sir Simon D'Ewes by Anne, dau. of Sir Wm. Clopton (1631), aged 10 days, in swaddling clothes, rel., C.

LETHERINGHAM. Sir John de Wyngefeld, lord of the manor, 1389, in arm. with arms on jupon; inscr. lost; large, now mur., N.A.

LOWESTOFT. Two large scrolls, c. 1490; the remains of a br. to a civilian and w., with 4 sons, 3 daus., and mcht. marks with initials N.H.; N.   Civilian and w. (head gone), c. 1540, mcht. mark, arms of the Saltfishmongers' Co.; children and inscr. lost; S.A.

MELFORD, LONG. Lady of the Clopton family, engr. c. 1480, in heraldic dress with arms of Francis on kirtle and Clopton on mantle, single canopy (mutil.); 3 shs.; inscr. and another sh. lost; rel., N.C.A.   Francis Clopton, son and h. of Wm. Clopton, esq., 1577, in arm., 2 shs.; inscr. lost; N.C.A.

MILDENHALL. Sir Hen. Warner of Mildenhall, 1617, in arm., also his son Edw. Warner, esq., 1618 (eff. lost), mar. Mary, 1 sh., mur., C.

ORFORD. John Coggeshall, thrice mayor, 1640, in civil dress, with 5 sons, and w. Elizth., with 2 daus., all kng., rect. pl., ach. on oval; inscr. in 8 Eng. vv. cut in stone; N.A.

PLAYFORD. Sir Geo. Felbrigg, 1400, in arm., with arms on jupon, single canopy now all lost but side shafts, marg. inscr. in Fr. much mutil., large, rel., now mur., C.

ROUGHAM. Sir Roger Drury (died 1410), in arm., and w. Margery (dau. and h. of Sir Thos. Naunton), 1405, in mantle, inscr. mutil.; shs. lost; large, N.A.

SAXHAM, GREAT. John Eldred, born at New Buckingham, Norf. alderman of London, travelled to Babilon, Egypt, Arabia and the Holy Land, aged 80, in civil dress, 6 Lat., 8 Eng. vv. and dedication plate, 2 achs. and 6 shs. including London, Clothworkers' Co., East India Co., Russia Mchts. and Turkey Mchts.; his son and h. Revett pos. in 1632; A.T., C.

SOTTERLEY. Thos. Playters, esq., patron of the ch., in arm., and w. Anne, sister and coh. of Roger Denneis of Tatyngton, esq., both died 1479, inscr. mutil., 1 sh. (2 others lost), effs. on C. floor, inscr. on wall.

STOKE-BY-NAYLAND. Lady in mantle, c. 1400; inscr. lost; S.C. *Possibly Kath., widow of Sir Thos. Clopton, w. of Sir Wm. Tendring, 1402.* Sir Wm. Tendring, 1408, in arm., bare headed with beard; inscr. lost; S.C.   Lady (Kath., dau. of Wm., lord Molyns, 1st), w. of John Howard, duke of Norfolk, mother of Thos. Howard, duke of Norfolk, died 1452, engr. later c. 1535, in heraldic mantle, 1 sh.; inscr. and 3 other shs. lost; S.C.

THURLOW, GREAT. Man in arm. with salade, and w. in widow's dress, c. 1460; inscr. lost; local, C.

UFFORD. Rich. Ballett, 'first goldsmith of the Balletts in London', 1598, aged 76, a skeleton on a tomb, rect. pl. with inscr., 10 Eng. vv. and arms of Goldsmiths' Co., mur., N.

WILBY. Civilian, c. 1530, and device of a running sheep; inscr. lost; local, N.

WOODBRIDGE. John Shorlond, 1601, aged 7, in civil dress, inscr. with 6 Eng. vv., 1 sh., now mur., C.

YOXFORD. Tomesin, dau. of Wm. Sydney, esq., by his w. Tomesin Baryngton, w. of Wm. Tendryng, esq., 1485, in shroud, with 3 sons and 2 daus. in shrouds and 2 daus. in ordinary dress with flowing hair, 1 sh. (3 others lost), large, now mur., C.

SURREY (LONDON)

BARNES. Edith and Elizth., daus. of John and Anne Wylde, 'died virgyns', 1508, with flowing hair, 1 sh., sm., rel. and now mur., S.A.

BEDDINGTON. Floriated cross for Margt. Oliver, servant to Nich. and Mercy Carru, 1425, mutil., sm., now under C. stalls. Nich. Carrew, esq., lord of the manor, 1432, in civil dress, and (1st) w. Isabel, fine double canopy, 4 shs., and slightly mutil. marg. inscr.; the inscr. mentions son Thos.; large, C.   Roger Elmebrygge, esq., sheriff of Surrey and Sussex, 1437, in arm., inscr. in 8 Lat. vv., 4 shs., under C. stalls.   Sir Rich. Carew, 1520, in arm. with tabard, and w. Malyn, in heraldic mantle; effs. and most of chamfer inscr. a modern restoration; A.T., S.C.

BETCHWORTH. Wm. Wardysworth, vicar, 1533, in mass vests., with chalice and wafer, now mur., C.

BYFLEET. Thos. Teylar, rector (1455-89), canon of Lincoln, in almuce, engr. c. 1480 (date not filled in), now mur., C.

CAMBERWELL, ST. GILES. John Scott, esq., a baron of the exchequer, 1532, in arm., and w. (Elizth. Skinner), kng.; 4 sons, 7 daus., shs., etc., lost.   John Bowyar, esq., 1570, civil dress, with 8 sons, and w. Elizth., dau. of Robt. Draper, esq., with 3 daus., all kng., 1 ach.; 2 shs. lost; the inscr. added in 1605 on the death of the lady, mentions her 2nd husband Wm. Foster, esq., by whom she had 1 son and 1 dau.   Mathye Draper, esq., 1577, civil dress, and w. Sence, dau. of Wm. Blackwell of London, esq., kng., 1 sh.; ach. and another sh. lost. *The brasses are now fixed to the back of the choir stalls, the palimps. in oak frames.*

CARSHALTON. Nich. Gaynesford, one of the esquires for the body to

Edw. IV and Hen. VII (died 1498), in arm. with 4 sons, the eld. in arm., the 2nd a priest in acad., and w. Margt. (Sidney, died 1503), one of the gentlewomen to Queens Elizth. (Widville) and Elizth. (of York), with collar of suns and roses, and enamelled dress, brass engr. c. 1480-90, dates on inscr. not filled in; 4 daus. and Trinity lost; 3 shs. above effs. and 4 on sides of tomb, mur., A.T., old chancel, now S.C.

CHEAM. John Compton, 1450, in civil dress, and w. Joan, 1458, hf. effs., rel., S.A.C. Inscr. and 2 shs. Barth., son and h. of Thos. Fromoundes of Cheam, gent., 1579; shs. palimp., cut out of 2 earlier shs; rel. and palimps. fastened down. Both in Lumley chapel.

CLAPHAM, ST. PAUL. Inscr. Wm. Tableer, 1401, filled in and now mur., N.

CLAPHAM, ST. PETER. Priest, c. 1470, in cope; inscr. recording its gift to the ch. in 1912 by Ethel Anne Marshall; mur., Sedilia.

COBHAM. Adoration of the shepherds, c. 1500, sm. rect. pl., now mur., C.

CROWHURST. John Gaynesford senior, esq., 1450, in arm., 1 sh., A.T., C.

CROYDON, ST. JOHN. Inscr. Elias Davy, citizen and mercer of London, 1455, restored, mur., N.A. He founded the almshouses in Croydon in 1447.

DITTON, LONG. (Rich. Hatton, 1616, aged 81, in civil dress, and w. Mary, dau. of Geo. and Rose Evelyn, 1612, aged 63); 3 sons, 6 daus., and inscr. lost; rel., mur., N.A.

DITTON, THAMES. Erasmus Forde, esq., son and h. of Walter Forde, treasurer to Edw. IV in his wars and 'at ye wynnyng of Barwyke', h. in descent to Sir Adam Forde, 1533, in arm., and w. Julyan, dau. and coh. of Wm. Salford by Elyn, dau. of Sir Rich. Chawrey, 1559, with 6 sons and 12 daus., all kng., rect. pos. with inscr., ach. and 2 shs., mur., N.C.

EGHAM. Anth. Bond, gent., citizen and writer of the court letter of London (scrivener), 1576, in civil dress, and 2 ws., with 1 son by 1st w., all kng., rect. pl. with 1 sh., inscr., and 4 Eng. vv., mur., S.A.

EWELL. Inscr. Edm. Dows, gent., one of the Clerks of the signet to Hen. VII, 1510. Lady Jane, dau. of John Agmondesham of 'Lede-red', Surrey, esq., w. of Sir John Iwarby of Ewell, knt., 1519, in heraldic mantle, 2 scrolls (1 lost) and 2 shs.

FARNHAM. Benet Jay (1586), in civil dress, and w. Elizth. (1594), with 3 sons and 3 daus., all kng., rect. pl. with ach., sh., and inscr. in 8 Lat. vv., mur., S.C.

GODALMING. Thos. Purvoche, 1509, in civil dress, and w. Joan, rel., C.

GODALMING, WYATT'S ALMHOUSES. Rich. Wyatt, gent., citizen and carpenter of London, founder of the almshouses, 1619, in civil dress, and w. Margt., dau. of Roger Sheers, with 3 sons and 3 daus., all kng., rect. pl. with 1 sh. and inscr. recording gift, mur. in chapel.

GUILDFORD, HOLY TRINITY. Civilian, c. 1500; inscr. lost; now mur. on board, Tower.   Maurice Abbot, aged 86, in civil dress, and w. Alice (Marsh), aged 80, both died Sept. 1607, mar. 58 years, with 6 sons 'all whome they left alive', all kng., rect. pl. with inscr., mur., N.

GUILDFORD, ST. NICHOLAS. Inscr. (chamfer). Arnold Brocas, B.C.L, canon of Lincoln and Wells, rector, 1395, A.T., More chapel.

HORLEY. Lady, possibly of the Salman family, c. 1420, with collar of SS. and son (lost) standing beside her, single canopy slightly mutil., large; foot inscr. and 2 shs. lost; another inscr. added to Joan, w. of John Fenner, 1516; now mur. in orig. slab, C.

HORSLEY, EAST. John Bowthe, bp. of Exeter, 1478, in episcopal vests. with mitre and crossier, kng., inscr. with 2 Lat. vv. and sh., mur., C.

KINGSTON-UPON-THAMES. Robt. Skern, 1437, in civil dress, and w. Joan, in mantle, inscr. in 12 Lat. vv.; ach. and 4 shs. lost; now mur. orig. slab. S.Tr.   Inscr. with 12 Eng. vv. 10 children of Edm.

Staunton, D.D, late minster of Kingston, now president of Corpus Christi Coll., Oxford, by his w. Mary, dau. of Rich. Balthrop, servant to the late Queen Elizth., 1653.

LAMBETH, ST. MARY. Lady Kath., sister and h. of John Broughton, esq., 1st w. of lord Wm. Howard (son of Thos., 2nd duke of Norfolk), 1535, in heraldic mantle; canopy and inscr. lost; rel., mur., N.C.

LAMBETH PALACE CHAPEL. Inscr. Matt. Parker, abp. of Cant., 1559-75, on a tomb erected by Wm. Sancroft, abp. 1678-91, to replace one destroyed in 1648.

LEATHERHEAD. Inscr., 14 Eng. vv. and ach. Robt. Gardnar, chief serjeant of the celler to Queen Elizth., 1571, aged 73, mur., S.A.

LINGFIELD. (Lady Elizth., dau. of Ralph, earl of Stafford, 1st w. of Sir Reginald Cobham, 2nd baron Cobham of Sterborough, 1375), in mantle, partly restored; inscr. and shs. lost; large, N.C. Sir Reginald Cobham, 2nd baron Cobham of Sterborough, 1403, in arm., marg. inscr. in 10 Lat. vv.; crest and shs. restored; large, A.T., N.C.

MOLESEY, EAST. Inscr. and sh. nth. Standen, gent., 3rd son of Edm. Standen, esq., cup bearer to the king of Scotland, some time lord Darnley, father to King James now of England, 1611, aged 71; his widow Elizth. pos.; mur., N.

MORTLAKE. Anne, dau. of Lewis Jeames, gent., 1608, aged 6, mur., N.

OCKHAM. Walter Frilende, rector, builder of chapel (1376), hf. eff. in mass vests., C.

OXTED. John Ynge, rector, 1428, in mass vests.; upper part of eff. lost; sm. mur. C.

PUTNEY. John Welbek, esq., 1476, in arm., and w. Agnes, 1478 (eff. lost), inscr. mutil. and palimp., on rev. another inscr. to John and Isabel Thorp, parents of Wm. Thorp, master of this college (St. Laur. Poutney, 1426-33, died 1437), mur., the inscr. on a hinge, N.C.

PUTTENHAM. Edw. Cranford, rector, 1431, in mass vests., rel., C.

REIGATE. Inscr. Memorandum of the erection of a porch or vestry by John Skynner, gent., 1513, mur., N.C.

RICHMOND. Robt. Cotton, gent., 'some time an officer of the re-mooving wardroppe of bedds' and groom of the privy chamber to Queen Mary, died yeoman of the wardrobe to Queen Elizth. (1591), in civil dress with 4 sons, and w. Grace Cawsen, with 4 daus., all kng., rect. pl. with inscr. and ach., mur., N.A.

STOKE D'ABERNON. Sir John D'Abernoun, 1277, in chain mail with enamelled sh. on arm, and holding lance; marg. inscr. in Fr. in single Lombardics lost; 1 sm. enamelled sh., large, C.   Sir John D'Abernoun, son of above, 1327, in arm. with sh., single canopy mutil., marg. inscr. in Fr. nearly all lost, large, rel. in 1912, C. Dame Anne, dau. and h. of Wm. Croyser, lord of the manor, w. of Sir Hen. Norbury, 1464, in widow's dress with 4 sons and 4 daus. standing on skirt, sm., now mur., N.C.

STREATHAM. Wm. Mowfurth, rector of Streatham and Mickleham, 1513, in mass vests., now mur., S.C.

WALTON-UPON-THAMES. John Selwyn, gent., 'keeper of her Ma'tis parke of Otelands under ye right honorable Charles Howard, lord Admyrall of England', 1587, in hunting dress with horn, and w. Susan, with 5 sons and 6 daus. surviving; above is a curious palimp. device representing a feat of agility performed by John Welwyn at a stag-hunt in the presence of Queen Elizth.; rel., the palimp. on hinges, mur., N.A.

WANDSWORTH. Nich. (Maudyt), serjeant-at-arms to Hen. V, 1420, in arm. with mace, head lost, marg. inscr. mutil., much worn, now mur. in orig. slab, C.

WEYBRIDGE. Thos. Inwood the elder, yeoman, 1586, in civil dress, and 3 ws., the 1st with 2 daus., the 2nd with 2 sons and 1 dau., all kng., rect. pl. with inscr. and 6 Eng. vv.

WOKING. John Shadet, 1527, in civil dress, and w. Isabell; children lost; now mur., S.A.

WOTTON. Inscr. Geo. Evelyn, esq., 1603. Inscr. Joan, w. 1613, aged 63.

SUSSEX

Woodman. 'The Sussex Brasses', by T. C. Woodman, 2 parts, 1903, reprinted from the 'Hove Gazette'.

AMBERLEY. John Wantele, 1424, bare-headed, in arm. with tabard, now mur., S.A.

ARDINGLY. Rich. Wakeherst, esq., 1454, in civil dress, and w. Elizth., dau. of Robt. Echingham, esq., 1464, engr. *c.* 1500, double canopy, foot inscr., 3 shs., A.T., C.   Rich. Culpepyr, esq., son of Walter Culpepyr of Goudhurst, Kent, in arm., and w. Margt., dau. of Rich. Wakeherst junior, 1504, double canopy, inscr. and 3 shs.; upper part of lady, canopy and shs. restored; rel., C.   Elizth., eld. dau. of Sir Wm. Culpeper of Wakehurst, bart, by his w. Jane, 1634, aged 7, inscr. and lozenge, C.

ARUNDEL. Thos. Salmon, esq., usher of the chamber to Hen. V, 1430, in arm. (only centre of eff. left), and w. Agnes 'alias dict' dolyver' nuper de Portugalia', principal lady to Beatrice, countess of Arundel, 1418, with SS. collar, double canopy with entablature much mutil., foot inscr. mutil., 1 sh. (3 others lost), large, fine.   John Threel, marshal of the household to Wm., earl of Arundel, 1465, in arm. with salade, livery collar and staff of office, inscr. in 10 Lat. vv. Inscr. with sh. The Rt. Hon. Thos., earl of Arundel, baron Maltravers and of Clime (Clun), KG, who mar. Margt., dau. and coh. of Rich Woodvile, earl Rivers, sister to Elizth., Queen of England, 1524; also Wm., earl of Arundel, his son, baron Maltravers and of Clime (Clun), KG, and w. Anne, dau. of Hen. Percy, earl of Northumberland, 1544, father of Hen., last earl of Arundel 'entombed in this church'; placed for remembrance by John, baron Lumley, in 1596; mur. *All in the Fitzalan chapel.*

BATTLE. John Lowe, 1426, in arm., inscr. in 12 Lat. vv.; another inscr. and 2 shs. lost; large, N.C.A.

BROADWATER. John Mapilton, rector, chancellor to (Joan of Navarre), queen of Hen. IV, 1432, in cope with initials on orphreys, single canopy, inscr. in 8 Lat. vv., C.

BURTON. Sir Wm. Goringe, knt. a gentleman of the privy chamber to Edw. VI, 1553 (kng. eff. in arm. lost), and w. Elizth., dau. of John Covert of Slaugham, 1558, in tabard, kng., with 5 separate groups of children, all kng., but effs. now lost, each with an inscr., mur., A.T., N.

BUXTED. Britell Avenel, rector (1408), hf. eff. in mass vests. in diapered head of floriated cross, stem mutil. as is also marg. inscr., C.

CHICHESTER CATHEDRAL. Two hands issuing from clouds and holding heart inscribed 'ihc', *c.* 1500.   Wm. Bradbridge, thrice mayor, died 1546, in civil dress, with 6 sons, and w. Alice, with 8 daus., all kng.; their dau. Alice, widow of Francis Barnham, sheriff of London in 1576, pos. in 1592; rect. pl. with inscr. and sh., mur., S.C.A.

CLAPHAM. John Shelley, esq., 1526, in arm. with tabard, and w. Elizth., dau. and h. of John Michilgrove of Michilgrove, esq., 1513, in heraldic mantle, Trinity, 4 shs., C.

COWFOLD. Thos. Nelond (prior of the Cluniac priory of Lewes, 1433), in monastic habit, triple canopy with B.V. Mary and Child, SS. Pancras and Thos. of Canterbury, marg. inscr. in 12 Lat. vv. mutil., sh. of the Trinity, another sh. lost, very large and fine, N.

CUCKFIELD. Hen. Bowyer (1589), in arm., with 3 sons, and w. Elizth., dau. and coh. of Thos. Vaux of Kater(len Hall, Cumb.), clerk controller to Hen. VIII (1601), with 2 daus., all kng., rect. pl.; inscr. and sh. cut in stone.; mur., S.A.

EASTBOURNE. Inscr. John Kyng, S.T.B, 'proprietarius' of the ch., treasurer of Chichester, 1445, mur., C.

ETCHINGHAM. Sir Wm., son of Sir Jas. de Echingham, died 'entour

my noet' (about midnight), 1388, in arm., head and single canopy lost, Fr. inscr. at feet and Lat. scroll over head stating he rebuilt the ch., large, C.   Sir Wm. Echyngham, lord of manor, 1412, in arm., and w. Joan (dau. and coh. of John Arundel, lord Maltravers), 1404, in mantle, also their son Sir Thos., lord of the manor, 1444, in arm., triple canopy and foot inscr., originally 9 shs. but only 1 and hf. another now remain, large, C.

FLETCHING. Sir — Dallingridge, in arm. with arms on jupon, and w. in mantle, *c.* 1380, double canopy with entablature mutil.; inscr. lost; large, A.T., S.Tr.

GRINSTEAD, EAST. Dame Kath. Grey, dau. of Thos., lord Scales, lady-in-waiting to Queens Elizth., ws. of Edw. IV and Hen. VII, 1505 (eff. lost), and her 2 husbands, Sir Thos. Grey, knt. and banneret, and Rich. Lewkenor the elder of Brambilletey, esq., both in arm., rel., now mur., S.A.   Dame Kath, and Rich. Lewkenor founded and endowed the ch. and an almshouse of 3 persons.

GRINSTEAD, WEST. (Sir Hugh Halsham, 1441), in arm., and w. Joyce, 1421, in mantle, double canopy slightly mutil., 1 sh., 1 banner (2 others lost), marg. inscr. nearly all lost. A.T., S.C.

HASTINGS, ST. CLEMENT. Thos. Wekes, 'juret of Hastyng', 1563, in civil dress, w. Margt. and dau. Elizth., effs. lost, N.   John Barley, mercer, 1601, aged 49, in civil dress, son Thos., 1600, aged 19 (eff. lost), and dau. Alyce, 1592, aged 7; the inscr. mentions his w. Mary, dau. of Robt. Harley, N.

HORSHAM. Thos. Clerke, 1411, in amice, albe, crossed stole, and cope with initials on orphreys; head and inscr. lost, C.

HURSTMONCEUX. Sir Wm. Fienlez, 1402, in arm., single canopy, marg. inscr. in Fr. with 26 days of pardon for saying a paternoster and an ave, canopy, marg. inscr. slightly mutil.; 4 shs. lost; large C.

LEWES, ST. MICHAEL. John Braydforde, rector, 1457, hf. eff. in mass vests., mur., N.A.

ORE. Civilian with anelace, and w., *c.* 1400, on a bracket (lost) under double canopy (mutil.); marg. inscr. and shs. lost; rel., S.A.C.

PETWORTH. Inscr. Nich. Smyth, a native of Bucks., scholar and fellow of Winchester and New Colls., bursar of Eton, rector for more than 30 years, 1591, aged 70, mur., C.

PULBOROUGH. Thos. Harlyng, canon of Chichester, rector of Ringwood and Pulborough, 1423, in cope, single canopy slightly mutil., marg., inscr., rel., now mur., N.A.

RUSPER. John de Kyggesfolde, in civil dress, and w. Agneys, *c.* 1370, hf. effs., Fr. inscr. inaccurately rel. and now mur., C.

RYE. Thos. Hamon, thrice burgess for parliament, 6 times mayor, long captain of the band, 1607, in civil dress, 6 Eng. vv., marg. inscr. mutil.; his w. Martha pos., C.

SHOREHAM, OLD. Inscr. with ach. Capt. Rich. Poole, aged 94, and only son Thos., aged 60, both died 1652, mur., C.

TICEHURST. Man in arm., *c.* 1370, large, to which has been added the smaller effs. of 2 ladies and an inscr. for John Wybarne, esq., died 1490, and his 2 ws. Edith and Agnes (died 1503), C.

TROTTON. Margarete de Camoys, in kirtle, cote-hardie, wimple and veil, *c.* 1310; 9 shs. on dress, single canopy, Fr. marg. inscr. in Lombardics, 8 shs., and devices, estoiles and other subjects powdering the slab, lost; large, C.   Thos., baron Camoys, 1419, arm. with garter, and w. Elizth. (dau. of Edm. Mortimer, earl of March, widow of Sir Hen. Percy, K.G. 'Hotspur', slain in 1403, she died in 1417), in mantle, both with SS. collars, holding hands, her son (Sir Rich.) standing by her side, double canopy with embattled entablature and engraver's mark on shaft, foot inscr., 3 shs. (another lost), 2 encircled by the garter, very large, A.T., C.

WARBLETON. Wm. Prestwyk (dean of St. Mary's Coll, in Hastings Castle), 1436, in cope with text from Job xix, 25, 26, on orphreys. single canopy (mutil.), with pelican in piety on centre finial, marg. inscr. in 11 Lat. vv. mutil., large, C.

WARWICKSHIRE

Badger, E. W. 'The Monumental Brasses of Warwickshire', 1895. Originally published in the 'Midland Naturalist', 1886. Not illustrated.

BAGINTON. Sir Wm. Bagot, 1407, in arm. with arms on jupon, and w. Margt. (Whatton), in mantle, both with SS. collars, large rel. and restored, mur., C.

COLESHILL. Wm. Abell, vicar, 1500, in mass vests. without stole and maniple, holding chalice and wafer, local, sm., C.

COMPTON VERNEY. Geo. Verney of Compton, esq., son of Sir Hen. Verney, died 1574, in arm.; by his w. Jane, dau. of Wm. Lucy of Charlcot, esq., he had 1 son and 4 daus.; 1 sh., br. engr. c. 1630, C.

ILMINGTON. Inscr. and sh. Long genealogical inscr. to the Brent family, 1531-1666, mur., N.Tr.

SOLIHULL. Wm. Hyll, gent., 1549, in civil dress, and 2 ws., Isabel and Agnes, 18 children in 3 groups, 4 sons, 11 daus., and 1 son and 2 daus., mur. on a board, C.   Wm. Hawes, aged 80, in civil dress, with 4 sons, and w. Ursula, Colles, aged 70, with 4 daus., both died 1610, all kng., rect. pl. with 6 Eng. vv. and 2 shs., mur., N.A.

STRATFORD-ON-AVON. Inscr. with 6 Lat. vv. Anne (Hathaway), w. of Wm. Shakespeare, 1623, aged 67, C.

SUTTON COLDFIELD. Josias Bull, gent., 1621, aged about 50, in civil dress, with 4 sons, Josias, Hen., Geo., John, and 1 dau. Anne, by his w. Kath., Walshe, widow, dau. of Wm. Botlier of Tyes, Essex, esq., 1 sh., mur., C.

WARWICK, ST. MARY. Thos. de Beauchamp, Earl of Warwick, 1401, in arm. with arms on jupon, and w. Margaret, dau. of Wm., lord Ferrers of Groby, 1406, in heraldic dress, large; canopy and inscr. lost; mur., S.Tr.

WARWICK, ST. NICHOLAS. Robt. Willardsey, 1st vicar, 1424, in mass vests., mur., over vestry door.

WIXFORD. Thos. de Cruwe, esq. (steward to Rich. de Beauchamp, Earl of Warwick, died 1418), builder of the chapel, and w. Julian, 1411, in mantle, double canopy, chamfer inscr. 5 shs. and badges of a foot, partly restored, large, A.T., S.C.

WESTMORLAND

GRASMERE. Inscr. Wm. Fleming of Coniston, esq., 1653, aged 44; his son and h. Daniel pos.; mur., C.

KENDAL. Alan Bellingham, esq., 1577, aged 61, in arm.; mar. (1) Cath., by whom no issue, (2) Dorothy, by whom 7 sons and 8 daus.; ach. and sh., rel., mur., N.C.

MORLAND. Inscr. John Blythe, vicar for 35 years and 4 days, 1562; palimp., on rev. a portion of an armed fig. with 1 son also in arm., and a frag. of inscr., c. 1520.

MUSGRAVE, GREAT. (Thos. Ouds, rector), c. 1500, in mass vests. with scroll on breast, 2 evang. symbols; inscr. and 2 other symbols lost; C.

WILTSHIRE

Kite. 'The Monumental Brasses of Wiltshire', by E. Kite, 1860.

BRADFORD-ON-AVON. Thos. Horton, founder of chantry (died 1530), in civil dress, and w. Mary (died 1544), Trinity and mcht. mark, br. engr. c. 1520 in lifetime as neither date is filled in, sm., now mur. in original slab, N.A.

CLIFFE PYPARD. Man in arm., probably of the Quintin family, c. 1380; insc. and shs. lost; S.A.

DAUNTSEY. Sir John Danvers, lord of the manor and patron of the ch. in right of his w., 1514, in arm, and w. Anne (dau. of Sir John Stradling), marg. inscr., 4 shs., A.T., C.

DEVIZES, ST. JOHN. John Kent, senior, gent., a benefactor to the town, 1630, aged 72, in civil dress, and w. (Mary Wyatt), inscr. with 4 Lat. vv., ach., S.C.

DRAYCOT CERNE. Sir Edw. Cerne (1393), in arm., and widow Elyne (1419), holding hands, Fr. inscr., C.

FOVANT. Geo. Rede, rector of the ch. at the time of the building of the new tower in 1492, in acad., kng., rect. pl. with Annunciation and inscr., engr., c. 1500, mur. in wooden frame, C.

LAVINGTON, WEST. John Dauntesay, esq., JP, 1559, aged 44, in arm., inscr. in 14 Eng. vv. stating he mar. 2 ws., by the 1st he had 5 children and by the 2nd 7; the vv. palimp., on rev. 9 lines of a Flemish inscr. recording the endowment of a mass (in 1518, see Norton Disney, Lincs., where are 33 lines of this inscr.) by Adrian Adrianson and Paesschine van den Steyne in the church of West-monstre (in the city of Middleburgh); rel., now mur., the palimp. on hinges, S.C.

MERE. John Bettesthorne, lord of Chadenwych, founder of chantry, 1398, in arm., inscr., and 2 Lat. vv.; marg. inscr. and 2 shs. lost; large, S.C.

SALISBURY CATHEDRAL. Robt. Wyvil, bp. for 45 years, during which time he recovered the castle of Sherborne and the chase of Bere for the ch. 1375, hf. eff. in episcopal vests. with mitre and crosier, stand-in in a castle, etc., with champion before the gate, marg. inscr. mutil., 3 shs. (2 others lost), large, N.E.Tr.   E. Geste, S.T.P. Camb., bp. of Rochester and high almoner for 12 years, bp. of Sarum for 5 years, bequeathed an immense number of books to the ch., 1578 (error for 1576), aged 63; Giles Estcourte, esq., one of his exors, pos.; N.E.Tr.

SALISBURY, ST. THOMAS. John Webbe, mayor (in 1561), died 1570, in civil dress, and w. Anne, dau. of Nich. Wylford, citizen and mcht.-tailor, with 3 sons and 3 daus., marg. inscr., 3 shs. (another lost), now partly covered, C.

STEEPLE ASHTON. Inscr. with mcht. mark. Peter Crooke, gave 20s. to the ch. and 40s. yearly to the poor, 1633; also Roger Crooke, gent., 1655, and Roger Crooks, gent., 1675, both added; S.A.

TISBURY. Laur. Hyde of West Hatch, esq., 1590, in civil dress, with 6 sons, and w. Anne, with 4 daus., rect. pl. with inscr., 6 Lat. vv. 2 shs. and crest, also a mutil. marg. inscr., C.

UPTON LOVELL. Priest, c. 1460, hf. eff. in mass vests., rel., C. Possibly Thos. Marchaunt, rector, 1462, or John Garton, 1469.

WARMINSTER. Elizth., w. of Thos. Carter, gent., 1649. aged 33, with 3 sons and 1 dau., all kng., rect. pl. with inscr. and 8 Lat. vv., mur., N.Tr.

WORCESTERSHIRE

ALVECHURCH. Philip Chatwyn, gentleman usher to Hen. VIII, 1524, in arm., 4 shs., mur., N.A.

BROADWAY. Anth. Daston, 1572, aged 66, in arm., inscr. in 10 Lat. vv. and ach.; partly palimp., on rev. of eff. a portion of an ach. from a large 16th cent. Flemish brass (for another portion of this br. see Westerham, Kent, 1563); mur., the palimp. fastened down.

FLADBURY. John Throckmorton, esq., under-treasurer of England, 1445, in arm., and widow Eleanor (Spiney), 5 shs.; marg. inscr. mentioning their son Thos. also 4 of the shs. restored in 1840; A.T., Tower.

KIDDERMINSTER. Maud (Harcourt), in mantle, and her 2 husbands, Walter Cookesey, esq. (1407), and Sir John Phelip, 1415, both in arm., all with SS. collars, triple canopy mutil., inscr. in 8 Lat. vv., 5 shs. (another lost), large, worn, C.

STOKE PRIOR. Hen. Smith, citizen and draper of London, left to this par. in which he was born £100 for the purchase of land, 40s of the rent of which was for 4 or 6 sermons to be yearly preached by strangers, and the rest for the schooling of poor boys, 1606, in civil dress, kng., mur., S.A.   Robt. Smith, citizen and draper of London, free and twice governor of the Mcht.-adventurers' Co. at Antwerp and Middleburgh, 1609, aged 75, in civil dress, and 2 ws.

Tomasin, and Susan, with 11 sons and 6 daus. by the 1st w., all kng., rect. pl. with inscr., ach. and 3 shs. above, mur., N.C.

STRENSHAM. Robt., son of Thos. Russell, lord of the manor, c. 1390, in arm., marg. inscr., shs. lost; C.   Sir John Russell, 1556, arm. with tabard, and only son Sir Thos. also in arm., and w. Edeth (Unton), 1562, in heraldic mantle, kng., ach. and 2 shs., mur., A.T., C.

WORCESTER, ST. HELEN. Stephen Maylard, registrary and proctor of the consistory court of Worcester, 1622, in civil dress, inscr. text and roundel, much worn and corroded, mur., Tower. Removed from the desecrated ch. of St. Michael.

YARDLEY. Isabel Wheler, dau. of Simon Norwych of Brampton, Northants, esq., 1598, and her 2 husbands, Wm. Astell, in civil dress, and Simon Wheler, esq., in arm., all kng.; she was a benefactor to the par.; rect. pl. and inscr., mur., C.

YORKSHIRE

ALDBOROUGH near BOROUGHBRIDGE (N. and W. R.). Wm. de Aldeburgh, c. 1360, in arm. with arms on jupon and sh., standing on a bracket with inscr., local, large, now mur., N.A.

BEVERLEY MINSTER (E. R.). Inscr. in 16 Eng. vv. Rich., son of Robt. Ferrant of Skipton-in-Craven, citizen and draper of London, 1560; mention is made of his w. Joan and their 7 sons and 5 daus.; worn, now mur., N.Tr.

BISHOP BURTON (E. R.). Joan, dau. and coh. of John Holme of Paulholme, esq., w. of Ralph Rokeby, esq., 1521, with her children (lost) Wm., Agnes and Rose, rel., C.

BRANDSBURTON (E. R.). Sir John de St. Quintin, lord of the manor, 1397, in arm. holding heart, head gone, and 1st w. Lora (dau. and coh. of Herbert de St. Quintin), 1369, marg. inscr. much mutil., 1 sh. (another lost), local, large, C.

CATTERICK (N. R.). Wm. Burgh, esq., his son and h., 1465, both in arm., inscr. and 2 shs. (other lost); the inscr. mentions the elder Wm's. wife Maud (Lascelles), 1432, and his son's w. Ellen (Pickering), 1446; local, under pews in Lady chapel, N.A.

COTTINGHAM (E. R.). Nich. de Luda (Louth), rector, prebendary of Beverley and of Salisbury, builder of the chancel (in 1374), died 1383, in choir cope, single canopy with super-canopy, marg. inscr. in 8 Lat. vv., large, rel. and restored, C.

COWTHORPE (W. R.). Eff. in judicial robes, church, bier, 1 sh., and 2 pieces of canopy work; the remains of the br. to Brian Roucliff, baron of the exchequer, rebuilder of the ch., 1494, in judicial robes without coif, and w. Joan, holding a church between them, C.

DONCASTER, ST. GEORGE (W. R.). Inscr. and ach. Rich. Flower of Impton, Radnor, clerk of the crown in the northern counties, 'heere ended his circuit', 1662, mur.

FLAMBOROUGH (E. R.). Inscr. in 26 Eng. vv. Sir Marmaduke Constable, knt., served in France with Edw. IV and Hen. VII, was at the 'winnyng' of Berwick and at Brankiston Field (Flodden) (died 1520), local, mur., C.

HARPHAM (E. R.). Sir Thos. de St. Quintin, lord of the manor, in arm., and w. Agnes (de Mauley), 1418, double canopy with shs. in pediments mutil., marg. inscr. much mutil., 3 shs. (another lost) local, large, N.C.   Thos. de St. Quintin, lord of Harpham, 1445, in arm. with livery collar, 3 shs. (another lost), local, N.C.

HELMSLEY (N. R.). Man in arm. of the Overton family and w., c. 1480, nearly effaced, *fine helmet and crest above:* inscr., shs., and children lost; Tower.

HULL, ST. MARY (E. R.). John Haryson, 'scherman', alderman, 1525, in civil dress with 3 sons, Thos., John., Wm., and 2 ws., Alys and Agnes, all kng., rect. pl. with Trinity (defaced) and inscr., mur., in wooden frame, S.A.

INGLEBY ARNCLIFFE (N. R.). Inscr. with 6 Eng. vv. Elizth., Maulverer

senior, 1674; the vv. 'made by herself 18 Jan. 1661; thos. Mann, Eboraci sculpt'. In churchyard?

KIRKBY MOORSIDE (N.R.). Lady Brooke, 1600, with 6 sons and 5 daus., all kng., rect. pl.; inscr. and 4 Eng. vv. cut in stone; mur., C.

KIRKLEATHAM (N. R.). Robt. Coulthirst of Upleatham, gent., mcht.-tailor, of London, 1631, aged 90, in civil dress holding book, marg. inscr. and 4 shs. of the Co., C.

LEEDS, ST. PETER (W. R.). Sir John Langton, 1459, in arm. with salade, and widow Eupheme (died 1463), local, mur., C. Rect, pl. with sm. effs. of 7 children, ach. and long inscr. giving births and deaths, also of their father Wm. Massie, mayor in 1689, died 1699, aged 65, bequeathed £100 to the chapel and school at Hunslet, and their mother Mary, who afterwards mar. Thos. Craven and died 1709, aged 72, local, mur., N.C.

LOWTHORPE (E. R.). Inscription with sh. John Pierson, esq., JP, 1665, aged 74; mar. Elizth. (Pierson), had 3 sons and 4 daus.; 'Tho. Mann Eboraci sculp.'; A.T.

NORMANTON (W. R.). Inscr. Rich., son of Wm. Mallett of Normanton, 1668, aged 45; 'Tho. Mann Eboraci sculp.'; A.T., S.C.

NUNKEELING (E. R.). Inscr. Geo. Acklam, benefactor to the par., 1629, aged 64; 'Gabr: Hornbie sculp.'; C.

OWSTON (W. R.). Robt. de Haitfeld (1417), in civil dress with anelace, and w. Ade, 1409, both with SS. collars, holding hands, Fr. inscr., N.A.

RIPLEY (W. R.). Chalice and inscr. Rich. Kendale, MA, rector, 1429, local, worn, C.

RIPON MINSTER (W. R.). Inscr. with ach. Sir Jordan Crosland, knt., constable of Scarborough Castle, 1670, aged 53, worn, now mur., S.Tr.

ROTHERHAM (W. R.). Robt. Swifte, esq., 1561, aged 84, in civil dress, with 2 sons, Wm., Robt., and 1st w. Anne, 1539, aged 67, with 2 daus., Anne, Margt., all kng., rect. pl. and inscr., 2 shs., A.T., N.C.

RUDSTONE (E. R.). Inscr. Kath., dau. of Edw. Hutchinson of Wikeham Abbey, esq., w. of John Constable of Carthorp, esq., 1677, 'Tho: Mann Eboraci sculp.', mur., Vestry.

SHEFFIELD, ST. PETER (W. R.). Two shs., one gartered, on tomb of Geo. Talbot, K.G, 4th earl of Shrewsbury, 1541, Shrewsbury chapel.

SPROTBROUGH (W. R.). Wm. Fitzwilliam, esq., lord of Sprotborough, died at Hathilsay 1474, in arm. with salade, and widow Elizth., dau. of Sir Thos. Chaworth, knt.; 4 shs. lost; local, C.

SUTTON-ON-DERWENT (E. R.). Inscr. Peter Cooke, rector for 30 years, 1625; his w. Anne pos.; C.

TADCASTER (W. R.). Inscr. Arthur Burton, 'buchar', 1608, local, Tower.

THORNTON-LE-STREET (N. R.). Inscr. and ach. Roger Talbot, esq., eld. son of John Talbot, 1680, aged 61; mar. Elizth., dau. of Ambrose Pudsey, esq., had 5 sons, and 7 daus. 'P. Brigges Ebor. sculp.'; mur., C.

TOPCLIFFE (N. R.). Thos. de Topclyff, 1362, in civil dress with anelace, and w. (Mabel), 1391, in mantle, under rich canopy with souls, angels, etc., marg. inscr. mutil., rect. pl., 70 in by 36 in, palimp., on rev. some unfinished portions of another br.; now mur., N.

WADDINGTON (W. R.). Inscr. with sh. Edw. Parker of Brownsholm, esq., graduate of Clare Coll., Camb., barrister of Grays' Inn, J.P. for Yorks. and Lancs., 1667, and w. Mary, dau. of Rich. Sunderland, esq., 1673; their 2nd son Robt. pos.

WENSLEY (N. R.). Sir Simon of Wensley, rector (1361-94), br. engr. c. 1375, in mass vests., hands folded, chalice on breast, head on cushion held by angels, Foreign, very fine; marg. inscr. lost; now mur., C.

YORK MINSTER. Wm. de Grenefeld, abp. of York, lord chancellor, 1315, in full vests., lower part of eff. stolen in 1829; canopy with saints at sides, inscr. lost; large, A.T., N.Tr.   Elizth., dau. of Sir

Edw. Nevell, knt., one of the privy chamber to Hen. VIII, widow of Thos. Eynns, esq., one of the gentlewomen of the privy chamber to Queen Elizth., 1585, large hf. eff. with open book with texts Ps. cxix, 30, 54, inscr. and 4 shs., mur.   Jas. Cotrel, esq., born Dublin, for about 20 years served the Queen's council in the north 'testes examinando', 1595, rect. pl. with ¾ eff. in civil dress with cap, 2 shs. and inscr., local, mur., S.A.

YORK, ALL SAINTS, NORTH STREET. Thos. Atkinson, tanner, sheriff (in 1627), died 1642, aged 72, rect. pl. with large hf. eff. in civil dress, and inscr., local, on slab, S.A.

YORK, ALL SAINTS, PAVEMENT. Inscr. Mary and Margery, daus. of Andrew Trew, alderman and lord mayor, 'both married in one day in this church and both buried in one sommer in this grave', 1600, aged 37, and 36, local, N.

YORK, ST. CRUX. Church demolished in 1886. Brasses, etc., kept in parish room built on the site. Mcht. mark and arms of the city of York; the remains of the br. to John Shaw, who died during his mayoralty 1537, and w. Agnes, local.   (Robt. Askwith, lord mayor in 1580 and 1593, died 1597, aged 67), rect. pl. with large ¾ eff. in civil dress with cap and signet ring, sh. in corner; inscr. lost; local.

YORK, ST. MICHAEL-LE-BELFRY. Inscr. Frances, dau. of Rich. James of Portsmouth, esq., w. of Wm. Farrer of Ewood 'within the viccar-idge of Hallifax', esq., 1680, aged 51; 'J. Mann, Ebor, sculp.'; N.A. Inscr. and sh. Thos. Dawny of Selby, esq., son of Thos. Dawny of Sutton manor in Coldfield, Warw., esq., 1683, aged 44; 'J. Mann sculp.'; worn, N.A.

YORK, ST. MICHAEL SPURRIERGATE. Inscr. Wm. Shaw, bachelor, mcht., son of Thos. Shaw, rector of Aldingham, Lancs., 1681, aged 40, bequeathed £100 to the poor of the par. for ever; 'J. Mann, Ebor. sculp.'; on slab.

YORK, ST. SAMPSON. Inscr. Wm. Richardson, 1680, aged 47; 'Joshua Mann sculp.'; S.A.

IRELAND

BANDON, CHRIST CHURCH, MILBROGAN (Cork). Inscr. Rich. Crofte, burgess, provost of Bandonbridge, 1629; his w. Anne pos.; mur., S.C.

DUBLIN, CHRIST CHURCH CATHEDRAL. Rect. pl. with gartered ach., 2 shs., 2 very sm. effs. on tombs, 1 in swaddling clothes, and inscr. The 2nd and 3rd sons of Sir Arthur Grey, K.G, Lord Grey of Wilton (lord deputy 1580-82), and of the Lady Jane Sibilla his w., which children died in Dublin castle during his 'deputacion', undated, c. 1580, mur., S.Tr.

DUBLIN, ST. PATRICK'S CATHEDRAL. Geoffrey Fyche, dean, 1537, rect. pl. with eff. in almuce kng. to an altar above which is a representation of Our Lady in Pity, device with initials and inscr., mur., C.

SCOTLAND

ABERDEEN, ST. NICHOLAS. Duncan Liddel, M.D., son of John Liddel, citizen of Aberdeen, 1613, aged 52, large Flemish rect. pl. with eff. seated in his study surrounded by books, etc., long inscr. below, marg. inscr. and sh., now mur. on south wall. The br. was engr. by Gaspard Bruydegoms of Antwerp.

EDINBURGH, ST. GILES. Rect. pl. with seated figs. of Religion and Justice, ach., etc., and inscr. by Geo. Buchanan. Jas. Stewart, Earl of Murray, regent of Scotland, assassinated at Linlithgow, 1569; palimp. on rev. portions of a male and female figure and part of an inscr., late 15th cent., now fastened down; mur., S.Tr. The work of James Gray, goldsmith.

GLASGOW CATHEDRAL. Man in arm., kng., rect. pl. inscr. to members of the Mynto family, 1605, mur., N.

WALES

BANGOR CATHEDRAL (Carnarvon). Inscr. with 4 Lat. vv. Hen. Rowlands, bp. of Bangor, 1616, aged 65, mur., S.A.

BEAUMARIS (Anglesey). Rich. Bulkley, mcht., in civil dress, with 2 sons (1 priest in almuce), and w. Elizth., with 1 dau., c. 1530, all kng., Trinity, B.V. Mary and Child, and St. John Evang., inscr. in 6 Lat. vv.; sh. lost; mur., C.

HAVERFORDWEST (Pembroke). John Davids, esq., 1651, aged 51, in civil dress, kng.; his w. Sage, died 1654, aged 62; rect. pl. with eff. of John Davids, inscr. and sh., mur., C.

LLANBEBLIG (Carnarvon). Rich. Foxwist, notary, 1500, mar. Joan, dau. of John Spicer, rect. pl. with eff. in bed holding sh. with the five wounds, penner, inkhorn, and another sh. at side, inscr. in 8 Lat. vv., sm., mur., C.

LLANDYSILIO (Montgomery). Inscr. with 15 Eng. vv. and lozenge, Mary, dau. of Wm. Eyton of Rosnant, esq., 1674, aged 26; 'Sylvanus Crue sculp.'. Now at Rhysnant Hall, near Llandysilio.

LLANGOLLEN (Denbigh), Inscr. with 6 Lat., 6 Eng. vv., and 2 shs., Magdalen, eld. dau. of John Trevor of Trevor, esq., 1663; 'Sylvanus Crue sculp'; mur., N.A.

LLANGYNFELYN (Cardigan). Jane Wilbertson, 1 May 1810, aged 41. Kng. rect. pl. inscr. Wife of Wm. Cobb Wilbertson, esq., of this parish, mur., C.

LLANRWST (Denbigh). Sir John Wynn of Gwedvr., knt. and bart., 1626, a bust, inscr., ach. and sh. Lady Sydney, w. of Sir John Wynn of Gwedvr, knt. and bart., 1632, a bust, inscr. and lozenge. Lady Mary, eld. dau. of Sir John Wynne of Gwedyr, knt. and bart., w. of Sir Robt. Mostyn of Mostyn, Flint, died 1652, aged 71, a bust, inscr. and 2 achs.; her son John pos. 1658; 'Silvanus Crue sculp'. Sir Owen Wynne of Gwedvr., bart., 1660, aged 68, a bust, inscr., ach. and sh. Dame Sarah, dau. of Sir Thos. Middleton of Chirke Castle, knt., w. of Sir Rich. Wynne of Gwyddvr, bart., 1671, ¾ eff. in frame, inscr. and 2 achs., very lightly engr., 'Guil. Vaughan sculpsit'. Gwyder chapel.

RUTHIN (Denbigh). Edw. Goodman, 1560, in civil dress with cap and scarf, inscr. in 4 Lat. vv. mur., N.A.   E. Goodman, burgess and mercer, 1560, aged 84, with 3 sons, Gawen, Gabriel (dean of Westminster 1561-1601), Godfrey, and w. Ciselye, 1583, aged 90, with 5 daus., Dorothy, Kath., Fides, Clare, Jane, all kng., mur., N.A.

SWANSEA (Glamorgan). Sir Hugh Johnys, 'made knight at the holy sepulchre of our lord ihu crist in the city of Jerusalem the xiii day of August 1441', knight marshal of France under John, Duke of Somerset, and knight marshal of England under John, Duke of Norfolk, who gave to him the manor of Landymor, in arm., and w. Dame Mawde (Cradock), with 5 sons (lost) and 4 daus., Resurrection and inscr., engr. c. 1500; 4 shs. lost; C.

WREXHAM (Denbigh). Humph. Lloyd of Bensham, esq., one of the masters in chancery extraordinary, 1673, rect. pl. with recumbent skeleton under arch, and inscr.; 'S. Crue sculp.'; mur., N. Inscr. with 6 Eng. vv. Joseph Critchley, churchwarden, 1647, aged 37; his fellow wardens pos.; 'S. Crue sculp.'; mur., N.

ISLE OF MAN

LEZAYRE near RAMSEY. Inscr. with sh. Margt., dau. of Peter Haywood of Heywood, Lancs., esq., by Alice, dau. of John Greenhalgh of Brannelsom, Lancs., esq., governor of the island, w. of Capt. John Garrett of Sulby, 1669, left 1 son and 3 daus., mur., N. Inscr. John Garrett of Sulby, captain, 1692, aged 99; also his grand-dau.-in-law Elizth., dau. of Wm. Sutcliffe, w. of John Garrett of Balabroy, 1745, aged 40, N.

MUSEUMS AND SOCIETIES

CAMBRIDGE, MUSEUM OF ARCHAEOLOGY. Lady and a group of 4 sons and 8 daus., *c.* 1530, palimp., on rev. positions of the head of lady in rebule head-dress, *c.* 1380.

CAMBRIDGE, FITZWILLIAM MUSEUM. Priest *c.* 1530, in mass vests., worn, East Anglican school, palimp. on rev. position of the centre of a civilian in mantle, 15th-cent. Group of 4 sons and one of 5 daus., *c.* 1550, both palimp. on rev. of sons, the feet of a civilian, *c.* 1520, on rev. of daus. a few lines of drapery.

LONDON, BRITISH MUSEUM. Head of a bp. or abbot, *c.* 1380, under fine canopy with soul, saints, etc., part, 27 in by 22½ in, of a large rectangular foreign brass.

Circular plate with head of a priest in amice surrounded by the heads of four boys and an inscr., *c.* 1420, sm., worn and dented; palimp., re-used in the 17th-cent., and engr. on the rev. with a mathematical instrument. Circular plate with hf. eff. of a priest in mass vests., *c.* 1460 (?) surrounded by an inscr. to Thos. Quythed (Whitehed), 'magister tercius istius collegii', sm.; palimp., re-used as no. (2) with a pair of open compasses on rev.

LONDON, VICTORIA AND ALBERT MUSEUM. The soul of an abbot or bishop in Abraham's bosom, part of an early 15th-cent. brass (small), some of the enamel still remains. Man in arm., *c.* 1430, with SS. collar. H. Oskens, chanter and canon, 1535, kng. with B.V. Mary and Child, St. Peter, and the Emperor St. Henry his patron saint, foreign, rect., pl. 34 in by 24 in, with sh. and inscr. Much of the original coloured composition still remains. From Nippes, near Cologne.

LONDON, SOCIETY OF ANTIQUARIES. Inscr. Dedication of a chapel in honour of St. Elio, 1446. From Tours, France. Yeoman of the crown, *c.* 1480, in arm. with badge on shoulder.

LONDON, WALLACE COLLECTION. Feet and portion of the legs of a man in chain armour, 13th cent. Foreign.

MAIDSTONE MUSEUM, KENT. Priest, *c.* 1440, in mass vests.

OXFORD, BODLEIAN LIBRARY. Man in arm., *c.* 1490. From Letheringham, Suff. Possibly Wm. Wingfield, esq., 1481.

SURREY ARCHAEOLOGICAL SOCIETY, GUILDFORD. Man in arm. of the Compton (?) family and w. in mantle, *c.* 1500, kng., rect. pl. powdered with firebeacons with scrolls, etc.

Continental Brasses

This list is by no means a complete one but it includes most of the important brasses. There is not an existing published list of all the known brasses of Europe, however, The Monumental Brass Society intend to issue a complete list in the not too distant future. During the 1939-45 war many brasses were lost or badly damaged. A few of these, it is hoped, may be now in other churches or museums. A few of the important lost brasses are illustrated in Creeny's volume (1884).

It is fairly certain that there are brasses on the Continent that have not yet been recorded or are not widely known. Eastern Europe is the most likely part in which to discover unrecorded brasses. If any such brass is found by a reader of this volume will he or she write to the publisher or The Monumental Brass Society, c/o Society of Antiquaries.

BELGIUM

ANTWERP (Cathedral)
1405 Philippe de Mezières. Kng. fig. of monk, Virgin and saints.

ATH (Bois de Lesinnes)
1572 Lambert de Warluzal. Fig. in arm. kng. to crucifixion; 60" x 34".

BRUSSELS (Musées Cinquintenaire)
1332-1398 John (1332) and Gerard de Heere (1398), uncle and nephew. Both under separate canopies, in arm. and jupons. Baldricks and swords. Savage men and lions at feet of each. Side staffs, niches, angels and saints, elaborate gables, towers and pinnacles. Large and small shields. Evang. symbols, marg. inscr.; 101" x 62".

1540-1567 Ricaldus and Joanna de Ribis, standing in wide niche, elaborate pillars supporting, embroided curtain behind. Emblazoned escutcheon hangs from Ricaldus' right arm, he is in armour. Lady in large loose gown, very elaborate brass, marg. inscr., 90" x 62".

1552 Guillaume de Goux and Wife. Shld., angel with lozenge; 108" x 60".

BRUGES
BÉGUINAGE
1410 Griel van Ruwescuere. Lady Superior in gothic niche, marg. inscr., 17" x 10"; chapel mur., n. wall.
1594 Elizabeth van der Voorde. 35" x 23"

CATHEDRAL (St. Sauveur)
1387 Wouter Copman. In shroud, marg. inscr.; 98" x 52".
1510 Pierre Meulenbeke. No further details available.

GRUUTHUOSE (Museum)
1509 Abel Porckett. Cain striking Abel. Rebus, 4 'porkers' in corners, marg. inscr.; 32" x 21".

HÔPITAL ST. JEAN
1527 Bernardin van den Hove. Civ. fig. on a lozenge.

ST. JACQUES
1460 Kateline d'Aut with Brother and Angel. Simple gowns, scrolls and scenes, 2 shs., evang. symbols, marg. inscr.; 77" x 45".
1577 Francisco de la Puebla and Wife (1572) and dau. All in period costume; escutcheons and mantling; marg. scroll inscr.; 79" x 45": Nave chapel.
1601 Anthonine Willebaert, first wife of Peter van der Mage, with 7 children; 29" x 26".
1615 Pierre de Valencia and Wife (palimp. c. 1380).

MUSEUM
1439 Joris de Munter and Wife (d. 1423). In shrouds, marg. inscr., shs.; 98" x 56".
1452 Martin de Visch, Lord of Capelle. In armour with tabard, shs., evang. symbols, marg. inscr.; 95" x 49".

1483 Jacob Schelewaerts, S.T.D. Seated at desk, 7 students and beadle, marg. inscr.; 82" x 43".
1518 Jehan de Liekerke and Wife, Jane de la Douve (1515). Man in armour, wife in plain gown; armorial and shs., marg. inscr.; 98" x 52".

COUTRAI (St. Martin)
1557 Pertseval Pollet and Family. Figures and crucifixion, inscr.; 15" x 18".

COURTRAI-VECHTE (St. Etienne)
1524 Florentine Wielant, in niche, head on pillow, columns either sides. Two angels hold lozenges impaled with arms. Roundels, dbl. marg. inscr. in Flemish; 64" x 35".

DAMME (Hôpital St. Jaen)
1531 Johannes de la Fontaine. Curé of a former church, cut out quatrefoil in which stands Johannes in eucharistic vestments with chalice. Rebus – a fountain on his right – on his left a merchant's mark. Rectangular inscr. away from quatrefoil framing it, evang. symbols in corners; 75" x 41".

DENDERONDE (Notre Dame)
1470 Pieter Esscheric and Wife Magriete. Seated Virgin and Child, on right kng. fig. of Pieter with St. Peter, on left wife with St. Margaret, scrolls, under is 24-line inscr., dates left blank; 36" x 23".
1560 Bartholomew Penneman. Virgin and Child, in centre 9 sons kng. with father with St. Bartholomew, wife kng. with 4 daus. and St. Bridget; shs, 6-line inscr. at base; 24" x 28".

DIXMUDE (St. Nicholas)
1499 Giles de Hertoghe and Wife. Resurrection with saints.

GHENT (Museum Van de Byloke)
1325-1352 William Wenemaer and Wife Margaret Sbrunnen. Man in armour holding sword with inscr. and sh. in other hand, mutilated; wife in long gown, widow's head-dress; each 84" x 30" (sep. brasses).

Cathedral
1599 Jonkheer Franchoys van Wychuus and Wife Marye Daneels-dochter van Pollynchove (1585). Rect. pl. with semi-circle at top containing achievement; effigy kng. in arm. and tabard, wife facing, kng., both to crucifixion; 9 sons kng. behind father, 3 daus. kng. behind mother; lozenge with arms; view of Jerusalem behind crucifixion, 4 shs. down each of two sides, 12-line inscr. below, Flemish.
1607 Leonard Betten, Abbot of St. Trond. Fig. in full pontificals; 108" x 48".

LIÉGE (St. Pierre)
Hognal Raso de Boric and Wife Marie Albouts. No other detail available.

MECHLIN (Musée de Metiers d'Art)
1608 Wilhem de Clerck, Margaret and Carel Clerck. Kng. fig. in armour with tabard, 44" x 28"; wife in long cloak kng., shs. (16), armorial, 16-line inscr.

NIEUPORT
1445 Jan van Clays and Wife. c. 1470. Angel and sh. (fragment); 30" x 22". Lost or stolen.

NIVELLES
16th cent. Marguerite de Scorney, Abbess. c. 1500. Crucifixion; 28" x 26", inscr. lost.

TEMPLEUVE
1615 Jacques Pottier and Wife. Figs., crucifixion and inscr.; 42" x 14".

THIELEN
1538 Louis van Lieefdail and Wife. Fig. in armour.

TOURNAI (St. Brice)

c. 1450 Jehans de Dours and Wife. Civilian and wife kng. to Holy Trinity with saints; 29" x 22½" (lost?).

ST. JACQUES

1574 Michel de Herry. Crucifixion and inscr.; 22¾" x 17".

1579 Lean Locelin and Wife. Both kng. to crucifixion with Jerusalem in background.

YPRES (Hospice de Notre Dame)

1410 Christoffels van Beissellaime. Inscr. only.

1457 Peter Lansame and wife. 36 line inscr. on rectangular plate, shs. in bottom corners, initials in centre; 42" x 28".

1489-87 Pieter Lansame and Wife Lizebette. Inscr. only on 4 sides of blank rectangular plate, 90" x 53"; between the inscr. are sm. illustrations of figures, 6 quatrefoils, 2 with shds. with arms.

DENMARK

RINGSTED (Zealand)

1319 King Eric and Queen Ingeborg. Both died 1319; crowned king, coronation robes and emblazoned sword and sceptre, face in alabaster (restored 1883); queen crowned, wimple (widow 5 months), simple gown, sceptre and book, face in alabaster; life-size effigies; saints in geometric niches, gothic shafts, canopies, marg. inscr., shs; 112" x 66"; altar tomb.

FINLAND

NOUSIS

Early 15th cent. St. Henry, Bishop and Martyr. In full pontificals, kng. fig. of bishop, the donor, elaborate canopy and side panels on tomb with scenes from life of St. Henry.

FRANCE

AMIENS (Cathedral)

1456 Bishop John Advantage. Sm. plate 25" x 22", Virgin and Child seated, bishop kng., St. John, birds and flowers, inscr.

BORDEAUX (Museum)

1392 John Scott and Wife. Civ. and wife under canopy; 60" x 31½".

DOUAI (Musée d'Antiquités)

1570 Priest in mass vestments with chalice; 54" x 22".

PARIS (Musée de Cluny) others, but not listed

1461 Guillaume de Helandice, Bishop of Beauvais. Mass order for chapel Jacobins Beauvais, octagonal plate.

Musée de Louvre

c. 1400 Peter Zatrylla. Civ. fig. on rectangular plate with canopy; 61" x 30".

ST. JUNIEN (Haute Vienne)

1513 Marcel Formier.

ST. JEAN D'ANGELY

Abbott in mass vestments; 78" x 37".

GERMANY (EAST)

ALTENBURG (Abbey Church)

1475 Gerart, Duke of Gulich. In armour, canopy, heraldic shs., evang. symbols., marg. inscr. of 3 lines all round; 134" x 68".

ERFURT (Cathedral)

1427 Herman Schindeleyb. Priest under canopy, chalice, sh., God the Father, angels and saints (part inscr. top multilated); 95" x 33".

1475 Honoldus de Platenberg. Dean, in cap and cope; 104" x 48".

1505 Dominus John de Heringen, licentiate in the decrees and of this church, cantor and canon, holding chalice (mutilated), hf. eff., shs., marg. inscr.; 84" x 47".

1560 Dominus Eobanus Zeigeler D.L. Cap, chasuble, chalice, 4 roundels, symb., marg. inscr.; 95" x 55".

GADEBUSCH

1432 Helena, Queen of Sweden, Duchess of Mecklenburg; 112" x 72".

HALBERSTADT (Dom Church)

1538 Priest in Almuce – Johann von Marnholt, Dean. (Several others).

LÜBECK (Dom Church)

1317-1350 Bishops Burchard von Serken (1317) and John von Mul (1350). Both in full vestments, each under sep. canopy, niches with saints, elaborate; prophets, St. M. Magdalene, God the Father in centre; scenes under feet, marg. inscr. (Lombardic); Burchard died aged 121; 142" x 73".

St. Mary's (Briefkapelle)

1369 Bruno von Warendorp. Proconsul of Lübeck, bearded, in simple gown, belted, roundels, evang. symbols.; 103" x 52".

Dom Church

1377 Bishop Bertram Cremen. Mitre, pastoral staff, full vestments, effigy cut to shape, 2 shs., 4 roundels, evang. symbols., saints in niches on border, small marg. inscr. (damaged); 115" x 73".

St. Catherine

1474-5 John Luneborch (civilian). Canopy, embroidered dress, bareheaded; hairy men at feet, crowned heads and griffins in border, inscr. inside marg. records two Johns, one died 1461; 111" x 60".

St. Mary's (Nave)

1550 Two figures in shrouds.

Cathedral

1561 Bishop John Tydeman. Doric portico tympanum, capitals and columns, figures; bareheaded and with beard the bishop holds mitre in right hand, pastoral staff in left; shield, roundels, evang. symbols; 123" x 90". *Damaged in 1939-45 war.* Illustrated in Creeny's volume.

1571 Gothardus ab Hovelin (Senator) and Wife. Mt. Olives, tablet above with inscr., two tablets below with inscr., two escutcheons; husband and wife at bottom facing; 98" x 56". Illustrated in Creeny's volume. *Damaged in 1939-45 war.*

MEISSEN

1463 Bishop Schönberg. Rectangular plate.

Cathedral

1464 Frederic the Good, Duke of Saxony. Fur-lined robe and tunic, sword, evang. symbols, marg. inscr.; 98" x 56".

1486 Ernst, Duke of Saxony (son of above). Plate armour, stdg. on pedestal holding banner; canopy, helmets, mantling, 11 shs., dble. marg. inscr. (German); 97" x 55".

1500 Albert, Duke of Saxony in full armour, stdg. on bracket. 3 helmets, mantled and crested, banner in right hand. 11 shs. dbl. marg. inscr. (German); 97" x 55".

1502 Ameleie, Duchess of Bavaria, daughter of Frederic the Good. Widow, in simple garb, rosary, 2 shs., marg. inscr. (German); 97" x 48".

1510 Sidonia, Duchess of Saxony (wife of Albert). Pious fig. in simple dress, 2 shs. at feet, dble. marg. inscr. (German); 95" x 48".

1510 Frederic, Duke of Saxony. Sm. canopy, plate armour, bareheaded, sword, 2 shs. (son of Albert and Sidona); marg. inscr. (dble. at top and bottom); 91" x 46".

George's Chapel

1534 Barbara, Duchess of Saxony. Embroidered cloak, ornate marg. border, 9-line inscr. bottom (German); 98" x 48".

Cathedral

1537 John, Duke of Saxony (husband of above). Armour, sword, shs., ornate marg. border, 6-line inscr. (German); 98" x 48".

1539 Frederick, Duke of Saxony (brother of above). **Armour,** sword, shs., ornate marg. border, 7-line inscr. **(German);** 98″ x 48″.

NAUMBURG (Cathedral)

1466 Bishop Dietrich von Buckenstorf. Canopy, alb, dalmatic, maniple, pastoral staff, textus, roundels, evang. symbols., marg. inscr. (restored); 85″ x 48″.

Cathedral Nave

1516 Bishop Schönberg. Figure of skeleton, canopy of branch tracery, 4-line inscr. above, scrolls down each side; 52″ x 23″.

NORDHAUSEN (Chapel St. Chriaci, Hospital)

The seven listed below are thought to have been destroyed in 1939-45 war. Some may have been looted. They are illustrated in Creeny's volume.

1400-1410 John Symo Segemund. Canopy with scrolls, in simple garb, sh., angels, roundels in corners, marg, inscr. sep.; 77″ x 42″.

1394 Henrich de Urbech. Simple canopy, kng. effigy, civilian, cote-hardi, local work, marg. inscr. 3 sides; 26″ x 15″.

1395 Jacob Capillanus. Simple canopy, chalice, cloak, maniple, marg. inscr. 3 sides, local work; 23″ x 19″.

1395 Herman de Werthere. Kng., cote-hardi, jäger's hat, sh., marg. inscr. 3 sides, local work; 25″ x 19″.

1397 Katherina Verter. Canopy, simple dress, kng. sh. (similar to Herman's); note spelling of surname; inscr. 3 sides, local work; 23″ x 20″.

1397 Heinrich Urbech (Snr.), father of Heinrich (1394). Canopy, kng., cote-hardi, sh., helmet, marg. inscr. 3 sides, local work; 23″ x 20″

1400 Half of brass figure under canopy facing left, hands held high, bells at waist, scrolle 'Miserere Mei', Trinity symbol; 45″ x 24″.

SCHWERIN (Dom Church mural)

1339-47 Bishops Ludolph and Henry de Bulowe. Both in eucharistic vestments, mitres, jewelled pastoral staffs, amice and chasuble ornamented with shs., dble. canopy, niches with saints-prophets, evang. symbols, 4 lge. shs., helmets, marg. inscr. (Lombardic); 115″ x 71″.

1314-75 Bishops Godfrey and Frederic de Bulowe (brothers of above). Both in eucharistic vestments, pastoral staffs, under elaborate canopies with staffs, saints in niches, elaborate gables, towers, pinnacles; diaper scenes, hairy men and a king feasting under feet of effigies, inscr. in wavy scroll all round; 151″ x 76″.

STRALSUND (St. Nicolas)

1357 Albert Hövener (Proconsul). Canopy, bareheaded, rich costume, niches with apostles and prophets, hairy men at base of feet, evang. symbols, shs., marg. inscr.; 100″ x 50″.

There are also brasses at Stolberg, Torgau and Zeitz.

GERMANY (WEST)

AACHEN (Aix-la-Chapelle, Cathedral Chapel)

1487 Arnold de Meroide. In 3 sections above inscr., 2 as dividers, 4 standards; Virgin and Child in middle, deceased kng. right, patron saint left, coloured, 12-line inscr.; 45″ x 28″.

1534 John Pollart. Canon, fig. of priest kng. to Virgin and saints; 59″ x 28″.

1560 Canon John Pael. kng. fig., Virgin and Child. St. John and St. Mary Magdalene. He was over 50 years in Holy Orders; 39″ x 27″.

BAMBERG (Cathedral, West Apse)

1399 Bishop Lampertus. Top half of effigy, mitre and crosier and pastoral staff; bottom half, emblazoned sh., 4 roundels, marg. inscr.; 63″ x 42″.

Cathedral (South Chapel)

1464 Georius, Count de Lewenstein. Canon, alb, dalmatic, almuce, cap, holding textus, lge. sh. with lion, 4 quatrefoils of shs. of arms, marg. inscr. 3 sides; 84″ x 39″.

1475 John de Limberg. Canon, almuce, alb, holding textus, lge. shield lower half, mantled and crested helmet, shs. in corners (worn), marg. inscr.; 68″ x 26″.

1505 Eberard de Rabenstein. Canon, effigy under canopy, almuce, chalice and textus, sh., mantling, crested helmet, 4 escutcheons, rebus, marg. inscr.; 73″ x 30″.

BRAUWEILLERS

1483 Adam Hertzogehrade. Abbot, fig. in mass vestments and almuce.

BRUNSWICK (St. Peter)

1376 John de Rintelen (*destroyed in 1939-45 war*).

BREMEN (Cathedral)

1477 John Rode. Priest in mass vestments with chalice.

CONSTANCE (Cathedral)

1416 Bishop Hallum of Salisbury, died while attending the Council of Constance. Fig. in pontificals, canopy; 87″ x 38″ approx.

COLOGNE (St. Mary)

1508 Henry de Berchem.

1535 Henricus Oskens (illustrated in Creeny).

1540 Catherine de Loe. Canoness.

(*These three and others lost in 1939-45 war.*)

COBURG (St. Maurice)

1553 John Ernst, Duke of Saxony. Coat of arms, crested helmets, marshalling, escutcheon, 16-line German inscr.; 83″ x 43″.

CUES (Chapel, Moselle)

1464 Cardinal Nicolaus Krebs, Bishop of Brixen. Effigy, lower half covered by inscr. (8-line), skull cap, jewel mitre, chasuble, amice, alb, glove with jewels, Rebus Krebs = crayfish; 79″ x 38″.

EMDEN (Schweizerkirke)

1507 Herman Wessel. Pastor, fig. of Christ, sm. effigy of priest; 92½″ x 50″.

FREIBURG

1541-1643 Thirty brasses to the royal family of Saxony.

HAMM (Agneskirche)

1461 Count Gerhard von Marck. In armour, canopied niche, evang. symbols, heraldic ach., lge. sh. base, marg. inscr.; 129½″ x 59½″. *Destroyed in 1939-45 war.*

HILDESHEIM (Cathedral)

Otto de Brunswick. Bishop, alb, stole, dalmatic, maniple and mitre, pastoral staff, holds model of Wolvenbergh; crisma on
1279 glove, marg. inscr. (Lombardic); 77″ x 30″. The third oldest brass with effigy.

1460 Eghard de Hanensee. Provost, cap, alb, dalmatic, maniple, escutcheon, holds textus, roundels, evang. symbols, marg. inscr.; 78″ x 30″.

KLEVE (St. Mary's)

1481 John I, Duke of Kleves and Elizabeth (1483). Brass on top of altar tomb with heraldic achievements on 4 sides. Bareheaded duke in armour standing on a swan. Lady in elegant robes with cloak over all, veiled head, two dogs at feet. Walled background, lower half covered by curtain. Small canopy of spiral bands with foliage, 5 achievements on either side of tomb, 3 ditto at both ends, no inscr.; Creeny gives size as 140″ x 101″ (splayed dimensions).

KORNELIMÜNSTER

1481 Abbot H. von Lüilsdorf. Half effigy in pontificals, rect. pls., part restored, lge. border inscr., medallions.

MÜNSTER (Cathedral)

1748 Friedrich Christian Josef, Freiherr von Galen, Dean and Canon of Münster, Paderborn, Osnabrück, Worms and Minden. Heraldic sh. in centre, marg. inscr., oval in square; 15¾". Rect. pl. 16" sq. Set angle-wise ach. and marg. inscr. in Latin in caps.

PADERBORN (Cathedral)

1340 Bishop Bernard de Lippe. In eucharistic vestments, standing in attitude of benediction, holding pastoral staff in his left hand. Two shields at angles on either side of long mitre. Early example of a continental cut to shape effigy, marg. inscr.; 97" x 51".

1394 Bishop Rupert. In vestments of a canon. Two angels holding his mitre, angels in niches of triple canopy, escutcheons in corners, men in armour at feet, 3 sides, marg. inscr. (name at top); 84" x 39".

REGENSBURG

1189 Gilded brass plate recording consecration of an altar, St. Emmeramkirche, dble. line inscr., Latin; the earliest brass recorded in Europe.

TRIER (Museum of Antiquities)

c. 1500 Crucifixion. Man and wife kng. under canopies, evang. symbols; 13" x 10".

VERDEN (Hanover)

1231 Bishop Yso von Welpe (oldest brass with effigy). Alb, dalmatic chasuble, pall, mitre, buskins, pastoral staff, holds models of castle and church in both hands level with head, 4 sides marg. inscr., Lombardic caps; 79" x 29".

HOLLAND

ALKMAAR, Nth. Holland (St. Lawrence, Transept)

1546 Pieter Claessoen Palinck and Josina van Foreest, wife. Shrouds, faces and parts of body uncovered, surrounded by scrolls with inscr. shs., armorial bearings, 6 sm. shs., marg. inscr.; 95" x 52".

AMERSFOORT (Flenite Museum)

1648 Margriete du Quesnoy. Inscription.

BREDA (Groote Kerk)

1539 Willem van Galen. Dean, effigy in mass vestments, canopy, angels with shs.

GOUDA (St. Janskerk)

1524 J. Johanzen van Crimpen. Inscr.

1568 (High dike-reeve of Schielant) Johan Dirck Hoenzoen van Suburich and Wife. Palimpsest c. 1500.

HAARLEM (Stadhuis)

c. 1480 Dirck Bleser. Engraved 1630 from tombstone c. 1480, married at III, one dau; engraved by Maetham; 42" x 26".

MIDDLEBURG (Museum)

1509 18-line inscr. recording foundation of masses for Ysenbaert family. 36" x 23¼".

NYMWEGEN (Guelderland, St. Stephen)

1469 Katherine de Bourbon. Effigy in cap and gown, jewells, escutcheons, marg. inscr.; altar tomb with 6 panels either sides and 2 panels at either ends; these panels of brass plates contain 12 saints, the end panels armorial bearings and figures; centre top plate 78" x 36". Engraved by William Leomansz of Cologne.

SLIEDRECHT (Dordrecht)

19th cent. Dutch Reformed Church. Four small plates from coffins, inscr. (*There is also a brass at Zevenaar.*)

ITALY

SUSA (Cathedral)

1368 Bonifacio Rotario of Asti. Triptych fig. in armour kng. to Virgin and Child, with St. George in attendance.

NORWAY

OSLO (Folk Museum)

1593 Erik Gertsøn. Kng fig., armour to crucifixion, achievement, 5-line inscr.; 8⅞" x 6¼".

1593 Eiller Brockenhus. Kng. fig., armour to crucifixion, achievement, 5-line inscr.; 8½" x 6¼".

1603 Elsebe Iul, Wife of Peter Brockenhus. Heraldic 9-line inscr.; 6⅞" x 5⅝".

The above three plates are gilded.

BERGEN (University, Museum of Antiquities)

1361 (engraved later) Godfried Sak. A 3-tower castle, 2 merchants' mks, 3-line inscr.; 19¾" x 16¾".

POLAND

GNIEZNO (Cathedral)

1480 Archbishop Jacobus de Senno. In amice, chasuble, mitre, pastoral staff and crozier, triple canopy, niches with saints, shields, symbols, marg. inscr.; 112" x 79".

KRACÓW (Cathedral)

1510 Cardinal Frederick Jagiello, son of Casimir IV, King of Poland. In alb, chasuble, amice and mitre; canopy, niches, saints Adelbert and Stanislaus; escutcheons, sm. shs.; 111" x 62". (Engraved by Herman Vischer The Younger.)

LUBIAZ

c. 1300 Duke Premizlaus of Steinau, died 1289. In armour, sh., and sword; simple canopy, marg. inscr., a separate inlay brass; 100" x 46". (Also three others c. 1300.)

NOWEMIASTO

1391 Sir Kuno von Liebensteyn. In armour, jupon, sh., angels, sm. shs., devices, roundels, marg. inscr.; 98" x 54".

POZNAN (Cathedral)

c. 1380 Priest in mass vestments and almuce.

1475 Lucas de Gorta. In armour and visor; triple canopy, side shafts, niches with saints, marg. inscr., shs.; 104" x 56". *Destroyed in 1939-45 war.* Illustrated in Creeny's volume.

1479 Bishop Andreas. Canopy, eucharistic vest., pastoral staff, niches with saints, shs., devices, evang. symbols, marg. inscr.; 99" x 50". *Destroyed in 1939-45 war.* Illustrated in Creeny's volume.

1498 Bishop Urielis de Gorka (son of Lucas de Gorta). Triple canopy, unusual, niches, saints, amice, chasuble, mitre, pastoral staff, book, shs, with devices, marg. inscr.; 113" x 68". *Destroyed in 1939-45 war.* Illustrated in Creeny's volume.

TOMICE

1524 Nicholas Tomiczi. In armour, Polish Ensign, 10-line inscr. at base; bareheaded, stndg. on tiled floor; architectural arches; 108" x 54".

TORUN (St. John)

1361 Johannes von Zoest and Wife. Canopies, architectural niches with saints, man in tunic and cloak, wild man, lady in cotehardi; scenes at base, people in woodland pastimes, marg. inscr.; 124" x 64".

WROCLAW (Cathedral)

Both damaged in 1939-45 war.

1456 Bishop Peter Nowak. Canopy, niches with weepers, 4 shields, mitre, pastoral staff, alb, tunic, stole, book, fishes, dragons etc., marg. inscr.; 92" x 57" (Face is 3 dimensional), damaged.

1482 Bishop Rudolphus von Rudesheim. Canopy, mitre, pastoral staff, S.S. John Bpst., John Evang., chalice, saints, shields, marg. inscr. (damaged). A brass to Bishop Henrich (1398) has been lost – probably destroyed in 1939-45 war.

There are brasses at Czarnkow and Wielgomblyny.

PORTUGAL
COIMBRA

1345 John Andrew. Precentor, leader of the Cathedral choir, inscr. in fine letters.

1348 Archdeacon de Sena. Inscr.

EVORA (Church St. John Evangelist)

1497 Ruy de Sousa. Plate 69" x 33¾" with foliage design of 8 linked ovals. Outside a dble. band inscr. in gothic minuscules.

1500 Branca de Vilhana, second wife of Sousa. Fig. of lady, canopy, gables, spires, turrets, tabernacles, figures, 4 quatrefoils, evang. symbols, marg. inscr., ornate; 75" x 44¼".

1530 Ruy Paeez and Wife, civilians. Figs. of Ruy and wife standing under arch of vine branches, plants on ground, both in simple gowns, head of lady in veil, man bareheaded; 2-line inscr. at base; 34¾" x 19¾".

LEÇA DE BALIO

1336 Fr. Stephen Vasques Pimental. No other data available.

MADEIRA (Funchal Cathedral)

1550 João Esmeraldo and Wife Agueda de Abreu, civilians. Two separate, cut-to-shape effigies, legs and feet of man lost; dressed in simple gowns, lady veiled, with rosary. 84" x 40".

PENAFIEL (St. Martin)

1537 João Correia, civilian. Effigy, three-quarter stndg., long gown, rosary on front, bareheaded; edged by two foliage columns, arch at top, 2 cherubs in top corners; floor chessboard design, inscr. on edges of casement; donor of chapel; 33½" x 17".

SPAIN
AVILA (Cathedral)

1455 Bishop Alfonso de Madrigal. Effigy in full pontificals, elaborate marg. inscr.; 63" x 25".

MADRID (Museo Arqueologico Nacional)

1373 Martin Ferrades De Las Continas, civilian. Under elaborate canopy.

SEVILLE (Museo Arqueologico)

1333 Damaged brass plate to Wife of Francisco Fernandes.

University Chapel

1571 Don Parafan, Duke of Alcala. Effigy cut to shape, stndg., quadrangular plate, 3 sides lost, base existing with inscr. of 8 lines; armour rich in detail, helmet and sword in hands, good action to figure; 97" x 66".

SWEDEN
UPPSALA (Vester Åker)

1327 Frau Ramborg de Wik. In long gown, single canopy and two angels with censers, 4 evang. symbols in corners, 2 shields, marg. inscr. in Lombardic caps; 73" x 37".

SWITZERLAND
BASLE (Museum)

1450 Isabella, Duchess of Burgundy. Pieta, taken from a 15th century painting; heraldic shs., Philip the Good kng., escutcheon, Isabella kng.; inscr. base, plate damaged; 27" x 39".

RHEINAU (Abbey Church)

1598 Abbot Theobald Werlin. In mitre and full processional vestments.

1642 Abbot Eberhard von Bernhausen. In mitre and processional vestments.

UNITED STATES OF AMERICA
NEW YORK (St. Anne's Protestant Episcopal Church, Brooklyn)

1883 Thomas Messenger. Warden, d. 1881. Angel seated on Christ's tomb, scene of resurrection under triple gothic canopy; top centre, medallion I.H.S., centre base inscription, shields either side, chancel; 93" x 42½".

Index

Entries in italics refer to plates.